D0934946

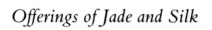

Offerings of Jade and Silk

OFFERINGS
OF
JADE AND SILK

Ritual and Symbol in the Legitimation of the T'ang Dynasty

HOWARD J. WECHSLER

Yale University Press

NEW HAVEN AND LONDON

Designed by James J. Johnson
and set in Bembo Roman.
Printed in the United States of America by
Halliday Lithograph, West Hanover, Massachusetts.

Library of Congress Cataloging in Publication Data

Wechsler, Howard J.
    Offerings of jade and silk.

    Bibliography: p. 283
    Includes index.
    1. China—Social life and customs—221 B.C.–960 A.D.   2. Rites and ceremonies—
China.   3. Legitimacy of governments.   4. Symbolism in politics.   I. Title.
DS747.42.W43   1985   394'.4'0951   84–15236
ISBN 0–300–03191–2 (alk. paper)

10 9 8 7 6 5 4 3 2 1

To my three *lao-shih*

MARY YIU

HYMAN KUBLIN

ARTHUR F. WRIGHT

Contents

Preface

When I first conceived this work, it was as a case study in dynastic legitimation that would employ the early T'ang dynasty as a typical example of how ritual and symbolic acts carried out on the state level served to generate political support during the first phases of Chinese imperial regimes. How naïve that thought proved to be! Proceeding with my research, I soon discovered that the early T'ang was, in fact, a rather special period in the history of Chinese ritual, one richly deserving that much abused designation, "watershed." First, it was a period in which the ritual theories of the third-century A.D. philosopher, Wang Su, finally emerged victorious over those of the second-century classical commentator, Cheng Hsüan. The story of the struggle for supremacy between the followers of the ideas of these two men, which lasted for more than four centuries, has largely remained untold. Second, whereas "case study" implies that the data one is employing is fully representative, I found a number of significant changes or shifts of emphasis in the ritual and symbolic acts performed by early T'ang emperors compared to those of previous ages, especially, for example, the Han. These changes and shifts of emphasis, I believe, form a comprehensible pattern: They seem to have been efforts by early T'ang rulers to ally themselves, in a variety of ways and to an unprecedented extent, with the hallowed Chinese political idea of *t'ien-hsia wei kung*, "the empire is open to all."

T'ien-hsia wei kung lay at the heart of the myth of two of China's most revered culture heroes, Yao and Shun, who passed their political power down to successors they deemed most worthy rather than to their own sons. The Chinese contrasted this idea with *t'ien-hsia wei chia*, "the empire belongs to one family."[1] Although the institution of dynasty is based on lineal succession, and thus is an embodiment of *t'ien-hsia wei chia*, early T'ang rulers did all they could to emphasize non-familial criteria as the basis of status elevation, especially their own moral virtue or that of their heirs. For example, the ideal of *t'ien-hsia wei kung* and the symbolism surrounding it suffuses, as never before, the early T'ang accession rites. Furthermore, the early T'ang dynasts undermined the quality of exclusiveness associated with family in a number of ways. They expanded the boundaries of the dynastic family by embracing, in many of the most important ritual and symbolic acts of the time, non-familial elements, especially their own high officials, forming what I have called an extended "political family." They depended less on the ancestral temple rites and on the power of lineal ancestors to legitimate their authority, and more on the suburban altar rites and the power of an all-embracing, universal Heavenly deity, Hao-t'ien shang-ti, who belonged not to one family only but to all the empire. Along with the emphasis on *tien-hsia wei kung* came a reduction in the secrecy that had formerly characterized certain rituals, such as the Feng and Shan sacrifices, which now became more public. Lastly, a symbolic vehicle like the calendar, which had formerly been closely linked to a given royal house, and therefore regarded as immutable during the lifetime of a dynasty, now broke free of familial bonds and was frequently altered for political ends.

At the same time, the new reliance on Hao-t'ien shang-ti as a sacrificial object at the expense of other deities in the Chinese pantheon had important repercussions for temporal power. The ruler's intensified worship and identification with an all-powerful Heaven enhanced his own standing as the "one man" in relation to the rest of the empire and thus helped establish the cosmological grounds for an enhanced absolutism. This trend, which became much more noticeable in the political practices and institutions of later Chinese dynasties, can be said to have been prefigured in the reformed state ritual of the early T'ang.

In the concluding chapter I suggest some possible reasons for these developments. First is the rise by early T'ang times of new conceptions of political power deriving from both Buddhism and Taoism, and also from the expansion of empire to an extent unprecedented in Chinese history. Second is the need for additional sources of legitimation made necessary by the increased number of activities that were now routinely undertaken by government but which had heretofore been self-legitimating components of the traditional cultural system.

My hope is that this study will encourage a re-evaluation of the kinds of sources thought important for the study of traditional China; challenge the notion that medieval Chinese ritual and ceremonial underwent little development or change and are thus topics lying beyond the purview of conventional historical scholarship; and generate a heightened appreciation of the interrelationship between ritual and symbolic activity and the wider Chinese political world.

Acknowledgments

The task of researching and writing this volume benefited from the generosity of numerous friends, colleagues, and academic organizations. In acknowledging their contributions, I do not in any way absolve myself of complete responsibility for the final product.

The University of Illinois at Urbana-Champaign provided me with a semester of released time in the fall of 1979 under its Faculty Study in a Second Discipline Program, which I spent in the Department of Anthropology, and another semester in the spring of 1981 as an Associate in the Center for Advanced Study. During 1980 and 1981 I was the recipient of a Grant for Research on Chinese Civilization from the American Council of Learned Societies. The Research Board of the Center for Asian Studies of the University of Illinois underwrote my travel expenses during a research trip to the People's Republic of China in the fall of 1980. The Research Board was again generous in providing financial assistance for the production of the final manuscript in the spring of 1983.

The staffs of the libraries of Fudan University, Shanghai, and of the Research Institute for Humanistic Studies of Kyoto University were exemplary in their dedication to lightening the burdens of an academic researcher. Thanks in this regard are also owed to Professor Zhang Guangda of the Department of History of Beijing University and Nunome Chōfū, formerly of the Department of Education of Osaka University, both of whom showed me warm hospitality while I worked in their respective countries.

I am especially indebted to the Japanese bibliographer of the University of Illinois Asian Library, Professor Yasuko Makino, for her tireless efforts on my behalf.

If, as Confucius said, we are to treat our friends by advising them to the best of our ability and guiding them properly, I am indeed blessed by friendship. Professors Blair B. Kling and Frederic C. Jaher of the Department of History, Patricia B. Ebrey of the Center for Asian Studies, and Norman E. Whitten of the Department of Anthropology, all at the University of Illinois, and Nathan Sivin, Professor of the History and Sociology of Science, University of Pennsylvania, commented on part or all of the manuscript and encouraged me in my work. Professor Richard C. Trexler, Department of History, State University of New York at Binghamton, shared his knowledge of bibliography concerning European royal rituals. Professor Ronald P. Toby of the Department of History, and Professors Seiichi Makino and Chieko I. Mulhern of the Center for Asian Studies, University of Illinois, advised me on matters of Japanese romanization. I am deeply grateful to all of them for their kindness and generosity.

Edward F. Winslow humored, consoled, and loved me during the long years of research and writing. His support made all the difference.

Last but not least, Werner Erhard enabled me to "get" that process can be as exciting and rewarding as completion. This book is a reflection of that realization.

Introduction

ON JUNE 12, 618 (THE FOURTEENTH DAY OF THE FIFTH LUNAR MONTH), a nobleman-general named Li Yüan, recent victor of a long and bloody campaign to take the capital city of the Sui dynasty (581–618), solemnly accepted the seals and ribbons of state from the last Sui monarch, the boy-emperor Kung-ti. Six days later he mounted the throne and founded a new dynasty, the T'ang (618–907), one of the great ages of Chinese imperium. Hundreds of officials participated in the determination and execution of his enthronement rites. The day of the ceremony was selected with great care: It was a propitious *chia-tzu* day, the first day of a sexagenary (sixty-day) cycle in the Chinese calendar and one which Li Yüan regarded as personally lucky. The event itself was announced to Heaven by a *ch'ai-liao* burnt offering sacrifice at a specially constructed altar in the southern suburbs of the capital. A general amnesty was declared, and the era-name was changed. The honorary noble rank of both officials and commoners was raised one step. All the districts through which the victorious T'ang troops had marched were declared exempt from taxes and compulsory labor service for three years; other districts under T'ang control were declared similarly exempt for one year. From a group of five elements, earth was chosen to symbolize the new dynasty; its correlative color was yellow. Three days later Li Yüan, whom we will hereafter refer to by his posthumous title, Kao-tsu, sumptuously banqueted his officials in the very hall where he had recently assumed the imperial mantle, and rewarded each of them with silk according to rank. Five days after this, on the twenty-eighth day of the month, the new emperor ordered work begun on the compilation of a dynastic code of laws.[1]

Kao-tsu conquered the Sui capital with an army said to have numbered more than two hundred thousand troops, and seized control of the Sui government with overwhelming force.[2] But force, while by no means an insignificant factor in the getting of power, does not in the long run constitute a stable base for the exercise and preservation of that power. One noted student of the problem concludes that "no power could stand if it relied upon violence alone, for force is not strong enough to maintain itself against the accidents of rivalry and discontent."[3] Talcott Parsons reminds us that "a power system in which the only negative sanction is the threat of force is a very primitive one which cannot function to mediate a complex system of organizational coordination."[4] Other writers similarly affirm that force is a "crude and expensive technique" for getting the job of government done.[5] In this respect, Kao-tsu required, shall we say, more refined and cheaper techniques of exercising and perpetuating his power.

The present study is an examination of some of the more refined and cheaper techniques that Kao-tsu and his two successors employed during the period of the formation and consolidation of the T'ang dynasty, covering the period from A.D. 618 to 683. It focuses on a number of ritual and symbolic acts carried out by them as they moved from reliance on military power to less coercive, more efficient means of control. It provides a brief historical background to each of these acts, tracing its evolution over time. Finally, it suggests that the early T'ang ritual and symbolic pattern departed in certain crucial respects from that of previous ages, especially the first great empire of Han; that this pattern was reflected in the victory, after a centuries-long struggle, of one school of classical exegesis and ritual theory over another; that this victory, in turn, may have been gained because the second Chinese empire required a qualitatively different kind of legitimation as compared with the first; and that this may have had important repercussions not only for the T'ang but for its successors all during the imperial period.

If we review Kao-tsu's actions in the days leading up to, including, and immediately following his enthronement, we can observe that he had already begun to implement techniques of control other than the employment of force. The stability of a regime, Max Weber has noted, is typically promoted by an appeal to the pecuniary motives of subjects or to their belief in the sanctity of custom. Kao-tsu's orders regarding exemption from taxes and compulsory labor service for specified periods, pardon from punishment for crimes already committed, and bestowal of honorary rewards can be viewed as constituting the former kind of appeal. Constituting the latter were his declaration of a new dynasty as opposed to a radically new form of regime, assumption in an age-old manner of the imperial mantle with all its traditional trappings, and adherence to ritual precedents of all kinds. He thereby reassured those who feared fundamental change and declared himself a staunch ally of tradition. But Weber postulates an even more important kind of appeal that might serve to promote political stability—*legitimacy*.

> An order which is adhered to from motives of pure expediency is generally much less stable than one upheld on a purely customary basis through the fact that the corresponding behaviour has become habitual. The latter is much the most common type of subjective attitude. But even this type of order is in turn much less stable than an order which enjoys the prestige of being considered binding, or, as it may be expressed, of "legitimacy."[6]

How Kao-tsu and his successors sought the firmer foundations of political legitimacy for their regimes provides one of the major foci of this study.

On another level of analysis, we can view Kao-tsu's enthronement policies as a means of gaining *support* for his regime. The concept of support is employed by David Easton in his systems analysis approach to political organizations. "We can say that A supports B either when A acts on behalf of B or when he orients himself favorably toward B. B may be a person or group; it may be a goal, idea, or institution."[7] There are two kinds of support. When support is generated as a consequence of some specific satisfaction derived from the system as a result of some demand made by its members, or in anticipation of such satisfaction, it is called *specific* or *direct support*. Specific support is a quid pro quo for the fulfillment of demands. But no political system could operate for long by depending on the specific support generated by specific outputs. For one thing, no system can meet all the demands of all its members all of the time, and considerable dissatisfaction over unmet demands is bound to arise. So a system must gain a more generalized acceptance through another kind of support that is not linked to particular decisions or to the granting of identifiable benefits. Such support is *diffuse* or *indirect support*. Diffuse support helps members tolerate political decisions they oppose or see as inimical to their interests by forming a reservoir of good will and generalized favorable attitudes toward the regime.[8]

How can diffuse support be generated? Probably the most effective device, according to Easton and others, including, as we have seen,

Weber, is the inculcation of a profound belief in the legitimacy of a political organization as a whole and of its authorities in particular.[9] Another is the employment of rites and symbols that arouse a deep sense of identification with the regime and its authorities and of a common interest among its members. Such rites and symbols can cause the regime and its authorities to be positively evaluated.[10] A second major focus of this study, then, will be certain rituals and symbols employed at the state level by the early T'ang emperors in order to secure diffuse support.

The policies associated with Kao-tsu's enthronement that provided material advantages and rewards to his officials and the common people can, in Easton's terms, be viewed as efforts to obtain specific support. All the others fall under the category of attempts to gain diffuse support by arousing among the public sentiments of legitimacy and a sense of identification with the T'ang order. These include the employment and manipulation of such rites and symbols as the seals of state, the accession ceremony itself, the sacrifice to Heaven announcing Kao-tsu's accession, the selection of the lucky *chia-tzu* day and of the element earth and the color yellow, and the order to compile a new code of a laws.

Yet another level of analysis of Kao-tsu's enthronement policies is provided by Amitai Etzioni's notion of compliance structures. Etzioni lists three major sources of control in an organization that can be allocated or manipulated: coercion, economic assets, and normative values. Each of these control sources is used in the employment of a specific type of power over any given subject.[11] Coercive power rests on the application or threat of application of physical sanctions (e.g., the inflicting of punishment, the issuing of jail sentences, the depriving of food). Remunerative power is based on control of material resources and rewards (e.g., the giving or withholding of salaries and fringe benefits, the determination of working conditions). Normative power relies on persuasion and the manipulation of esteem, prestige, and ritual symbols (e.g., issuing a coat-of-arms, using flags or emblems, granting honorary offices or titles, performing a sacrificial act).[12]

Power is employed to gain *compliance*, a relation consisting of the employment of power by superiors to control subordinates, and the orientation of subordinates to this power.[13] Patterns of compliance may vary within a single organization, but most organizations can be labeled according to the relative emphasis given the predominant pattern. For example, prisons and concentration camps, where force is the major means of control applied, achieve *coercive compliance*. Blue collar and white collar industries, where remuneration is the major form of control, achieve *utilitarian compliance*. Churches, political parties, and some educational institutions, where normative power is the major source of control, achieve *normative compliance*. Although all political organizations (or at least the elites of these organizations) pursue power goals, power is usually pursued in order to control or change the allocation of coercion, material resources, or normative patterns, or various combinations of these.

Etzioni postulates that certain types of goals and certain types of compliance structures are associated, that is, they are "congruent," because certain compliance structures are most effective in attaining certain goals. The goals of a political organization may change over time, however, as when a revolutionary party must turn to governing over the long term a country it has just seized control of. Here, Etzioni offers a dynamic hypothesis: "Organizations tend to shift their compliance structure from incongruent to congruent types," and "organizations which have congruent compliance structures tend to resist factors pushing them toward incongruent compliance structures." [14]

We can observe this process of shifting compliance structures in the case of the T'ang if we once more return to our description of the activities surrounding Kao-tsu's accession. By the time of his enthronement Kao-tsu had begun the process, in Etzioni's terms, of shifting the compliance structure of his political organization away from coercive and more toward utilitarian and normative compliance. Naturally, force or the threat of force continued to provide a source of direct support, through fear of the consequences of non-compliance among his subordinates and the people at large. But now, by means of granting material and other rewards, Kao-tsu had begun to appeal to the calculative orientation of those he governed. His acceptance of the seals of state, fulfilling the requirements of the accession ritual, making the sacrifice to Heaven, using the *chia-tzu* day, and so forth, were all aspects of persuasion and the manipulation of esteem, prestige, and ritual symbols—the bases of normative power.

That Kao-tsu would have begun shifting from coercive to other types of compliance is not surprising, even within a Chinese context. Etzioni's dynamic hypotheses of compliance structures had, in fact, been stated in a somewhat cruder and less systematic way more than nine hundred years before the T'ang by Lu Chia, counselor to the founding emperor of the Han dynasty, another Kao-tsu (rg. 206–195 B.C.). When Lu advised Han Kao-tsu to heed the lessons of government found in certain of the Confucian classics, the emperor derided his counselor:

"All I possess I have won on horseback!" said the emperor. "Why should I bother with the *Odes* and *Documents*?" "Your Majesty may have won it on horseback, but can you rule it on horseback?" asked Master Lu. "Kings T'ang and Wu in ancient times won possession of the empire through the principle of revolt, but it was by the principle of obedience that they assured the continuance of their dynasties. To pay due attention to both civil and military affairs is the way for a dynasty to achieve long life."[15]

The goals of ruling were not the same as those of military conquest, Lu was saying. Although he did not explicitly express himself in this manner, his message was that now that the empire had been won and military concerns had largely been replaced by problems of civil administration, the new emperor would have to shift his compliance structure away from coercion toward more congruent modes. This is precisely what T'ang Kao-tsu had begun doing.

Easton's concept of diffuse support and Etzioni's concept of normative compliance are related in that both are associated with the manipulation of esteem and prestige symbols and the performance of ritual. They are further linked through the concept of legitimacy: Normative compliance may occur as the result of the orientation of an actor toward an organization or its authorities that he is led to believe are legitimate.

Up to now we have been relating various modes of analysis only to the policies associated with Kao-tsu's enthronement ceremonies. But the concepts of diffuse support, normative compliance, and legitimation can be related to a far wider range of activities that the T'ang founder and his successors undertook in the formative and consolidation phases of the dynasty. Any ritual or symbolic act performed by the authorities of a regime is potentially legitimating or may generate support or compliance, especially when it is perceived as conforming to tradition, the orthodox ideology, or approved norms. Every regime in medieval China thus attempted to continue hallowed political and ritual practice, at least along generalized lines. On the other hand, every regime also attempted to dissociate itself from its predecessor, since the latter had become morally bankrupt, a fact reflected in its loss of the Heavenly Mandate. Thus, soon after the beginning of the T'ang, the Grand Astrologer, Fu I, complained that the dynasty had been tardy in creating its own distinctive institutions and ceremonial by which it might be distinguished from the failed Sui. He advocated that the T'ang proceed immediately to change the calendar, the color of court dress, the code of laws, the names of bureaucratic offices, as well as to establish its own music and ritual, all of which, he maintained, would "refresh the eyes and ears" of the people and allow them to perceive its surpassing moral qualities.[16]

The rituals and symbolic acts I will be treating in this volume were essentially designed with Fu I's words in mind.[17] They are what Derk Bodde has called "institutional" in that they are shaped by the conscious theorizing of ritualists, cosmologists, and government administrators.[18] In addition, they share most or all of the following characteristics: (1) The emperor is the major actor or major focus; (2) there is a *locus classicus* in the Confucian canon; (3) they are relatively well documented, and have a history that can be traced down to T'ang times; (4) they constituted a focus of court discussion or debate during the early T'ang; (5) an official decision was made to implement them; (6) and even if they were not actually carried out, emperors typically sought their legitimating properties and felt a certain incompleteness without them.

A common feature of ritual behavior is the manipulation of powerful symbols. Symbols are nearly always manipulated, consciously or unconsciously, in the struggle for and maintenance of political power.[19] Social scientists identify two basic types of political symbols, *credenda* and *miranda*. Credenda are things to be believed. They offer us reasons why we should give our approval to the continuance of authority, and are set forth in political doctrine, theory and ideology, and such written documents as constitutions, charters, and declarations. Miranda are things to be admired. Their function

> is to arouse admiration and enthusiasm, setting forth and strengthening faiths and loyalties. They not only arouse emotions indulgent to the social structure, but also heighten awareness of the sharing of these emotions by others, thereby promoting mutual identification and providing a basis for solidarity.... Flags and anthems, ceremonials and demonstrations, group heroes and legends surrounding them—these exemplify the importance of miranda in the political process.[20]

Miranda provide specific foci for emotions, reinforcing and intensifying the relatively generalized responses produced by the credenda. Thus, although the Constitution may seem rather dry and remote from us, we have all experienced the power of our national flag or an Independence Day ceremony to move us. Here, we will be as much concerned with miranda as with credenda, with the concrete ceremonial or symbolic vehicles generating sentiments of legitimacy or support as with the abstract ideology or values that lay behind them.

The contents of this volume are organized as follows. Chapter 1 provides a theoretical background for our inquiry, with a comparative examination of the concepts of legitimacy, ritual, and symbol as understood by Western scholars and their traditional Chinese counterparts, especially those of the early T'ang. Chapter 2, by way of providing a historical and political background, discusses the general history of the period, the filiation of the early T'ang ritual codes, the ideological basis for the major ritual controversies of the day, the central government ritual apparatus, and the careers of the officials most instrumental in determining ritual policy. Chapters 3 to 11, the bulk of the volume, each deal with a different imperial ritual or symbolic activity: its potential for generating sentiments of legitimacy and political support; its origins and history prior to the T'ang; its role during the reigns of Kao-tsu, T'ai-tsung, and Kao-tsung; and, finally, the inferences that can be drawn from the above. Chapter 12 provides, as a general conclusion, an overview of the preceding material.

CHAPTER 1

Legitimacy, Ritual, and Symbol in Modern Western and Traditional Chinese Perspective

> O ceremony! show me but thy worth.
>
> Shakespeare, *Henry V*

CHINESE WRITERS UP TO AND INCLUDING THOSE OF THE EARLY T'ANG PERIOD cannot be said to have wrestled with the concepts of legitimacy, ritual, and symbol in as systematic and sophisticated a manner as twentieth-century Western social scientists and humanists. Nevertheless, they were repeatedly drawn to discuss such questions, if often in specific contexts rather than in the abstract. In doing so they reveal a surprising number of points of agreement with their Western counterparts. Ritual, in particular, was a subject of intense interest because the Chinese considered the proper observance of ritual and, in its more mundane form, social etiquette to be the very hallmark of a civilized people. They believed, moreover, that a ruler's performance of ritual coupled with correct moral behavior could actually influence the cosmos in a manner beneficial to mankind. One reflection of this interest is the sheer space devoted to the subject in the histories and institutional compendia. For example, only one of the nineteen Standard Histories that contain topical essay (*chih*) sections lacks a chapter devoted to ritual; and fully one-half of the two hundred chapters of the *Comprehensive Institutions* (*T'ung-tien*), a T'ang encyclopedia, is devoted to the same subject. With the rise of the unitary state and of Confucianism to a position of dominance as state orthodoxy at about the beginning of our era, Confucians served as experts in the field of ritual, discoursing on its proper forms and manipulating it for political ends, both on behalf of and against monarchical power. At the same time, in their roles as historians, ritualists, and scriptural exegetes, they served as the guardians of political legitimacy and as some of the most powerful

9

manipulators of its symbols. Since early times in China, legitimacy, ritual, and symbol have, as elsewhere, been inextricably commingled.[1]

LEGITIMACY

"The desire for legitimacy," notes one scholar, "is so deeply rooted in human communities that it is hard to discover any sort of historical government that did not either enjoy widespread authentic recognition of its existence or try to win such recognition."[2] Max Weber, the father of modern legitimation theory, concludes that "no system of authority voluntarily limits itself to the appeal to material or affectual or ideal motives as a basis for guaranteeing its continuance. In addition every such system attempts to establish and to cultivate a belief in its 'legitimacy.'"[3] Political legitimacy can be said to adhere to a regime and its authorities when the governed are convinced that it is right and proper to obey them and to abide by their decisions.[4] Moreover, because in some way the governed see the regime as conforming to their own values or moral principles, they believe that it will produce decisions that accord with their expectations. Legitimacy is thus an "evaluation that imputes future behavior of an expected or desired type."[5]

According to Weber, claims to legitimacy might be based on (1) *rational* grounds—on the belief that rules and laws are "legal," and that the authorities have the right under such rules to issue commands; (2) *traditional* grounds—on the belief in the historical sanctity of timeworn traditions and the legitimacy of the status of those exercising authority under those traditions;[6] (3) *charismatic* grounds—on the devotion to the holiness, heroism, or exemplary character of some person, and on the moral values and order revealed or prescribed by that individual. The legitimacy adhering to a particular person on the basis of charisma may endure beyond that person's lifetime by means of a process Weber calls "routinization of charisma," in which charisma comes to be viewed as an objective, transferable entity that can be transmitted by ritual means from one bearer to another or may be created in a new person. The transmission of religious authority by anointing, consecration, or the laying on of hands, and of royal authority by anointing and coronation, are examples of this process.[7]

David Easton approaches legitimacy from the vantage point of his concept of support. Support in this respect may derive from three sources: agreement with the ideological principles of a regime and its authorities, attachment to the structure and norms of the regime, or devotion to the authorities because of their perceived personal qualities, particularly their exemplary morality. These three types of legitimacy Easton calls *ideological, structural,* and *personal.*[8]

Some mechanisms possess what Easton calls omnibus effects in that they may stimulate sentiments of legitimacy in more than one way. An ideology constitutes one such mechanism. So, too, do ritual, ceremonies, and the physical symbols of the regime—the miranda—which reinforce the effects of ideology:

> Accession and installation ceremonies, display of the physical symbols of authority such as coats of arms, wands, or seals of state, favored ceremonial treatment for individuals representative of the special character of the regime, special penalties for offenses against such representative persons, displays on patriotic holidays and events, all stand as specific and variable responses that nurture diffuse support. By focusing on the major political values of the system, on the exemplary character of the incumbents of authority roles, or on their conformity to the regime, such procedures are able to contribute to the reinforcement of sentiments of legitimacy, ideological, personal, or structural, as the case may be.[9]

Peter Berger sees legitimation as a way of explaining and justifying the social order. It answers questions "about the 'why' of institutional arrangements." There are two kinds of legitimation, according to Berger. The first, *primary legitimation,* legitimates purely by its objective facticity, by simply being; it tells the ways things really are, for example, "Tribe X lives on this side of the river, and we on the other." The other type is called *secondary legitimation,* which is made necessary by challenges to this facticity. Socialization is never complete: resistance always persists to some extent. Here, facticity is not enough; legitimating "answers" or "formulas" are required to remind the old or to instruct the young. These answers take such forms as affirmations of tradition ("This is how things have always been done"), and theoretical justifications ranging from simple proverbs and moral maxims, to more complex myths, legends, and folktales, to sophisticated political ideologies.[10]

It needs to be stressed that legitimation is an ongoing process that is never completed. There are always newcomers to the political system who must be politically socialized. "The child in any system needs to be bound for the first time to the regime and its authorities through perceptions of their legitimacy."[11] Moreover, the authorities can never take their legitimation for granted. Even adults who may have at one time felt that the regime and its authorities were legitimate may no longer be quite so sure. "Reserves" of legitimacy can be quickly depleted. Thus even old and established regimes must continually renew sentiments of legitimacy on the part of their members.[12] In addition, the authorities may from time to time need to reassure themselves that they are indeed legitimate.

The Chinese were forced to confront the question of political legitimacy at least as early as the very beginnings of their historiographical tradition: for, which regimes were to be considered legitimate (and so, have their histories written) and which ones not? Yet even sources predating the beginnings of true historiography in China, known as *ching* or "classics," can be said to have touched on the problem of legitimacy. The *Book of History* (*Shu-ching*, sometimes called, more aptly, *Book of Documents*), contains propaganda speeches justifying the conquest of the Shang dynasty by the Chou around 1100 B.C. The speeches present perhaps the earliest articulated Chinese views on political legitimacy and the obligations of monarchy.[13] A popular view of the chronicle known as the *Spring and Autumn Annals* (*Ch'un-ch'iu*), which covers the period 722–481 B.C., is that Confucius, its purported author, offered moral judgments regarding men and their actions by nuances in his wording.[14] Such judgments sometimes involved the legitimacy of the positions the men occupied.

Of these two works, the *Book of History* is especially important in that it introduces two key ideas that influenced Chinese notions of political legitimacy for some three thousand years, down to our own century. The first is the famous Mandate of Heaven (*t'ien-ming*) doctrine, which, as Herrlee Creel points out, represents to the premodern Chinese what divine right of kings did to monarchical Europe and "governments derive their just powers from the consent of the governed" does to the United States.[15] In the *Book of History*, the Duke of Chou, younger brother of the Chou founder, first enunciates the Mandate of Heaven doctrine to the officials of the Shang to explain how the Chou came to conquer them.[16] According to the view expounded by the Duke of Chou, Heaven (*t'ien*) selects someone of outstanding virtue and ability and confers a mandate (*ming*) on him and his lineal descendants to rule all under Heaven. The chosen monarch is literally Son of Heaven, *t'ien-tzu*. The Mandate can be justified only by the continued good rule of the monarch; should it no longer be forthcoming, Heaven revokes its Mandate and transfers it to some other worthy and his progeny. This theory served to explain to the Chinese the periodic shift of political power from one dynastic house to another during their long history.

The second key idea introduced in the *Book of History* is that of cession of the throne or yielding of power, narrated in the very first section of the work, "The Canon of Yao." Here the sage-ruler Yao chooses the commoner Shun instead of his own son to succeed him as ruler. After testing Shun for three years and finding him entirely worthy, Yao abdicates power and turns the throne over to him.[17] According to other accounts, Shun in turn ceded his throne to Yü rather than to his own son because of Yü's greater virtue. It was Yü who for the first time passed the throne to his own son, thus inaugurating the first Chinese dynasty, the legendary Hsia. The cession of the throne to a moral worthy is clearly incompatible with the idea of enduring dynastic houses in which power is routinely passed from father to son, or at least to some close family member. Thus rose a tension between political ideal and political practice that characterized the entire traditional period of Chinese history. It is our contention that many of the ritual and symbolic activities of the early T'ang emperors were designed to help resolve this tension.

By Han times there arose a belief that Heaven not only could grant or revoke a Mandate to rule, but also constantly supervised a ruler's administration by means of its power to reveal auspicious or calamitous omens. Heaven-sent anomalies of nature—comets, eclipses, droughts, floods, earthquakes, and the like—were especially intended to warn the ruler that he was in danger of losing the Mandate. The view was put forth, among others, by the Han philosopher Tung Chung-shu (179?–104? B.C.), who once wrote:

> Whenever the state was on the verge of failures stemming from the loss of the Way, heaven first would send forth calamities and prodigies as warning. When (the rulers) were incapable of correcting themselves, it again would send forth strange and extraordinary phenomena in order to worry and frighten them. When they still did not change their ways, injury and downfall then came upon them.[18]

According to the doctrines of *t'ien-ming* and of Heaven-sent portents, there was a mutual interaction between Heaven and man, especially between Heaven and the ruler.[19] Such doctrines gave rise, during Han times and afterward, to incessant and vocal warnings by counselors that rulers had to practice virtue and avoid idleness, and also to frequent penitential edicts that were provoked by various calamities, in which fearful rulers verbally flagellated themselves for not pursuing virtue ardently enough. On the other hand, all would-be dynastic founders and insecure rulers searched hungrily for any phenomena that could be interpreted as signs that they indeed were the rightful occupiers of the throne.

The theory of portents is tied to yet another theory about the way in which Heaven and man interact. This is the theory of the Five Elements (*wu-hsing*), which was popular during Ch'in and Former Han times, propagated most notably by the Former Han scholar, Tsou Yen. The Five Elements are earth, wood, metal, fire, and water. The *Lü-shih ch'un-ch'iu*, a source of about the third century B.C., explains how the Five Elements work:

> Whenever any Emperor or King is about to arise, Heaven must first make manifest some favorable omen among the lower people. In the time of the Yellow Emperor, Heaven first made a large (number of) earthworms and mole crickets appear. The Yellow Emperor said: "The force of the element earth is in the ascendancy." Therefore he assumed yellow as his color, and took earth as a pattern for his affairs.

Next come descriptions of the powers and colors in ascendancy during the dynasties of Hsia (wood/green), Shang (metal/white), and Chou (fire/red). The text predicts that Heaven next will make the ascendancy of water manifest, which will replace fire, and that black will be assumed as its color. Following this entire sequence, the cycle will once more revert to earth.[20]

According to this view, each of the Five Elements controls natural and human events during the time of its ascendancy, then declines, to be replaced by the next element in the cycle. Every Chinese dynasty has a governing element that determines its character and institutions. Large-scale changes among men are manifestations of changes among these powerful natural and cosmic forces.[21] The theory of the Five Elements was, then, yet another early Chinese statement regarding the process of legitimate political succession.[22]

Until fairly late in Chinese history there was no general term that can be equated with our own abstraction, "political legitimacy." The Han dynasty historians Ssu-ma Ch'ien and Pan Ku both employed the term *t'ien-t'ung*, roughly meaning a sovereignty ordained by Heaven, to suggest the quality of legitimacy.[23] But in his *History of the Former Han Dynasty* Pan also introduced the term *cheng-t'ung*, legitimate or orthodox line of succession in a dynasty or of descent in a family. The term appears in the "Monograph on Suburban Sacrifices" (*Chiao-ssu chih*), where it is recorded that "when Hsüan-ti became emperor, he sprang from the legitimate line of Wu-ti [*Hsüan-ti chi wei, yu Wu-ti cheng-t'ung hsing*]."[24] To understand the reference fully, we need to know that Hsüan-ti (rg. 73–48 B.C.) was the great-grandson of Wu-ti (rg. 141–87 B.C.), in his direct line, and that the intervening ruler, Chao-ti (rg. 86–74 B.C.) was a younger brother of Wu-ti. In another section of Pan Ku's work the term appears again, this time in conjunction with the observation that the reason special mourning was observed for parents was to "distinctively revere one's own ancestors and to stress the orthodox line of descent" (*ming tsun pen-tsu erh chung cheng-t'ung*).[25] Similarly, part of an imperial edict issued by the Northern Chou emperor Hsüan-ti in A.D. 580, concerning his abdication of the throne and designating the crown prince as his successor, reads: "The Crown Prince Yen occupies the position of eldest legitimate son; to him belongs the orthodox succession [*cheng-t'ung*]."[26] Although as used by these writers *cheng-t'ung* had a rather narrow meaning, it gradually evolved into a broader concept that we might loosely equate with our own "legitimacy."

The process appears to have been completed by the Sung dynasty (960–1279), when many of the major literati and historians of the age, such as Ou-yang Hsiu, Su Shih, Chu Hsi, and Ssu-ma Kuang discussed in detail their respective criteria for legitimate dynastic succession, which they referred to as *cheng-t'ung*.[27] The term may have received some currency on the basis of the writings of the late T'ang dynasty scholar Han Yü (768–824), who spoke of *tao-t'ung*, or line of transmission of the Truth or Orthodox Teaching, which he conceived as stretching from the culture-heroes Yao and Shun, through the Chou dynastic founders, down to Confucius and Mencius—and then no further.[28] *Cheng-t'ung* may well have evolved as a political parallel to the moral sequence of *tao-t'ung*. In the pre-Sung period, however, questions of legitimacy were with only a few exceptions approached on a piecemeal and highly specific basis: Individual dynasties were judged legitimate or not, and lines of orthodox political succession from dynasty to dynasty were drawn, but rarely, if ever, did writers treat legitimacy as an abstraction worthy of discussion in its own right.

The disintegration of the Han dynasty late in the second century and its formal abolition early in the third was followed by almost four hundred years of political and cultural fragmentation known as the Period of Disunion (220–589). During much of this time China was ruled simultaneously by two or more dynasties, mainly non-Chinese regimes in the North and Chinese colonial regimes in the South. The patchwork of poli-

ties presented a thorny problem for historians, which sometimes led to
sharp disagreement over which were legitimate. Perhaps the earliest example of the problem occurred in the mid-fourth century, when a question arose over which of two regimes, Ts'ao-Wei or Shu, was the rightful
successor to the Han.[29] In the histories compiled later during the Period of
Disunion, southerners tended to consider northern regimes illegitimate,
and vice versa. Early in the T'ang seven Standard Histories which came to
be regarded as the definitive treatments of past regimes were compiled.
The T'ang historians tended to adopt the prejudices of their predecessors
in the Northern and Southern Dynasties whose documents they depended
on for their own compilations. This led to a confusing situation in which
southern regimes were considered legitimate in the histories of the southern dynasties of Liang and Ch'en, whereas northern regimes were considered legitimate in the histories of Northern Ch'i, Northern Chou, and
Sui.[30] To make matters even more complex, the T'ang ruling house reckoned that it had inherited its legitimacy from the Sui, by way of the
Northern Chou and Western Wei dynasties.

In the period immediately preceding the T'ang perhaps the fullest discussion of the question of historical legitimacy appears in the writings of
the Sui dynasty Confucian philosopher Wang T'ung (584?–617), also
called Wen-chung-tzu.[31] Two works have been attributed to Wang, the
Primal Classic (*Yüan-ching*) and the *Discourses on the Mean* (*Chung-shuo*).
The former is no longer extant in its original form, but in the latter
Wang T'ung says that he compiled the *Primal Classic* in order to demonstrate the historical legitimacy (lit. *t'ien-ming*) of certain regimes, much, he
said, as the *Spring and Autumn Annals* had been written to demonstrate
the legitimacy of the Chou dynasty.[32] "Was not my writing of the
Continued Classics [*Hsü-ching*] and *Primal Classic* all about a knowledge of
t'ien-ming?" he once asked rhetorically.[33] From other comments made by
Wang we can see that he traced a line of legitimate succession from the
Han dynasty to Western Chin (265–317), Eastern Chin (317–420), Liu-
Sung (420–79), Northern Wei (386–535), Northern Chou (557–81), and
Sui (581–618).[34] This line seems a bit strange in light of the progression
from Liu-Sung, a southern Chinese regime, to Northern Wei, a "barbarian" regime of the North, but it may have been conditioned in part by
Wang's family background: His great-grandfather, who first lived under
the Liu-Sung, later decided to resettle under the Northern Wei.[35] Wang's
great-grandfather's transfer to the North, moreover, personified a much
wider trend of the times. Ch'en Yin-k'o's work on the Sui and T'ang

demonstrates that much of the culture, law, and institutions of the Northern Wei originated among the southern states, and that the non-Chinese Northern Wei in its turn contributed to further development in these areas in such northern regimes as the Northern Ch'i, Sui, and eventually the T'ang.[36] In this light, Wang's line of dynastic legitimacy becomes somewhat easier to comprehend.

Wang's criteria for legitimacy are expressed most explicitly in relation to the Northern Wei, a dynasty from which he traced his own descent via his great-grandfather, in a discussion with one of his disciples, Tung Ch'ang:

> Tung Ch'ang inquired: "Why in the *Primal Classic* are Northern Wei [rulers] referred to as emperors [i.e. treated as legitimate]?" The Master replied: "'Amid such distress of disorder and dispersion, Whither can I betake myself?'"[37] They who serve Heaven and Earth and protect the living people are my sovereigns. As to they who occupy the land of the Former Kings and receive the Way of the Former Kings, how can I, being [one of] the people of these Former Kings, not also refer to them as such?"[38]

Wang thereby implies the existence of four criteria for the presence of political legitimacy. A regime must (1) serve Heaven and Earth, presumably by means of the rituals dedicated to them; (2) nourish and protect the common people; (3) physically occupy the territory ruled by former legitimate rulers of China; and (4) follow the rituals and procedures of former rulers. Unlike the Sung theorist Ou-yang Hsiu, Wang did not regard the presence of a unified empire as a sine qua non of legitimacy.[39] Also, unlike most other Sung scholars, Wang seems to have been favorably disposed to non-Chinese dynasts who maintained Chinese ritual and rules of etiquette. Legitimacy, then, was to be conferred even on "barbarians" as long as they preserved and promoted traditional Chinese culture, a thought that would have been anathema to most Sung Neo-Confucians, intent as they were on stressing native Chinese traditions.[40]

To what extent Wang T'ung's ideas regarding legitimacy influenced thinkers during the early T'ang period is difficult to say. Elsewhere I have expressed a number of reservations regarding the view, put forth in the *Discourses on the Mean*, that Wang served as teacher to a large group of men who later rose to positions of considerable influence in early T'ang government.[41] There appears, however, to be little among Wang's four criteria for legitimacy that men of the early T'ang would have found fault with. Points 1 and 2 are very much in tune with classical *t'ien-ming* doctrine. By compiling the Standard Histories of several coeval regimes during the Period of Disunion, early T'ang historians demonstrated that in their view legitimacy could be based on the physical control of just part of the territory historically occupied by the Chinese, as in point 3. Finally, as we will see in later chapters, the T'ang certainly thought of itself as the inheritor of the rituals and procedures of former Chinese rulers, and thus as the receptor of the Way of Kings. Regarding point 4, then, being themselves of partially "barbarian" background, the T'ang dynasts could not have but applauded Wang T'ung's view that non-Chinese regimes might be as legitimate as native ones if they cherished native culture and preserved it for posterity.

There is a work surviving from the early T'ang period which reflects some contemporary ideas regarding the dynamics of dynastic change and the founts of political legitimacy. This is the *Brief Discussion of (Former) Rulers* (*Ti-wang lüeh-lun*), in five *chüan*, by Yü Shih-nan (558–638), a former Sui official who served at T'ang T'ai-tsung's court.[42] The work was written about 627, ostensibly to provide T'ai-tsung with examples of good and bad rulers of the past: successful rulers to provide him with patterns to emulate, failed rulers to provide him with cautionary warnings. Because of the brevity of most sections and their episodic style, we can formulate conclusions regarding Yü Shih-nan's historical and political views only with difficulty. Nevertheless, it is possible to trace certain judgments the author has made about the line of legitimate dynastic succession. For example, the Northern Chou dynasty is treated more favorably than the Northern Ch'i, reflecting the T'ang view that its line stretched from the Northern Chou through the Sui and not through the coeval Northern Ch'i. It is also interesting to note that, for whatever reason, Yü entirely neglects to discuss the failed last emperor of the Sui, Yang-ti, even though he might have provided an excellent minatory example for T'ai-tsung. On the other hand, the section on the Han founder, Kao-tsu, is comparatively long—over eight hundred characters—mirroring the intense early T'ang interest in the Han dynasty, to which it often compared itself and which it regarded, at least indirectly, as the fountainhead of its own legitimacy.[43]

The most interesting portions of the work, for our purposes, deal with a perennial historical question for the Chinese: What forces most affected the rise and fall of dynasties? The theme is stated in the preface in a dialogue between two imaginary characters, a Young Gentleman (*kung-tzu*) and his Teacher (*hsien-sheng*). The Young Gentleman inquires: If we successively examine good and bad rulers from earliest times to the present, we see that some endured for long periods whereas others were prematurely extinguished. What, then, is the principle behind their flourishing or destruction? Is it the Will of Heaven or the actions of men? The Teacher replies: The length of a ruler's reign is dependent on the quality of his rule. If he rules well, then Heaven sends down blessings, and good omens appear. If he rules badly, then Heaven responds with natural calamities, and evil omens arise. Heaven's will and man's intentions both contribute toward producing the result.[44] According to Yü, then, legitimacy derives from a combination of human action and Heaven's Mandate, with the former serving to elicit the latter. This theme informs much of his book, providing it with a leitmotif.

T'ien-ming, or, simply, *ming*, while often translated as "Mandate of Heaven" or "Heaven's will," is in some contexts also understood as "fate" or "destiny."[45] The concept of predetermination occupied a prominent place in Confucianism from Han times.[46] Yü Shih-nan explicitly addresses the question of fate in *chüan* 4 of his work, in a section dealing with the last ruler of the southern dynasty of Ch'en. Here the Teacher notes that even though the southern region was small and its army weak, from the end of the Han onward it had been consolidated and made strong by means of the proper use of men and topography. But at the end of the Ch'en, try as its rulers might, they could not save the dynasty from the Sui conquerors. Although the South had long been consolidated, now it could not be preserved: This was due to *ch'i-yün*, literally, the turn of fate. When the Young Gentleman inquires what *ch'i-yün* was, the Teacher narrates a story that took place in 557, the first year of the Ch'en. In this year a soothsayer predicted that the Ch'en would endure through five rulers and thirty-four years, which was precisely the case. From this, concludes the Teacher, we see that a dynasty's allotted time is not determined by men's actions alone.[47] For Yü Shih-nan, then, historical explanation only partially rests with historical man; the rest is up to Heaven or fate.[48]

That this was a generally accepted early T'ang view about dynastic change and dynastic legitimacy is suggested by remarks made in the *Sui History* (*Sui-shu*) by the historian Wei Cheng (580–643), another Sui official who rose to the rank of chief minister under T'ai-tsung. In the "Comments of the Historian" section of the "Basic Annals" of the Sui founder, Wei observed that the rapid conquest of the Northern Chou by the Sui was based "not merely on the plotting against them of men, but also on the assistance lent by Heaven. Taking advantage of this turn of fate [*chi-yün*, almost identical to *ch'i-yün*], they transferred the [Northern] Chou vessels [of sovereignty to the Sui]."[49] In the early T'ang, then, dynastic success and, by extension, dynastic legitimacy—were viewed as the outcome of a combination of men's actions, Heaven's will, and fate. If the former was important, the latter two were decisive.

RITUAL

Whatever discipline they work in, Western students of ritual theory can, broadly speaking, be divided into two groups, each containing antithetical elements. The first group consists of those who view ritual more in terms of what it does and what it accomplishes, that is, its instrumental qualities (functionalists), and those who view ritual more in terms of what it says or means, that is, its expressive qualities. The second group consists of those who see the workings of ritual, as well as myth, religion, and various non-verbal communications systems like music and art, as analogous to the workings of language (structuralists), and those who do not. Whereas most structuralists are also functionalists, the reverse is not necessarily the case.

What do we mean by the term "ritual"? Jack Goody's functionalist definition seems a good place to start: "By ritual we refer to a category of standardized behaviour (custom) in which the relationship between the means and the end is not 'intrinsic,' i.e. is either irrational or non-rational."[50] Goody divides ritual into three basic types: magic, religious ritual, and ceremonial (or what might be called secular ritual). Whereas most ritual, he believes, is designed to achieve some end, he emphasizes that ritual in fact possesses nothing intrinsic that empowers it to bring about the desired end, and so from the observer's viewpoint it can be considered irrational or nonrational. Religious ritual among the three types is the only one to make reference to mystical beliefs or powers, that is, the supernatural.[51] To this definition we might want to add only the commonly made observation that ritual operates primarily on the symbolic level; it is a form of symbolic statement.[52]

The functionalist approach to ritual tends to emphasize what is accomplished in the social and political realms by virtue of its performance. Among social scientists, from Durkheim onward, there has been a stress on the positive role of ritual in the maintenance of social systems, especially on the way in which ritual enhances social unity and integration. Durkheim saw ritual as a way for the individual to experience corporate selfhood, to reaffirm common bonds, and to reinforce social solidarity. When men periodically gather to celebrate the rites, they renew interpersonal relations and create an enhanced collective consciousness. Communion with the gods is at the same time communion with society. The goals of ritual, either directly or indirectly, are always collective or social.[53] This theme has been elaborated upon and extended by those writing after Durkheim, who have tended to emphasize that, especially where the forces of social fragmentation and interpersonal or intergroup conflict are strong, ritual serves as a vehicle for integration and unity.[54]

Ritual seems to be capable not only of producing social unity but also of clarifying and reinforcing social differences. For example, ritual affirms status differences, in that ritual actors adopt special modes of dress that emphasize in an exaggerated way the formal social distinctions among them. Ritual actors move in ceremonial procession in an order that further comments on their relative social status. Ritual reflects, expresses, and affirms the peculiar structural arrangements of a society and reinforces its social values. It confers legitimacy upon the particular social interpretation a society has of itself.[55] This leads us to a consideration of ritual as a powerful force for conservatism and authority.

It has been said that political authority, being an abstraction, can be verified only through the rituals and symbols it employs.[56] These, by endowing authority with mystical values and legitimacy, serve not merely to reflect authority but also to recreate and reinforce it. By such means the extent to which people are persuaded to accept a given authority goes far beyond the obedience normally elicited by force.[57] We have seen that the emotions aroused by rituals and symbols can serve to generate diffuse support for incumbent regimes and their authorities. Rituals, impressive ceremonies, and pomp of all kinds lend a powerful mystique to rulers, surrounding them with grandeur, exalting their status, and ultimately facilitating their sovereignty.[58]

The power of a ritual to elicit political acquiescence may be not only a function of its external physical trappings, but may also spring from the inner dynamics of ritual itself. Mary Douglas sees ritual as operating in a manner similar to a kind of language, called a restricted code, which is frequently found in small-scale, local societies whose members all share the same fundamental assumptions. This language is characterized by a rigid syntax and a narrow range of alternate forms. It allows for little or no expression of individuality among actors, thus promoting social solidarity and conformity. Ritual is in this respect viewed as a system of control as well as of communication.[59] Maurice Bloch believes that it is the formalized speech employed in ritual that allows it to exert a controlling authority over participants. Ritual's formalized oratory, he points out, typically employs an archaic vocabulary; a limited number of syntactical forms, usually those considered most polite or impersonal; maxims, proverbs, or historical allusions from a limited traditional body of texts; the use of a special style of delivery; and a rigidly traditional overall structure. Formalization of speech can become a form of power or coercion because it dramatically restricts what can be said, and because one speaker, uttering statements in unchallengeable form, can coerce the response of another.[60]

Ritual helps rulers to exercise authority over others by reaffirming the positions of those already in power. When the hearer in a ritual initially accepts the restricted language of ritual, it implies that he is also accepting the speaker, the one who is on top.[61] Because ritual presents its materials "authoritatively, as axiomatic, stated in a form to render it unverifiable," it discourages inquiry.[62] Disagreement is ruled out because one cannot disagree with the right order of a ritual or the language it employs. Thus, there is the saying "one cannot argue with a ritual."[63]

Instead of viewing ritual as operating to influence this world or the other to bring about some external result, some scholars treat it primarily as an activity with no identifiable practical ends. Even if a ritual achieves certain ends, they maintain, there is no reason to assume that it was expressly intended to achieve such ends. It is practiced, they believe, for no other reasons than its own. It is to be understood in terms of its effects not on the collectivity but on the individual. Although some social scientists, especially anthropologists, are increasingly open to this view, its major proponents have heretofore been psychiatrists, philosophers, semanticists, and theologians.[64] For them ritual is concerned not with practicality but with human drives and emotions.[65]

If we were to catalogue those characteristics most commonly attributed to ritual, we would probably end up with something like the following list:[66]

    1. *Order* or *regularity*. A ritual is a structured event having an orderly sequence of action (although the order may not in all cases be understood by the actor or observer). So important is the order of a ritual that the slightest irregularity in procedure can render it ineffective.

    2. *Repetition*. A ritual is repeated because what it does is continually required. What is repeated is the occasion, content, or form of the ritual, or any combination thereof.

3. *Distinctiveness.* A ritual is set apart from the normal routine of daily life in terms of time, place, and the physical implements employed. Special behavior or stylization characterizes the ritual actor's movements. The actions and symbols employed are extraordinary.

4. *Dramatic effects.* A ritual is not essentially a spontaneous activity but is self-consciously acted. It dramatizes its content and the roles of participants. It is "staged" for dramatic effect, to capture the attention of the audience and to intensify their commitment.[67]

5. *Collective aspect.* An audience implies a collective aspect to ritual. Ritual is performed in a collective setting; it is a shared rather than a private experience.

6. *Symbolism.* Ritual is above all symbolic activity and a symbolic mode of communication.

A useful way to conceptualize how a ritual might work comes from Edmund Leach, who compares a ritual to an orchestra performing a Beethoven symphony. Stated briefly, the music is divided into movements, the themes from one being likely to appear in direct or transposed form in another. To the listener the various musical lines, movements, and the symphony as a whole form a system of interrelated parts. Although the music may take an hour to be performed, the message is transmitted as if everything happened simultaneously. If the performance is successful, the combination of noises the orchestra makes adds up to a mental impression in the audience not markedly different from the statement Beethoven originally wished to make.[68] Although made in another context, the words of Frederik Barth seem particularly apposite here. Barth observes that just as a Beethoven symphony cannot be "explained" other than by listening to it and experiencing its effect, so must ritual be experienced rather than merely explained. If explanation were possible or sufficient, there would be no need ever to perform the rite.[69]

The Chinese term for ritual, *li*, encompasses not only the kind of religious ritual discussed above, but many other notions as well. An early form of the character for *li* already appears in the oracle bone inscriptions—the earliest evidence of writing in China—of the second millennium B.C. It depicts a sacrificial vessel (*li*) with what may be two pieces of jade above it. Later, during Ch'in or Han times, the character assumed its modern form when it was joined to a radical, *shih*, representing either the reeds used in ancient milfoil divination or else a phallic symbol for earth.[70] Both parts of the character suggest the ancient meaning and function of *li*. In the earliest Chinese texts, such as the *Book of Poetry* (*Shih-*

ching) and the *Book of History*, *li* is used almost exclusively in the sense of sacrificial rites associated with ancestral or fertility cults for the securing of supernatural protection and blessings.[71] By the time of Confucius a trend toward increased rationalism in Chinese thought had resulted in an expansion of the meaning of *li* to include the kinds of carefully thought out behavior that formed the code of conduct of the noble lords (*chün-tzu*). Still later it became a code of conduct for all men. *Li* includes such meanings as good manners, etiquette, courtesy, honesty, decorum, decency, cultivation, social obligation, chivalry, custom, and tradition.[72] *Li* was "the embodied expression of what is right" in any given situation.[73] It thus embraced religious ceremonial, sanctioned social practice, and notions of morality and culture. It came to be regarded as the very principle upon which Chinese civilization was based, and thus constituted a major focus of traditional Confucian learning.

The ancient Chinese, like their modern Western counterparts, viewed ritual in both its instrumental and expressive dimensions. But more than the latter, perhaps, they regarded the two functions as inseparable. The Chinese began evolving general theories about *li* toward the end of the Chou dynasty and early in the Han.[74] This was the period when the teachings of the philosophers were first recorded, and the three classics on ritual, the *Rites of Chou* (*Chou-li*), the *Book of Rites* (*Li-chi*), and the *Ceremonial and Ritual* (*I-li*) were all set down in their final form.

Instrumentally, the early Chinese saw *li* as a tool for cultivating moral values and regulating social conduct. As it is said in the *Book of Rites*, "Of all the methods for the good ordering of men, there is none more urgent than the use of ceremonies."[75] Just as the doctrine of the Mandate of Heaven and the theory of portents constituted restraining forces on unbridled absolutism, the *li* were considered a tool for the restraint of civilized mankind as a whole. *Li* regulated human emotions that would otherwise be unrestrained, so as to keep people within bounds, and also gave them a refined expression.[76] Ritual was employed to order the cardinal human relationships in society, "to regulate the relationship between ruler and subject, to insure affection between father and son, peace between brothers, and harmony between husband and wife."[77] *Li* served also to maintain the social gradations necessary to avoid conflict among men.[78]

Ritual facilitated the ordering of the state because, as Confucius observed, when rulers were punctilious in their ritual observances, the people were punctilious in fulfilling their duties to superiors, and thus it was easy to rule. When the ruler acted morally and adhered scrupulously to ritual, "the whole country would 'surrender' to his goodness," and the people would by themselves "flock to him from all sides with their babies strapped to their backs."[79] Ritual served the function of control because it lent a certain uniformity and therefore predictability to people's behavior: "The Master said, 'If the people be taught by lessons of virtue, and uniformity sought to be given to them by the rules of ceremony, their minds will go on to be good.'"[80] Thus ritual assumed a kind of magical potency in its ability to sway the people in the ruler's favor. It is easy to see how ritual might have been manipulated by Chinese monarchs seeking to establish or reaffirm their legitimacy or to consolidate their authority.

The well-known story of the Han founder, Kao-tsu (rg. 206–195 B.C.), well illustrates this point. Kao-tsu had been a peasant before his rise to power and was ill at ease with the niceties of protocol. When he founded his dynasty he therefore abolished the elaborate and bothersome Ch'in ritual code. Unfortunately, his followers, many of whom were rough-and-ready fellows like him, did not show him the courtesy proper to his august position. They often made a shambles of court audiences, getting drunk, hurling insults at one another, and hacking up the wooden pillars of the palace with their swords. To introduce some decorum to his court, Kao-tsu was moved to appoint an erudite named Shu-sun T'ung to provide him with a court ritual consonant with his modest personal capacity for performing ceremonial. When it was completed, and Kao-tsu found it to his liking, he held a court audience with all his subordinates in attendance. The spectacle was dramatic: The emperor was carried into the audience hall on a litter, hundreds of officials carried banners and announced his arrival, and officials came forward to present congratulations to him. All then rose and drank a toast to the emperor in order of rank. Best of all, even after much reveling following the ceremonies, no one dared to become drunk or misbehave. Pleased by this new state of affairs, Kao-tsu exclaimed, "Today for the first time I realize how exalted a thing it is to be an emperor!"[81] Ritual thus served as a powerful tool for dignifying and strengthening the ruler's position and for controlling the behavior of subordinates. It emphasized the large gap between the position of emperor and that of mere bureaucrat, prevented former associates from presuming upon past friendships, and helped keep subordinates agreeably subservient.

With the rise of a belief in the interrelationship of man and nature late in the Chou and during the Han, as reflected in the theories of portents and

of the Five Elements, ritual became linked to the notion that its performance directly influenced the cosmos. According to this notion the human
and natural worlds were linked together so that actions in one brought a
corresponding reaction in the other. The linchpin connecting these worlds
was the ruler, whose behavior on earth found resonance in the cosmos.
The emphasis was on harmonizing human conduct with the rhythms of
the universe. Thus, for example, the "Monthly Instructions" (*Yüeh-ling*)
chapter of the *Book of Rites* portrays the ruler as conforming his ritual
behavior to the calendar. In the Ming-t'ang or Hall of Light, ancient
Chinese monarchs are depicted as moving from room to room, changing
the color of their dress, adjusting their musical tubes, performing rituals,
and issuing decrees all according to the month and the season, thus signifying the basic unity of Heaven and Earth. Conversely, ritual performed
out of season or without the proper mental or emotional attitude might,
according to this doctrine, disturb the cosmic harmony and generate corresponding natural calamities on earth.

As powerful as ritual was in achieving general social order and preserving the harmony of Heaven and Earth, early Chinese thinkers did not
fail also to stress the effect ritual had on the individual ritual actor. Indeed,
man, not the ancestors, spirits, or gods, was always at the center of ritual
activity. Confucius says in the *Analects*, "If I am not present at the sacrifice, it is as though there were no sacrifice," that is, whether or not the
spirits are present is not as important as the state of mind of the sacrificer
and the personal value he obtains from his ritual performance.[82]

The ancient Chinese did not conceive of ritual as divinely inspired;
rather it was simply an outgrowth of human feelings.[83] The third century
B.C. philosopher, Hsün-tzu, one of the most thoughtful early commentators on the subject, attributed the origin of ritual to the ancient kings of
China, who established ritual principles in order to curb contention and
wrangling among men, and to train their desires.[84] Ritual thus had a secular rather than religious basis. Its value, moreover, was largely subjective,
filling, according to Hsün-tzu, a deep emotional need in man:

> The sacrificial rites originate in the emotions of remembrance and longing for
> the dead. Everyone is at times visited by sudden feelings of depression and
> melancholy longing. A loyal minister who has lost his lord or a filial son who
> has lost a parent, even when he is enjoying himself among congenial com-
> pany, will be overcome by such feelings. If they come to him and he is greatly
> moved, but does nothing to give them expression, then his emotions of re-
> membrance and longing will be frustrated and unfulfilled, and he will feel a
> sense of deficiency in his ritual behavior.[85]

Ritual also provided a richly satisfying sensory and aesthetic experience in terms of the food, flora, utensils, music, and physical setting employed:

> Rites are a means of satisfaction. Grain-fed and grass-fed animals, millet and wheat, properly blended with the five flavors—these are what satisfy the mouth. The odors of pepper, orchid, and other sweet-smelling plants—these are what satisfy the nose. The beauties of carving and inlay, embroidery and pattern—these are what satisfy the eye. Bells and drums, strings and woodwinds—these are what satisfy the ear. Spacious rooms and secluded halls, soft mats, couches, benches, armrests and cushions—these are what satisfy the body. Therefore I say that rites are a means of satisfaction.[86]

Rites were made for man by man, and the emotional, sensory, and aesthetic elements of ritual satisfied corresponding human needs. Rites were made not for the gods or the deceased but for living ritual actors.[87]

Intermingled with this profoundly humanistic approach to ritual was a skeptical rationalism regarding its efficacy. Hsün-tzu recognized a difference between the attitude toward ritual on the part of the educated and unlettered masses: If for the latter they were matters pertaining to the spirits, for the former they were merely human practice.[88] Such rationalism was carried to the extreme by the first-century thinker Wang Ch'ung, who spoke out against the almost universal Chinese belief of his time that upon his death man was transformed into a ghost possessing superhuman power, a belief underlying the practice of ancestor "worship." Sacrificial rites to the dead had absolutely no efficacy, Wang claimed, since there were no beings to receive sacrificial offerings. But if there were no such things as ghosts, there was still reason behind sacrifice. Men performed the rites for the purpose of avoiding the appearance of ingratitude for the virtues and contributions of past men.[89] Such skepticism about the nature of rites on the part of Chinese intellectuals provided a means by which they could exploit the sentiments of and influence those who thoroughly believed in supernatural conceptions—the masses.[90]

The post-Han disunion period was not a time for seminal thoughts on ritual. Perhaps the anti-ritualism professed by the third-century poet Juan Chi ("The rites were not set up for the likes of me!") better represents an age in which Confucianism was widely held in political disrepute and Taoism and Buddhism often held greater sway.[91] One scholar who bucked the trend of the times was the Sui Confucian philosopher, Wang T'ung, whom we have already met and who seems to have surpassed all of his contemporaries in his manifest devotion to li. Wang not surprisingly derided Juan Chi's statement that the rites were not for the likes of him.[92]

For Wang they were everything! It is said that when he was residing at home he did not for a moment set aside the *Rites of Chou*. When a disciple inquired about it, he replied, "Since I esteem the great sages of Chou, how could I neglect their *li*?"[93] Modeling himself on Confucius, he sought to embody the same passionate concern for the preservation and propagation of the ancient rites and music. When a disciple asked the meaning of *tao*, Wang freely borrowed from the *Analects* (XII.1) to reply, "Make no movement that is contrary to *li*, look not at what is contrary to *li*, listen not to what is contrary to *li*."[94]

Ritual, according to Wang, nurtured the moral and spiritual values essential to a state's well-being:

> The Master said: "If the capping ceremony is done away with the empire will be without adult [males]; if the marriage ceremony is done away with the empire will be without upright households; if the mourning ceremonies are done away with all in the empire will neglect their relatives; if the sacrificial rites are done away with all in the empire will forget their ancestors."[95]

To ignore the ancient rites and music was to embrace disaster, the fate of the Chin and Southern Dynasties during the disunion period, according to Wang. "Alas! Wasn't it because they abandoned the rites and music of Former Kings that they came to this?"[96] Indeed, it was precisely because a regime preserved the ancient rites and music that Wang considered it politically legitimate, even when, as we have seen, the authorities of that regime were not Chinese.[97]

Legitimacy was a function both of the preservation of the ancient ways and of *the* Way: the Way (*tao*) or Way of Kings (*wang-tao*), on the one hand, and rites and music on the other, were mutually dependent, in Wang's opinion. When one of his disciples once asked about the Way, Wang replied: "When *li* are fulfilled the Way is preserved."[98] Another time, when asked about rites and music, Wang answered: "When the Way of Kings flourishes, rites and music in turn also thrive. But they do not do so now."[99] Although ritual, by Wang's estimation, had been on the decline since the time of the sage-rulers, he believed he could stem the tide by writing his *Continued Classics*, which he envisaged as extending the teachings of the six Confucian classics, including those on rites and music: "Even when the Way of Kings has long been confused," he asked rhetorically, "cannot the rites and music still be regulated?"[100] Unfortunately, Wang T'ung's fervor for ritual does not seem to have been matched by any theoretical originality.

Although the T'ang was an age in which Confucianism had once more moved toward center stage, the strength of its scholarship on ritual lay in the annotation of the ritual classics and the compilation of successive ritual codes rather than in the area of theoretical speculation. Much of our knowledge of early T'ang views on ritual emerges from the *Sui History* "Monograph on Ritual" (*Li-i chih*), compiled by a group of contemporary scholars; official documents concerning ritual matters that survive in a number of T'ang sources; recorded discussions at court; and scattered jottings.

When ritual matters were addressed during the period, platitudes and classical quotations often served in place of thoughtful comment. It is nevertheless possible to identify certain characteristics ritual was believed to possess that were stressed during the early T'ang. First, ritual derived not from any supernatural source but from man himself. This theme, raised many times during the period, was succinctly expressed in 640 in a joint memorial to T'ai-tsung by an ad hoc group of officials investigating ritual: "Ritual descends not from Heaven nor does it spring from Earth. [It is based] only on men's feelings."[101] This led to a second view that ritual was supple and flexible and could adapt to changes in human sentiments or attitudes. T'ai-tsung forcefully expressed this idea in the first month of 629 at the time of the spring plowing ceremony, when he rejected the opinion of one of his counselors that the site he had selected "was not in accord with ancient ritual." T'ai-tsung remarked: "Since rituals arise out of men's feelings, how then can they remain permanent?" The site was therefore not changed.[102]

Ritual matters often served as a smoke screen in a tug of war for political power between monarchy and bureaucracy. If emperors for whatever reason wanted to alter ritual procedures or simply ignore them, their officials just as often wanted to hold them to their letter. A third early T'ang view of ritual was that it might serve to restrain imperial absolutism and set certain limits on a monarch's behavior. Repeatedly during the early T'ang, officials urged their rulers to observe the ritual prescriptions.[103] In a good number of these cases officials probably were acting out of a sincere belief that violation of the old regulations would in some way impair the efficacy of the ceremonies and cause a decline in good government. But just as often officials sought to hold the emperor to the ritual regulations in order to make his behavior more predictable, dissuade him from acting out of purely selfish concerns, and limit his ability to treat his subordinates capriciously. The oft-invoked injunction of T'ai-tsung's trusted counselor, Wei Cheng, that "the rules of ritual cannot be exceeded" can thus be better understood in the context of bureaucratic attempts to control imperial behavior.[104]

T'ai-tsung was not unaware that ritual in practice served to control his own behavior. He once gave a banquet where everyone was called on to compose a prose-poem (*fu*). The emperor's *fu* spoke of the many bad rulers who had given free rein to their emotions, and the few enlightened rulers who had been able to control theirs. Wei Cheng then wrote a *fu* on the Former Han, which alluded to the story narrated earlier in this chapter about the founding emperor and his need to restore decorum to his court:

> In the end [Kao-tsu] depended on Shu-sun T'ung's rites,
> Only then did he know how exalted it was to be an emperor.

T'ai-tsung then replied: "Wei Cheng never fails to restrain me with ritual."[105]

Ritual was a two-way street, however. If the emperor might be constrained or more readily controlled by the requirements of ritual, so might his officials and the wider populace as a whole. In perusing the materials related to ritual for the early T'ang, on several occasions we encounter the phrase *an shang chih min*, taken from the *Book of Rites* and the *Book of Filial Piety*: "Confucius said 'For giving security to superiors and good government to the people [*an shang chih min*], there is nothing more excellent than the rules of propriety [*li*].'"[106] The phrase appears, for example, in imperial edicts of 624 and 637.[107] When Tsu Hsiao-sun completed his "New Music" in 628, T'ang-tsung observed that rites and music were used by the ancient sages to regulate (*tsun-chieh*) the people and to establish good government.[108] T'ai-tsung's counselor Wei Cheng noted in his *Sui History* that the state could be governed by four methods: the first, benevolence and righteousness; the second, regulation by ritual; the third, codified law; and the fourth, punishment. Benevolence, righteousness, and regulation by ritual were the "trunk" of government, and codified law and punishment the "branches," Wei maintained.[109] How similar these sentiments appear to another passage from the *Book of Rites*: "The end to which ceremonies, music, punishments, and law conduct is one; they are the instruments by which the minds of the people are assimilated, and good order in government made to appear."[110] Thus, the fourth early T'ang view of ritual was that it served as a tool for controlling the masses (and officialdom as well), and for rendering the position of the ruler more secure. It was a view with which few modern functionalists would disagree.

SYMBOLISM

Modern scholars mark oral speech, writing, mathematical notation, flags, and even certain behavior patterns as symbols.[111] The creation of symbols appears to be universal among men.[112] Symbolism is so basic to man and the forms it takes so elemental that it may transcend barriers of both language and culture. On the other hand, the ways in which different societies conceptualize such symbols as kinship systems, moral codes, religions, and ideologies are sufficiently distinct that they have served students of behavior as a basis for characterizing and classifying those societies. For cultural anthropologists, culture is conceived as a system of symbols.[113]

In this study we are particularly interested in the relation of symbolism to ritual, and, further, to political control.

The *Oxford English Dictionary* defines symbol as "something that stands for, represents, or denotes something else (not by exact resemblance, but by vague suggestions, or by some accidental or conventional relation); *esp.* a material object representing or taken to represent something immaterial or abstract, as a being, idea, quality, or condition...."[114] Symbolic forms are multifarious and self-transcendent: "The ways in which a symbol can mean are potentially as many as the ways in which one thing can stand for and lead the mind to something else...."[115] Symbols possess many of their "meanings" simultaneously, a quality variously known as polysemy, multivocality, or multivalency.

One of the ways symbols have been employed is as an instrument of power and social control. All societies, it has been said, "manipulate people through the symbols that engage them."[116] Certain symbols are so powerful in this regard that they are referred to as "master," "dominant," "core," or "key" symbols. Those in authority attempt to legitimate their rule by making it appear as if they possess an exclusive relationship to these kinds of representations—moral symbols, sacred emblems, orthodox ideologies, and so on.[117] "Descended from the gods," "divine right of kings," and "the will of the majority" are among such central conceptions. In traditional China the Mandate of Heaven belongs to this category. Symbols can serve as handmaidens of authority because of their ability to unify an audience around a common focal point. They do not themselves create unity; rather they provide "units of discourse which are fundamental to all thinking and doing, units of feeling around which emotions of loyalty and assurance can cluster."[118] For example, a powerful symbol like a national flag enables coalitions to form among groups or individuals that might otherwise remain hostile to one another.[119]

The complexity of symbolic associations allows symbols to serve as focal points of emotion and sentiment. Among the various kinds of signifiers, symbols may well be the most potent in terms of feelings stirred and action-impelling properties.[120] Raymond Firth provides us with a useful example of the difference between the least potent of signifiers, a sign, and a symbol. A red flag in the middle of the road (a sign) usually means that there is some obstacle ahead and that we should for safety's sake slow down. However, the same flag placed on a Parisian students' barricade stands for a complex, not very specific set of ideas and actions, that is, it is a symbol. It may stand for the general idea of defiance of established authority, but at the same time for more elaborate and vaguely delineated ideas of moral values and political justice. The red flag, moreover, now generates strong emotions that are intermingled with intellectual concepts.[121] Symbols, unlike signs, possess a dynamic quality. Their multivocality and ability to stir emotions can trigger responses among people in the public arena.[122] We can see that this is especially true of dominant symbols, like the Christian Cross or, in the Chinese case, the River Chart (Ho-t'u) and Lo Writing (Lo-shu), sacred documents of remote antiquity supposedly guaranteeing the holder's possession of the Mandate.[123]

Symbols can aid constituted authority by generating "quiescence" among members of a political system. Skillfully employed political symbols—such as slogans and theories, commemorative events and monuments, music and song, flags and decorations, mass ceremonials and parades, and so forth—can produce emotional catharses and the resolution of tensions which serve to nullify dissent and defuse potentially threatening action.[124] By setting rough limits to thought, symbols affirm certain ideas while virtually excluding others. A given political system or ideology may persist therefore simply because, given the tyranny of the prevailing symbolism, no one can conceive of potential alternatives. They are thought to be a "natural" part of the universe and therefore unalterable.[125]

One kind of symbol, the religious, serves among its various functions to unify man not with other men but with the beyond, whether God, gods, deified ancestors, or some such. Religious symbols are regarded as having the power to lead man toward a relationship with the divine or to levels of experience from which he is normally excluded.[126] They reveal a whole rather than a partial reality, what Clifford Geertz has called the "really real."[127] Since these symbols are thought of as life-givers and death-dealers, they are "besought, trusted, feared, and placated with service and sacrifice."[128]

Symbols have played their part in China as in all other societies. We have only to mention, for a start, the trigrams and hexagrams of the *Book of Changes*, yin-yang dualistic cosmology, and the reckoning of time by the ten heavenly stems and twelve earthly branches. Rather than comment on the number and variety of Chinese symbols, I want here to provide an introduction to the ways in which the Chinese traditionally understood the concept of symbol and how it functioned.

In the Former Han period the numerological correlations of the yin-yang school were adapted to the *Book of Changes*, producing a body of literature called *wei-shu*, or apocrypha, which sought to give a systematic explanation of the cosmos and its movement, but was judged by later Confucians to be a hodgepodge of superstition. Although most of the apocrypha on the *Book of Changes* are now lost, they appear to have been concerned with the study of the relations between emblems or graphic representations (*hsiang*) of natural objects and the numerical categories (*shu*) that were assigned to these representations. In the apocrypha the *hsiang* are the eight trigrams, which, according to the *Book of Changes*, were created by the culture-hero Fu Hsi after he first carefully observed the natural objects around him. The trigrams served as the springboard for the numerological symbolism employed in the apocrypha.[129]

The character *hsiang* is an important element in our discussion of the Chinese understanding of symbolism. Karlgren has traced several meanings for *hsiang* in the ancient literature, among them figure, to represent, to imitate, image, shape, appearance, to depict, pictured, emblem, and symbol.[130] The character *hsiang* provides, in fact, perhaps the closest approximation in pre-modern Chinese for our words "symbol" or "symbolize" in the sense of substitution for or representation of physical objects. The *Book of History* speaks of the twelve symbols or emblematic forms of the ancient rulers (*ku jen chih hsiang*) which were worn on the monarch's robes: sun, moon, constellation, mountains, dragons, pheasants, bronze libation cups, water weeds, flames, seeds of grain, ax, and *fu*-symbol (a mark of distinction).[131] The twelve emblems seem to have been representations of the universe and its component elements. A passage on the suburban sacrifices in the *Book of Rites* suggests the cosmological nature of some of the emblems:

On that day, the king assumed the robe with the ascending dragons on it as an emblem [*hsiang*] of the heavens. He wore the cap with the pendants of jade-pearls, to the number of twelve, which is the number of heaven. He rode the plain carriage, because of its simplicity. From the flag hung twelve pendants, and on it was the emblazonry of dragons, and the figures of the sun and moon, in imitation [*hsiang*] of the heavens. Heaven hangs out its brilliant figures, and the sages imitated [*hsiang*] them. This border [i.e., suburban] sacrifice is the illustration of the way of heaven.[132]

The twelve emblems survived throughout imperial times in China as symbols of royal authority.

During the early T'ang the scholar Yang Ch'iung discoursed on the twelve emblems in a memorial to the throne dated 662, in which he explained the symbolic function of each, using the character *hsiang* no less than nine times. The sun, moon, and constellation symbolized the enlightenment of the ruler shining down upon all mankind; the mountains, by scattering clouds and rains, symbolized the wise ruler's deluging his people with benefits; the dragon, whose transformations were numberless, symbolized the wise ruler's issuing of laws and instructions according to the temper of the times, and so forth.[133]

The twelve emblems was only one example of a whole treasure trove of political symbols—*miranda*—that served to exalt and legitimate royal power in China. The nine caldrons attributed to the culture-hero Yü, which were successively moved to different dynastic capitals during the Hsia, Shang, and Chou, became symbols of the transmission of political authority. Founding a new dynasty was thus referred to as "establishing the caldron" (*ting ting*).[134]

Another group of symbolic objects that functioned in dynastic transitions, also nine in number, were the so-called nine gifts or nine conferments (*chiu-hsi*). In ancient times the gifts were given as rewards to meritorious subordinates by the Son of Heaven. They consisted of special carriages and horses, clothing, musical instruments, doors and stairways, and other marks of distinction.[135] The nine gifts figured in a majority of dynastic transitions from the Three Kingdoms period through the T'ang.[136]

Like their modern Western counterparts the ancient Chinese understood the process of symbolization to encompass not just physical objects but human actions as well. The chapter in the *Book of Rites* on the suburban sacrifices says: "When the Son of Heaven went on his inspecting tours to the princes, the viands of the feast to him were composed of a [single] calf.... [The feasting of him in such a manner] was to do honour to the idea of sincerity."[137] Reading through the chapter on the suburban sacrifices, it seems apparent that almost every gesture, employment of ritual utensils and victims, placement of ritual actors and altar, and so on, had a symbolic meaning.

The symbolic nature of ritual was greatly appreciated by that most sensitive of commentators, Hsün-tzu:

> In the funeral rites, one adorns the dead as though they were still living, and sends them to the grave with forms of symbolic life. They are treated as though dead, and yet as though still alive, as though gone, and yet as though still present. Beginning and end are thereby unified.[138]

Our discussion of Chinese symbolism has barely scratched the surface. We have, for example, not even mentioned literary, Taoist, or Buddhist symbolism. Nor have we dealt with such important matters as color codes, taboos, or ceremonial protocol, all of which operated symbolically in the political arena of the imperial court. Nevertheless, it should be clear that thinking Chinese were keenly aware of much of the symbolism that operated in their society. They took pains to identify symbols and to associate them with possible referents. But judging by a lack of relevant material, such "deeper" questions as how the symbolic mechanism operated, what the properties of symbols were, and in what ways symbols influenced politics for the most part failed to occur to the Chinese or, more likely, simply did not interest them.

The manipulatory dimension of ritual and symbol suggests that they can be purposively fabricated by individuals or groups with particular goals in mind. This seems not to be the case, however. No one makes up ritual or symbol any more than anyone makes up language. Ritual and symbol arise without intention or adaptation to conscious purpose; they seem to be collective products worked out by numberless anonymous men over long periods of time.[139] Consequently, elites cannot consciously mold political myths or rituals to serve selfish ends, since these attempts at manipulation usually are discovered, and so fail.[140] According to this way of thinking, elites can seize on the manipulatory opportunities afforded by pre-existing rituals and symbolic associations, but they cannot systematically create them de novo. Ironically, it appears that rituals and symbols must in some way already be regarded as "legitimate" in order for them to confer legitimacy on those who employ them.

To say that ritual and symbol can be manipulated for effect implies the existence of an audience that serves as the target of manipulation. But who is this audience?[141] Here we must introduce Easton's concept of the "politically relevant members" of a political system. "It should be clear," notes Easton, "that there is no structural difference between those who introduce demands and those who react to outputs.... They are part or all of the politically relevant members of a system, those who can and do participate in the political process."[142]

Insofar as the mass of T'ang commoners exerted through their potential for insurrection at least a negative input into the political system, they can be regarded as having participated in the system in some limited way, and thus as having been politically "relevant." No doubt this is one basis, as we will see in a later chapter, for the initiation of T'ang imperial tours of inspection, which, by "showing the flag" and the emperor's personal concern for his people, served positively to engage the emotions of the populace encountered along the imperial route. The same holds true for those ritual and symbolic activities that directly touched the lives of the people living in the T'ang capital and its environs, the setting for a majority of the state rituals.

For the most part, however, the masses were only indirectly the intended audience of manipulation. Equally or even more powerful in terms of its ability to generate indirect support for regimes in traditional China was the elite scholar-official class, consisting of retired, incumbent, or potential officials and their families, which many times before had demonstrated its ability to nourish or quickly destroy a newborn regime. It was they and, more properly, their representatives who, in Easton's terms, routinely participated in the political process. In the early T'ang ritual and symbolic activities we treat in this volume, the major actors in all cases are either emperors, their officials, or both. This leads us to a consideration of the idea that whereas T'ang officials, along with the emperor, normally had a hand in determining the patterns of state ritual and symbolic behavior, they themselves, broadly speaking, were also the intended primary audience for such behavior. Leach underscores this notion by observing that in a ritual there is usually a master of ceremonies or chief priest whose actions provide guideposts for all the other participants. "But there is no separate audience of listeners," he cautions. "The performers and listeners are the same people. We engage in rituals in order to transmit collective messages to ourselves."[143] This also seems to have been the case with the collective messages transmitted by the T'ang emperors and their officials in the state rituals. Here, ritual actors and ritual audience were for the most part one and the same.

CHAPTER 2

The Early T'ang Ritual Background

THE DYNASTY KAO-TSU FOUNDED WAS ONE OF THE MOST SUCCESSFUL AND widely influential in all of Chinese history. During the T'ang, in the words of Arthur Wright and Denis Twitchett, China became "the radiating center of civilization for the whole of East Asia."[1] From its great fountainhead, political and institutional models, Confucian and Buddhist moral and ideological precepts, and the latest fashions in literature and dress flowed freely to other states within the Chinese cultural orbit. Its capital, Ch'ang-an, the greatest city in the world of its time, attracted religious pilgrims, students, leaders of tribes and petty states, diplomatic emissaries, merchants, and entertainers from all over Asia. Much of the success of the T'ang was owed to its predecessor, the Sui (581–618), which had reunited China in 589 after centuries of political and cultural fragmentation. Although in power for less than forty years, the Sui provided much of the institutional foundation for the new regime. During the founding and consolidation period of the T'ang, comprising the reigns of Kao-tsu (618–26), T'ai-tsung (627–49), and Kao-tsung (650–83), the dynasty did not need, therefore, to undertake vast new public works projects, reorganize its government, or radically transform its basic institutions and political practices.[2] Dynastic energies were expended instead on institutional adaptation and improvement, the creation of domestic peace and material prosperity, and the expansion of empire.

Like their immediate predecessors, the T'ang royal house claimed descent from the northwestern aristocracy and had married heavily with Turkish and other non-Chinese nobility. Indeed, Kao-tsu was closely related on his mother's side to the royal houses of both the Northern Chou

(557–81) and the Sui. By 617, years of expensive and fruitless military campaigns against Korea, general administrative decline, and the effects of natural calamities unrelieved by a demoralized bureaucracy had generated widespread opposition to the Sui. Kao-tsu, a member of the social elite that had furnished rulers for successive regimes in North China, and commander of the large T'ai-yüan garrison in the central part of modern Shansi province, was in a perfect position to lead a revolt against the Sui. In a year's time he had become a Son of Heaven. Although much of his reign was spent wiping out opposition to the T'ang among other contenders for the throne and extending central power to the countryside, Kao-tsu succeeded in establishing the institutional and political framework of the dynasty. Sources of revenue were increased by the reimposition of the Sui system of land-tenure and direct taxation; irrigation and canal systems were extended; a law code was promulgated; the civil service system was revived; a school system designed to train candidates for the examinations was re-established; and local militia units were organized, stationed most heavily in the capital region. By the conclusion of his reign, the dynasty had been placed on solid administrative, economic, and military foundations.

The last years of Kao-tsu's reign were marked by a struggle for power between his second son, T'ai-tsung, who had successively vanquished rebel holdouts against T'ang authority, and his first son, the crown prince, who became jealous of his brother's military successes and fearful that T'ai-tsung's growing popularity would destroy his own chances of inheriting the throne. The climax of this struggle came early in the sixth month of 626, when T'ai-tsung and a band of his supporters slew the crown prince and one of his followers, a younger son of Kao-tsu, at the Hsüan-wu Gate, the northern entrance to the imperial palace. The Hsüan-wu Gate incident, which brought T'ai-tsung to power, irrevocably changed the course of the dynasty and inaugurated the first high point of T'ang history.[3]

T'ai-tsung spent his period in power consolidating and extending the achievements of his father. T'ang administration was rationalized and improved, attaining a degree of efficiency and fairness and generating an abundance of bureaucratic morale, that remained benchmarks for future ages. The economy prospered, helped by domestic peace, good weather and harvests, as well as new measures, such as the "relief granary" system which afforded the population some protection against the ravages of natural disaster. The new prosperity enabled T'ai-tsung to undertake an interventionist foreign policy. T'ang control was extended over the Turks of Inner Mongolia, the Central Asian oases of the "Silk Road," the T'u-yü-hun of modern Tsinghai province, and the Hsüeh-yen-t'o of modern Sinkiang. Only the northern Korean kingdom of Koguryŏ remained beyond the emperor's grasp. Successive campaigns against Koguryŏ occupied his last years on the throne and brought him the bitter and unaccustomed taste of defeat. Despite this setback, T'ai-tsung's reign created a sense of national well-being and a widespread mood of self-confidence unknown in China since the heyday of the great Han dynasty. Later ages celebrated T'ai-tsung's reign as a model that combined exemplary civil government with unrivaled military success. They attributed his dramatic achievements not only to his own conscientiousness and wisdom but also to his willingness to heed the excellent counsel of his ministers, themselves outstanding statesmen. It seemed to them that T'ai-tsung was the embodiment of a Confucian ideal: a modest sovereign willing to accept correction out of a sincere concern for his people.

The next emperor, Kao-tsung, was not among his father's first choices as heir. But when personal scandal and political intrigue eliminated two of his brothers from the succession, Kao-tsung was promoted to crown prince despite T'ai-tsung's reservations concerning his ability to lead the country. The emperor had good reasons for doubt. T'ai-tsung's kind of administration demanded qualities and a sheer force of personality that Kao-tsung simply did not possess. Moreover, Kao-tsung was hobbled by poor health—bouts of dizziness and impaired vision brought upon, perhaps, by strokes—which frequently left him incapacitated. The resulting political vacuum at court was quickly filled by the beautiful and enticing Wu Chao, who in 655 had Kao-tsung set aside his legitimate wife, the childless Empress Wang, and elevate herself to the position of empress. Confucian historians have been entirely hostile to Empress Wu, a woman who dared after her husband's death to rule China with the title of "emperor." But it is nevertheless apparent that she possessed abundant gifts and, although completely ruthless and vindictive, had a natural genius for politics.

By and large, Kao-tsung and Empress Wu proved to be effective caretakers of the T'ang legacy. There was, after all, little need for administrative innovation: The basic machinery of government had been established under Kao-tsu and improved and rationalized under T'ai-tsung. T'ang codes of law and administrative regulations were updated. The civil service examination system was reorganized: The *chin-shih* examination degree came to confer far greater prestige than any other, and the first palace examinations were inaugurated. Under the joint leadership of Kao-tsung and Empress Wu the T'ang rose to a level of military power and prestige surpassing even that of T'ai-tsung's time. For a brief moment, in the late 650s and early 660s, China controlled territory of unprecedented dimensions, stretching from the Sea of China to the borders of Persia. Even Koguryŏ, unconquered all during the Sui and early T'ang, fell under T'ang suzerainty for a time.

By the end of the period signs of internal stress and crisis had become apparent, however. Extravagant military expenditures and the costs associated with a swollen civilian bureaucracy had imposed a heavy burden on the peasantry, who fled in ever greater numbers to undeveloped areas in order to escape taxation. The ravages of flood and drought, an increasingly serious problem as time went on, were not being ameliorated. The court, moreover, did not know how to cope with the situation. The dynasty, which had become militarily overextended and was suffering the increased power of foreign rivals, especially the Tibetans and revivified Turks, lost much of its recently acquired territory. Although traditional Chinese historians have been quick to criticize Kao-tsung and, especially, his consort, for this decline, it is also true that they presided over a period of general domestic peace and administrative stability lasting longer than the reigns of Kao-tsu and T'ai-tsung combined.

THE EARLY T'ANG RITUAL CODES

It had long been fashionable by early T'ang times for Confucians to bewail the state of ritual practice and knowledge, which were considered to have declined precipitously from the Golden Age of Hsia, Shang, and Chou. As recently as 582 a former Northern Ch'i dynasty official, Yen Chih-t'ui, had reported in a memorial to the Sui founder that "it has already been a long time since the rites and music collapsed into ruins."[4] Confucius in his own age already deplored the superficial quality of ritual—all surface effects with none of the feelings and attitudes appropriate to the occasion. In the *Analects* he had cried, "Ritual, ritual! Does it mean no more than offerings of jade and silk? Music, music! Does it mean no more than bells and drums?"[5] Confucius' comment was much in the minds of those who discussed ritual at the early T'ang court.[6] It was also alluded to in an imperial edict of 637, where the implicit, pious hope was that the new ritual and music would be more than just jade and silk, bells and drums.[7] Nevertheless, the early T'ang commentators took for granted that ritual had become elaborate, empty, and confused, and that despite the efforts of successive ages ritual procedure was still largely in disarray.[8]

The introduction to the "Monograph on Ritual" of the *Sui History*, written during the early T'ang, traces the beginning of the decline to the demise of the Western Chou dynasty and the establishment at Lo-yang of a much-weakened eastern successor regime in the eighth century B.C. Later, Confucius had wanted to save his age with ritual and music, but the rulers of the various feudal states had paid no heed to him, and ritual had declined even further. The Ch'in had inherited Chou ritual, but Shih-huang-ti had utilized only those rituals that exalted his personal power and restrained his officials, and had dealt ritual a crushing blow with his infamous decree ordering the Burning of the Books. Although ritual was reconstituted under the Han, it soon became elaborate and empty, with little to esteem. The introduction concludes with a routine listing of the various ritualists during the Period of Disunion and the Sui who had lent their hand to compiling the ritual codes of their respective regimes.[9] In the end, one senses a certain lack of enthusiasm on the part of the early T'ang scholars for the labors of these ritual experts of the disunion period.

Perhaps the picture they painted was a bit too dismal. Despite political fragmentation and internecine strife, traditional Confucian studies had proceeded apace from the end of the Han down to the T'ang, with ritual serving as the most popular field of study. Studies on ritual, both in terms of the number of titles and total number of chapters, occupy first place among all the categories of classical scholarship treated in the *Sui History* "Monograph on Literature," a preponderant majority of which was compiled during the post-Han through Sui period.[10] The interest in ritual was to a large extent focused on mourning regulations, a reflection of the aristocratic bent of society during the disunion period. Mourning regulations, with their emphasis on distinctions between near and remote relations, were a means of shoring up the aristocratic family system.[11] In the South emphasis on ritual studies was also placed on the ceremonial, music, carriages, and clothing employed at court. In the North there was a much greater stress placed on the *Rites of Chou*, an idealized Han dynasty depiction of the Chou bureaucracy, of dubious historical value. The mixed Chinese-"barbarian" dynasts of the northern regimes sought to benefit from the sentiments of legitimacy surrounding a regime that was regarded as the fount of Chinese culture. Su Ch'o (498–546), minister under the founder of the Western Wei dynasty, Yü-wen T'ai, used the archaic nomenclature of the *Rites of Chou* to rename all the offices of government. In the middle of the sixth century the Yü-wen family went on to proclaim themselves rulers of the "Chou" dynasty, later referred to as the Northern Chou to distinguish it from its illustrious predecessor. In the Northern Ch'i dynasty, which was coeval with the Northern Chou, *Rites of Chou* scholarship also flourished. Hsü An-sheng, renowned as an interpreter of the text, gathered about him a large body of disciples.[12]

The Sui reunification of China in 589 created the need for a ritual code reflecting the establishment of a centralized empire and a monarchy with expanded powers. A commission of several high officials, presided over by Niu Hung, worked on drafting the Sui ceremonial, which was published in 602 in 130 sections (*p'ien*) and 100 chapters (*chüan*).[13] Ch'en Yin-k'o has demonstrated that although the Sui was in many institutional respects a legatee of the Yü-wen house, with respect to ritual it for the most part followed not the unrealistic *Rites of Chou*, which harked back to a decentralized feudal regime, but rather the codes of the southern regimes of Liang and Ch'en and the northern regime of Ch'i.[14]

At the very beginning of the T'ang, before the dynasty had time to compile its own ritual regulations, the Sui code was followed virtually *in toto*. Only in T'ai-tsung's time did the T'ang complete its first ritual code, the so-called *Chen-kuan li*, after T'ai-tsung's reign-name, which was in 138 sections divided into 100 chapters. While adding some new topical sections, it was essentially based on the old Sui code. The *Chen-kuan li* was presented to the throne and an edict issued ordering it put into practice in the first month of 633.[15]

The chief compilers of the *Chen-kuan li* were Fang Hsüan-ling and Wei Cheng, two of T'ai-tsung's most influential ministers. There is an interesting story involving Fang and Wei, of contemporary date, which suggests that many of the deficiencies medieval Chinese saw as characterizing ritual knowledge ever since the Golden Age of Chou had lingered into the early T'ang as well. The story, which may well be apocryphal, was set down in 646 by Wang Fu-chih, third son of the Sui Confucian philosopher Wang T'ung, and it is contained in the *Complete T'ang Prose* (*Ch'üan T'ang-wen*).[16] Its characters comprise some of the more illustrious figures of the early T'ang government who were alleged to have once been disciples of Wang T'ung: Wei Cheng, Fang Hsüan-ling, Wen Yen-po, and Tu Yen.[17] According to the narrative, when Wei Cheng fell ill sometime during T'ai-tsung's reign he was visited by a younger brother of Wang T'ung, Wang Ning. Wei mentioned to Ning that at the end of the Sui, when he, Fang, and the others were all serving Wang T'ung, the Confucian teacher had praised several of his other disciples as outstanding in their knowledge of the rites and music. This had made Wei, who presumably knew far less than they, somewhat uncomfortable.

Later, when Wang T'ung and his disciples who were authorities on rites and music had all died, Wei, Fang, and the others found themselves serving T'ai-tsung in high advisory positions. One day the emperor invited them to attend a banquet, during the course of which he inquired which rites of the Hsia, Shang, and Chou dynasties were suitable to employ for the T'ang. A grave silence fell over the table. Only after Fang and Tu had glared at him for some time did Wei make the rather obvious point that the ritual of the Hsia and Shang could no longer be studied in much detail, and then quoted Confucius to the effect that since the mirror of Chou was in the previous two ages, he followed the ritual of Chou. If His Majesty wished to select from the regulations of the former ages to demonstrate the Way of Kings, Wei opined, he could do no better than put the rites of Chou into practice. Upon hearing this, T'ai-tsung became very happy.

The next day T'ai-tsung summoned Tu, Fang, and Wei to his chambers and told them that he had spent all the previous night reading the *Rites of Chou*, which, he informed them, was truly the work of sages. He had concluded from his reading of the text that good government could not be achieved without reviving such ancient Chou institutions as the well-field system, the *feng-chien* "feudal" system, and others. He ordered them to return to their government offices and lodge there while deliberating on how this policy was to be best implemented. After several fruitless days of discussion, however, Wei asked to be excused from this impossible task. Diplomatically, the emperor did not again bring up the matter of the *Rites of Chou*.

Nevertheless, at another banquet which was held soon afterward, T'ai-tsung again pressed his counselors about devising rites and music appropriate to their time. He was extremely sorrowful that the rites and music had fallen into ruin, he said, and it was only for this reason that he had been urging them on so. If they did not succeed in this venture, the Ancients would grieve over it. Wei Cheng quickly reassured T'ai-tsung that the question of rites and music might still be settled. The emperor once more apologized for his urgency, and he requested that they retire without any further thoughts on the matter. Mortified and trembling with fright, Wei, Fang, and the others kowtowed and immediately departed.

Once out of earshot of the emperor, Fang turned to Wei and blamed their ignorance of rites and music on the fact that their teacher, Wang T'ung, had never instructed them in this field. If Wang's other disciples were here now, he rued, they would not be in such a mess!

Whether or not this story is true is not as important, I think, as the reflection it provides of a contemporary perception about the depressed state of ritual knowledge, and of the difficulties faced even by so-called experts in fashioning a suitable ritual blueprint for their own time. Despite this perception—or, perhaps, because of it—during the reign of T'ai-tsung an emphasis was placed on ritual texts in the *ming-ching*, or classics examination. Candidates were expected to have studied both the *Rites of Chou* and the *Ceremonial and Ritual*.[18]

The *Chen-kuan li* remained in force during the rest of T'ai-tsung's reign and into the early years of the reign of his successor. Eventually, after several lacunae had been discovered in it, Kao-tsung ordered that a new set of regulations be compiled. Known as the *Hsien-ch'ing li*, the ritual code of the Hsien-ch'ing ("Manifest Felicitation") reign-period, it was presented to the throne in 130 chapters in 658. Kao-tsung personally provided its preface. The consensus of contemporary scholars was, however, that the new work did not come up to the standards of the old. Moreover, ambiguities in the text caused confusion in carrying out its provisions. Thus, in 676 an edict was handed down returning ritual usage to the regulations of the Chen-kuan period. The following year yet another edict was issued stating that since the *Hsien-ch'ing li* had in several respects not accorded with ancient practice, state ritual was henceforth to conform to the practice of Chou times. But since this was not a real possibility, and the ritual officials had little else to work with, they relied in practice on both the *Chen-kuan li* and *Hsien-ch'ing li*, and neither was actually discarded.[19]

CHENG HSÜAN VERSUS WANG SU

It is important to note that the transition from the *Chen-kuan li* to the *Hsien-ch'ing li* was not simply a matter of the displacement of one corpus of ritual regulations by another. The transition also reflected, in many respects, the victory of the ideas of one school of classical exegesis and ritual theory over another. In this context, we need to know something about two thinkers of the Later Han and Three Kingdoms periods, Cheng Hsüan and Wang Su.

Cheng Hsüan (127–200) was born into a locally prominent family in modern Shantung province.[20] He spent his early years studying the classics, and after exhausting his tutors' knowledge of the subject he left home for the Han capital, where he studied for a time under the renowned scholar Ma Jung (79–166). He and Ma eventually became the two most esteemed commentators of the Later Han dynasty. Giles rightly calls him "one of the most voluminous of all the commentators upon the Confucian Classics."[21] Indeed, Cheng made the entire domain of the classics his own, attempting to provide a consistent interpretation over the complete body of the canon. He especially excelled in the area of ritual exegesis, writing commentaries on all three of the ritual classics, the *Book of Rites*, the *Rites of Chou*, and the *Ceremonial and Ritual*, a feat unprecedented among Confucian scholars of the Han.[22] Although in his classical commentaries Cheng basically cleaved to the Old Text school of thought, he also attempted to reconcile it with New Text interpretations and thus eliminate the distinctions between the two schools.[23] The New Text school was heavily influenced by Five Elements and yin-yang cosmological speculation, and the prophetic and apocryphal texts known as *ch'an-wei*. *Ch'an* were prognostication or divination texts. *Wei*, or "weft" texts, were considered complementary to the "warp" (*ching*) texts of the orthodox canon. *Ch'an-wei* were regarded as omens sent directly by Heaven. They appear to have originated at the beginning of the Later Han dynasty, when their texts were employed to demonstrate that the Later Han founder, Kuang-wu-ti, had gained Heaven's Mandate.[24] Whereas the New Text school tended to identify the political world with the operation of the universe, the Old Text school placed less emphasis on the cosmos, and its adherents were oriented more toward man than toward the divine.[25]

Wang Su (195–256) was the son of the scholar-official Wang Lang, who occupied high office under the Three Kingdoms Wei dynasty founders, Ts'ao Ts'ao and his son, Ts'ao P'ei.[26] As a young man Wang Su earned a reputation as a brilliant scholar, and he quickly rose to high position in the central government. He wrote extensive commentaries on the classics, including all three texts on ritual. His scholarly training combined work in the Old Text and New Text traditions, as had that of Cheng Hsüan. But whereas Wang was generously disposed toward the scholarship of such Old Texters as Chia K'uei (30–101) and Ma Jung, he was more critical of the New Texters, among whom he seems to have lumped Cheng Hsüan. Wang so disliked Cheng's interpretations of the classics that he is said to have compiled an entire book deriding Cheng's views, called *Discussions Attesting the Truth of the Sage* (*Sheng-cheng lun*). It is now lost.[27] But we know that in the *Sheng-cheng lun* Wang generously quoted from *The School Sayings of Confucius* (*K'ung-tzu chia-yü*), a work he himself had largely forged, to counter Cheng's ideas regarding several ritual matters. These included the number of ancestral temples the imperial house should have, the number of altars that should be built in the near suburbs of the capital and what deities should be worshiped there, and the nature of Heaven, or Hao-t'ien shang-ti.[28] These are all subjects we will treat in later chapters of this volume.

One of the major foci of the debate between Cheng Hsüan and Wang Su, and between their later adherents as well, was the nature of Heaven. Whereas Wang saw Hao-t'ien shang-ti as a single, supreme deity, Cheng combined him with the so-called Five Heavenly Emperors to form the Six Heavens (*liu-t'ien*). During the Period of Disunion the debate over the nature of Hao-t'ien shang-ti intensified, with Cheng's and Wang's views alternately prevailing. At the beginning of the Chin dynasty, during the reign of Wu-ti (rg. 265–90), for example, Wang Su's interpretations of the classics triumphed, probably owing to the fact that he was the maternal grandfather of the emperor. His versions of the classics were studied in the schools, and his ideas regarding the ritual at the ancestral temple and suburban altars were all followed to the exclusion of those of Cheng Hsüan. But later in the dynasty, there was a shift in intellectual currents more in the direction of Cheng Hsüan's textual interpretations.[29]

The world of scholarship, split into northern and southern camps during the Period of Disunion, was likewise split in its allegiance to the views of Cheng and Wang. Generally speaking, the so-called School of Northern Learning (*Pei-hsüeh*) esteemed the *Book of History*, *Book of Changes*, *Book of Poetry*, and *Book of Rites* all in their Cheng Hsüan versions.[30] The School of Southern Learning (*Nan-hsüeh*) was a somewhat more complex affair, accepting some of Cheng Hsüan's interpretations of canonical texts, such as the *Book of Changes* and *Book of History*, but also favoring the commentaries of scholars like Tu Yü and Wang Su. It was also heavily influenced by neo-Taoism, as interpreted most notably by Wang Pi (226–49). While Cheng Hsüan's ideas were more influential on the ritual practice of the Northern Dynasties, those of Wang Su were more influential among the regimes of the South. Gradually, Southern scholarship began to incorporate the interpretations of Northern Learning, and vice versa. But whereas Northern Learning as a whole declined by the late sixth century, Southern Learning flourished.[31]

Ritual scholarship in the early T'ang was merely part of a much larger effort to reunify Chinese thought after centuries of fragmentation between North and South, and to settle those areas of inquiry that had served as the traditional focus of classical learning. In the middle of T'ai-tsung's reign, sometime around 638, the emperor ordered the compilation of official commentaries on the Confucian canon. Known as the *Five Classics with Orthodox Commentary (Wu-ching cheng-i)*, in 180 *chüan*, it was designed to be used by candidates studying for the *ming-ching*, or classics degree, one of the degrees offered in the renascent examination system.[32] The commission that initially compiled the work was headed by K'ung Ying-ta, a northerner. Soon after its promulgation in 642, further investigations were apparently made into the commentaries comprising the *Wu-ching cheng-i*, but these remained unfinished during T'ai-tsung's time. After further revision during 651 and 652, it was published in 653 by a group of scholars supervised by Kao-tsung's uncle, Chang-sun Wu-chi.[33] The work sought to bring order and unity to the diverse and frequently conflicting commentaries on the classics that scholars had produced since Han times, by removing individual authors' attributions and creating a seamless, harmonious synthesis.[34] The *Wu-ching cheng-i* provided the basis for classical education throughout the T'ang.

The commentaries that were chosen duly reflected the predominant intellectual current of the age, especially the shift toward Southern Learning, although interpretations of the School of Northern Learning were by no means excluded.[35] The trend toward Southern Learning was, however, overwhelming. An authority on the history of Chinese classical scholarship, P'i Hsi-jui, observes that "after the unification of classical learning, there was Southern Learning but no Northern Learning."[36] Thus, for example, the Tso commentary on the *Spring and Autumn Annals* used in the *Wu-ching cheng-i* derived largely from the version of Tu Yü, who, as we have seen, was a scholar of the School of Southern Learning.[37] Wang Pi's commentary on the *Book of Changes*, which had been utilized during the Chin and the southern dynasties of Sung and Liang but not in the North, now replaced that of Cheng Hsüan, previously championed in the Northern Wei and its successors.[38] Similarly, Cheng Hsüan's version of the *Book of History* was substantially done away with in favor of the Old Text edition (a forgery) attributed to K'ung An-kuo but actually the work of Wang Su and others. This Old Text version had earlier been popular in the South, but had gained currency in the North only in Sui times.[39]

Although by the Sui and early T'ang, Wang Su's interpretations of the classics had in some areas displaced those of Cheng Hsüan, the same does not yet appear to have been true of ritual. Lu Te-ming, writing in the late sixth century, noted that "nowadays the three [texts on] rites are all dominated by Cheng (Hsüan)."[40] K'ung Ying-ta, the head of the project that first compiled the *Wu-ching cheng-i*, referred to ritual exegesis simply as *Cheng-hsüeh*, the study and application of the ritual theories of Cheng Hsüan.[41]

The history of early T'ang ritual, through the reign of Kao-tsung, can be viewed to a significant degree as a struggle between proponents of the theories of Cheng Hsüan and Wang Su. Beginning in T'ai-tsung's time many of Cheng Hsüan's most important ideas on ritual were gradually abandoned and their place taken by those of Wang Su. A climax of sorts was reached early in Kao-tsung's reign, in 657, when Chang-sun Wu-chi, perhaps the most respected voice of the age, and Hsü Ching-tsung, the president of the Board of Rites, along with other officials, launched a broad-ranging attack on Cheng Hsüan, charging that since his ritual theories had been based on the unorthodox weft texts (i.e., New Text school theories), they were filled with errors. Kao-tsung thereupon ordered that several changes be made in T'ang ritual, which were later incorporated into the revised T'ang ritual code, the *Hsien-ch'ing li*. We will review some of these changes in detail in succeeding chapters. Although Cheng Hsüan's ideas were partially revived beginning in 666, the overall trend in the most important areas of T'ang state ritual was nevertheless in favor of Wang Su. Between 726 and 732 state ritual was again reformulated, producing the so-called *Ta-T'ang K'ai-yüan li*, in 150 chapters, the crowning achievement of codified ritual in the T'ang, named after a reign-period of the emperor Hsüan-tsung (rg. 712–56).[42] The *K'ai-yüan li*, which provided the basis for ritual practice during the remainder of the T'ang, blended together the theories of Cheng Hsüan and Wang Su. But in most important respects it followed the provisions of the *Hsien-ch'ing li*, serving to perpetuate the shift away from Cheng Hsüan's ideas.[43] Thus, the trend in classical scholarship away from the theories of Cheng Hsüan and toward those of Wang Su was replicated in the realm of ritual.

One of the areas in which the Cheng Hsüan-Wang Su conflict may have had the greatest practical impact was in the growth of the political power of the emperor. As we will see in chapter 5, for example, Wang Su's ideas on the suburban altar rites elevated the Heavenly deity Hao-t'ien shang-ti to an unrivaled status among objects of sacrifice. This appears to have reinforced the concept of one supreme sovereign on earth, and consequently helped to provide a theoretical justification for the growth of the autocratic power of the emperor in medieval and later times in China. In this sense, the *Hsien-ch'ing li* of Kao-tsung's time occupies a key place not only in the history of T'ang ritual but also of traditional Chinese state ritual in general.[44]

THE EARLY T'ANG RITUAL ESTABLISHMENT

Matters of ritual during the T'ang were handled by the Board of Rites (*li-pu*), one of six boards managed by the Department of State Affairs (*shang-shu sheng*). There were four subdivisions of the Board of Rites, also called *pu*, which I will refer to as "bureaus" to avoid confusion: (1) the bureau of rites (*li-pu*); (2) the bureau of sacrifices (*ssu-pu*); (3) the bureau of sacrificial provisions (*shan-pu*); (4) the bureau in charge of guests (*chu-k'e*). The jurisdiction of the bureau of rites covered such matters as ritual, music, clothes, tallies and seals, portents, and gifts for funeral expenses to families of deceased court officials and harem women. The bureau of sacrifices was in charge of all state sacrifices, offerings to the imperial ancestors, ceremonies on the anniversary of the death of an emperor or empress, and divination by tortoise shell and milfoil, among other responsibilities. The bureau of sacrificial provisions looked after all the food and wine consecrated to the objects of sacrifice at the imperial tombs and imperial ancestral temples. The bureau in charge of guests was responsible for supervising the descendants of the Sui and Northern Chou imperial houses, who, as we will see, occupied a special ritual status under the T'ang, and all envoys from foreign vassal states who had come to pay homage at court. The Board of Rites was governed by a president (*shang-shu*), who was assisted by a vice-president (*lang-chung*) and an assistant secretary (*yüan-wai lang*).[45] This bureaucratic structure, reflecting the system of government at high T'ang, may not have been as well developed during the early years of the dynasty.

The ceremonies of T'ang ritual were divided, according to tradition, into five categories, the *wu-li*. The first, rites of auspicious occasions (*chi-li*), included all sacrifices at the suburban altars, at the Ming-t'ang, at the imperial ancestral temple, at the imperial tombs, in conjunction with imperial tours of inspection, the Feng and Shan sacrifices, and so forth. The bulk of the rites we examine in this volume are *chi-li*. The second, rites concerning guests (*pin-li*), included all those ceremonies related to the entertainment of foreign rulers and envoys who came to court. The third, military rites (*chün-li*), were performed on the occasion of T'ang military expeditions abroad, whether personally led by the emperor or not, various activities concerned with the training and instruction of the military forces, and sacrifices to various deities associated with military pursuits. The fourth, rites of happy occasions (*chia-li*), was a broad category covering various fortunate changes of status within the royal house, including the coming of age and marriage of emperors or crown princes; the presentation of congratulations by imperial family members or court officials on such occasions; cappings and marriages in official families; and the dispatch of court emissaries to the provinces. Less joyous occasions, such as those connected with illness and death at court, were covered by the fifth category, rites of sad occasions (*hsiung-li*).[46] There were one hundred and fifty-two T'ang rites in all, of which the largest category, rites of auspicious occasions, numbered fifty-five.[47]

During the first half of the T'ang, officials already serving in various capacities in the central government were appointed to *ad hoc* commissions to discuss and formulate ritual procedures. They did not need to be assigned to offices with formal ritual jurisdictions in order to carry out their tasks. This was a way of bringing as much knowledge from as wide a group of sources as possible to bear on the historically vexing problems associated with the re-establishment of the ancient ceremonies. The first instance of this practice occurred in the Wu-te period (618–26), when the officials Wen Ta-ya, Tou Wei, and Ch'en Shu-ta were assigned to determine certain ceremonial regulations.[48] Later, when the *Chen-kuan li* was being compiled, the president of the Secretariat, Fang Hsüan-ling, and the director of the Imperial Library, Wei Cheng, were both assigned to oversee the project. In Kao-tsung's time such eminent officials as the grand commandant, Chang-sun Wu-chi, and the president of the Secretariat, Tu Cheng-lun, along with several other high officials were all assigned to compile the *Hsien-ch'ing li*.[49] Although it is difficult always to ascertain the individual inputs of scholar-officials, I do not think it necessary to agree with the T'ang writer Su Mien, a critic of early T'ang ritual scholarship, who sought to absolve men like Fang Hsüan-ling and Wei Cheng of any wrongdoing by claiming that their busy official schedules allowed them little or no time to devote to their tasks.[50] The sources reveal that men like Fang, Wei, Chang-sun Wu-chi and many others, all statesmen with heavy official burdens, participated in many of the most momentous ritual debates of the time, and therefore exerted significant influence on ritual decision-making. Later, this influence was translated into various regulations embodied in the ritual codes.

Scores of scholars labored on various projects associated with state ritual early in the T'ang. We might pause briefly here to summarize the careers of the most important of these, whom we will be encountering from time to time throughout this study.

Of all the many T'ang commentaries on the *Book of Rites*, only that of the great exegete K'ung Ying-ta (574–648) survives.[51] K'ung's native place was in modern Hopei province. A precocious student, he soon became an expert in all the Confucian classics, both in their Cheng Hsüan and Wang Su versions. At the beginning of Sui Yang-ti's reign he achieved high place in the *ming-ching* examination and served for a time as a scholar at Lo-yang. During the civil wars at the end of the Sui, he joined T'ai-tsung's staff, becoming a scholar in his brain trust, the College of Literary Studies (*Wen-hsüeh kuan*). After the formation of the T'ang, he served both Kao-tsu and T'ai-tsung, rising to the posts of grand secretary in the Secretariat and tutor to the crown prince. Most of his official duties, however, were in the world of scholarship. It is said that when discussions on the calendar and the Ming-t'ang were held, most of the scholars yielded to his opinion. When K'ung participated in the project that compiled the *Chen-kuan li*, his learning and decisiveness allegedly carried the day. For his labors on this project, as well as on the compilation of the *Wu-ching cheng-i*, he was generously rewarded, yet he never attained highest office in the central government.

Yen Shih-ku (581–645) was the grandson of Yen Chih-t'ui (531–91), himself descended from a scholarly family stretching back to the Three Kingdoms Wei period.[52] Although the family was originally from modern Shantung province in the northeast, it began tracing its native place to the northwestern Shensi region beginning in Chih-t'ui's time. Inheriting his family's scholarly tradition, Shih-ku began his official career during the latter half of Sui Wen-ti's reign, but soon lost his post and had to earn his living as a tutor. When the T'ang arose, he followed Kao-tsu on his campaign to conquer the Sui capital. From this time forward he occupied successive posts in the T'ang central government, largely in the Secretariat and Imperial Library. T'ai-tsung assigned him the task of compiling a definitive edition of the Confucian classics, known as the *Wu-ching ting-pen*. When the project was completed, it is said that none of the other Confucians could find fault with it. Later, he was one of the scholars assigned to work on the compilation of the *Chen-kuan li*. In 637 he was ordered to annotate Pan Ku's *History of the Former Han Dynasty* for the edification of the crown prince, a work of scholarship still in use today. When T'ai-tsung was making preparations to perform the Feng and Shan sacrifices, and those assigned to determine the proper ritual could not agree, Yen insisted that his commentarial work, the *Feng-shan i chu shu*, be taken as the basis of discussion; thereupon, most of the scholars followed his ideas on the matter. Before his death in 645, he rose to the post of president of the Imperial Library and a scholar of the College for the Development of Literature (*Hung-wen kuan*).

One of the most powerful and highly honored statesmen of the early T'ang period was Chang-sun Wu-chi (ca. 600–59), elder brother of T'ai-tsung's consort, the Wen-te Empress.[53] Chang-sun was descended from a Northern Wei noble family, bearing the original surname of T'o-pa. He was about the same age as T'ai-tsung, and they were close friends from the time of their youth. Trusted by T'ai-tsung as a thoroughly loyal supporter, in 626 he was one of the men who engineered the future emperor's coup against his brothers at the Hsüan-wu Gate. From the beginning of Chen-kuan (627–49), Chang-sun served as the emperor's most influential adviser, even though he often held only honorary office. By a special edict he was permitted unrestricted access to the imperial apartments, and in 628, when T'ai-tsung first personally performed the round altar sacrifice to Heaven, he was one of two officials given the honor of returning to the palace in the imperial carriage. Upon T'ai-tsung's death, together with Ch'u Sui-liang, he was chosen to receive the emperor's last will and testament. Early in the reign of his nephew, he assumed the role of an *éminence grise*, wisely guiding Kao-tsung's regime and serving as one of his most outstanding scholars. During 651 and 652 he supervised the revision of the *Wu-ching cheng-i*, and later he was one of the chief compilers of Kao-tsung's ritual code, the *Hsien-ch'ing li*. Nevertheless, his star rapidly fell owing to the machinations of Wu Chao, whose elevation to empress in 655 he had strongly opposed. In 659 he was fasely accused by one of the Empress's followers of conspiring to rebel against the throne and was banished, without an inquiry, to a remote border region in modern Kweichow province where he was eventually hounded by henchmen of the Empress into committing suicide.

After Chang-sun Wu-chi perhaps the most influential official of T'ai-tsung's time was the minister Fang Hsüan-ling (578–648), whose native place was in modern Shantung province.[54] As a young man Fang mastered both the classics and history and was adept at composition. He passed the Sui *chin-shih* examination at the tender age of seventeen, and he served that dynasty, as had his father before him, in various offices both local and central. Shortly after the T'ang occupation of the Sui capital, Fang joined

T'ai-tsung's retinue and soon became an intimate of the future emperor, accompanying him on his military campaigns and serving as both adviser and secretary. He was one of the masterminds, along with Chang-sun Wu-chi, of T'ai-tsung's Hsüan-wu Gate plot against his brothers for the succession. Under T'ai-tsung, Fang served as chief minister, dominating the Department of State Affairs for thirteen years, between 629 and 642. Along with Wei Cheng, he was in charge of supervising two important scholarly projects: the compilation of five Standard Histories of regimes of the preceding disunion and Sui periods, and the compilation of the Chen-kuan ritual code. As a bureaucrat Fang attained an enduring reputation for pragmatism and practicality, as opposed to the narrow moral idealism of some of his colleagues.

Representing the idealistic wing of Confucian politics at T'ai-tsung's court was Wei Cheng (580–643), a descendant of a minor official family in the modern Hopei region.[55] Wei entered T'ang political life in 618, when he arrived in Ch'ang-an following his former master, the defeated "rebel" leader, Li Mi. Although he was again on the losing side in the succession struggle of 626, having been employed by the former heir apparent, Li Chien-ch'eng, T'ai-tsung discerned extraordinary qualities of loyalty and frankness in Wei and immediately placed him on his staff. Under T'ai-tsung, Wei rose to the posts of director of the Imperial Library and president of the Chancellery, with chief minister status. He is renowned in Chinese history as a fearless and blunt remonstrator, an unswerving moral conscience of his emperor, and a restraint on unbridled imperial power. Along with Fang Hsüan-ling, Wei compiled the *Chen-kuan li*. On his own he produced yet another work on ritual, known as the *Classified Ritual* (*Lei-li*), or *Continued Book of Rites* (*Tz'u Li-chi*), in twenty chapters, which arranged the canonical *Book of Rites* into topical categories graced with the best of earlier exegesis on the text. The work was not, however, widely disseminated, and it disappeared in the eighth century.[56]

Hsü Ching-tsung (592–672) is classified among the "evil ministers" (*chien-ch'en*) in the biographical chapters of the *New T'ang History*, doubtless owing to his role in furthering the career of Empress Wu.[57] He was a southerner, his native place being Hangchow in modern Chekiang province. As a youth he was good at literary composition, and he was one of the few men of the Sui to attain the highest degree of *hsiu-ts'ai*, going on to serve Yang-ti in a number of modest offices. Soon after the establishment of the T'ang, Hsü's growing reputation led T'ai-tsung to recruit him for his staff. During Chen-kuan he served in a number of posts in the Chancellery and Secretariat, and concurrently worked on compiling the history of the first two reigns of the T'ang. He briefly occupied the office of chief minister in 649, before being demoted as the result of a scandal. Early in Kao-tsung's reign he twice served as president of the Board of Rites, and continued to work on the compilation of T'ang history. By the time he again occupied the chief ministership, beginning in 656, he had succeeded in consolidating his political power by acting as a devoted supporter of Empress Wu, actively participating in the political intrigues which systematically removed her opponents and left her the dominant figure at court. Hsü was one of the chief compilers of Kao-tsung's ritual code, the *Hsien-ch'ing li*, and participated in several other projects affecting ritual. In contrast to his ritual scholarship, Hsü's work on T'ang history has been singled out for condemnation by traditional Chinese scholars, for it is known that he wielded a "crooked brush" and falsified several incidents.

Beyond their ritual activities, the above group of men appears not to have been politically aligned in other respects. Represented among them were northeasterners, northwesterners, and southerners; "artistocrats" and those of humbler social origins; high-powered officials and those of more modest rank; dyed-in-the-wool Confucians and practical administrators. Even the concerted attack on Cheng Hsüan's ritual theories early in Kao-tsung's reign seems not to have mirrored any factional alliances. The campaign against Cheng was, after all, led by Chang-sun Wu-chi and Hsü Ching-tsung, bureaucrats who, as we saw, were on opposite sides of the struggle over the continued influence at court of Empress Wu.[58] Chang-sun dearly paid with his life for his brave stand, while Hsü rose to become one of the most influential lights of the age. Chang-sun and Hsü's support of Wang Su as a ritual guide may, then, be viewed as the outcome of a shared ritual and cosmological vision which served to transcend the usual partisan politics. In this respect, ritual issues at the early T'ang court could occasionally unite rival elements and provide a happy, if unaccustomed, arena for political cooperation.

CHAPTER 3

Plum Trees and Flood Waters: The Management and Manipulation of Portents

> Whatever procedure is used for selecting among the possible successors, whether by bullet or ballot, the human choice often requires the affirmation of divine authority. Either the electors themselves are seen as chosen by God (or by his clergy), or else they resort to some material device in order to divine the wishes of the unseen powers.
>
> Jack Goody, introduction to *Succession to High Office*

IN TRADITIONAL CHINA, OF ALL THE MIRANDA SURROUNDING THE ASSUMPTION of power by a new dynasty, perhaps the most powerful in its ability to generate sentiments of political legitimacy and diffuse support was the auspicious omen. Even before a dynasty was formally inaugurated, typically it had already long engaged in the management and manipulation of auguries and presages demonstrating that it had received the Mandate of Heaven, or the blessing of some central holy figure in Taoism or Buddhism, or both.

The Chinese belief in the validity of portents can be traced back as far as the so-called oracle bones of the Shang dynasty (ca. 1700–1100 B.C.), where predictions of future events were made on the basis of cracks artificially generated in the scapula of oxen and plastrons of tortoises, which were then "read" by diviners. By Former Han times the doctrine of the interrelationship of Heaven and Earth had spawned the notion that changes in the Mandate would be preceded by appropriate natural phenomena proclaiming the fact. As the *Doctrine of the Mean* observes: "When a nation or family is about to flourish, there are sure to be happy omens; and when it is about to perish, there are sure to be unlucky omens."[1] The *Lü-shih ch'un-ch'iu* states: "Whenever any Emperor or King is about to rise, Heaven must first make manifest some favorable omen among the lower people."[2] From the end of the Former Han onward, auspicious omens were regarded as indispensable symbolic affirmations of the legitimacy of founding rulers, palpable signs that they possessed the surpassing virtue required by the Mandate of Heaven doctrine.[3]

Auspicious omens were typically manipulated for political advantage not only by a prospective regime but by individuals or groups seeking to curry favor with that regime in order to obtain material rewards. By "discovering" and presenting favorable portents, they helped generate mass support on its behalf. Auspicious omens were thus not only devices serving to help generate political support for a new dynasty, they were signs that confirmed the existence of popular support for that regime, crude yardsticks by which such support might be measured. Omens represented, by metaphorical and symbolic means, according to Miyakawa Hisayuki, the "will" of the general public, which normally had difficulty in expressing itself politically, short of rebellion and similar acts of violence.[4]

Although serious contenders for power during political interregna all manipulated portents in their favor, the ultimate winner was presumably blessed with the most efficacious and therefore the "best" portents. To the extent that these portents were eventually judged best by the public at large and also accepted by the vanquished contenders for power, who figuratively bowed under their cumulative weight, the effective use of such symbols accelerated the establishment of peace and order by a new regime. Putting the onus of selection upon luck or the gods, Jack Goody observes, helps remove an element of friction from the affairs of men.[5] Political normalcy can thus be restored sooner.

As used here the term "portents" encompasses at least three distinct Chinese categories, the contents of which, nevertheless, occasionally overlap. The three categories are reflected in the names of various treatises (*chih*) devoted to them in the Chinese Standard Histories. Auspicious influence (*fu-jui* or *hsiang-jui*) portents include such diverse phenomena as colored vapors, bright lights, providential fauna and flora, strange stones and gems, sweet dew, and even vivid dreams. Five Elements (*wu-hsing*) portents consist largely of meteorological phenomena—earthquakes, thunder, lightning, wind, fire, flood, clouds, rain and so forth, but also include such things as the songs sung among the people predicting future events. Astrological/astronomical (*t'ien-wen*) portents concern anomalous movements of the heavens and the appearance of marvelous celestial phenomena of all kinds: meteors, comets, eclipses of sun and moon, strange lights, and so forth.[6] Certain of these portents were regarded by the Chinese as serving both to predict the transfer of political power from one regime to another and to indicate precisely to whom Heaven had granted its new Mandate. The art of political prognostication in China also involved the use of prophetic and apocryphal texts, *ch'an* and *wei*. Although the interpretations derived from *ch'an* and *wei* were often of considerable political utility to dynastic founders, because of their revolutionary potential there was a tendency to suppress them once the social order had been re-established.[7]

In early imperial times the Han usurper Wang Mang (rg. A.D. 9–23) made perhaps the fullest use of portents to justify his assumption of power.[8] But portents figured significantly in the great majority of dynastic transitions from Wang Mang's time down to the T'ang.[9] Omens appear to have played a particularly important role in the legitimation of the Sui dynasty, predecessor of the T'ang. The *Sui History* notes that "when the emperor first received the abdication of the [Northern] Chou, fearing that the masses were not yet content, he often spoke about auspicious omens in order to dazzle them. Those [portents] which others fabricated and presented were countless."[10] So important did the Sui founder regard these symbols of legitimacy that at his accession the president of the Board of Rites bore a register of auspicious omens and auspicious influences (*fu-ming chi hsiang-jui tieh*), listing prophetic signs that had figured in the Sui rise to power.[11] Wen-ti's personal infatuation with omens is also reflected in a work compiled sometime during the first part of his reign by the official Wang Shao, known as the *Record of Auspicious Signs Favoring the Imperial Sui* (*Huang-Sui ling kan chih*), which was presented to the throne and promulgated throughout the empire. Containing such items as songs of prophecy sung among the people, *ch'an* and *wei* prognostications, auspicious signs, and even Buddhist omens, it was thirty chapters long, and took, it is said, a full ten days to recite to a captive audience of assembled officials.[12]

Early T'ang portents are treated in a number of sources. The *Old* and *New T'ang History* each contain treatises on the Five Elements (*Wu-hsing*) and astronomy/astrology (*T'ien-wen*). Although they furnish considerable information on these two categories of portents, since most were regarded as inauspicious they are largely unrelated to the T'ang founding.[13] For auspicious omens relating to the establishment of the dynasty, we must turn to the *Collected T'ang Statutes* (*T'ang hui-yao*), the encyclopedic compilation *Ts'e-fu yüan-kuei*, scattered items in the Sui and T'ang Standard

Histories, and, especially, Wen Ta-ya's *Diary of the Founding of the Great T'ang Dynasty* (*Ta-T'ang ch'uang-yeh ch'i-chü-chu*). Much of the T'ang interpretation of portents appears to have derived from Five Element doctrine dating from Han times, especially from such weft texts as the *Wu-hsing chuan*, a commentary on the *Book of History*, now lost.[14]

T'ang portents were divided into four basic types: grand (*ta*), superior (*shang*), intermediate (*chung*), and lesser (*hsia*). The most numerous type was the grand, comprising a total of sixty-four varieties. Grand portents were to be reported to the throne immediately upon their discovery, and officials were forthwith to go to the palace to offer their congratulations to the emperor. All the other types of portents were saved until the end of the year, when they were formally announced and a sacrifice of thanks performed at the ancestral temple.[15]

The early T'ang attitude toward portents was not fixed, but rather seems to have varied according to the situation. Whereas lucky signs and evil omens were regarded as inevitable by-products of the interaction between Heaven and Earth, men of the early T'ang did not believe that such signs always bore equal significance. For them omens, especially unfavorable ones, possessed only a conditional validity, since the outcomes they predicted, they believed, might be entirely avoided. Such an attitude is clearly revealed in the introduction to the "Monograph on the Five Elements" of the *Sui History*, written during the period 629–56. The introduction notes that there were sure to be natural anomalies and supernatural events whenever mankind was guilty of transgressions. Mere belief in such signs and devoted service to the gods, however, did not ensure prosperity. Rather, the key to good fortune lay in a man's cultivation of virtue (*te*) and righteousness (*i*), by which means he might change bad to good. This idea was underlined by a quote from the *History of the Former Han*: "Virtue overcomes that which is unlucky and righteousness suppresses that which is unfavorable." Thus, concludes the introduction, the sage-rulers of old always were able to neutralize misfortune by means of their virtue and righteousness.[16]

A similar attitude is expressed by the early T'ang official Yü Shih-nan. In his *Brief Discussion of (Former) Rulers*, mentioned in chapter 1, the Teacher and Young Gentlemen discuss signs from Heaven. Here Yü uses the Teacher to present his own ideas on the function of portents. He says: "If Mount T'ai were to collapse it would certainly follow upon the rooting up of its soil. If trees were to snap in two it would all be the result of grubs and larvae. If a dynasty were to be destroyed there certainly would be omens of misfortune." The Teacher goes on to affirm that when rulers govern well Heaven sends down blessings and auspicious signs; when they rule poorly Heaven replies with calamities and omens of misfortune. "Just like sounds corresponding to voices and shadows following their forms, this is certainly the natural principle of things." Thus were Heavenly events and human affairs inextricably intertwined, he concludes.[17]

Yet Yü also felt that there were limits to the power of portents to predict prosperity or misfortune. When a comet was sighted for a period of more than one hundred days in 634, and T'ai-tsung took it as a Heavenly warning against defects in his administration, Yü took pains to set his mind at ease. He pointed to the case of a ruler in early Chinese history who so cultivated his virtue after the sighting of a comet that the comet disappeared in a mere ten days. "If Your Majesty does not cultivate virtuous government," he said, "even though unicorns and phoenixes be seen repeatedly, in the end of what advantage is it? But if you make your administration be without deficiencies and the common people peaceful and happy, although there be calamities and abnormalities, how are they harmful to the age?" He concluded that if T'ai-tsung was scrupulously attentive to government, even the sighting of comets would be no cause for worry.[18] Another of T'ai-tsung's counselors, Wei Cheng, agreed with Yü, opining that when rulers cultivated their virtue portents would subside, so that even though there had been a portent, there would be no calamity.[19] From this it can be seen that during the early T'ang the significance of inauspicious portents was played down by officials when they regarded the quality of government as otherwise satisfactory. The attitude toward portents, then, could be shaped by the political needs of the moment.

The attitude of early T'ang emperors toward portents likewise seems to have been largely politically determined. Kao-tsu, as Wen Ta-ya's *Diary* attests, "was enlightened and exceptionally rational, and did not speak of spirits or the supernatural."[20] Yet, as we shall see, the T'ang founder made excellent use of portents in his rise to power. On the other hand, he also knew that auspicious omens might be potent weapons in the hands of various anti-T'ang rivals, who might be equally persuasive in interpreting such signs in their own favor. Thus, on the twentieth day of the sixth month (July 17), exactly one month after taking the throne, Kao-tsu prohibited discussion of auspicious influences (*fu-jui*), thereby closing the books on further speculation concerning those signs and influences portending his or anyone else's coming to power.[21]

Kao-tsu's son, T'ai-tsung, was similarly enlightened, and fond of scoffing at earlier Chinese emperors who had relied on favorable signs as evidence of their own just rule. In the ninth month of 628, albino magpies built their nests in linked pairs on trees on the palace grounds. The association of white birds with paired nests was particularly auspicious. But when his officials began congratulating him, the ever-practical T'ai-tsung grew enraged, exclaiming: "I have always laughed at Sui Wen-ti's fondness for speaking about auspicious omens. A worthy man is an auspicious omen. How are white magpies beneficial to our affairs?" He thereupon ordered the nests torn down and the birds released in the wilds.[22] In the same month, the emperor, complaining about the numerous recent reports of lucky omens by his officials, issued an edict placing restrictions on what omens might be reported directly to the throne and what might be said about their significance. In his edict T'ai-tsung claimed that security and peril lay in human actions, fortune and misfortune in the art of governing. If a ruler was tyrannical, good omens could not make him better. If his government was good, bad omens could not make him evil. Omens, he concluded, could therefore not be depended upon.[23] However, T'ai-tsung's edict was something less than a complete repudiation of auguries. After all, it permitted the direct reporting to the throne, "as of old," of such grand omens as unicorns, phoenixes, tortoises, and dragons, although only a physical description and the place of their discovery might be memorialized, and no "embellishments" were to be permitted.[24] Moreover, on occasion a flattering interpretation lent to an omen by his officials could still visibly please the emperor.[25]

Since legitimation is never completed, each ruler in a dynasty must legitimate himself, replicating the process undertaken by his predecessor. Omens were, in this context, a useful vehicle for exploitation, of which T'ai-tsung was well aware. Kao-tsu's edict of abdication in 626, which may well have been written under his son's tutelage, claimed that when T'ai-tsung was young there had been auspicious omens portending his later rise to power.[26] In his command ordering his son to ascend the throne, Kao-tsu likewise noted that T'ai-tsung's rise had accorded with various lucky signs. The implication was that T'ai-tsung's legitimacy rested at least in part on omens and the heavenly grace they symbolized.

THE AUGURIES OF KAO-TSU

Wen Ta-ya's *Diary of the Founding of the Great T'ang Dynasty* presents the fullest picture anywhere of those portents during the Sui-T'ang transition that were interpreted by contemporary men as predicting the success of the T'ang and of Kao-tsu's accession to the throne.[27] The *Diary* reveals many of the types of portents serving to shape attitudes about and opinions toward the T'ang by the wider populace. It also shows how these portents were interpreted and manipulated by the T'ang dynasts and their supporters to make it seem as if the T'ang house alone, among the many contenders for power at the end of the Sui, was predestined to gain the Mandate. In the T'ang Standard Histories only a modest number of portents is associated with Kao-tsu, who is, after all, generally portrayed as a ruler of only modest qualities and accomplishments. By contrast, auspicious omens and signs are mentioned with a frequency and regularity in the *Diary* fully consonant with its depiction of Kao-tsu as a great hero and true founder of the T'ang. It also raises the suspicion that Wen Ta-ya's compilation may have been intended not simply to stand as an eyewitness record of the founding of the regime but also to help legitimate T'ang power in general and that of Kao-tsu in particular.

According to the *Diary*, as early as 616 Kao-tsu had begun to interpret certain events as auspicious signs in his favor. In 572, at the age of seven *sui*, he had inherited the nominal title Duke of T'ang. Although the title gave Kao-tsu no actual territorial authority, the site of T'ang lay in T'ai-yüan, the same region to which Kao-tsu had been assigned to put down banditry and anti-Sui rebellion. T'ang (also known as T'ao) was an area traditionally associated with the legendary sage-emperor Yao, who was sometimes called T'ao-T'ang after the two names of his patrimony. Now, the *Diary* notes, "Thinking that the common people of T'ai-yüan were the old folk of T'ao-T'ang, and that [the region for which] he had received his pacification commission was the same as his own [nominal] fief, the emperor [i.e. Kao-tsu] was secretly joyous at this turn of events, attributing it to Heaven's conferment."[28] Similarly, the next year, 617, he is depicted as commenting to his son, T'ai-tsung: "T'ang is assuredly our patrimony, and T'ai-yüan is its territory. My coming here now is Heaven's grant. If it be granted and we do not take it, calamity will befall us."[29]

About this time Kao-tsu failed to stem the tide of Turkish invasions into the Shansi region, and Sui Yang-ti had dispatched an envoy from his capital at Chiang-tu to seize him and bring him back to court for punishment. But a few days later an imperial edict arrived in T'ai-yüan pardoning the T'ang leader. Although all the roads from Chiang-tu to Kao-tsu's headquarters had been cut off by the general fighting in the region, a lone Sui envoy bearing the imperial pardon had miraculously been able to get through without encountering any difficulties. The event was naturally interpreted by Kao-tsu and the rest of the T'ang camp as yet one more sign that he possessed Heavenly favor. Kao-tsu exclaimed excitedly: "The remaining years of my life have truly been granted by Heaven!"[30]

Even more palpable signs of Heaven's favor were soon made manifest. In the first month of 617 a bright light, like a great fire, lit up the night sky above Chin-yang, Kao-tsu's headquarters in T'ai-yüan. Shooting flames blazing bright hovered directly west of the city above Dragon Mountain (*Lung-shan*), pointing southwest as far as the eye could see.[31] Here the traditional symbol of Chinese emperors, the dragon, is linked with Kao-tsu; southwest, the direction of the Sui capital, was where he would have to march if he were to succeed to the Mandate. At the same time, a purple vapor like a rainbow cut horizontally through the fire and mounted upward to the Big Dipper, lasting from the first through the third watch before being extinguished. "On top of the city wall all those who kept the watches saw it, but no one was able to explain it and none dared speak."[32] The Big Dipper was an asterism also traditionally linked to the imperial position.[33] The purple vapor, like the flames hovering over Dragon Mountain, promised an exalted future for Kao-tsu. But this was not the first time that his destiny had been presaged by such atmospheric phenomena. The *Diary* notes that earlier, when Kao-tsu had been appointed the commander-administrator (*chün-shou*) of Lou-fan, located in the vicinity of T'ai-yüan, an expert in interpreting vapors (*ch'i*) noticed that there was what he called a "Son of Heaven vapor" (*t'ien-tzu ch'i*) emanating from the northwest of the imperial palace at Lo-yang and thus strongly linked with the T'ai-yüan region.[34]

At this point in its narrative, the *Diary* speaks for the first time of the prophetic folk ditties which had long been sung by the common people of T'ai-yüan.

When the law is kept,	*Fa-lü ts'un*
And the Way and its Power are present,	*Tao-te tsai*
Then a white-bannered Son of Heaven	*Pai-ch'i t'ien-tzu*
Will emerge from the Eastern Sea.	*Ch'u tung-hai*

The people also often spoke of a "white-robed Son of Heaven" (*pai-i t'ien-tzu*) in their songs, the *Diary* notes.[35] The specific reference to the Way and its Power (*tao-te*) marks this ditty as one of many Taoistic omens in the Sui-T'ang transition period. Such omens served as powerful molders of behavior during these anxious times.[36]

The second ditty is called "Peach-plum Li":

Peach-plum Li,	*T'ao-li tzu*
Be not extravagant in speech.	*Mo lang yü*
As a yellow heron you fly round the hill,	*Huang-ku jao-shan fei*
And turn about in the flower garden.	*Yüan chuan hua-yüan li*

The *Diary* claims that the ditty concerns T'ang Kao-tsu. Li, or plum, is of course the family name of Kao-tsu. The *t'ao*, or peach, is a homonym of the *t'ao* of T'ao-T'ang, which, as we saw, was the region associated with the T'ang and also with the sage-ruler Yao. Finally, the reference to the flower garden in the last line appears to be another allusion to Kao-tsu. According to the *Diary*, Kao-tsu's officers had earlier requested that he choose the color white for his banners, as Wu-wang had done when he exterminated Chou, the bad-last ruler of the Shang dynasty. But the T'ang leader demurred, saying that it was premature to use the color white before at least entering the suburbs of the Sui capital. Instead, he suggested using banners of red and white, red representing the old Sui color (since he was nominally still in the service of the Sui), and white representing the old tradition of Wu-wang. Kao-tsu had thus met his officers halfway. When the banners, made of red and white cloth seamed together, were displayed in all directions from the camp walls and city ramparts of Chin-yang, the *Diary* notes that "red and white shone on one another like a flower garden."[37]

As Woodbridge Bingham has demonstrated, it is possible to interpret the "Peach-plum Li" ballad, which seems to have had at least three versions other than the one recorded by Wen Ta-ya, as referring not to T'ang Kao-tsu but to certain of his rivals for the throne, particularly the rebels Li Mi and Li Hung.[38] As Anna Seidel has shown, the name Li Hung appeared many times during the Han and disunion periods as a messianic figure in religious Taoism.[39] The "Peach-plum Li" ballad and prophetic references to Li Hung moved the increasingly paranoiac Yang-ti to desperation. In 615 he executed his official Li Hun and the latter's relative Li Min, along with almost their entire clan.[40] Li Min was killed because he was also known as Li Hung-erh, the *hung* of his name meaning "flood," virtually homonymous in T'ang times with the *hung* ("great") of Li Hung. As the *Sui History* notes, "The emperor suspected that the character *hung* accorded with the prophecies. . . ."[41] Yang-ti was not the only one caught up in the excitement generated by the prophetic omens. After hearing the ditties sung by old and young on the streets of T'ai-yüan, Kao-tsu, claiming that he was their subject, observed that he would have to travel one thousand *li* to conquer the Sui capital, and thus accord with the prophecies.[42]

Two white sparrows were the next auspicious signs to appear in Kao-tsu's camp. The first was discovered and presented by a Buddhist monk whose secular name was Li. The other alighted on a tree directly in front of Kao-tsu and was seized by his followers.[43] White birds had since Han times, especially in the weft texts, been regarded as special signs of Heaven's favor, comparable to the settling of sweet dew.[44] Moreover, white was associated in yin-yang and Five Element cosmology with the west, and all during the period after the T'ang uprising in T'ai-yüan, Kao-tsu's main forces were moving westward toward the Sui capital. It was altogether appropriate, then, that small white birds in great number were sighted and presented to Kao-tsu from this time forward, since white birds were spirits of the west.[45]

The very last omens to appear before Kao-tsu left T'ai-yüan were purple clouds, sighted at dawn one morning directly above the spot where he was seated. After some time they began to break up into clouds of five colors, each in the shape of a dragon or some other beast. This phenomenon was repeated for three mornings in all, and everyone in Tai-yüan was said to be able to observe it.[46] Five-colored clouds in the shape of dragons were auspicious omens associated with a Son of Heaven.[47] Later they would be treated as a grand portent by the T'ang. Although his civil and military officials paid calls on Kao-tsu to congratulate him on these auspicious signs, the T'ang leader, it is said, "resisted them and would not accept [reports of the portents]."[48] Prospective emperors could not be seen as too eager to embrace signs presaging their future.

In the seventh month of 617, on their way to the Sui capital, the T'ang army became bogged down by torrential rains near the town of Huo-i, midway down the Feng River valley. Directly to the east, a mountain called Huo-t'ai overlooked a strategic pass leading toward Huo-i, which was guarded by twenty thousand enemy troops. After it had rained steadily for more than a week, on the sixteenth day (chia-tzu) there appeared a white-robed rustic (pai-i yeh-lao) who claimed that he had been sent by the god of the mountain. He advised Kao-tsu to take a side road on the southeast side of the mountain toward Huo-i and promised that the rains would let up at the beginning of the eighth month and that the mountain god would destroy the Sui army for the sake of the T'ang. As the old rustic had predicted, the rains ceased on the first day of the eighth month, after more than three weeks. Kao-tsu ordered a shrine erected to the mountain god and sacrifices made to him. A few days later, after getting its weapons and provisions in order, the T'ang army set out on the mountain-side road toward Huo-i, which concealed its advance from the enemy and thus contributed to its first major victory against the Sui.[49]

At the end of the eighth month a piece of lapis lazuli in the shape of a tortoise was discovered in T'ai-yüan. It bore an inscription of four characters in red: "Li will rule for ten thousand generations." The blue-green of the stone and the red of the letters were "naturally dazzling.... it was an object of divine workmanship." Kao-tsu, the *Diary* says, at first refused to believe in the genuineness of the stone and ordered that his officials try to wash off the letters in order to test its authenticity. But even a whole night's rubbing had no effect. Indeed, the more they rubbed, the clearer the characters became. When his subordinates came to congratulate him, Kao-tsu once more assumed the role of the reluctant ruler. "The bright Mandate of High Heaven is bestowed amidst ten thousand auspicious signs," he acknowledged. But he claimed that he was deficient in virtue and therefore did not want reports of the discovery to be proclaimed among the people. Instead, he ordered that a sacrifice be made to the stone tortoise, and that those who had discovered it were to be ennobled.[50] News of the discovery of this sacred tortoise nevertheless must have spread far and wide—just as Kao-tsu had planned.

On the very same day as the discovery of the stone tortoise, an auspicious blade of grain (*chia-ho*) was found in the region of the Sui capital and presented to Kao-tsu. Auspicious blades of grain were produced, according to Chinese tradition, when sweet dew fell and wind and rain were timely, and were characterized by great size and abundant ears. They were signs of the conferment of the divine Mandate.[51] To mark this propitious event, Kao-tsu issued an order granting honorary office to the discoverer of the plant. In the text of the order he noted that such plants were good omens that had appeared in past ages. Now that the T'ang house had arisen, he happily observed, it was receiving similar signs of divine favor.[52]

During the ninth month Kao-tsu led his forces across the Yellow River, whose spirit was propitiated with a sacrifice, into the region within the Passes, Kuan-chung, gateway to the Sui capital.[53] Moving westward, the T'ang leader stopped at the confluence of the Wei and Lo Rivers, some miles downstream of the city. There all the boats needed for the river crossing proved rotten beyond repair, so Kao-tsu was forced to go upstream along the Lo River, several tens of *li*, where finally he was able to obtain boats in navigable condition. Unfortunately, however, rocks and sandbars abounded in the shallow water and it was impossible to move downstream to the Wei River. No one had any solution to the problem, but during the night, under an altogether clear sky, the river level suddenly rose several feet and the boats were able to float to a point where they could cross the Wei River. All were amazed by this stroke of luck, comparing Kao-tsu's good fortune with that of Han Kuang-wu-ti (rg. 25–57), who, also without boats, was able to cross the Hu-t'o River when it iced over.[54] Although his officials clambered on board to congratulate him, Kao-tsu professed that it was simply a chance occurrence: "What virtue do I have to be worthy of it?" Nevertheless, he prudently ordered that sacrificial offerings be made to the Lo and Wei rivers and also to Hua-shan, one of China's "holy" mountains located in the vicinity of the capital.[55]

The T'ang forces captured the Sui capital in the tenth month of 617, and Kao-tsu now began making preparations in earnest for the political transition from Sui to T'ang. By this time the auspicious omens had already worked a considerable amount of magic on his followers. In the eleventh month, when Kao-tsu set up the puppet Kung-ti as the successor to Yang-ti, the supporters of the T'ang leader noisily clamored without success for him "to accord with the auspicious omens" and himself assume the imperial mantle.[56] Nevertheless, in the months following, the T'ang camp sought to reinforce the positive responses already generated by the portents, folk ditties, and other signs by interpreting them even more forcefully and unambiguously than before in Kao-tsu's favor. This effort can be seen especially in the carefully engineered petitions begging Kao-tsu to ascend the throne. The petition of P'ei Chi and "more than two thousand men" sent in during the fourth month of 618 observes that the T'ao-li of the "Peach-plum Li" ballad tallied with Kao-tsu's surname and also was related to the region of the sage-ruler Yao, a further link to the T'ang, "all of which accords with the way of Heaven." The petition goes on to interpret other lines drawn from the folk ditties as referring to Kao-tsu and the T'ang, even those which might just as readily have been linked to the water-and-flood symbolism associated with Li Hung's name.[57]

According to tradition, Kao-tsu had to decline the throne three times before accepting. This gave P'ei Chi and other officials further opportunities to present their case for interpreting various signs in Kao-tsu's favor, including two new songs said to have been sung among the people, which Wen Ta-ya duly records. The first is a song by the "holy man" (shen-jen) of T'ai-yüan, Hui Hua-ni.[58] The Chinese characters for "the son of eighteen" (shih-pa tzu) mentioned in the first line can be combined to form the character for Kao-tsu's surname, Li. Similary, the *chia-tzu* day referred to in a later line not only further connotes the Li surname; it also refers to a day Kao-tsu found personally lucky as well as to the specific date of the T'ang uprising in T'ai-yüan. Other lines are similarly significant:

> In his hands he holds a pair of white sparrows;
> On his head he wears purple clouds.
> ....
> The northwestern Heavenly fire illumines Dragon Mountain,
> The bright lad's fiery rays connect with the Big Dipper.

All these images were, as we saw, specifically associated with Kao-tsu while he was still in T'ai-yüan. The repeated use in the song of a character pronounced *t'ang*, meaning variously "hall" or "majestic," served to evoke the dynastic name T'ang. The ballad thus seems to have been carefully crafted to meet the specifications and personal history of the T'ang founder.

The same can be said of the second folk song, in sixteen lines, which the *Diary* claims was written in the year 570 by Wei Yüan-sung of the Northern Chou dynasty.[59] According to a note in the *History of the Northern Chou Dynasty (Chou-shu)*, Wei Yüan-sung "was fond of predicting the future," and was very successful at it. The text of the poem attributed to him has been discussed at some length by Bingham, who views it as a whole as representing "a remarkably accurate prophecy" of the fall of the Sui and the founding of the T'ang, with several lines clearly referring to Kao-tsu.[60] For example, the fifth line, "At eighteen becomes a man" (or, alternately, "Ten and eight make a male child") echoes the first line of Hui Hua-ni's ballad and indicates the surname Li. The next line, "Flood waters lodge at the side of the sword," may refer even more specifically to Kao-tsu, whose *tzu*, or given name, was Yüan. According to one source of T'ang date, *yüan* means "flood waters."[61] Line fourteen, "The plum-tree (*li-shu*) rises majestically (*t'ang-t'ang*)," and line sixteen, "Deep waters drown the yellow poplar (*yang*)," similarly seem to point to Kao-tsu. The *li*, *t'ang-t'ang*, and deep waters all evoke images of the T'ang leader who is about to submerge the Yang (homophone of the yellow poplar) house of the Sui. Indeed, the fit is just too good. The poem has been so well tailored to Kao-tsu's requirements that Bingham suspects it to have been a forgery "mostly if not entirely invented to heighten the prestige of the new dynasty." He places its composition in the year 618 or later.[62]

I would suggest that one line from the poem, line twelve, which is incomplete and contains only two characters, places the date of the com-

position attributed to Wei Yüan-sung squarely in the year 618, immediately preceding Kao-tsu's enthronement. The two characters represent Yü,
legendary founder of the Hsia dynasty, and T'ang, founder of the Shang
dynasty, rulers that Bingham believes the folk song intends in some manner to compare with T'ang Kao-tsu, who is founding a dynasty of his
own. But why these two particular rulers? Yü and T'ang founded their
dynasties each in a different manner, the first by inheritance based on moral virtue, the second by force of arms. As we will see in the next chapter, a
great propaganda effort was launched in the spring of 618 by Kao-tsu and
his advisers to legitimate his accession by demonstrating that he had united
the venerable qualitites of moral virtue and military merit in his one
person.[63] The appearance of Yü and T'ang in the same line of this poem
was thus no mere accident.

Auspicious omens continued to be discovered in the period following
Kao-tsu's enthronement, and for these we must turn to sources other than
Wen Ta-ya's Diary, which leaves off at this point. Six days after the inaugural ritual, Venus, the "Grand White" (T'ai-po), was seen in the daytime.
Although Venus is often regarded in Chinese astrology as a negative
omen, on this occasion it was conveniently taken to be a positive sign. The
omen read, "Soldiers arise, the vassal is strengthened," alluding to Kao-
tsu's recent good fortune in vanquishing the Sui.[64] In the twelfth month of
the year the usually turbid water of a stream cleared up, meaning, according to tradition, that the empire was at peace.[65] In addition, during this
year "auspicious wheat" (chia-mai) and auspicious blades of grain were
presented to the throne, and auspicious colored clouds (ching-yün and
ch'ing-yün) were observed in the capital and elsewhere.[66]

During the remainder of the reign favorable omens were seized upon
and exploited by a regime forced to meet military challenges on several
fronts and thus faced with the necessity of periodically demonstrating its
legitimacy anew. Such omens not only augured a successful future for the
dynasty; by powerfully swaying public opinion, they also helped guarantee that future. True, the portents witnessed were by no means entirely
propitious; there was the usual number of earthquakes, eclipses, and other
anomalies of nature and of the Heavens, and the auguries taken upon their
discovery sometimes boded ill. But in an era in which the quality of government was good and the monarch cultivated virtue, these might be, as
we saw earlier, conveniently dismissed as relatively harmless. On the
other hand, there was a profusion of special signs reflecting Kao-tsu's
continued favor with Heaven and furnishing reassurance that he was indeed the rightful possessor of the Mandate: white birds and red birds;

more auspicious blades of grain and colored clouds; much falling of sweet dew; trees, especially plum (*li*) trees, whose branches grew together; auspicious stones bearing inscriptions predicting that the T'ang would rule for ten thousand years, and so forth.[67]

THE TAOIST AND BUDDHIST CONTRIBUTIONS

Taoism occupied a special position during the T'ang among the three teachings of Confucianism, Taoism, and Buddhism. Early in the dynasty, the imperial house began claiming descent from Lao-tzu, the Taoist "founder," and in 624 Kao-tsu awarded highest place to Taoism at a court debate among representatives of the three teachings. Taoist precedence was reaffirmed by T'ai-tsung and Kao-tsung, although both these rulers were also motivated by a pragmatic concern not to alienate the followers of the other two beliefs.

The Taoist contribution, both material and ideological, to the founding of the T'ang appears to have been more substantial than previously thought.[68] During its campaign to topple the Sui, the T'ang were the beneficiaries of generous Taoist support in terms of both manpower and supplies for their troops. At the time of Kao-tsu's rising in the fifth month of 617, his daughter, a resident of the Sui capital, responded by fleeing the city and raising troops on her father's behalf. She encamped them near a Taoist temple, which supplied the army with rations from its stores.[69] Later, in the eighth month, after the fall of the town of Huo-i, Taoist monks in the vicinity joined up with the T'ang army and marched with Kao-tsu on the Sui capital.[70] In addition, a number of Taoist portents variously prognosticated the T'ang victory over the Sui or indicated that Lao-chün, the patron deity of Taoism, had given his blessing to the T'ang cause. Such portents must have been widely disseminated among the masses and could not have but aided the T'ang rebels. Wen Ta-ya does not specifically identify as Taoist the old rustic who appeared before Kao-tsu near Mount Huo-t'ai in the seventh month of 617. But Miyakawa Hisayuki has shown that in Taoist literature the gods of Mount Huo-t'ai were identified as Taoist deities.[71] Moreover, the Shansi region had long been a stronghold of Taoism. It was while Kao-tsu was assigned to combat banditry in Shansi that a Mao-shan Taoist, Wang Yüan-chih of Chin-yang, site of the T'ang headquarters in T'ai-yüan, secretly presented him with auspicious omens and predicted that he was destined to gain the Mandate.[72]

On the whole, not much is made of Taoist omens in the T'ang official sources, and few details are provided. This is not the case with Taoist texts, however, although these need to be read critically and with some skepticism. Of especial importance to the T'ang cause before it achieved power was the Taoist establishment called Lou-kuan, located not far from the Sui capital. One Taoist source claims that as early as 611 a priest by the name of Ch'i Hui, who was later to become the abbot of Lou-kuan, predicted that someone descended from Lao-tzu would become the next emperor. It was Ch'i Hui who provided Kao-tsu's daughter with rations from Lou-kuan's stores. When Kao-tsu's troops arrived in the vicinity of the capital at P'u-chin Pass, Ch'i Hui is portrayed as declaring that "the Perfect Ruler [chen-chün] has come. He will pacify [p'ing-ting] the Four Quarters." So saying, he changed his given name to P'ing-ting, and sent more than eighty Taoist monks to greet the T'ang leader.[73] According to the same source, later that year, on the eighth day of the eleventh month of 617, Kao-tsu sent an envoy to Lou-kuan to pray for good fortune for his revolutionary movement. During the ceremony a white cloud descended like a curtain over the altar, merging with the rising smoke of the incense. At the same time, a pair of white deer came to the gate beside the main hall of the complex, departing only after letting out several long cries. These auspicious omens apparently presaged the culmination of the T'ang conquest of the Sui capital, which took place the very next day.[74]

Yet another Taoist prophecy of Kao-tsu's victory supposedly took place in 617, delivered by no less a figure than Lao-chün, the highest Taoist deity. On this occasion, we are told, Lao-chün descended on Chung-nan Mountain, located about ten miles west of the Sui capital. There he told the hermit (and famous T'ang mathematician) Li Shun-feng that "the Duke of T'ang is going to receive the Mandate of Heaven." Li thereupon is said to have decided to come down from the mountain and join the T'ang ranks.[75]

Perhaps the most dramatic narrative of a Taoist prophecy concerning Kao-tsu took place in 620, when forces led by T'ai-tsung were arrayed against one hundred thousand "rebel" holdouts against T'ang power in the lower Feng River valley of southern Shansi province.[76] At this time the deity of Mount Yang-chiao, scene of the epiphany of 617, appeared before a man named Chi Shan-hsing. The deity was garbed in white and astride a white horse with a red mane and red hoofs. Red and white were, as we saw, Kao-tsu's colors during his anti-Sui campaigns. The deity said to Chi Shan-hsing: "Tell the T'ang Son of Heaven Li so-and-so for me: 'Now you have gained the sagely rule. If your altars of state are long to endure, you should establish the An-hua temple east of Ch'ang-an and install Taoist images there, then the empire will have a Great Peace (*t'ai-p'ing*).'" He then disappeared into the air. When the message was finally delivered to Kao-tsu and a stone tortoise, on whose back written "The empire is at peace; your descendants will flourish a thousand myriad years," was presented in confirmation of the prediction, Kao-tsu was extremely pleased. He rewarded Chi, and also ordered a temple built at the site of the epiphany.[77] The next time the deity appeared before Chi, he identified himself in the following manner: "I am the Immortal Nonpareil [*wu-shang shen-hsien*], surnamed Li, *tzu* Po-yang, *hao* Lao-chün. I am the emperor's ancestor." He then predicted that at the Lao-tzu Temple in Po-chou, a withered tree would spring to life as proof of his words. He also pledged to aid the T'ang by chastising its enemy, the "rebel" Liu Hei-t'a, in that year.[78] Both predictions came true.

Those Taoist individuals and institutions instrumental to the T'ang cause were duly rewarded for their contributions. Around 619 Kao-tsu ordered new halls of worship built at Lou-kuan, presented Lou-kuan with ten *ch'ing* of land, and appointed Ch'i P'ing-ting (Ch'i Hui) as its abbot.[79] The following year the emperor donated to it twenty *shih* of rice and one thousand rolls of silk, and changed its name to Tsung-sheng kuan, the Temple of the Imperial Ancestor.[80] It may have been on this occasion, or else in 619, that Kao-tsu first claimed Lao-tzu as the imperial ancestor and formally inaugurated his cult.[81] About the same time, in 620, the Mao-shan Taoist, Wang Yüan-chih, was summoned to court, given an official title, and generously rewarded for his predictions about Kao-tsu's gaining the Mandate. Miyakawa believes that Wang may have been behind the divine manifestations on both Mount Huo-t'ai and Mount Yang-chiao.[82] If this were so, the T'ang owed him a debt it could never repay. In 624 Kao-tsu paid a visit to Lou-kuan, where he personally sacrificed to Lao-chün.[83]

According to Wen Ta-ya's *Diary*, Kao-tsu was "extremely skeptical" about Taoism and Buddhism, and "had no deep faith."[84] Nevertheless, Taoist messianism was a potent ideological force stimulating popular support for various anti-Sui rebels, many of whom had their own active bands of Taoist adherents. The linking of the imperial house with Taoist millennial expectations must have served to bolster troop morale while T'ang armies were marching on the Sui capital or while they were locked in combat with rival forces after Kao-tsu ascended the throne. It must also have been designed to reinforce the political support lent the regime by

Taoist-oriented officials at the court and their families. This was the audience most likely targeted by Kao-tsu when he ranked Taoism first at the court debates on the three teachings and when, at the lectures on the three teachings at the National College during the following year, he granted Taoists precedence over Buddhists in the seating arrangements.[85]

The position of Buddhism in the early T'ang was naturally influenced by the official doctrine of the imperial family's descent from Lao-tzu. It may have been for this reason that early T'ang monarchs, particularly T'ai-tsung, never assumed the mantle of a Buddhist Ćakravartin king, turner of the Wheel of Law and universal monarch, as had the Sui founder, Wen-ti.[86] On the other hand, there were just too many adherents of Buddhism among all classes of Chinese society for rulers to ignore the teaching in attempting to obtain support for their rule. Even Kao-tsu, perhaps the least devout and the harshest Buddhist critic among early T'ang monarchs, made friendly overtures to Buddhists while on the throne. This was because Buddhism was able to supply the regime with the same kind of prophetic, religious, and material support as its Taoist rival.

According to the *Continued Biographies of Eminent Monks* (*Hsü Kao-seng chuan*) by the T'ang Buddhist writer Tao-hsüan, sometime during the reign of Sui Wen-ti a Buddhist monk named Ching Hui, an expert in the art of prognostication, predicted Kao-tsu's later triumph. If true, this would have constituted the earliest prophecy concerning the T'ang founder. After the establishment of the dynasty, in gratitude for Ching-hui's prophecies, Kao-tsu established the Sheng-yeh Temple in the quarter north of the eastern market of Ch'ang-an for him.[87] It is difficult to ascertain, however, whether Kao-tsu was aware of the prophecies at the time they were first made. Another source records a portent concerning Kao-tsu which took place just before he rose in revolt. One night, he dreamed that he had died and that his body had fallen from his bed onto the ground, where it was eaten by maggots. When he awoke he consulted a Buddhist priest, Chih-man, who interpreted the dream as follows: You are going to gain the empire. When you died your body fell beneath (*hsia*) the bed. The many maggots eating you means that the common people will all hasten to your side. Because we do not dare use the term Son of Heaven, we say "below the stairs" (*pi-hsia*) to indicate the position of emperor. Thus, the *hsia* is a sign of your impending rise to the highest status. Chih-man remained by Kao-tsu's side all during his march on the Sui capital, making other prognostications with the same message, and undoubtedly contributing mightily to morale among the T'ang forces. When Kao-tsu took the throne, he rewarded the priest by restoring his old temple and granting him permanent residence in the emperor's former residence in T'ai-yüan.[88]

THE AUGURIES OF T'AI-TSUNG

Portents played a more minor role in the coming to power of Kao-tsu's son, perhaps reflecting the fact that now that the dynasty's power had been established on a fairly firm footing there was less need for them. Nevertheless, since all rulers have normal legitimation needs, and since T'ai-tsung came to the throne in an especially violent manner, stories of auspicious signs and prophecies foretelling his greatness were sedulously propagated. For example, at the time of his birth it is said that two dragons sported outside his dwelling, departing only after three days.[89] Later, when he was four *sui*, a self-styled physiognomist predicted that before Kao-tsu's son had reached the age of twenty he would "benefit the age and soothe the people" (*chi-shih an-min*). As soon as the physiognomist had departed, Kao-tsu began to fear that his prediction would spread among the people and bring harm to the family; he thus deputed men to pursue and kill him. But the physiognomist had seemingly disappeared into thin air and could not be found, raising suspicions that he was actually some sort of spirit. Kao-tsu therefore selected his words for T'ai-tsung's given name, Shih-min.[90]

As T'ai-tsung did indeed benefit the age and soothe the people, yet other prophecies were forthcoming. While battling anti-T'ang rebels in 621, accompanied by his adviser Fang Hsüan-ling, T'ai-tsung paid a call on the Mao-shan Taoist, Wang Yüan-chih. Although T'ai-tsung was in disguise and Wang did not know his identity, he nevertheless discerned that "there is a sage [i.e., future emperor] among us," and dubbed him a "Son of Heaven of the Great Peace" (*t'ai-p'ing t'ien-tzu*).[91] When T'ai-tsung ascended the throne a few years later, he promoted Wang to the high rank of second degree, second class, and allowed this Taoist the unprecedented honor of wearing the imperial purple. In 635 he established a monastery on Mao-shan in modern Kiangsu province for him.[92] Around the same time, another Taoist priest, Hsüeh I, who was a calendrical expert and good at foretelling the future on the basis of celestial phenomena, secretly revealed to T'ai-tsung that heavenly phenomena indicated he would be victor in the struggle with his brothers for the succession and

that he was destined to rule the empire. As a reward, T'ai-tsung recommended that he be appointed to an official post. When he became emperor,
T'ai-tsung appointed Hsüeh abbot of a temple he had constructed at the
site of his own future tomb, on Chiu-tsung Mountain northwest of
Ch'ang-an. At the temple an observatory was built so that Hsüeh might
keep his eyes trained on the Heavens and report any anomaly, along with
his interpretation, to the throne.[93]

At the same time that Taoist portents were predicting T'ai-tsung's
rise to power and confirming his legitimacy, Buddhist signs were also
making themselves known to him. During either 621 or 622 T'ai-tsung
sighted a Kuan-yin p'u-sa, the Buddhist goddess of mercy, in the sky.
Taking this as a fortunate omen regarding his future, he ordered that a
Buddhist temple be built on the spot.[94]

In his edict transferring power to T'ai-tsung in the eighth month of
626, Kao-tsu referred to the fact that since an early age his son had
accorded with various auspicious omens, and that in more recent times
auspicious signs had appeared in great numbers portending T'ai-tsung's
rise to power.[95] The emperor was apparently referring to the portents
discussed above.

THE AUGURIES OF KAO-TSUNG

Of the first three T'ang emperors, the recorded portents preceding and
accompanying Kao-tsung's rise to power appear to be the most ambig-
uous. This may reflect the judgment of later men that his reign was only
a mixed success: Although the limits of T'ang suzerainty in Asia were
pushed to their furthest point, it was Kao-tsung who unwittingly aided
the rise of the infamous Wu Chao, who in her quest for power and legitimacy almost destroyed the dynasty. Kao-tsung was appointed crown
prince on the seventh day of the fourth month (April 30), 643. The first
omen accompanying his appointment, appearing in the same month, was
judged inauspicious. It was a blue-green vapor, which wound around the
Eastern Palace, traditional abode of the heir apparent.[96] A second portent
was more favorable. In the ninth month of 643, twenty-four stalks of a
purple *chih* fungus, in the shapes of dragons and phoenixes, were produced
in the crown prince's chambers.[97] The fungus, which can be preserved for
a long time, was a symbol of long life and prosperity.

On the whole, portents during Kao-tsung's time were neither particularly numerous nor particularly remarkable. Like his father before him,

the emperor was careful to cultivate the image of an enlightened monarch who was openly skeptical about the significance of omens. On one occasion he derided Sui Yang-ti (that convenient early T'ang scapegoat) for his reliance on such signs and maintained that genuine portents were only those that could be verified by several observers; the rest did not bear credence.[98] Yet, this did not prevent him from seizing upon the sighting at the end of 663 of what was said to have been a unicorn in the southern part of modern Shansi province, and unicorn tracks in front of a hall of the Ta-ming Palace, to change his reign name at the beginning of the following year to Lin-te, "Unicorn Virtue."[99]

CONCLUSIONS

In the late Sui civil wars, auspicious omens and lucky signs constituted indispensable weapons in the arsenals of all the contenders for power. Such signs of Heaven's favor and popular will were much sought after because they could be shrewdly parlayed into even more public support. Since great symbolic and political significance was attached to these signs, reporting them was a serious business, with serious consequences. After the battle of Hsi-ho in Shansi province in the sixth month of 617, a local Sui official, Kao Te-ju, was captured by the T'ang. Kao had earlier reported to Sui Yang-ti sighting an auspicious omen in the form of the fabulous *luan* bird. When Kao was brought to the T'ang camp, both Kao-tsu's eldest son, Chien-ch'eng, and T'ai-tsung excoriated him for having falsely turned a mere wild bird into a *luan*, and compared him with other despicable villains in China's past who had similarly deluded their sovereigns. Such evil men deserved death, they decided. Kao was summarily beheaded.[100]

Nonetheless, deception was the stock-in-trade of all those who dealt in portents. As we saw at the beginning of this chapter, contemporary men generally adopted a very practical approach to the matter. If inauspicious omens could be conveniently ignored for political reasons, could not auspicious omens be manipulated—even fabricated at will—also for political reasons? It is apparent that Kao-tsu and his successors, or, at the very least, their supporters, engineered portents or else interpreted prophetic signs in their favor. While it may be useful in this discussion to attempt to distinguish between those portents that were consciously fabricated from those that occurred "spontaneously" without any apparent human intervention, such a task is difficult at best. Stone tortoises, folk ballads, even white-robed rustics could be produced with relative ease. Colored clouds in fantastic shapes, bright lights, winds, tides, and other atmospheric phenomena were presumably more difficult to fake. But even in these cases people were subject to the power of suggestion, especially when there was already present among them the will to experience certain phenomena in a favorable light.

It might be argued that since the active supporters of the T'ang had already willingly bound themselves to the regime, the primary audience for the portents and the legitimating function they served were those who had not yet committed themselves—the masses at large. This would presumably explain the considerable reliance placed by the T'ang on religious symbolism in its portents, especially that of Taoism. It is impossible to estimate the portion of the general populace that would have been swayed by such Taoist appeals, but Kao-tsu, who was "extremely skeptical" about religious belief, surely would not have devoted so much energy to Taoist prophecies and signs had the returns been so meager. The popularity of Taoism was by no means confined, moreover, to strongholds in the T'ai-yüan region of Shansi or even around Mao-shan in Kiangsu. For example, after the pacification of the rebel Liu Hei-t'a in southern Hopei in 623, Kao-tsu assigned a new prefect, Yen Yu-ch'in, to administer Lien prefecture. Yen's regime was uncommonly compassionate and lenient, giving rise to a song among the people pervaded by a deeply Taoist tone:

Lien prefecture's Yen has the Way;	*Lien-chou Yen yu tao*
His conduct is like that of Chuang and Lao.	*Hsing-hsing t'ung Chuang Lao*
He loves the people like a newborn babe;	*Ai min ju ch'ih-tzu*
He would not even kill untimely weeds.	*Pu sha fei-shih ts'ao*[101]

Yet it would be wrong to maintain that portents laden with Taoist or Buddhist symbolism were aimed primarily at the masses whereas those suffused with Confucian imagery were targeted exclusively toward the elite. Many high officials at the early T'ang court were ardent Buddhists or Taoists. The official view, introduced it now appears as early as Kao-tsu's time, that Lao-tzu was the ancestor of the ruling Li-T'ang house, conferred a kind of orthodoxy on Taoism that must have served to increase the power of Taoist symbolism even among the scholar–official class. As Michel Strickmann has recently suggested, moreover, millennial expectations were shared not just by the masses but also by members of the sophisticated southern aristocracy, who were influenced by Mao-shan

Taoism. Some of the latter became important advisers at the early T'ang court.[102] On the other hand, when widely publicized, as they usually were, portents bearing such "Confucian" content as the Mandate of Heaven, color symbolism associated with Chinese epic heroes, and the like, must have been powerful propaganda devices affecting all classes of society.

CHAPTER 4

Merit and Virtue Conjoined: The Early T'ang Accession Ceremonies

Thus the Chinese emperor more resembled the Babylonian in ideology, being a representative of the gods placed in ritual and administrative charge on earth, and concurrently the representative of man before heaven. He is under responsibility. But the rites of accession, being more juridical or triumphant than dynamic, are rather more Egyptian. The accession crisis of death, chaos, and renewal remains a historical myth, under heaven, rather than being entirely assimilated to death and resurrection like that of Osiris or Marduk.

Robert S. Ellwood, *The Feast of Kingship*

AMONG MANY PEOPLES ROYAL ACCESSION HAS BEEN A SUPREMELY SACRED RITE in which the renewal of kingship becomes a renewal of an entire society. On the one hand, as a rite of political continuity it underlines individual human fragility and the inevitability of death. On the other, it joins human society to the sempiternal cosmic cycle and underlines its continuity with nature. Such themes are often encompassed in a ritual enactment of myth, in which the king (as king/god) dies and is resurrected or fights a cosmic battle, or in a ritual recitation of the creation epic. Seen in this way, the accession ceremony is a recreation of the act by which the world came into being.[1] "Almost everywhere," Mircea Eliade observes, "a new reign has been regarded as a regeneration of the history of the people or even of universal history. With each new sovereign, insignificant as he might be, a 'new era' began."[2]

The theme of death and resurrection also informs the accession ceremony considered as a rite of passage. At the beginning of this century, Arnold van Gennep observed that in any society the life of an individual was "a series of passages from one age to another and from one occupation to another." Such passages, he said, include sexual initiations, marriages,

78

ordinations, funerals, royal enthronements, that is, every change of place, state, social position, and age. For every one of these there were ceremonies whose essential purpose was to pass from one defined position to another.[3] According to van Gennep, rites of passage are divisible into three stages: (1) rites of separation, or "preliminal" rites; (2) rites of transition, or "liminal" rites; (3) rites of incorporation, or "postliminal" rites.[4] Victor Turner, who built upon van Gennep's theories, observes that rites of liminality characteristically begin with the symbolic killing of the subject or his separation from ordinary secular or profane relationships, and conclude with his symbolic birth or reincorporation into society. In moving from one status to another in a rite of passage, the former self must be destroyed so that the new self can be created.[5]

Weber viewed accession/installation ceremonies as vehicles for the routinization of charisma. Charisma, according to Weber, can be transmitted by ritual means from one bearer to another by dissociating it from a particular individual and making it an objective, transferable entity. The belief in legitimacy is then no longer attached to the individual but to the ritual acts by means of which he first achieves his status and to the qualities he is believed to acquire by means of them.[6]

Easton treats accession ceremonies in terms of his concept of support. Because such ceremonies take place at the very beginning of an incumbency, usually before the authority of a ruler has been fully recognized or demonstrated, such ceremonies are designed to enhance his legitimacy and to generate additional support on his behalf. Easton notes that diffuse support is generated by identifying the ruler with the dominant political symbols: both the traditional or sacred physical symbols of authority (miranda) and the grand political myths and doctrines of state (credenda). Favored ceremonial treatment for individuals or groups closely associated with the regime and the distribution of amnesties and rewards among the wider populace, acts that are often associated with accession rituals, serve to nurture both specific and diffuse support.[7]

The event of accession is virtually always surrounded by ceremonial. The anthropologist Meyer Fortes suggests that this is because ritual possesses an important moral component: It works not only incontestably to proclaim the successor to an office but also to bind him to that office and all the obligations attached to it. In the accession/installation ritual, in return for mobilizing "incontrovertible authority behind the granting of office and status," and thus guaranteeing its legitimacy, society "imposes accountability for its proper exercise."[8] Once in office, the incumbent must show his devotion to that office by dressing his part, and also living his part by observing a number of distinctive and onerous ritual restrictions. The emblems and insignia of office symbolize for Fortes not so much the authority of that office as its responsibilities, attaching the holder to his office by ritual sanctions. The religious character of accession/installation ritual thus derives not from concepts of divine kingship but from the need to invest with "binding force the moral obligations to society for its well-being and prosperity...."[9]

With these theoretical speculations in mind, let us now examine traditional Chinese forms of the acession ceremony, especially those of the early T'ang.

ACCESSION CEREMONIES IN PRE-T'ANG TIMES

There are two basic types of accession ceremonies in traditional China. The first involves the rites surrounding the transition between two different dynasties and the coming to power of a founding ruler, which we might refer to as different surname succession. The second involves the rites surrounding an internal dynastic transition and the coming to power of a descendant or blood relative of a dynastic founder, which we might refer to as same surname succession.[10] By accession ceremonies in general we mean to include (1) the specific transaction carried out following the demise of one ruler and the transfer of authority to his successor; as well as (2) all the forms and rites carried out in conjunction with the exaltation of the successor to the imperial position, such as state announcements, transfer of regalia, sacrificial proclamations, the granting of rewards or benefits, and the like. Accession ceremonies as a term employed here thus includes rites both consummating and commemorating all aspects of attaining royal authority.[11]

Before an accession takes place, there has to be a transfer of political power. In instances of different surname succession there are essentially two archetypes of transfer, by voluntary yielding (*shan-jang*) and by conquest of arms (*fang-fa*). The first method is epitomized in the myths of Yao and Shun, and Shun and Yü, dating from about the late Chou period, in which the sage-ruler Yao is portrayed as having voluntarily ceded his power, that is, passed on the Mandate, to Shun on the basis of the latter's superior moral virtue, a process later replicated in the transfer of the throne from Shun to Yü.[12] Because of its association with sage-rulers, *shan-jang* became in Chinese eyes a sacred political instrument by which

power was transferred and, simultaneously, legitimated. Beginning with
the Ts'ao-Wei regime in the third century, whose founder made it appear
as if he had assumed power by means of *shan-jang*, it became a much-
abused practice, empty of all significance.[13] The second method involves
the forceful chastising of tyrannical rulers and the seizing of their power,
as in the case of T'ang's overthrowing the villainous last ruler of Hsia and
King Wu's defeating the last ruler of Shang. It was the way in which most
regimes actually came to power in China.

There are also two basic types of transfer in same surname succession.
The first occurs when a deceased ruler is succeeded by a relative, usually a
son. The second involves the abdication of a ruler in favor of a relative,
who is also usually a son.

In the early T'ang we find an interesting mix of power transfers. The
T'ang came to power by a method that is clearly of the *fang-fa* type,
although it was, for symbolic reasons, also portrayed as a *shan-jang*. Kao-
tsu ruled for eight years before abdicating to his son, T'ai-tsung. The third
T'ang emperor, Kao-tsung, succeeded to power upon the natural death of
his father, T'ai-tsung. All four types of political succession thus figured in
early T'ang history.

There was an inherent contradiction between the notion that power
was to be inherited, as in the case of same surname succession, and the
principle of succession on the basis of manifest virtue, as in *shan-jang*. In
her structuralist study of the Yao and Shun myth and its correlates, while
noting the universal aspect of the opposition between heredity and virtue,
Sarah Allen emphasizes the significance of the tension generated in the
Chinese case:

> "Virtue," as I have used the term in this study, is essentially a response to the
> demands of the larger community or state, even when these demands conflict
> with the interests of one's family or kinship group. Heredity is the protection
> of family or kinship interests. This opposition is inherent in any human socie-
> ty that differentiates one nuclear family or kinship group from another, but
> it increases in importance with the complexity of the political and social
> organization of the community. In the settled agricultural community of
> traditional China, with its complex system of kinship organizations
> existing alongside a political organization with an hereditary king and a
> non-hereditary officialdom, this opposition assumed unusual importance.[14]

The tension between heredity and virtue was given substance in the Confucian canon. In the "Evolution of Rites" (*Li-yün*) section of the *Book of
Rites*, we read:

When the Great Way was practiced the world was shared by all alike [*t'ien-hsia wei kung*]. The worthy and the able were promoted to office and men practiced good faith and lived in affection. Therefore they did not regard as parents only their own parents, or as sons only their own sons.... Now the Great Way has become hid and the world is the possession of private families [*t'ien-hsia wei chia*]. Each regards his parents as only his own parents, as sons only his own sons; goods and labor are employed for selfish ends.[15]

In this passage the quality of *kung* is equated with a spirit of magnanimity and cooperation transcending the parochialism of family or kinship ties, whereas *chia* is equated with partiality toward family or kin group and the protection of family interests.[16] In the Golden Age of the past, men had lived their lives and conducted government on the basis of *kung* rather than *chia*, but now the world had degenerated into selfishness. Although the passage does not directly address the institution of hereditary monarchy, the message is clear: *Kung* is a moral analogue to the political concept of succession on the basis of virtue, whereas *chia*'s political analogue is hereditary succession. Throughout the rest of the study we will see the enormous moral and political appeal exerted by the *t'ien-hsia wei kung* concept, which serves as a leitmotif surrounding many of the ritual and symbolic acts performed by early T'ang monarchs.

The Chinese classics on ritual contain no accounts of an accession, perhaps reflecting a tendency to emphasize order and stability, that is, a permanent annual calendar of ceremonial, at the expense of chaos and instability, that is, a rite of political transition.[17] The *Book of History* contains what are probably the earliest depictions of Chinese accession ceremonies. The sage-kings Yao and Shun both seem to be portrayed as accepting the Mandate of Heaven in or around some kind of temple or shrine.[18] Some commentators have claimed that the *Book of History* also suggests that at the time of the accession of the young heir of the Shang dynasty founder, T'ang, a sacrifice was made either at T'ang's temple or in front of his corpse to announce the accession of his son.[19]

A much longer and more detailed narrative of an accession ceremony is found in a later chapter in the *Book of History* called "The Testamentary Charge" (*Ku-ming*), which describes the coming to power of the Chou King, K'ang (trad. rg. 1078–52 B.C.), following the death of his father, King Ch'eng.[20] Here the dying King Ch'eng lays a testamentary charge on the grand protector (*t'ai-pao*) and other high officials, naming his successor and commanding them to assist him in facing the difficulties of his new position. Immediately following the king's death, the grand protector orders the king-designate escorted to an apartment near the place where his father's corpse reposes. Two days after the king's death a record is made of his testamentary charge that his son should succeed him. Seven days after his death he is encoffined. Now it is time to enact his charge and to display and transfer his regalia: precious gems, jade scepters, tortoise shell, drum, carriages, and much more. On this same day the king-designate, wearing a hempen cap and a skirt adorned with emblems of royal authority, enters a hall in the building containing his father's body to assume the royal mantle. High officials bearing special ceremonial objects are also in the hall, along with all the Feudal Princes (*chu-hou*). The grand historiographer (*t'ai-shih*) carries the testamentary charge and importunes the king-designate to accept it. The latter repeatedly bows and declares he is unqualified to assume such an onerous burden. He then receives the ceremonial objects and sacrifices with them three times, signifying that he has accepted the charge. He has now become a *wang*, or king, and also a Son of Heaven.

The next chapter in the *Book of History*, "The Announcement of King K'ang" (*K'ang-wang chih kao*), details the audience which the new king conducts for all his officials and the Feudal Princes immediately following his accession. No mention is made of any sacrifice or ancestral temple, but it has been widely assumed that after the accession ceremony was completed and before the new king's inaugural audience, an announcement of his accession was made before the corpse of his father.[21] The "Testamentary Charge" and "Announcement of King K'ang" chapters provided an early model for the accession ceremonies of generations of subsequent Chinese monarchs.[22]

The Chou ceremony was rather modest in comparison with the more elaborate accession rituals that evolved in Han and later times. The enthronement of the Han emperor Wen in 179 B.C. reveals a relatively complex rite with most of the major components of the T'ang accession ceremony already in place: the transfer of the imperial seals and credentials; the promulgation of an imperial edict announcing the inauguration of the new regime; the general amnesty of the empire; the granting to the common people of one step in honorary noble rank; the conferment of titles; and a visit to the ancestral temple.[23] Emperor Wen's accession ceremonies provided a model for the rite during much of China's imperial age. Nevertheless, this model was modified all during the period leading up to the T'ang. Some of these modifications are summarized below.

Time of enthronement. During the Former Han dynasty only Wu-ti (rg. 141–87 B.C.) assumed the imperial position on the same day as the death of his predecessor, suggesting that same-day succession was not an operational principle during this period. During the Later Han, however, same-day succession seems to have been the rule, if not always practiced.[24] Overall, in both the Former and the Later Han, the accession of a new emperor preceded the interment of his predecessor.[25]

Place of enthronement. It appears that early in the Former Han accession ceremonies took place in the ancestral temple of the founder, Kao-tsu, but that about the time of Chao-ti (rg. 86–73 B.C.) the ceremonies began to take place before the deceased emperor's coffin. Nishijima Sadao hypothesizes that the change in practice may have come about as a result of a growing interest in the Confucian classics during the time of the previous ruler, Wu-ti. The Kung-yang commentary to the *Spring and Autumn Annals*, which notes the practice of accession in front of the coffin of the deceased, may have been influential in this development.[26] All of the Later Han enthronements took place before the coffin of the deceased emperor.[27] Even after this practice became the rule, the Han continued having the new ruler personally visit the ancestral temple of the founding emperor, site of the first Han accessions.

Reading of the will and appointment of the previous emperor. From the Han dynasty onward the issuing and public reading of written communications from previous emperors, both living and dead, played a crucial role in the accession ceremonies and the wider process of political legitimation. The *locus classicus* of this practice, as we have seen, was the "Testamentary Charge" chapter of the *Book of History*. The written communications were known as *chao* and *ts'e* (or *ts'e-ming*). The *chao* usually contained the will of the previous emperor, whereas the *ts'e* contained the appointment of his successor.[28] They were devices for passing on the Mandate from one dynasty to another or from one dynastic family member to another.[29]

Especially in instances of different surname succession it was essential to demonstrate that a dynastic founder had rightfully inherited the Mandate. This was accomplished in part by having the last ruler of the previous dynasty issue *chao* and *ts'e* in praise of the moral virtues and accomplishments of his successor. Ogata Isamu, who has studied the transition from Later Han to the Ts'ao-Wei dynasty in some detail, notes that the last ruler of the Later Han, Hsien-ti, indicated his willingness to cede the throne to Ts'ao P'ei, the Wei founder, in no fewer than four *chao*.

Later, Hsien-ti issued a *ts'e* in which he observed that the Mandate did not remain in one place forever but belonged to him who was most virtuous. Just as in the time of Yao, who had ceded the Mandate to Shun, the Mandate had now been transferred to the virtuous Ts'ao P'ei.[30] Both the *chao* and *ts'e* thus denied the concept that the empire belonged to one dynastic house alone (*t'ien-hsia wei chia*) in favor of the doctrine that the empire belonged to the most virtuous (*t'ien-hsia wei kung*).

It is easy to see how the *t'ien-hsia wei kung* doctrine might have provided a theoretical basis for different surname succession. Perhaps surprisingly, then, the doctrine also played an important role in the transfer of power within a dynasty, especially in cases of abdication. In such instances the abdicating emperor sometimes suggested that Yao and Shun had operated under special constraints that did not pertain to their own situations. For example, in A.D. 471, at the time of the abdication of the Northern Wei emperor, Hsien-wen, in favor of his son, the emperor issued a *chao* in which he noted that Yao and Shun would have passed power on to their own sons except for the latter's moral imperfections. But since his own progeny was morally unblemished, he alone deserved to succeed to the throne.[31] Other emperors might claim that their motives in ceding the throne to moral worthies, who happened to be their own sons, were no less altruistic than Yao's or Shun's. In 508 the Northern Chou emperor, Hsüan-ti, stated in a *chao* that the doctrine of *t'ien-hsia wei kung* did not rule out succession within a family, and therefore he was appointing his eldest son as his legitimate successor.[32] The promulgation of *chao* and *ts'e* thus served to gloss over the ideological weakness of the *t'ien-hsia wei chia* element of same surname succession, by making it seem as if the transfer of power within one family was being carried out in accord with the open character of political succession embodied in the Yao and Shun myth; that is, it was only because the dynastic descendant possessed virtue that he was inheriting the Mandate of the dynastic founder. Seen in this way, *chao* and *ts'e* represent in graphic form the moral components of accession ceremonies discussed by Fortes. By emphasizing the virtue possessed by political successors, they in effect laid a claim against the future conduct of those successors and bound them more closely to the duties of office. They were also, in Weberian terms, instruments by which the charisma of the previous ruler was transferred to his successor.[33]

Assuming the position of ruler. At least beginning with the Later Han, a distinction was made between assuming the position of Son of Heaven (*t'ien-tzu*) and that of emperor (*huang-ti*). The "Monograph on Ritual and Ceremonial" of the *History of the Later Han Dynasty* records the following sequence of activity at an accession ritual. The Three Dukes (*san-kung*) read the "Testamentary Charge" chapter of the *Book of History*. The crown prince assumes the position of Son of Heaven (*chi t'ien-tzu wei*) in front of the coffin of the deceased. Then all the officials entreat him to assume the position of emperor; he yields to their entreaty. The officials exit from the hall and return wearing clothes suited for festive occasions. The testamentary charge of the deceased is read, the crown prince receives the imperial seal and then assumes the position of emperor (*chi huang-ti wei*).[34]

What was the significance of the distinction between assuming the position of *t'ien-tzu* and that of *huang-ti*? The title *huang-ti* was created in 221 B.C. by the first emperor of China, Ch'in Shih-huang-ti, in order to set himself apart from the Chou rulers who had called themselves king (*wang*) and also Son of Heaven (*t'ien-tzu*). Whereas *t'ien-tzu* connoted power limited by the will of Heaven and dependent on moral rectitude, the new title *huang-ti* seems to have connoted no such limitations, representing power untrammeled by any heavenly or earthly considerations. During the Han, however, these distinctions appear to have blurred somewhat as Confucians attempted to surround the *huang-ti* concept with precepts of moral responsibility and the doctrine of the provisional conferment of the Mandate that had been at the heart of Confucianism for more than half a millennium. At the same time the concept of *huang-ti*, which appears nowhere in the Confucian classics, began to be formally included in Confucian political theory.[35] As the concepts gradually became sorted out, *huang-ti* and *t'ien-tzu* were seen as possessing somewhat different functions or jurisdictions. *Huang-ti* came to be associated with the emperor's stewardship of the state and his control over domestic government, whereas *t'ien-tzu* was associated with his role as a bridge to the deities of Heaven and Earth and his authority over "all under Heaven," including foreign tributaries of China.[36]

The *huang-ti/t'ien-tzu* distinction in accession ritual persisted in the post-Han period through the end of the T'ang dynasty. When a ruler ascended the throne he separately assumed, in a two-stage ritual, the position of both *huang-ti* and *t'ien-tzu*. But how he did so depended on whether power was being passed from one dynasty to another or within a dynastic family. In different surname succession the new ruler first received the imperial seals and assumed the position of *huang-ti*. Following this, he carried out the sacrifice to Heaven, announcing that he had been ceded the position of emperor and begging to be confirmed in this position and to receive the Mandate. By this second ritual he thereby acceded to the status of *t'ien-tzu*.[37] However, in cases of same surname succession the process was reversed: The ruler first became *t'ien-tzu* and only afterward became *huang-ti*.[38]

Transfer of the imperial seals and ribbons. Most accession ceremonies involve the transfer of regalia symbolizing both the acquisition of the right to rule and the continuity of political power from one source to another. Forms of regalia, while enormously diverse, serve similar functions. They act in a magical way to protect their possessors and ensure the safety of the state. They outlast the lives of individual men and regimes and ensure the passage of power across the break of human death or political demise. They legitimate political succession.[39] Their transfer also "demonstrates de facto strength, whether of arms, followers, or craftiness," and may serve to announce the resolution of a disputed succession.[40]

By Later Han times the acquisition of certain regalia, the imperial seals and ribbons, had become a central element of the accession ritual. No emperor was considered a true Son of Heaven if he did not physically possess them.[41] Thus, the imperial seals were to the Han and later ages what the nine caldrons had been to the Three Dynasties of Hsia, Shang, and Chou—supreme vehicles of legitimation.

There were six imperial seals made of white jade, each a little more than an inch square, topped by a handle with coiling dragons and tigers. Each had a different text: Three of them began with the term Son of Heaven (*t'ien-tzu*) and three with the term emperor (*huang-ti*). The *huang-ti* seals were generally employed in matters relating to domestic affairs, whereas the *t'ien-tzu* seals were used in matters relating to foreign affairs.[42] They were impressed upon some kind of purple clay to make a seal. The seals were transferred to a new ruler either when he made a formal announcement of his assumption of duties at the ancestral temple or else in front of the coffin of his deceased predecessor at the time of enthronement.[43] In either case, the meaning was that the seals had been transferred to the new ruler by his own ancestors, or by the last ruler of a defunct regime and *his* ancestors.

In addition to these six seals there was a special seal which was considered *primus inter pares* among all the imperial seals in its ability to confer political legitimacy on its possessor. The seal was not, like the other impe-

rial seals, employed by the emperor on state documents, but served only
as an emblem of his power.[44] Because it was handed down from generation to generation in the Han house, it was called the "seal by which the
Han transmits the state" (*Han ch'uan-kuo hsi*).[45] Although, according to
the *History of the Former Han Dynasty*, the Han founder obtained the seal
from the last ruler of the Ch'in, this tradition is suspect. The seal may well
date, in fact, from Later Han times.[46] The transmission of the seal in the
post-Han period is also clouded with uncertainty.[47] Many of the regimes
of the disunion period claimed to possess it, but it is more than likely that
the seal was lost or destroyed one or more times during the chaotic period
of successive dynastic transitions, and that it was counterfeited as needed
to serve the legitimating interests of various dynastic founders. After
examining the history of the transmission of the *ch'uan-kuo* seal down
to the Mongol Yüan dynasty (1279–1368), the Ch'ing scholar, Chao I,
concluded simply that "every age manufactured its own seal."[48]

Announcement to Heaven. Although it is recorded that Han Kao-tsu
built an altar at the time of his accession, it is not clear whether he ascended
it personally to perform the sacrifice to Heaven to announce the fact.
Perhaps such a practice had not yet come about. But at the beginning of
the Later Han, its founder, Kuang-wu-ti, made a burnt offering to Heaven
at the time of his accession. From Ts'ao-Wei and Chin times it became the
general rule that founding emperors who had just received the Mandate
personally sacrificed to Heaven to announce their accession.[49] Although
the names of the sacrifices and their objects differ somewhat in the sources,
their purpose was in all cases to offer thanks to Heaven or to the Lord-on-
High, Shang-ti, for having conferred the Mandate on the dynastic
founder.[50] A sacrificial animal was burnt, creating smoke which ascended
to Heaven, by means of which it was believed that Heaven or Shang-ti
understood the meaning of the sacrifice and granted approval of the
founder's enthronement. Altars (*t'an*) for these sacrifices were usually built
in the southern suburb of the capital, although they were in a few instances
established elsewhere.[51]

Adoption of an era-name. The practice of selecting an era-name (*nien-
hao*) began in 163 B.C. under Emperor Wen of the Han, some seventeen
years after his enthronement.[52] At first, era-names merely indicated the
relative chronological position of the era measured against the entire
reign—such as "first era," "second era," and so forth. In 114 B.C. Emper-

or Wu's officials first formulated the doctrine that an era was to be named
for some sign of Heaven's favor.[53] Thereafter ear-names possessed special
significance for a ruler, and they were selected to convey specific meanings. This sometimes led to a proliferation of era-names during individual
reigns, and it is often possible to correlate the names with the major pre-
occupations or goals of a regime at the time they were selected.[54] During
the third century A.D., in the state of Shu-Han, one of the three successor states to the Later Han dynasty, the practice was inaugurated whereby
in cases of same surname succession rulers who had just come to power
waited until the beginning of the New Year to announce their first era-
name. To do so during the same year as the death of the previous ruler was
henceforth considered unlucky.[55]

Choosing an element. From Han times onward as part of their accession ritual founding emperors chose one element among the Five Elements
to symbolize the power behind their dynasty. As we have seen, the practice of tying the concept of the royal virtue to the Five Elements arose with
the philosopher Tsou Yen around the third century B.C. Tsou Yen believed that the Five Elements operated by mutual conquest, that is, they
overcame one another in a set order. By the end of the Former Han a new
scheme known as mutual production, by which elements were believed to
arise out of one another in a set order, had gained currency. The mutual
production scheme was seized upon by the Han usurper Wang Mang to
legitimate his regime. Thereafter, it remained the principle by which
dynasties were believed to succeed one another.[56]

The adoption of a new era-name and, especially, the selection of a
new element can be viewed as symbolic acts underlining the renewal and
regeneration aspects of the Chinese accession/installation ceremony. Here
I would like to return to the idea that an accession is a rite of passage in
which the former self must be destroyed before the new self can be born,
and that the ceremony represents a recreation of the world. Many years
ago, Marcel Granet pointed out that there is literary evidence that in
ancient China, before the establishment of dynastic succession, the authority of a chief depended on his killing or chasing out the old sovereign and
expelling the noxious forces associated with him. But in so doing, he pol-
lutes himself and must therefore expiate his act. He does this by dis-
membering a victim and throwing his limbs out of the four gates of the
city. The victim merely substitutes for the chief himself, who is thereby
purified.[57] The choosing of a new element (and color) for his regime by a

dynastic founder ritually symbolizes this ancient expulsion of noxious forces.[58] It announces that the ruler is reborn and the world created anew.

Announcement of a general amnesty. General amnesties for condemned criminals were a pre-dynastic Ch'in practice, which can be traced as far back as the seventh century B.C. The first amnesty issued in conjunction with an accession occurred in 250 B.C. with the coming to power of the Ch'in king, Hsiao-wen. The act was reinforced by Hsiao-wen's son in turn when he came to power. As Brian McKnight notes, by issuing an amnesty at the beginning of his reign a ruler manifested his compassion, reassured potential enemies that their previous acts were forgiven if not forgotten, and declared his ability to restore order to the empire.[59]

Granting of rewards. Rewards were generously bestowed on commoner and official alike at the time of an accession. During the Han and afterward it was common practice for new emperors to bestow one order of aristocratic rank on the general populace (*tz'u min-chüeh i-chi*). Such orders determined both a man's obligations to the state and the privileges the state owed him.[60] Taxes for certain classes of people were also commonly reduced or remitted for specified periods. Officials were either rewarded with aristocratic ranks or with cash. Accession ceremonies were often the time when emperors announced appointments to staff positions in their administrations. The granting of amnesties, rewards, and appointments was obviously aimed at securing specific support for new rulers and their regimes.

Visit to the ancestral temple. The burial of the previous emperor and a special visit to the ancestral temple (*yeh-miao*) by the new emperor were the two steps serving to bring the accession ceremonies to a conclusion.[61] In the Former Han, newly enthroned monarchs paid a visit to the temple of the dynastic founder, Kao-tsu; under the Later Han, rulers generally first visited Kao-tsu's temple and afterward visited the temple of the Later Han founder, Kuang-wu-ti.[62] According to the theory of Nishijima Sadao, the practice of visiting the ancestral temple may have become important when the site of the enthronement ceremony was moved from the ancestral temple to in front of the deceased emperor's coffin, as a way of continuing the old rite in a new form.[63] The visit symbolized that even after his death, the state belonged to Kao-tsu, its founder. Any new Han emperor had to announce his accession to Kao-tsu's spirit in order to gain his approval.

The ancestral spirit possessed such power in the first place because Kao-tsu had been the first to receive the Mandate. When a ruler assumed power in the Han, then, it was believed that power came not directly from Heaven but rather by means of the mediation of the dynastic founder. In this way the conflict inherent in the Mandate of Heaven doctrine (based on virtue) and the system of dynastic succession (based on heredity) was partially resolved.[64]

Since both the visit to the ancestral temple and the announcement to Heaven at the southern suburban altar ostensibly served the same purpose, the expression of gratitude for having received the Mandate, questions sometimes arose concerning which of the two ceremonies was more appropriate. For example, at the time of the accession of Emperor Yüan of the Eastern Chin dynasty in A.D. 317, one of his officials sent a letter to a colleague noting that there were two views on the matter and asking him which one he recommended. The second official advocated an announcement at the ancestral temple.[65] Later, in A.D. 498, a debate was held at the court of the Southern Ch'i monarch, Ming-ti, on whether it was appropriate for a new ruler to be presented at the ancestral temple or not. Opponents claimed that there were no records of the practice in antiquity. Proponents, pointing to Cheng Hsüan's view that a newly enthroned monarch personally had to sacrifice to his ancestors, and the many examples of the ritual recorded in the classics and the two Han histories, won the day.[66]

KAO-TSU'S ACCESSION

In discussing the accession ceremonies of the T'ang founder we are blessed with relatively rich documentation. The accession ceremonies of an emperor usually received fairly cursory treatment in such basic sources as the Standard History of a dynasty. In the best of cases we are usually offered a few sentences regarding the circumstances surrounding the accession, perhaps a severely truncated text of an edict of abdication by an outgoing emperor, or some abbreviated speeches of officials urging the future emperor to accept the Mandate, the latter's repeated refusals before accepting, and finally a bland notation that on such-and-such day the emperor assumed power and carried out the usual activities associated with an accession. Sometimes we are merely told that the emperor assumed power on a given day, and not much else.

In Kao-tsu's case, in addition to the usual sources bearing on an acces-

sion ceremony, we also possess Wen Ta-ya's *Diary of the Founding of the
Great T'ang Dynasty*. Almost the entire last chapter, approximately 5,000
out of 6,300 characters, is devoted to the series of ritual steps by which
Kao-tsu ascended the throne. Although some of its documentation is
duplicated elsewhere, it nevertheless remains the longest and most detailed
version of the first T'ang accession. Unfortunately, the *Diary* contains
almost no physical description of the accession ceremony itself, and it is
weak in chronology. Other sources do not overcome the former deficien-
cy, but they readily repair the latter. The narrative of events the *Diary* and
these other sources together present is as follows.

On the seventeenth day of the eleventh month of 617 (December 20),
while the second Sui emperor, Yang-ti, was cloistered at the city of
Chiang-tu, the puppet boy-emperor Kung-ti, who had himself assumed
power at Kao-tsu's behest only two days previous, appointed the T'ang
leader chancellor (*ch'eng-hsiang*) and enfeoffed him prince of T'ang (*T'ang-
wang*). In effect, Kao-tsu now controlled the entire Sui government, being
forbidden to perform only those sacrifices normally reserved for an
emperor. In the months ahead he amassed further honors and perquisites
of rank much on the model of the Han usurper, Wang Mang. With the
murder of Yang-ti at Chiang-tu in the middle of the third month of 618,
the stage was properly set for the formal political transition from Sui to
T'ang. On the twenty-third day (April 23), Kung-ti announced that he
"desired to carry out the ritual of ceding the throne (*shan-jang*)."[67] He
promoted Kao-tsu to chancellor of state (*hsiang-kuo*) and offered him the
nine gifts, which, as we saw, were a traditional reward to those who were
soon to assume the imperial mantle.[68] The T'ang leader's rank was now
higher than that of any other noble in the land. Much of the *ts'e* which
announced the conferral of these honors was taken up with a profuse de-
tailing of Kao-tsu's accomplishments in restoring order to the country.[69]
Each of the fifteen sections describing his achievements ended with
the ritual intonement: "This also was your merit [*kung*]." The *ts'e* thus
sedulously imitated those employed in earlier dynastic transitions on
the *shan-jang* model.[70]

With the offer to Kao-tsu of the nine gifts and the promulgation of the
ts'e indicating Kung-ti's intention to step down in his favor, the T'ang
accession ceremonial had begun in earnest. But the protocol of *shan-jang*
ritual required a prospective ruler to deny all intention of seeking the
Mandate. Kao-tsu began fulfilling his assigned role in this time-honored
charade by "secretly" addressing his staff, affirming his undying loyalty to

the Sui, and suggesting that opportunists had taken advantage of the emperor's youth to make him heap such honors on the T'ang leader, which he himself had never sought. He thus refused to accept the nine gifts.

His subordinates were, however, armed with weighty precedents: Hsiao Ho of the Former Han and the Duke of Lu during Chou times had both been granted such special privileges; they had not refused them, nor should he. Kao-tsu declined to be compared with those two worthies. He ridiculed the founders of the Wei and Chin dynasties who sought to create favorable conditions for their usurpations by eliciting *chao* from their predecessors that sung their praises, or the nine gifts with which they boasted of their merits. Nor did he approve of the founding rulers of dynasties during the Period of Disunion, who, modeling themselves on their predecessors in Wei and Chin, had hoped to make it appear that their gaining power was by *shan-jang*, in order to exalt themselves. "I have not heard," he said, "that the descendants of Chou and Chieh ["bad-last" rulers, respectively, of the Hsia and Shang] voluntarily ceded their thrones at the beginning of Shang and Chou. Speaking like this, the principles [by which they gained power, i.e., military conquest] can be known. Why did [later rulers] carelessly [seek to] change the Mandate of Heaven in order falsely to honor themselves? Whenever I read past history and encounter such examples, I always clap my hands and laugh."[71] When again pressed by his subordinates to accept the nine gifts, Kao-tsu vowed not to follow the examples of Ts'ao Ts'ao and Ssu-ma Yen, founders of the Ts'ao-Wei and Chin dynasties, who had accepted the nine gifts and other similar honors on their way to becoming emperors in falsely fabricated *shan-jang* rites, since he would be ashamed one day to be included in the same chapter of a history as they![72]

If Kao-tsu were dutifully playing a prescribed role in a venerable set piece, his subordinates, ever mindful of their own parts, yet again encouraged him to accept the proffered honors. This time Kao-tsu presented an even more elaborate case for his reluctance to accept the Sui emperor's abdication. Since the time of Ts'ao Ts'ao and Ssu-ma Yen, he said, when dynastic transitions had come under the influence of Confucian scholars, they had been made to appear as voluntary abdications even when dynastic founders had won the throne by military means. The truth of the matter had been conveniently concealed and the *shan-jang* procedure had become an empty convention. The cession of the throne from Yao to Shun had illustrated that power was to be transmitted on the basis of virtue and was not to be the private possession of one family (*t'ien-hsia wei kung*). But by

the time of the Shang and Chou there were no longer any Yaos and Shuns
to cede power to the most virtuous, and the founders of these dynasties
won their positions by military victory. In ancient times there were thus
two different methods of transmitting dynastic power: on the basis of virtue (*te*) and on the basis of military achievement (*kung*). Each method had
its own time. In later history, however, neither virtue nor merit had
figured in the transmission of power.[73] Having stated his piece, the T'ang
leader made a compromise gesture of accepting the position of chancellor
of state, but commanded that the nine gifts be distributed among his
subordinates.[74]

After conferring further honors on Kao-tsu, on the fourteenth day of
the fifth month (June 12), the Sui boy-emperor formally announced his
abdication.[75] In a *chao* issued on this day, Kung-ti observed that Heaven
had sent disaster down on the Sui, and that Yang-ti had been murdered in
Chiang-tu. Because of his youth he could not himself set things right. But
Kao-tsu had come to save the world at the right time. He had marched
everywhere to exterminate the rebels, become leader of the Chinese and
barbarians and protected commoners and the emperor alike. The people's
hearts had gone over to him. To treat him like a mere subject would thus
be opposed to the Heavenly Mandate. In ancient times Shun had ceded his
throne to Yü. Now that his own dynasty had been destroyed, he wanted
to follow such a precedent and retire to his family estate. All were now to
serve the T'ang dynasty and, following ancient practice, speedily offer the
imperial title to his successor. He then ordered that his own officials were
not to present any further memorials to him, signifying that he was, in
effect, no longer emperor.[76] Kung-ti's last official act before departing the
capital was to dispatch the Grand Protector, Hsiao Tsao, and the Grand
Commandant (*t'ai-wei*), P'ei Chih-yin, to offer Kao-tsu the imperial seals
and ribbons.[77] Acceptance of the seals by the T'ang leader would have
been tantamount to his becoming emperor.

Some two thousand T'ang supporters, led by P'ei Chi, now peti-
tioned Kao-tsu to assume the imperial mantle. "We have heard that the
empire is shared by all the people [*t'ien-hsia chih kung*] and is not solely the
possession of one surname," they reminded him. Recounting with much
hyperbole his many accomplishments, they compared him with the legendary emperor Chuan-hsü (trad. rg. 2513–2435 B.C.) and the Chou dynasty
founder, King Wu. They enumerated the various omens that had presaged
his rise to power. Finally, they arrived at their primary object, offering
Kao-tsu the throne. "The Mandate of Heaven is not constant," they

noted, "but is conferred on him who is worthy." In ancient times Shun had passed the throne on to Yü. Following ancient precedent, they now dared to offer Kao-tsu the imperial designation. It was now up to Kao-tsu to carry out his part in the hallowed ritual, which was to refuse their offer for the first time. Undaunted, P'ei Chi and the others reminded him that he owed the Sui emperor no blind loyalty and that it was correct to establish a dynasty of his own. "Although long ago Chou and Chieh ["bad-last" rulers of the Hsia and Shang] were both unworthy, they each had sons. But we have not heard that T'ang and Wu [founders of the Shang and Chou] served these sons as officials [i.e., they had founded their own dynasties]." Kao-tsu smiled and promised to consider the proposal, but did not yet accept their petition.

P'ei Chi and the others now pressed their case yet once more, describing the many other omens foretelling that Kao-tsu would become emperor. Kao-tsu should found his own dynasty so as to accord with these lucky signs, for to disobey Heaven would lead to misfortune. This time Kao-tsu replied by paraphrasing Han Kao-tsu's words at the time he accepted the throne from his followers: "Since you lords have thrust such high honor on me and think that my assuming the position of emperor would greatly benefit the people of the empire, then it may be done." He then asked coyly, "How could I differ with [those words]?" In this manner, he indicated his acceptance of the throne.[78] P'ei Chi and the others bowed repeatedly and danced with joy. They shouted "Long life!" to the T'ang leader and departed.

With Kao-tsu's assent obtained, preparations for the actual accession ceremony could now proceed apace. P'ei Chi and another official, named Ting Hsiao-wu, along with several hundred others, worked feverishly to devise a proper ritual. At Kao-tsu's request, they selected a *chia-tzu* day for the accession. On this day, the twentieth day of the fifth month (June 18), Kao-tsu assumed the position of *huang-ti* in the T'ai-chi Front Hall (*T'ai-chi ch'ien-tien*) of the imperial palace. A special altar had been established in the southern suburbs of the capital, which served as the site for the announcement to Heaven by means of a burnt sacrifice (*ch'ai-liao*) presided over by P'ei Chi and Hsiao Tsao.[79]

With the announcement to Heaven, Kao-tsu carried out the ritual of assuming his second regnal position of *t'ien-tzu*, Son of Heaven. The text of the announcement to Heaven once again returns to the themes Kao-tsu's followers had raised in offering him the throne. Since the creation of man, the text begins, Heaven had established leaders over him. The Mandate of Heaven, however, was never constant. Shun and Yü had been ceded their thrones and had established the Yü and Hsia regimes. T'ang and Wu had also benefited their ages: By employing military force they had established the Shang and Chou. Although the methods of the two pairs were different, their merits and achievements were identical. All those who had later established dynasties of their own had selected one or another of their methods. Kao-tsu then went on to list his many accomplishments in putting down the late Sui disorders, mentioning also the various portents predicting his coming to power. The young Sui emperor, knowing that the fortunes of his own dynasty had run out, had abdicated the throne in his favor. He was thus now announcing his accession to Heaven.[80]

The T'ang founder then issued an edict granting a great amnesty to the empire, announcing the adoption of an era-name, raising the honorary rank of officials and commoners one degree, and exempting certain areas from taxes and labor service for specified periods. He employed the edict to restate yet one more time the basic theme of his accession ritual: that cession of the throne on the basis of virtue and conquest by military merit were essentially two different sides of the same coin. At the end of the Sui he had responded to the chaos of the time to set in order all within the empire, recreating it anew. The Sui, seeing that their own time was past, had respectfully abdicated power and had transferred it to him.[81] At the same time Kao-tsu followed time-honored practice by selecting earth as his element, along with the color yellow. Three days later, he banqueted his officials at the T'ai-chi Hall and rewarded them with silk according to rank. Except for the many appointments to office and noble rank Kao-tsu made during this time, this essentially completes the sequence of events surrounding his accession.

In reviewing the accession ceremonies of the T'ang founder we cannot but be struck by his repeated claims, made at almost every opportunity, that he had gained the throne not simply by virtue of his superior morality but also by military achievement. Moreover, there was no essential difference, he maintained, between the Yao-Shun-Yü and T'ang-Wu models of dynastic succession, that is, between *shan-jang* and *fang-fa*: Both had the equal sanction of history and tradition. Thus Kao-tsu's accession can be seen as a curious example of a combination of *shan-jang*, a model he only falsely claimed to detest, and of *fang-fa*, a model he sought far more ardently to embrace. In this respect, Kao-tsu broke with the practice of the past several hundred years, giving rise to the question of "why?"

Miyakawa Hisayuki has studied cases of *shan-jang* procedure from the Later Han and Ts'ao-Wei dynasties through the T'ang-Sung dynastic transition. He concludes that in pre-T'ang times *shan-jang* was a tool employed by the aristocracy in order to control various military contenders for the throne, who desired to cover up the real facts of their rise to power. In their need to gain the political legitimation that *shan-jang* conferred, military leaders became the pawns of the aristocracy, who had the knowledge and experience successfully to manipulate the ritual trappings of dynastic transitions. By T'ang times, according to Miyakawa, conditions had changed sufficiently—the power of the aristocracy had declined in the face of increasing political centralization at the end of the Northern Dynasties and Sui—that T'ang Kao-tsu might feel free to criticize the *shang-jang* procedure. Moreover, those who surrounded Kao-tsu, primarily disaffected former Sui officials, really wanted him to succeed, Miyakawa asserts, and so willingly lent him their support. Since political support was already his, Kao-tsu was free to carry out his accession ritual without the need completely to play up its *shang-jang* aspects.[82]

Although Miyakawa has, perhaps, put his finger on some broader elements affecting the style of Kao-tsu's accession, I would also emphasize more personal factors. Kao-tsu's self-image was as a founder of a dynasty in the *fang-fa* tradition of the great Chou and, especially, the Han. Throughout his accession documents, he heaps praise on the Chou and Han while denigrating the regimes of the post-Han period, especially the Ts'ao-Wei, Chin, Liu-Sung, and Ch'i. His use of Han Kao-tsu's own words in granting the petition of his subordinates that he assume the position of emperor, and, as we shall soon see, his adoption of a term associated with Han Kao-tsu for his era-name, were carefully calculated gestures fully in keeping with his self-image as a political descendant of the Han founder. There is a speech in Wen Ta-ya's *Diary* made by Kao-tsu to his two elder sons, Chien-ch'eng and T'ai-tsung, dating from the period before the T'ang conquest of the Sui capital, in which he stresses the importance of personal merit (*kung*) in gaining the throne.[83] The speech suggests that Kao-tsu's emphasis on personal merit in achieving success may have been a sincerely held belief rather than just an idea crassly manipulated for political gain.

At the same time, Kao-tsu was unwilling completely to relinquish the notion that virtue had also served as the basis of his Mandate. This can be seen in the era-name he chose at his inauguration: *Wu-te*, or Military Virtue. The term first appears in the *Conversations of the States* (*Kuo-yü*), a quasi-historical work of late Chou date, and also later in the *Records of the Historian* by Ssu-ma Ch'ien. It was also the name of a dance (and its music) first performed during the time of Han Kao-tsu to symbolize the role of military action in restoring order to the empire.[84] T'ang Kao-tsu's Office of the Chancellor (*ch'eng-hsiang fu*) had, furthermore, been located in the Wu-te Hall of the Sui imperial palace.[85] His choice of an era-name was a brilliant stroke. With its allusion to Han Kao-tsu, it reinforced the idea that the T'ang founder was a successor to the Han Mandate. And as a statement about the basis for Kao-tsu's past victories and those still to come against various holdouts against T'ang power, it was a vehicle well suited to the propaganda needs of the moment. But more important, it once again raised the twin issues of virtue and merit in the transmission of dynastic power that had figured so importantly in his accession ritual. Its use of *te* brought to mind the cession of the throne to someone of superior moral worth. Its use of *wu* reinforced the idea that the new emperor possessed superior military talents and accomplishments. Both virtue and merit were thus united in his one person. In this way Kao-tsu's regime was represented simultaneously as the way of Yao-Shun-Yü and also the way of T'ang-Wu, precisely the same message he had sought to convey throughout his accession ceremonial!

At this point I would like to return to the question of the place of myth in accession ritual. Robert S. Ellwood maintains that although the Chinese accession ritual shares certain characteristics with those of other societies—for example, the transfer of regalia, ancestral veneration, themes of renewal—it ultimately lacks the reenactment of a creation myth, the death and resurrection of the king/god, a cosmic battle, and so forth. Instead, the expression of kingship in the rites is "historical and political, enacted in actual rather than ritual combat, in the battles which the dynasty having received the mandate of heaven must wage in order to win security for the throne," or in the "historical" (i.e., only quasi-mythological) accounts of the founding of regimes by the sage-kings of old. The choosing of a new element becomes, in this context, not a vestigial symbol of the ruler's resurrection but the ritual expression of a historical imperative. In this way, history itself becomes the ritual reenactment of the creation scenario.[86] I think that this point is made especially well by Kao-tsu's accession ceremonies, which are suffused at every level by the symbolism of *shang-jang* and *fang-fa*, key themes in the historical myths of the ancient regimes, and also by the *t'ien-hsia wei kung* symbolism surrounding the triumphs of Shun and Yü. Kao-tsu even goes so far as to repeat the words the Han founder uttered upon his acceptance of the throne, which are found in the Han history. The T'ang accession ceremony is not a sacred re-enactment of the creation but a secular rite whose ground of being is the recorded past.

Several other aspects of Kao-tsu's accession ritual deserve comment. First, the time of the ritual. The date selected was a *chia-tzu* day. It was considered an especially propitious time for inaugurating new enterprises because it was the first day of the Chinese sixty-day cycle. The Sui founder had, for example, also ascended the throne on a *chia-tzu* day.[87] But for Kao-tsu *chia-tzu* possessed additional significance. In the theory of the Five Elements *chia* was associated with the element wood. The character for wood combined with the character *tzu* forms the character *li*, which was Kao-tsu's family name. A *chia-tzu* day was thus considered particularly auspicious for Li-family undertakings. It was for this reason that Kao-tsu launched his revolt in T'ai-yüan against the Sui, had the Sui puppet emperor appoint him chancellor, and ascended the throne all on *chia-tzu* days.[88]

Second, the transfer of the imperial seals. The "Kung-ti Annals" of the *Sui History* and the "Kao-tsu Annals" of the two T'ang Standard Histories all depict the Sui puppet emperor as transferring the imperial seals to Kao-tsu as his last official act prior to quitting the capital.[89] It is doubtful, however, whether the Sui emperor possessed any genuine imperial seals to transfer to the T'ang, since at the end of the Sui the seals appear to have been lost either to rebel enemies of the T'ang or else to the Northern Turks. Wen Ta-ya's *Diary* records that after Yang-ti's murder in Chiang-tu, his empress, harem women, concubines, treasures, and imperial seals all fell into the hands of the rebel Tou Chien-te. Later, "reckless persons" reported that Tou had sent the empress, concubines, and treasures to the Turks in order to bribe them and seek their assistance in his efforts to conquer the empire.[90] A different story concerning the fate of the Sui imperial seals appears in the biography of Tou Chien-te in the T'ang Standard Histories, which records that when Tou was defeated by the T'ang in 621, Tou's wife along with some of his former officials offered up the *ch'uan-kuo* and seven other imperial seals as tokens of their surrender.[91] Yet another source reports that when the Sui was destroyed, Yang-ti's empress and the crown prince took the seals and fled northward to the Turks. The seals did not come into the possession of the T'ang until 631, the year of the Turkish conquest.[92] Wen Ta-ya's account suggests that it was only rumored that the seals found a home among the Turks, and that in reality they remained in the camp of Tou Chien-te, a version of events

supported by Tou's biographies in the T'ang Standard Histories. A Yüan
dynasty writer, Yang Huan, who attempted to trace the history of the
ch'uan-kuo seal down to his own time, felt that there was no basis whatsoever to the story that it came into the possession of the Turks at the end
of the Sui.[93] Whichever of these narratives one chooses to believe, it is
apparent that there were no genuine imperial seals for the last Sui emperor
to transfer to Kao-tsu at the time of his accession, and that therefore they
must have been fabricated especially for the occasion.

Third, the announcement to Heaven. Earlier it was noted that in the
post-Han period founding emperors ascended the altar in the southern
suburb personally to make the announcement to Heaven. In Kao-tsu's
case, however, he merely deputed officials to act as proxies for him at the
altar. Such a practice appears to have commenced with Sui Wen-ti, who
also deputed proxies to carry out the ch'ai-liao sacrifice to Heaven.[94] The
appointing of proxies suggests that the ch'ai-liao no longer functioned to
legitimate imperial power to the same degree it had earlier.

Lastly, the question of the visit to the ancestral temple. We have seen
that during the Han newly enthroned emperors paid a visit to the ancestral
temple to announce their accession and gain the approval of the dynastic
founder. Data on the yeh-miao rite for the Period of Disunion is somewhat
spotty and not entirely consistent.[95] It appears, however, that within a
short time after ascending the throne an emperor of a southern regime
usually made a special visit to the ancestral temple. An exception was in
cases in which he assumed power after having served as crown prince,
since crown princes already had visited the ancestral temple upon their
designation as imperial heirs, and it was deemed unnecessary to obtain the
approval of the dynastic founder a second time. In northern regimes no
distinction seems to have been made regarding the visit to the ancestral
temple between emperors who had been crown prince and those who had
not. But whether in the North or South, it appears that the most important ritual associated with an emperor's accession was no longer the visit to
the ancestral temple, but rather the rites he personally performed at the
suburban altars (chiao-ssu) acknowledging his receipt of the Mandate.

For example, in the Northern Ch'i dynasty, where the first altar rites
of an emperor usually took place in the first month of the year following
his enthronement, the visit to the ancestral temple took place on the day
after the altar rites, or the day after that. Although the visit to the ancestral
temple had by no means been abandoned, the temporal sequence suggests
that it was less important than the altar rites. From T'ang times onward it

became general practice for newly enthroned monarchs not to personally visit the ancestral temple at all to announce their accession.[96] Thus, fifteen days after his accession, Kao-tsu had the tablets of four of his ancestors placed in the ancestral temple, but made no announcement to them.[97] From this it can be inferred that the power of the ancestors to legitimate political authority, symbolized by the *yeh-miao* rite, had been replaced in the early T'ang by a more direct and therefore more powerful device that did away with the need for ancestors to serve as intermediaries between Heaven and the emperor—the suburban altar rites (see following chapter).

T'AI-TSUNG'S ACCESSION

The materials on T'ai-tsung's accession are not nearly as detailed as those for his father's. The T'ang Standard Histories merely record that Kao-tsu abdicated in favor of T'ai-tsung and that the latter ascended the throne in the Hsien-te (Manifest Virtue) Hall of the Eastern Palace, the residence of the crown prince, a position T'ai-tsung had occupied since his elder brother's death.[98] In fact, all the evidence points to the conclusion that T'ai-tsung forced his father from power. The accession took place on a *chia-tzu* day, the ninth day of the eighth month (September 4), 620.[99] P'ei Chi was appointed to announce the accession with a burnt sacrifice to Heaven at the southern suburban altar.

The new emperor then distributed a generous grab bag of rewards to various ranks of the populace. Issuing a great amnesty, he pardoned all crimes, whether already discovered or not, that had been committed prior to dawn of the day of his accession, and permitted all those who had been banished for crimes during his father's reign to return home. He advanced the honorary rank of commoners one step, and variously augmented the honorary noble ranks of his officials. Six prefectures in the capital region had their *tsu* and *tiao* taxes remitted for two years; all the rest of the empire was excused from taxes and labor service for one year. Rewards of grain and silk were granted to the very aged; others who were disadvantaged were also assisted.[100] Lastly, he released from service more than three thousand of Kao-tsu's harem women, sent them home to their relatives, and gave them permission to remarry.[101] Following custom, T'ai-tsung did not announce his era-name until the first day of the New Year (January 23), 627.[102] It was *Chen-kuan*, True Vision, adopted from the *Book of Changes*: "Heaven and Earth in their course [give forth] a true vision; the sun and the moon in their course [emit] a true light."[103]

The content of two documents associated with T'ai-tsung's accession are worth noting. The first is Kao-tsu's *chao* announcing his intention to abdicate, promulgated on the eighth day of the eighth month.[104] Near the beginning of the document, Kao-tsu provides the legitimating basis for both his cession of the throne and his son's succession.

> In ancient times the throne was yielded to the most worthy. But from the Three Dynasties onward, the empire belonged to one house [*t'ien-hsia wei chia*]. [The practice of] inheritance by birth continued on this basis, and descendants succeeded one another in turn. Thus, they were able to offer filial sacrifice at the ancestral temple.

He had been on the throne for nine years, he continues, his strength was now exhausted, and he desired to rest from his burdens. When T'ai-tsung was young there had been auspicious omens concerning his future. Heaven had granted him divine military talents and a sharp mind. The raising of "righteous" troops against the Sui, the successes of the early T'ang campaigns, and the conquest of the Sui capital were all owing to T'ai-tsung's efforts, he maintains. He then lists his son's great victories against the many rebel leaders after the founding of the T'ang. "His merit [*kung*] reaches the sky, his virtue [*te*] embraces the universe." Auspicious omens and lucky signs had amassed in great quantity, presaging his accession. All of China was now awaiting him to fulfill the prophecy of the popular ballads sung by the masses. Thus, Kao-tsu was now passing the position of ruler on to his son, and he called on everyone, from officials on down to the common people, to obey his will in this matter. Characteristically, he ends his *chao* with a reference to Han Kao-tsu, who had treated his father with great respect and had accorded him the title *t'ai-shang huang*, Retired Emperor, which T'ang Kao-tsu himself was now assuming.[105]

The second document is a *ts'e* ordering T'ai-tsung to ascend the throne, which was promulgated on the day of his accession.[106] As in the *chao* of the day previous, Kao-tsu states the basis for T'ai-tsung's legitimacy near the very beginning of the document: "From the time of Hsia and Yin [i.e., Shang], when power was transferred, it was by inheriting the throne. The rule that it went to the eldest son certainly originated with them." Kao-tsu expresses the wish to be relieved of the heavy burdens of ruling and again praises T'ai-tsung's intelligence and exceptional military accomplishments. And once again he points to the ballads sung among the people and lucky signs announcing that T'ai-tsung had inherited the Mandate. Therefore, in accordance with signs from Heaven, and bowing to the will of the people, he is duly transferring the throne to T'ai-tsung. He then orders P'ei Chi and Hsiao Yü to confer the imperial seals and ribbons on his son, signifying that he had indeed become emperor.

With the transfer of power from Kao-tsu to T'ai-tsung, two new qualities were imparted to the T'ang accession ceremonies. First, it was the initial instance in the T'ang of same surname succession. Second, it was one of the few instances in the dynasty of abdication. T'ai-tsung's accession ceremonies thus possessed certain characteristics that set them apart both from his father's and also from those of most of his dynastic successors.

It was probably just because of the circumstances surrounding his accession, particularly his murder of his brothers and his strained relationship with Kao-tsu, that T'ai-tsung took advantage of the occasion to demonstrate publicly his great filial piety and respect for his father. His selection of a *chia-tzu* day for the ritual, and the appointment of P'ei Chi to announce the accession to Heaven, dutifully replicated his father's acts at the time of his own enthronement. T'ai-tsung ascended the throne not in the main hall of the imperial palace but in the crown prince's residence, thus deferring to his father's position as a retired but still living emperor. His policy of amnesty and generous rewards was further calculated to place him in the best possible light and to overcome any latent hostility to him that might have existed among various sectors of officialdom and the populace at large. It was necessary for him to be far more generous than his father, who had assumed the imperial mantle amid far less controversy. On the other hand, T'ai-tsung's offering of a *ch'ai-liao* sacrifice to Heaven, normally a ritual undertaken only by founding emperors, may have symbolized his claim to being not just a successor emperor but a "founding" emperor in his own right.[107]

The *chao* and *ts'e* that were promulgated in the name of the father but likely commissioned by the son and his cohorts, similarly, not only served the exigencies of ritual but of what we now refer to as public relations, burnishing T'ai-tsung's recently tarnished image as they strengthened his claim to the throne. Thus, there was a repeated emphasis on the *t'ien-hsia wei chia* doctrine, which, as he was the eldest legitimate son, legitimated his claim to the T'ang throne in general, and the auspicious omens, lucky signs, and other propitious phenomena said to have been personally associated with T'ai-tsung, which legitimated his claim to the throne in particular. There was also an echo of the theme of Kao-tsu's accession documents here: the stress, certainly exaggerated, on T'ai-tsung-s merit in the founding of the dynasty and in putting down opposition to T'ang rule in the years immediately afterward. But T'ai-tsung was said to possess not just merit but a virtue that embraced the universe. In this way hereditary succession was portrayed, more than ever before, as simultaneously fulfilling the requirements of both *t'ien-hsia wei chia* and *t'ien-hsia wei kung* doctrine.[108]

Ogata believes that the *chao* and *ts'e* of T'ai-tsung's accession were the first examples of a device that came to be fully formalized during the T'ang, in which the notion could be widely circulated abroad that the next emperor possessed virtue, and was thereby deserving of the throne beyond his mere blood relationship to the imperial house. Eventually, he speculates, the concept of virtue itself became family-linked, and the *chao* and *ts'e* served as mechanisms by which the *te* or charisma of T'ang ancestors could be passed down, or "routinized" in a Weberian sense, to descendants who inherited the Mandate.[109]

KAO-TSUNG'S ACCESSION

After the special cases of his grandfather and father, it may be said that Kao-tsung's enthronement was the first "normal" accession in the T'ang, flavored by neither the sweetness of dynastic conquest nor the bitterness of fratricide and usurpation. Perhaps it is for this reason that there is a relative paucity of materials on the event when compared to those for his two predecessors.[110]

T'ai-tsung died on the twenty-sixth day of the fifth month (July 10), 649, at his summer retreat at Black Horse Mountain (*Li-shan*), located about thirty-five miles east of the capital. Kao-tsung, who had been vacationing with his father at the palace, was hurriedly escorted back to Ch'ang-an by a large military guard. T'ai-tsung had left behind a testamentary edict, drafted by his counselor Ch'u Sui-liang, commanding that his son ascend the throne in front of his coffin "according to the old system of Chou and Han." He also gave a number of instructions regarding his encoffinment, which was to be carried out seven days after his death on the model of the "Testamentary Charge" chapter of the *Book of History*, the mourning to be observed for him by various ranks of officials, the frugality to be practiced in his burial arrangements, and other topics, including the cessation of Chinese hostilities against Korea.[111] This edict was formally proclaimed on the twenty-ninth day (July 13), coincident with the beginning of mourning for the late emperor at the T'ai-chi

Hall.[112] Two days later, on the first day of the sixth month (July 15), Kao-tsung assumed the imperial mantle in front of his father's coffin, at the age of twenty-two *sui*. The day was *chia-hsü*, the first *chia* day following T'ai-tsung's death.[113] Kao-tsung then declared the usual general amnesty and, perhaps because of the unremarkable circumstances of his accession, allotted only modest rewards to various groups in the empire. Only one prefecture in the capital region, along with all those who had recently performed heavy labor service, was exempted from taxes and corvée for one year.[114] On the first day of the New Year (February 7), 650, he inaugurated his first era-name, *Yung-hui*, Forever Honorable.[115]

Kao-tsung had been neither the favorite son of T'ai-tsung nor the favorite of his father's ministers. Indeed, even after T'ai-tsung had appointed his ninth son crown prince, some of the most respected and powerful statesmen in the land had pleaded with him to change the succession: They feared that Kao-tsung would prove to be too weak to lead the government effectively. T'ai-tsung was steadfast in his support of Kao-tsung but knew that other minds were less than enthusiastic over the prospect of his rule. In his testamentary edict he therefore endeavored to allay their fears about Kao-tsung's leadership qualities, lend him a bit of legitimacy, and remind them of their duty to obey him in his decision:

> The imperial crown prince, Chih, is greatly filial and communicates with the spirits. His is a virtue that springs from Heaven. He has accumulated much experience in tending the administration and is well acquainted with important matters of government. All you officials high and low are to "perform your duty to me, the departed, and serve him, the living."[116] Do not disobey my will.[117]

Given the fact that Kao-tsung had heretofore demonstrated a general lack of remarkable qualities and that his father had rather little to work with, the testamentary edict can be seen as a last-minute, somewhat desperate attempt by T'ai-tsung or his close associates to make a *t'ien-hsia wei kung* case for his son's assumption of power and, even more, to bind his subordinates to his will on the basis of sentiments of loyalty.

T'ai-tsung must have had good reason to worry that his chosen heir would not succeed him. Indeed, upon the emperor's death, his most trusted counselor, Chang-sun Wu-chi, immediately packed Kao-tsung off to the capital, even before the rest of the imperial party returned with the emperor's corpse. Special wooden tablets, in which bird feathers had been inserted, to signify that they were to be carried as quickly as a bird flies, were issued to raise four thousand troops from among regional militia forces. They and veteran T'ang generals formed a protective shield around Kao-tsung, escorting him back to Ch'ang-an[118] When Kao-tsung arrived at the capital with this force, they arrayed the imperial carriages and horses "as if it were an ordinary day" in order not to raise anyone's suspicions that T'ai-tsung was dead. The troops then encamped in the vicinity of the Liang-i Hall deep inside the palace compound, continuing to protect the prospective emperor.[119] The accession ritual itself appears to have been carried out with some haste. Although T'ai-tsung had specified that he was to be encoffined the prescribed seven days after death, the accession ceremony took place before his coffin a scant five days later. All this suggests that there was anxiety over how smoothly the succession would proceed, and even over the possibility of a coup to thwart Kao-tsung's assumption of power.

CHAPTER 5

The Suburban Sacrifices and the Cult of Heaven

As for the rites, none is more important than sacrifice. As for sacrifice, none is greater than that to Heaven. Heaven is the ruler of all the deities. The Son of Heaven is the ruler of all the people. Therefore, only the Son of Heaven sacrifices to Heaven once each year.

Ch'in Hui-t'ien, *Wu-li t'ung-k'ao*.[1]

BY T'ANG TIMES, OF ALL THE PERIODIC RITES OF STATE, THE SUBURBAN SAC-RIFICES (*chiao-ssu*) especially the sacrifice to Heaven at the round altar (*yüan-ch'iu*), had become the most important. According to the *New T'ang History* "Monograph on Rites and Music," there was a total of twenty-four sacrifices per year that the emperor might personally perform.[2] Following Sui practice, the T'ang divided their state sacrifices into three categories: great (*ta*), intermediate (*chung*), and lesser (*hsiao*).[3] The emperor had the exclusive right personally to perform the great and intermediate rites or to assign surrogates to carry them out in his place. Lesser rites were performed by the emperor's officials. The suburban sacrifices, along with those at the ancestral temple, were classified as great rites. These opulent ceremonies vividly substantiated the emperor's temporal power as well as his special relationship with Heaven, Earth, and the imperial ancestors. In the suburban sacrifices, so called because the altars on which they were performed were located in the near suburbs of the capital, the emperor personally acknowledged the Mandate bestowed upon him and thanked Heaven for its favor. It was an acknowledgment that all things spring from Heaven.

In T'ang times the suburban altar rites came to play a pivotal role in confirming imperial authority. In the Han dynasty the rites at the ancestral temple had mainly served this function. As we saw in the last chapter, soon after ascending the throne the emperor made a special *yeh-miao* visit to the ancestral temple to announce his assumption of power and to secure the blessings of his lineal ancestors. No altar rites were associated with the imperial accession. But by T'ang times, in order for an emperor to express fully the legitimate nature of his power, it had become necessary for him personally to perform sacrifices to Heaven and Earth at the suburban altars at some time following his accession, usually within three years. The T'ang suburban sacrifices emphasized the emperor's direct link to Heaven, symbolized in the course of the ceremonies by his use of the phrase, "The Son of Heaven, Your Servant, X" (*t'ien-tzu ch'en mou*) in reference to himself while communicating with Heaven.[4] Because the sacrifice to Heaven reflected the emperor's direct link with it, unmediated by either ancestors or other spirits, it served to enhance his personal authority. The emperor, moreover, was the only person in the empire allowed to sacrifice to Earth (*ti*); all others could merely sacrifice to lesser gods of the soil (*t'u*).[5]

Whereas the Han *yeh-miao* rites and all routine, seasonal ancestral temple sacrifices can be considered as essentially the "private" rites of the imperial family, the suburban sacrifices were dedicated not to blood relations of the dynastic founders but to gods who belonged to no individual family or class, gods of all the people. Moreover, in contrast to the ancestral temple rites, which were performed in enclosed structures often located inside the imperial compound, the suburban sacrifices were carried out on open-air platforms situated well beyond the precincts of the imperial family or court. Compared to the ancestral sacrifices, then, the altar rites possessed a more "public" character. In this respect, they functioned much like the *chao* and *ts'e* of the T'ang imperial accession ceremonies, legitimating the incoming emperor's authority by means of a public declaration regarding his great achievements and the appropriateness of his inheriting the Mandate, irrespective of his family ties.[6] Political legitimacy in the T'ang had become less dependent on blood relationships than in the Han. T'ang rituals and symbols of legitimation, as we will see in the following chapters, had opened up and out to embrace more "public" objects of worship and more numerous individuals or groups as participants and spectators.

It should be noted, however, that while ostensibly serving as sacrifices to "public" gods, the suburban rites also had affinities with traditional Chinese ancestor worship. Opinions have varied concerning how closely the suburban sacrifices were at first linked to ancestral worship.[7] But it has been pointed out that the worship of Heaven cannot completely be distinguished from the worship of ancestors, since the ancient Chinese concept of Heaven (*shang-ti* or *t'ien*) was itself linked in some hazy manner to the royal ancestors.[8] The link to ancestors in the suburban sacrifices was demonstrated on another level by the practice of naming lineal ancestors as ancillary sacrificial objects in relation to Heaven. This status was known as *p'ei* "coadjutor (of Heaven)" or "associated (ancestral) deity." The first of these associated sacrificial objects appears to have been Hou Chi, "Ruler Millet," the legendary ancestor of the Chou royal house.[9] In Han times stars came to be thought of as the embodiment of ancestors, and star worship became popular. The weft texts reveal a belief that after a person died his spirit ascended to Heaven to reside in a star. The royal ancestors, it was thought, resided in the center of Heaven, in the region of our Polaris.[10] In the Later Han dynasty, many stars served as *p'ei* in the suburban sacrifices. Finally, in the suburban sacrifices Heaven served symbolically as the father of the emperor. Thus the sacrifices incorporated, at various levels, the idea of ancestor worship. On the other hand, by means of the sacrifices it became possible for emperors to distinguish themselves from all those other social classes in the empire who practiced their own ancestral rites. The suburban rites had important political overtones: They were an imperial monopoly linking the emperor to an "ancestor" who was also a universal deity.

SUBURBAN SACRIFICES THROUGH THE SUI

The origins of the suburban sacrifices can be traced back to the Chou period and the pre-dynastic era of Ch'in.[11] The *Rites of Chou* speaks of a sacrifice to Heaven at a round altar (*yüan-ch'iu*) at the time of the winter solstice and a sacrifice to Earth at a square altar (*fang-ch'iu*) at the time of the summer solstice.[12] The *Book of Rites* notes that the sacrifice to Heaven was made by burning the animal victim on a blazing pile of wood, and that to Earth by burying the victim in an earthen mound.[13] In the *Book of Rites* the sacrifices to Heaven and Earth are assoicated with a ritual known as the border or suburban sacrifice (*chiao*), but there is no mention of a round or square altar. This later gave rise to conflicting theories about the precise location of the rites.

The suburban sacrifices were not considered major rites until well into the Former Han dynasty, when, under the growing influence of Confucian ritualists, a major reform of state ritual was undertaken. Altars were established in the northern and southern suburbs of Ch'ang-an shortly after the accession of Ch'eng-ti (rg. 33–6 B.C.), who inaugurated the personal worship of Heaven and Earth by an emperor. At the same time the imperial worship of several other deities was discontinued. Even afterward the suburban sacrifices were performed only intermittently, becoming firmly established as a state ritual only from the beginning of the Later Han.[14] According to the general Han understanding of the ritual, Heaven was to be worshiped in the southern suburbs (*nan-chiao*) at the time of the winter solstice, and Earth at the northern suburbs (*pei-chiao*) at the time of the summer solstice.[15] What we refer to as Heaven (*t'ien*) was also called Hao-t'ien shang-ti or Shang-ti, a deity superior to all others who was to be worshiped personally by the ruler in a rite of the utmost sanctity.[16]

During the subsequent Period of Disunion the suburban sacrifices underwent a transformation, greatly increasing in importance from about A.D. 317, the time of the transition from the Western Chin to Eastern Chin dynasty. In the Ts'ao-Wei and Western Chin not many emperors took a personal role in carrying out the suburban sacrifices. But from Eastern Chin onward emperors typically performed them within a year or two following their accession, a sign that the rites were now held in far greater esteem than previously.[17]

Suburban ritual practice differed greatly in North and South China during the Period of Disunion.[18] Southern Dynasties practice was heavily influenced by Wang Su, who held that the southern suburban and round altars mentioned in the classics were one and the same, as were the northern suburban and square altars; rites at the former were dedicated to Heaven and at the latter to Earth.[19] Thus, for example, in the late Southern Dynasties period of Liang and Ch'en the southern suburban/round altar was dedicated to Hao-t'ien shang-ti, with various ancestral deities as *p'ei*. It was located south of the capital and consisted of two levels. The Liang round altar was 27 Chinese feet tall, with a top tier diameter of 110 feet and a bottom one of 180 feet. The Ch'en round altar was somewhat smaller: 22 feet high with a diameter for the top tier of 100 feet. The northern suburban/square altar was situated north of the capital. In the Liang it was on two levels, 100 feet per side on the top tier and 120 feet per side on the bottom. Each tier was 10 feet high, and there were stairs ascending each of the four sides. In the Southern Dynasties the suburban sacrifices were performed at the northern and southern altars in alternate years, each on the first *hsin* day of the first month.[20]

Northern practice relied on the ideas of Cheng Hsüan, who, heavily influenced by the weft texts, held that the southern suburban and round

altars were separate entities dedicated to different deities.[21] According to
Cheng Hsüan, the deity Kan-sheng ti was worshiped at the southern suburban altar on the first *hsin* day of the first month of the year. *Kan-sheng*
literally means "moved" or "impelled to life." According to Five Element
theory it was believed that the ancestor of each dynastic house had been
given life by a god who was the essence of one of the Five Elements. Thus,
depending on the governing element (and color) of a dynasty, a different
god was worshiped as its Kan-sheng ti at the time of the prayer for grain
(*ch'i-ku*).[22] On the other hand, the god Hao-t'ien shang-ti was, according
to Cheng, worshiped at the round altar at the time of the winter solstice in
the eleventh month. This deity Cheng equated with the god called T'ien-
huang ta-ti (Heavenly Illustrious Great Emperor), also known as the
Northern Chronogram (*pei-ch'en*) and Radiant Moon-Soul Gem (*Yao-p'o
pao*), all names for a northern star spirit, our Polaris.[23] Cheng similarly
considered the square and northern suburban altars as two distinct places
dedicated to different gods. The earth deity K'un-lun was worshiped at the
square altar, and the earth deity Shen-chou, an embodiment of the ancient
Nine Provinces of China, was worshiped at the square altar.

Cheng Hsüan's cosmological model was called the theory of the Six
Heavens (*liu-t'ien chih shuo*) because of his idea that, in addition to the
heavenly deity Hao-t'ien shang-ti, there were five other heavenly deities
known as the Five Emperors (*Wu-ti*) or Five Heavenly Emperors (*Wu-t'ien
ti*).[24] The *locus classicus* of the Five Emperors is the *Rites of Chou*.[25] They
first became associated with the five colors, green, red, yellow, white, and
black in Ssu-ma Ch'ien's *Records of the Historian*, written in the first century B.C., and later with the five directions.[26] Wang Su opposed the exalted status lent the Five Emperors by Cheng Hsüan, claiming that he was
influenced by the false weft texts.[27] During the Chin dynasty, Wang Su's
views that the Five Emperors were not the same as Heaven won out, and
as a consequence their cult was briefly abolished between 266 and 289.[28]
Worship of the Five Emperors continued in the post-Chin period under
the Northern and Southern Dynasties and also under the Sui.[29] According
to the view of Cheng Hsüan, the appropriate places to sacrifice to the Five
Emperors were the four suburban altars and the Ming-t'ang, where their
spirit-thrones were arranged all during this period and into the early
T'ang.

In both the Northern Ch'i and Northern Chou dynasties the round
altar was located south of the capital and consisted of three levels. In the

Northern Ch'i the altar was about 45 feet high, each tier measuring 15 feet in height. On the upper and middle levels were stairs facing the four directions; the bottom level had stairs in eight directions. The top level of the altar was 46 feet in diameter, the bottom 270 feet. In the Northern Chou each of the three levels of the round altar was about 12 feet high. The diameter of the top was about 60 feet, and there were 12 staircases. The southern suburban altars were also located south of the capital. They were smaller than the round altars and consisted of only one level. The southern suburban altar of the Northern Ch'i dynasty was round, 36 feet in diameter, and only 9 feet high, with stairs pointing in the four directions. Its counterpart in the Northern Chou was square, 40 feet on a side and 12 feet high. Sacrificial victims at the southern suburban altars were burned, like those at the round altars. The northern suburban altar of the Northern Ch'i dynasty was round, like the southern suburban. But that of the Northern Chou dynasty was square, like its southern suburban altar, 40 feet on a side and 10 feet high. The Northern Chou "square" altar actually appears to have been octagonal in shape. Sacrificial victims at both the northern suburban and square altars were buried, not burned.[30] Such was the rather confusing picture of sacrificial altars established during the Northern Dynasties under the influence Cheng Hsüan's ritual theories.

The Sui inherited the altar system of the Northern Dynasties and passed it on to the T'ang. The Sui round altar was on four levels, ranging from 200 feet at the base to about 50 feet on the summit tier. The southern suburban altar was separated from the round altar by about a third of a mile, and was located a little more than three miles south of the imperial palace. It was 40 feet in diameter and 7 feet high. The square altar was located almost five miles north of the palace. It comprised two tiers each 5 feet high; the lower tier was 100 feet per side, the upper 50 feet.[31] There does not seem to be any physical description of the Sui northern suburban altar. It was taken for granted by the Chinese of this time that ritual imperfectly performed would evoke corresponding responses from Heaven. Thus in 614, when Sui Yang-ti performed the winter solstice sacrifice to Hao-t'ien shang-ti at the round altar and did not observe the appropriate regulations regarding the matter of seclusion (chai) prior to the ceremony, a price was paid. A great wind sprang up on the day of the ceremony, and when the rite was completed, the emperor's mount became sick, forcing him to return in haste to his palace.[32] It was seen as a divine signal portending the end of the Sui, soon confirmed by the many bands of rebels roaming the countryside.

THE EARLY T'ANG SUBURBAN SACRIFICES

The history of the suburban sacrifices of the early T'ang represents a shift away from the ideas of Cheng Hsüan toward those of Wang Su. At first, during Kao-tsu's period, since there was no time to develop new rituals, the Sui ritual system of four suburban altars dedicated to different deities was adopted *in toto*.[33] The T'ang round altar was located less than a mile southeast of the main southern gate of Ch'ang-an. It consisted of four tiers, each slightly over 8 feet high. The diameter of the lowest tier was 200 feet while that of the summit tier was 50 feet, the same as at the Sui round altar.[34] At the time of the winter solstice, sacrifices on the summit tier were dedicated to Hao-t'ien shang-ti, with Kao-tsu's grandfather, Li Hu, serving as the associated ancestral deity, or *p'ei*. Other deities received sacrifices on the lower tiers or on earthen mounds located in the immediate vicinity. The square altar, located about three and a half miles north of the palace, consisted of two tiers, the bottom 100 feet on a side and the top 50 feet. Sacrifices were dedicated on the upper tier to the God of Earth (*Huang ti-ch'i*) at the time of the summer solstice; Li Hu was again designated *p'ei*. On the first *hsin* day of the first month of the year, Kan-sheng ti was sacrificed to at the southern suburban altar in a prayer for grain, with Kao-tsu's father as *p'ei*.[35] Since the T'ang element was earth and its color yellow, its Kan-sheng ti was Han shu-niu, an embodiment of the Yellow Emperor, Huang-ti.[36] The earth deity Shen-chou was sacrificed to at the northern suburban altar in the tenth month, with Li Hu as *p'ei*. In addition to these rites, the Five Heavenly Emperors received offerings at the southern suburban altar, the Ming-t'ang, and at altars in the eastern, southern, western, and northern suburbs of the capital according to the season of the year. These ceremonies were all based on the ideas of Cheng Hsüan. Except for designating his father, Kao-tsu, as the associated ancestral deity at both the round and northern suburban altars, T'ai-tsung made no major changes in the altar rites all during his reign.[37]

Kao-tsu's first personal performance of a suburban sacrifice appears to have occurred in the eleventh month of 621 at the southern suburban altar, some three and a half years after he came to power.[38] A shorter period of time seems to have elapsed between T'ai-tsung's accession and his first suburban ceremony, which took place at the round altar in the eleventh month of 628, a little more than twenty-eight months following his accession.[39]

T'ai-tsung deftly employed the suburban sacrifices for various politi-

cal as well as more immediate religious ends. The rites served, first of all, as
an occasion for him to demonstrate his personal generosity by granting
rewards to various groups in the empire.[40] But T'ai-tsung was also capable
of manipulating the ceremonies in a more sophisticated manner. It is said
that during his father's reign, when he was locked in a struggle for the
succession with his two brothers, at the time of the suburban sacrifices he
would display his personal bow and arrows at the head of all the ritual
articles used in the ceremonies. These weapons, twice as large as those
normally employed, and removed from the T'ang armory especially for
the occasion, served to symbolize T'ai-tsung's great physical prowess and
numerous military triumphs—at the expense of the reputations of his
brothers.[41] During his own reign, at the suburban rites of 628, T'ai-tsung
ordered two of his highest officials, P'ei Chi and Chang-sun Wu-chi,
together to ascend the imperial carriage as a special mark of his favor, a
gesture designed to reward their personal loyalty to the emperor and to
heighten bureaucratic loyalty in general.[42] In the eleventh month of 643,
just a few months after he had appointed the future Kao-tsung as crown
prince, the emperor employed the occasion of the suburban rites to help
legitimate the appointment of his new heir, ironically at precisely the moment that he was experiencing serious doubts about Kao-tsung's ability to
lead the T'ang.[43] In the ceremonies, the crown prince followed his father
in making an offering of jade and silk to Hao-t'ien shang-ti. Earlier in the
year a stone had been discovered with an inscription predicting the long
life of the dynasty. In the text of his announcement to Hao-t'ien shang-ti,
T'ai-tsung made sure to suggest that the receipt of this auspicious omen
reflected a Heavenly endorsement of the passage of power from Kao-tsu
through T'ai-tsung to the new heir, and that Kao-tsung fully shared with
his father in Heaven's blessings. Thus did he sanction his son's special role
in the ceremonies.

Curiously, the description of the suburban rites of 643 almost precisely parallels that of T'ai-tsung's first visit to his father's tomb early in 639.
(See chapter 7.) For several days it had been cloudy and snow had fallen,
and on the day of the ceremony clouds and fog had cast gloom over everything. But when T'ai-tsung ascended the altar the clouds miraculously
dispersed and the weather cleared. All the ritual objects shone in the sun-
light.[44] It surely must have been interpreted by those in attendance as a
further sign of T'ai-tsung's heavenly favor, and of the appropriateness of
the appointment of Kao-tsung.

The year 643 appears to have been the last time that T'ai-tsung personally performed a suburban sacrifice to Heaven. The next sacrifice to Heaven by an emperor was made by his son, in the eleventh month of 651, thirty months after ascending the throne.[45] It was during Kao-tsung's reign that a major change was made in T'ang ritual that radically altered the nature of the suburban rites and affected their performance in China for more than a millennium to come.

In 657 Chang-sun Wu-chi, perhaps the most respected voice of the age, along with the President of the Board of Rites, Hsü Ching-tsung, and other ritual officials, launched a broad-ranging attack on Cheng Hsüan, charging that his theories had been based on the unorthodox weft texts and were therefore filled with errors. They singled out for condemnation Cheng's belief that Hao-t'ien shang-ti was the same entity as the Northern Chronogram/Radiant Moon-Soul Gem, asserting that this star was not the same as Heaven. They cited various evidence, including a report by the Grand Astronomer Li Shun-feng, that at the suburban sacrifices Hao-t'ien shang-ti should be sacrificed on to the summit tier of the altar, whereas the Northern Chronogram/Radiant Moon-Soul Gem should be sacrificed to on the next lower level. This proved that they were not identical and that, rather, Hao-t'ien shang-ti was supreme. Similarly, they argued that the Five Emperors were merely deities representative of the essences of the Five Elements who had become associated with specific stars. The Five Emperors did not, contrary to Cheng Hsüan's theory of the Six Heavens, possess the same status as Heaven. As they rhetorically inquired, "There is only one Heaven [t'ien-shang wu erh]; how then can there be six?" They supported Wang Su's belief that the round and southern suburban altars, on the one hand, and the square and northern suburban altars, on the other, were one and the same. Up to this time T'ang ritual practice had embodied Cheng Hsüan's ideas. It was now time for a fundamental change, they concluded. Upon receiving their memorial, Kao-tsung ordered that worship of the Five Emperors was to be preserved at the southern suburban altar only, but that in other respects Cheng Hsüan's ideas were to be discontinued as the basis of T'ang ritual practice.[46]

The major change in the suburban sacrifices at this time was the discontinuation of the sacrifice dedicated to Kan-sheng ti and the amalgamation of the southern suburban altar rites and those at the round altar into a single sacrifice dedicated to Hao-t'ien shang-ti, who was worshiped, as before, at the time of the winter solstice. Similarly, the rites at the northern suburban and square altars were also combined; the sacrifice to Shen-chou was discontinued, leaving only that to the God of Earth. The sacrifices to the Five Heavenly Emperors at most of the suburban altars with which they had traditionally been associated and at the Ming-t'ang were also terminated.[47]

Yet another policy advocated by Chang-sun Wu-chi and Hsü Ching-tsung symbolized the relative decline of the ancestral temple sacrifices vis-à-vis the altar rites, a trend that was discussed in the last chapter. Earlier, the memorialists pointed out, the number of food baskets and platters employed in sacrifice had varied greatly, depending on the type of sacrifices performed. At the ancestral temple, for example, twelve baskets and twelve platters were employed on each sacrificial occasion. But at the sacrifices to Heaven and Earth and various other deities at the suburban altars, only four of each were used. Since the status of a sacrifice was indicated by the number of vessels employed, "the numbers [of vessels] at the ancestral temple sacrifices could not exceed those at the altar sacrifices," they concluded. By imperial decree the numbers used at both rites were now fixed at twelve, and the change was appended to the ritual regulations.[48] In this way the previous superiority in the material realm enjoyed by the ancestral temple rites was officially ended.

It is important to observe that during the time of Kao-tsung's predecessors, Kao-tsu and T'ai-tsung, Hao-t'ien shang-ti was just one of several deities to whom rites were dedicated at the suburban altars. Now Hao-t'ien shang-ti had clearly emerged supreme: He was the main object of sacrifice not only at the winter solstice rite but also at the prayer for good harvests, which had formerly been dedicated to Kan-sheng ti, and at the Ming-t'ang, whose sacrifices had formerly been dedicated to the Five Emperors.[49] The reforms advocated in the memorial of 657 by Chang-sun Wu-chi and Hsü Ching-tsung came to be codified in the *Hsien-ch'ing li*, completed in 658.[50]

However, the reaction against Cheng Hsüan's ritual theories proved at first to be somewhat tentative in terms of policy-making. Beginning in 666, Kao-tsung began returning to some recently discarded ideas. Kan-sheng ti was restored as the object of worship in the prayer for good harvests.[51] Shen-chou worship was also reinstated, and a new altar dedicated to him was established north of the capital.[52] The following year, Cheng Hsüan's ideas regarding the designation of associated ancestral deities at suburban sacrifices and at the Ming-t'ang were once again followed. At the same time, the Five Heavenly Emperors were restored as objects of sacrifice at the Ming-t'ang, joining Hao-t'ien shang-ti.[53] These decisions all reflected the rehabilitation of Cheng Hsüan as a ritual guide.

Kao-tsung was almost apologetic in his edict of 667 announcing his changes, blaming them on the confused state of ritual theory from Han times onward. By 676 court ritualists seem to have become even more disenchanted with the reforms embodied in the *Hsien-ch'ing li*, which they felt was inferior to the *Chen-kuan li*, and Kao-tsung was persuaded to order that ritual matters were now to be decided on a much broader scale than before according to the regulations of the Chen-kuan period.[54] A year later another edict was handed down stating that since the Hsien-ch'ing regulations had in several respects not accorded with ancient practice, state rituals were henceforth all to conform with the regulations contained in the ancient *Rites of Chou*—apparently a euphemism for the ideas of Cheng Hsüan. Nevertheless, notes the "Monograph on Rites and Ceremonies" of the *Old T'ang History*, from this time onward the *Chen-kuan li* and *Hsien-ch'ing li* were both employed as the basis for ritual decision-making.[55] This means that for most of Kao-tsung's reign, Cheng Hsüan's theories were largely in eclipse and the supreme ritual status of Hao-t'ien shang-ti was never successfully challenged. In most important respects, as we saw in chapter 2, the *K'ai-yüan li*, which was compiled during Hsüan-tsung's reign in the eighth century and served as the basis for T'ang imperial ritual for the remainder of the dynasty, followed the *Hsien-ch'ing li*. Although the Five Emperors were once again worshiped, in the regulations for the various sacrifices of Hsüan-tsung's time and afterward it is clear that they always played a subordinate role to Hao-t'ien shang-ti and were never conceived of as the equals of Heaven, thus preserving the early T'ang movement away from Cheng Hsüan's theories.[56]

THE RITUAL REGULATIONS

The altar rites, carried out with all the resources the dynasty could muster, presented one of the most impressive and colorful of ceremonial spectacles. Attending were great numbers of participants and spectators: Li family members, court officials from grades one through nine, military servicemen, foreign dignitaries and others. The ritual performers were richly garbed, the sacrificial vessels and utensils were crafted by the finest artisans of the imperial atelier, the musicians were highly skilled, and the dancers were dressed in costumes of marvelous contrivance. Music and song punctuated the various stages of the sacrifice. During Kao-tsu's time the music of the Sui dynasty was employed for the great T'ang state rites. But in 626 Tsu Hsiao-sun was assigned the task of composing new music, which was completed and promulgated in 627, a year after T'ai-tsung ascended the throne. It was known as the "Court Music of the Great T'ang" (*Ta-T'ang ya-yüeh*). Later, during T'ai-tsung's time, Chang Wen-shou continued and revised Tsu's work. Tsu's music contained twelve suites (*ho*), based on the number of Heaven, intended to be performed at all court rituals.[57]

There is no description of T'ang altar rites for the early part of the dynasty. Rather, we have only a detailed plan of the rites as they were supposed to be performed by the emperor or his surrogates during high T'ang, contained in the *K'ai-yüan li*. We can, nevertheless, gain a fairly good idea of how an altar rite, such as the round altar sacrific to Hao-t'ien shang-ti at the time of the winter solstice, might have been performed in the early T'ang based on the *K'ai-yüan li* description. According to this source, there were seven major phases of the round altar ritual, which are summarized as follows:[58]

(1) Observance of the seclusion regulations. The emperor observes seven days of seclusion (*chai*) prior to the sacrifice. Four of these days consist of low intensity or relaxed seclusion (*san-chai*) in a special hall of the imperial palace, where the emperor's basic activities are carried on with only minor restrictions.[59] The next three days consist of high-intensity or strict seclusion (*chih-chai*), two at the T'ai-chi Hall of the palace and one at a detached palace, especially constructed for the occasion near the altar site, where the emperor is supposed to focus all his mental and emotional energies in order to attain an inner state of being appropriate to the solemnity of the ritual.

(2) Establishment of the ritual positions. Three days before the ceremony, positions for all the participants and invited spectators, as well as for the ritual vessels, sacrificial victims, and other paraphernalia are marked out at the altar site. The imperial great canopy and canopies for participating officials are laid out first. Then positions for spectators are arranged according to their office or rank. A day before the ceremony the spirit-throne (*shen-tso*) of Hao-t'ien shang-ti is placed on the summit tier of the altar, at the northern end facing south. The spirit-throne of the *p'ei*, Kao-tsu, is established on the eastern side, facing west. The spirit-thrones of other deities also worshiped at the round altar are set up, in order of descending importance, on the lower three tiers and the other mounds at the site.

(3) Inspection of the sacrificial victims and vessels. On this day (a day prior to the sacrifice?) the entire altar is placed off limits to non-ritual

personnel, and the various vessels, stands, washing utensils, baskets, and associated ritual paraphernalia are positioned on the altar at their previously assigned places. The altar is then swept clean. After this, the sacrificial victims are examined by the inspectors and pronounced "fat." The sacrificial animals are led off to the kitchen, where the cooking utensils are also examined. On the day of the sacrifice, before dawn, the sacrificial victims are slaughtered; the hide and blood of the animals are used to fill dishes that later will be placed before the spirit-thrones of the gods on the altar, and the flesh of the animals is cooked.

(4)   The imperial carriage leaves the palace. At dawn the emperor is escorted by his officials, amidst panoply and music, from the T'ai-chi Hall to the detached palace at the site of the round altar. The detached palace is the scene of the emperor's last day of strict seclusion prior to performing the sacrifice to Heaven. After arriving at the detached palace, the emperor meets in audience with his civil and military officials, who afterward return to the imperial palace.

(5)   Presentation of jade and silk. Before dawn on the day of the sacrifice, the ritual officers place offerings of jade and silk in round baskets and food in various vessels. They are then carried to the round altar, which is now swept clean. Musicians, dancers, presiding ritual officers, and spectators all take their places. Shortly before dawn, the emperor is borne by palanquin out of the detached palace. He mounts his carriage of state and is escorted as far as the great canopy, to which he is again borne by palanquin, and where he rests. Precisely at dawn the emperor changes his robe to one traditionally worn by rulers sacrificing to Heaven, and is led into the inner precincts of the altar. Emperor, participants, and spectators all make double obeisances toward the spirit-thrones of Hao-t'ien shang-ti and the *p'ei*, Kao-tsu. The ritual officials then kneel and remove the jade and silk offerings from their baskets. The emperor mounts the altar by the southern stairs and faces north, as subject, now, not as sovereign. Receiving the jade and silk, he kneels and places them at the spirit-throne of Hao-t'ien shang-ti. The emperor prostrates himself, rises, and is led to the spirit-throne of the associated ancestral deity, Kao-tsu, where, facing east, he makes another offering of silk. He then descends the altar.

(6)   Offerings of cooked food. As the emperor had been making his offerings of jade and silk, ritual officers had brought trays of food consecrated to Hao-t'ien shang-ti to the outer precincts of the altar. They are now brought to the various staircases of the altar proper. The dishes of skin and blood from the sacrificial animals are taken up to the top tier and

placed before the spirit-throne of Hao-t'ien shang-ti. The emperor is led to a washstand, where he laves his hands and the ritual winecup and dries them carefully. He then mounts the altar via the southern staircase. A ritual officer ladles wine into the winecup, and the emperor is led to Hao-t'ien shang-ti's spirit-throne. Facing north, he kneels and places the wine-cup down before the spirit-throne. An officer now intones the sacrificial prayer in which the emperor refers to himself as "Your Subject, X, who has succeeded to the position Son of Heaven" (ssu t'ien-tzu ch'en mou). The emperor makes a similar offering of wine before the spirit-throne of the associated ancestral deity, while another prayer is intoned, this time refer-ring to the emperor as the p'ei's such-and-such generation descendant, "Emperor and Subject, X" (huang-ti ch'en mou). After performing a double obeisance, the emperor is again led to Hao-t'ien shang-ti's spirit-throne and handed the ritual winecup. Kneeling before the spirit-throne, the emperor sacrifices the wine, sipping it. He replaces the winecup, pros-trates himself, and rises. The trays containing the sacrificial flesh are now brought in and given to the emperor, who hands them in turn to his atten-dants. The emperor kneels, takes up the winecup again, and drains the wine. He prostrates himself, rises, makes a double obeisance, and descends the altar. Secondary (ya-hsien) and tertiary offerings (chung-hsien) are made to Hao-t'ien shang-ti and the associated ancestral deity by other ritual par-ticipants, and the more minor deities on and around the round altar are also sacrificed to.

Afterward, the emperor is led to the station for "observing the fire," where he assumes his customary place facing south. Ritual officers approach the spirit-thrones on the round altar with baskets, removing the jade and silk offerings and the prayer-tablets. They take these, along with the dishes containing the sacrificial flesh, millet, glutinous rice, and the ritual wine and descend the altar via different staircases, proceeding to yet another altar constructed of firewood. All the articles removed from the round altar are placed on the firewood. The wood is ignited, and when it is half-consumed by the fire the ceremony is pronounced completed. The emperor is now led back to his great canopy.[60]

(7)   Return of the imperial carriage to the palace. The emperor rests for a while at the great canopy and takes the opportunity to change his costume. The ritual officers also change from their ceremonial costume to normal court attire. The emperor then mounts his palanquin, is trans-ferred to his carriage of state, and is escorted back to his palace.

AN ANTHROPOLOGICAL APPROACH TO THE ALTAR RITES

We can view the round altar rite, as Edmund Leach does, in terms of a crossing of metaphysical space and metaphysical time. At the round altar the emperor moves into a sacred area and liminal zone which bridges the gap between the temporal world inhabited by mortal men and the Other World inhabited by immortal and omnipotent gods. The emperor's ritual performance establishes a bridge across space by means of which the power of the gods flows toward man. As the emperor mounts the round altar he passes not only into sacred space but into a different quality of time, a sacred non-time in which past, present, and future coexist simultaneously. This is the "abnormal" time of the gods. After the rite is completed, the emperor descends from the altar and makes another transition from abnormal back to normal time. The crossing of the boundary to sacred space and sacred time and back is marked in various ways. The emperor prepares for the rite by secluding himself from the normal affairs of the world. He changes his costume while at the great canopy before ascending the altar. He walks to and climbs up the altar staircase rather than being carried or riding, as he was just minutes before. He washes his hands to remove the pollution of the world before entering the presence of the gods. He changes his clothes again after descending the altar.

Animal sacrifices such as those made at the round altar can be looked at in two complementary ways, according to Leach. In the first, animals are gifts or tribute to the gods made by man in the expectation of reciprocity—that the gods will bestow benefits on him in return. The gift must be killed so that its essence can be transferred to the Other World. In the Chinese case the essence of the animal is believed to be transmitted to Heaven by means of the smoke produced by the fire. Here, sacrifice is a mode of communication between linked entities. It is at the same time a sign of submission of donor to receiver. In the second, the sacrificed animals are stand-ins for the sacrificer. Death is conceived of as a separation of the ghost-soul from the corpse and a purification of the soul. The sacrifical ritual serves to separate the sacrificer into pure and impure parts. When the animal is killed, the donor by vicarious association is also purified. Leaving his impure part behind him, he is initiated into a new ritual status.[61]

With Leach's comments in mind, it is easy to see why the sacrifice to Heaven was a jealously guarded imperial prerogative. Although throughout the ceremony the emperor was compelled graphically to demonstrate

his position of inferiority relative to Hao-t'ien shang-ti, because it established a direct link between Heaven and its Son, it actually served to exalt
the emperor's position. In liminal space and time the emperor appears to
be relatively weak and helpless: He is handed all the ritual objects, taking
nothing by himself; he is escorted by others everywhere about the altar;
his physical movements, largely prostrations and obeisances, communicate humility and dependence. Yet paradoxically, the emperor's status and
power are affirmed at this very moment of powerlessness. He is humbled
and leveled, as Victor Turner says, to make him "fit for a higher status or
state."[62] It is precisely in the liminal space of ritual that the participant
achieves come deeper kind of knowledge or some higher form of power
than before. Having successfully communicated with Heaven, the emper-
or descends the round altar and emerges from the ritual space greatly vital-
ized, not enfeebled, by his experience. By means of the ritual, moreover,
he has powerfully demonstrated to outsiders his exclusive relationship
with that most puissant of cosmic forces, Hao-t'ien shang-ti. The basis of
his authority is perceived as being "public" as much as "private." It is
therefore all the more persuasive.

Yet until Kao-tsung's time, as we have seen, Hao-t'ien shang-ti was
only one among several gods who were sacrificed to at the suburban
altars. The *Hsien-ch'ing li*, rejecting the ideas of Cheng Hsüan, raised Hao-
t'ien shang-ti to an exalted level; Kan-sheng ti and the Five Emperors,
heretofore his rivals, were virtually eliminated as primary objects of sacrifice. This strengthened worship of Hao-t'ien shang-ti reflected the cosmological concept of *t'ien-shang wu erh*, "There is only one Heaven," a
broadside aimed at Cheng Hsüan's Six Heavens theory, which we find in
various contemporary public utterances.[63] The condition of one supreme
deity in Heaven was congruent with that of one supreme autocrat on
earth; here terrestrial social hierarchy echoed cosmological structure—and
was legitimated by it. The emperor's worship of Heaven thus validated his
own status relative to the rest of the empire, a status whose parameters and
operating principles were becoming clear only gradually, as the T'ang
continued the centralization policies initiated by their Sui predecessors and
expanded the territory of the Chinese empire to unprecedented limits. It is
not surprising, then, that the *K'ai-yüan li* of T'ang Hsüan-tsung's time,
another expansionary era, should have adopted the *t'ien-shang wu erh* view
embodied in Kao-tsung's ritual code. The *K'ai-yüan li* not only provided
the cosmological and ritual model for the rest of the T'ang, but set a pattern for the state sacrifices of later, increasingly autocratic ages.

CHAPTER 6

The Ancestral Cult and the Cult of
Political Ancestors

[T]he problem of death is such a deep-rooted and powerful human issue
that power groups everywhere seize on it and exploit it for their ends.
                                        Abner Cohen, "Political Symbolism"

ANCESTOR WORSHIP HAS BEEN REGARDED AS A CENTRAL ELEMENT OF THE
ancient Chinese religion.[1] Its overall importance in early times may be
gauged, perhaps, by the fact that the great majority of references to ritual
in the Confucian classic, the *Book of Poetry*, is related to the ancestral cult.[2]
According to C. K. Yang, on a religious level the cult encouraged hopes
among men for supernatural aid and assuaged fears of supernatural re-
tribution; it also satisfied their desire to provide for the welfare of the
departed souls of kinsmen. On a secular level it inculcated such kinship
values as filial piety, loyalty to family, and the perpetuation of the family
line.[3] But in China, as in many other societies, the ancestral cult also had a
political dimension. Because ancestral cults are exclusive rather than inclusive, they tend to represent selfish and sectional interests and the conflict
over them, and affect power divisions and classificatory distinctions within and among political groups. They therefore help to shape political
alignments, territorial divisions, and the organization of authority.[4]

In antiquity, the ancestral temple was considered the most important
part of a home. The *Book of Rites* says that when a superior man (*chün-tzu*)
builds his house, "the ancestral temple should have his first attention, the
stables and arsenal the next, and the residences the last."[5] The physical
place of royal ancestor worship was the royal ancestral temple (*tsung-miao*
or *t'ai-miao*). The *tsung-miao* was a symbol of political, not just religious,
power, ranking with the altars of state (*she-chi*) as collective representations of the state. From ancient times the royal ancestral temple and lavish

sacrificial rites performed therein symbolized dynastic might and helped to stabilize the political order in China.[6] Nor were these functions of the ancestral temple unknown to the ancient Chinese. Speaking in 40 B.C. of the establishment of Han ancestral temples throughout the country earlier in the dynasty, Emperor Yüan (rg. 48–32 B.C.) observed: "This was the best expedient by which power was established, subversive intentions eradicated, and the people unified."[7]

By positing that its own ancestors constituted some of the most powerful spirit-protectors of the incumbent regime, and then claiming exclusive access to them by means of the ancestral rites, a ruling house created a powerful device for generating support for itself among those groups lying outside the magic dynastic kinship circle. By the time of the first historical dynasty of Shang in the second millennium B.C. ancestor worship was already providing, David Keightley maintains, "powerful psychological and ideological support for the political dominance of the Shang kings. The king's ability to determine through divination, and influence through prayer and sacrifice, the will of the ancestral spirits legitimized the concentration of power in his person."[8] The intense ceremonialization of the royal ancestral cult in ancient times was at least partly a function of the impressive political advantages afforded a ruling house from exclusive communication and identification with its own ancestors.

By the time of Confucius the dynastic house of Chou had lost its monopoly on the form, if not the content, of the royal ancestral rites—the royal cult was closely imitated in many of the states nominally under Chou control—a development Confucius found repugnant.[9] Moreover, Confucius, who tended to avoid speculation about the afterlife, admitted that he knew very little about sacrificing to the ancestors:

> Someone asked for an explanation of the Ancestral Sacrifice. The Master said, I do not know. Anyone who knew the explanation could deal with all things under Heaven as easily as I lay this here; and he laid his finger upon the palm of his hand.[10]

In this respect Confucius weakened the purely religious aspect of ancestor worship. But exclusive access to the dynastic ancestors remained an important tool and symbol of monarchical power, attested to in the Han dynasty by the ritual visit to the ancestral temple (yeh-miao) soon after an emperor's accession.

In the post-Han period, however, as we have seen, the "power" of the dynastic ancestors to legitimate royal authority gradually declined as emperors increasingly established a more direct relationship with Heaven by means of the altar rites. In the Southern Dynasties the *yeh-miao* ceremony following enthronement was employed only when a person ascending the throne had not previously been crown prince. In the Northern Dynasties the overall situation is less clear, but there are recorded instances (in the Northern Ch'i, for example) in which emperors conducted sacrifices at the ancestral temple within a day or two after taking the throne, constituting a kind of *yeh-miao* ritual.[11] *Yeh-miao* visits to the ancestral temple continued as a practice for newly appointed crown princes all through the period from the Wei, Chin, and Northern and Southern Dynasties into the T'ang.[12] For example, in 698 the newly appointed T'ang crown prince performed the *yeh-miao* ceremony, and in 720 the crown prince did the same on the occasion of his capping.[13] The chapter of the *K'ai-yüan li* which concerns the capping of the crown prince contains a section entitled "The crown prince visits the ancestral temple" (*T'ai-tzu yeh t'ai-miao*), indicating the routine association of the capping ceremony with *yeh-miao*.[14] The link to the royal ancestors was thus reforged at the time of the establishment or capping of the dynastic heir. In this way the T'ang ancestors continued to have a legitimating role, even if attenuated, in the formation of an emperor's power.

The ancestral cult, one of the most significant institutions of traditional Chinese religion and kingship, has been the subject of intense debate from the Han dynasty down to modern times. Almost every aspect of ancestral worship has come under question: How should the ancestral temple be arranged internally? how many ancestors should have temples dedicated to them? which ancestors could have temples devoted to them in perpetuity, and which ancestors were eventually to have their temples "destroyed" and their spirit-tablets (*shen-chu*) removed? what criteria governed designating certain ancestors as Great Ancestor (*t'ai-tsu*) or First Ancestor (*shih-tsu*)? what was the proper time to perform the various ancestral sacrifices? and on and on. Although T'ang scholars dutifully assumed the roles of the disputants of earlier periods, they contributed precious little that was new to the debate, nor did they appear to achieve any permanent solutions.

Judging from archaeological, epigraphical, and literary evidence, there was little or no differentiation in ancient times between such structures as the royal residence, the hall of government, the ancestral temple, or even such "cosmic" edifices as the Hall of Light (*Ming-t'ang*).[15] The palace was a temple and vice versa. Even in Western Chou times the ancestral temple appears to have been an integral part of the royal palace, the place where kings enfeoffed loyal followers and issued orders to their officials.[16] But as government became more complex, the buildings associated with it became more specialized. The ancestral temple, now liberated from the palace as a separate structure, also underwent evolution over time. Whereas originally it appears that each ancestor had a separate building dedicated to him, beginning with the Later Han there was only a single structure, with separate rooms consecrated to individual ancestors.[17]

But how many ancestors simultaneously had temples devoted to them in ancient times? Like many of the other debates over ritual that were endemic in medieval China, the one over the number of ancestral temples arose from outright contradictions in the canonical texts and also from the way certain textual ambiguities were interpreted. The Confucian classics yield royal ancestral temple numbers of four, five, seven, or even nine depending on how the texts are read. The *Book of Rites* alone furnishes mutually contradictory numbers, possibly reflecting the fact that the Han compilers charged with producing a canonical edition of the work chose to include sections reflecting both New Text and Old Text theories.[18] Perhaps some of the parts of the text addressing the problem are merely corrupt.[19] Matters are further complicated by the propensity of some of the most influential thinkers on ritual, such as Cheng Hsüan, to depend for their interpretations on the weft texts, which were often unreliable. Cheng Hsüan believed that in ancient times founding rulers established four temples for ancestors within the mourning circle, and an additional temple for the First Ancestor, thus making a total of five.[20] Under the Wei, the Chin, and the Northern Dynasties the views of Cheng Hsüan generally prevailed. This was also the situation during the Sui dynasty and, as we will soon see, at the very beginning of the T'ang.

THE EARLY T'ANG ANCESTRAL TEMPLE SYSTEM

The T'ang imperial ancestral cult can be traced back to the third month of 618, still some nine or ten weeks prior to his accession, when Kao-tsu established his ancestral temple at the old Li-family mansion in Ch'ang-an, located in the T'ung-i quarter, a little south of the imperial city (*huang-ch'eng*). The temple was dedicated to his four nearest lineal ancestors.[21] It was not until after his accession in the fifth month, however, that the spirit-tablets of the four ancestors were transferred from the old temple into the formal T'ang ancestral temple, located just inside the southeast wall of the imperial city, and regular seasonal sacrifices (*shih-hsiang*) to them inaugurated.[22] At the same time the four were given posthumous honorary designations. Kao-tsu's great-great-grandfather, Li Hsi, was called Duke of Hsüan-chien; his great-grandfather, Li T'ien-tz'u, was called Prince of I; his grandfather, Li Hu, was called Emperor Ching; and his father, Li Ping, was called Emperor Yüan. His grandfather was given the special temple-name (*miao-hao*) Great Ancestor and his father was given the temple-name First Ancestor.

The term Great Ancestor had been used in China since the time of the earliest historical dynasties, according to classical accounts. In the T'ang period a Great Ancestor was generally thought of as the person who was first enfeoffed with the land or property that became the patrimony of the lineage. The temple of a Great Ancestor was never to be destroyed as long as the dynasty survived. The meaning of First Ancestor seems to have been less clearly understood by the men of T'ang.[23]

Kao-tsu's decision to go back only four generations in establishing his ancestral temple may have been based on several factors. The "Monograph on Ritual" of the *New T'ang History* suggests that founding rulers sometimes encountered difficulty in finding a sufficient number of forebears who possessed the high moral virtue or eminent official careers required of someone worshiped as a dynastic ancestor.[24] Yet the next three generations of ancestors claimed by Kao-tsu seem also to have possessed these requisite qualities. The ancestry of Li Hu, Kao-tsu's grandfather, is not absolutely certain. The T'ang traced Li Hu's ancestry back to the ruling house of one of the Sixteen Kingdoms of the disunion period, the Western Liang (400–420), centered in western Kansu province. Li Hu's putative fifth-generation ancestor (the seventh-generation ancestor of Kao-tsu), Li Hao, was founder of the Western Liang, head of a prominent local lineage, and a descendant of the Han general, Li Kuang. Li Hao's son, Li Hsin, followed him on the throne, but Hsin's son, Ch'ung-erh, Kao-tsu's putative fifth-generation ancestor, was forced by the barbarian Hsiung-nu to abandon his throne and flee to southern China; later he took service under the Northern Wei, rising to the position of prefect.[25] Any or all of these ancestors conceivably could have been enshrined in the T'ang ancestral temple without shame. An insufficiency of eligible ancestors seems, then, to provide the weakest explanation for Kao-tsu's establishment of only four temples.

More likely is that Kao-tsu had canonical authority for this number as well as the backing of the exegete Cheng Hsüan. The "Record of Small Matters Pertaining to Mourning Dress" (*Sang-fu hsiao-chi*) chapter of the *Book of Rites* says: "At the great royal sacrifice to all ancestors, the first place was given to him from whom the founder of the line sprang, and that founder had the place of assessor to him. There came thus to be established four ancestral shrines."[26] Cheng Hsüan relied on the weft texts to put forth the view that the sage-rulers Yao and Shun both established five ancestral temples, consisting of four temples dedicated to ancestors within the mourning circle (*ch'in-miao*), and an additional temple for the First Ancestor (*shih-tsu miao*) who could be beyond the mourning circle. Kao-tsu's temples were *ch'in-miao*. Another possible factor behind Kao-tsu's decision were the precedents set by other dynastic founders, most recently during the preceding Sui dynasty, when Wen-ti established four temples to his ancestors after his accession.[27] Kao-tsu's establishment of his four temples even before the formal establishment of the T'ang also had a recent historical precedent. The founder of the Northern Ch'i, Wen-hsiang, who died late in 549, founded four temples to his ancestors just before his own death and the formal inauguration of the dynasty by his younger brother in 550.[28]

DEBATES ON THE NUMBER OF ANCESTRAL TEMPLES

As we have seen, the four-temple configuration was only one of several possible organizing models for royal ancestral temples found in the Chinese classics. It was not long before these other models began to be discussed at court. The ritual controversy which resulted might well have been predicted, since the question had been discussed intermittently for centuries prior to the T'ang.[29] Around 629 the possibility was raised of expanding Kao-tsu's initial four-temple configuration to seven temples, and designating Li Hao (351–417), Kao-tsu's seventh-generation ancestor, as First Ancestor. Although such eminent statesmen of the time as Fang Hsüan-ling supported the plan, the vice-president of the Secretariat, Yü Chih-ning, raised a lone voice against it on the grounds that Li Hao was a remote ancestor who had little connection with the founding of the dynasty and was therefore unsuited to be awarded such an exalted title.[30] No further action was taken at the time. But a few years later, in 635, Kao-tsu's death prompted T'ai-tsung to reopen the matter. He ordered his courtiers to hold a full-scale debate on the ancestral temple system.[31]

By T'ang times the royal ancestral temple system had already been discussed and debated so thoroughly by generations of scholars that scarcely any new arguments could have been brought to bear on the question.[32] This fact did not prevent an outpouring of comment. The remonstrating counselor Chu Tzu-she briefly traced the ideas of previous discussants, such as Wei Hsüan-ch'eng of the Han, who thought that Sons of Heaven and Feudal Princes should both have five temples, and Liu Tzu-chün, who maintained that the temples of the Feudal Princes should always number two fewer than those of the monarch. He then cited passages in the classics that supported the notion that persons of different statuses deserved correspondingly different rituals. He therefore recommended the establishment of seven temples in order suitably to exalt the imperial position.[33]

Ts'en Wen-pen, vice-president of the Secretariat, noted that since the Burning of the Books in Ch'in times, documents on the ancestral temple system had been in disarray, and since the time of the two Han, Wei, and Chin dynasties, despite efforts to rectify the records, different opinions had persisted. Basically, these opinions could be divided into two schools: the four-temple (actually five-temple) configuration of Cheng Hsüan, and the seven-temple configuration of Wang Su. No one had yet been able to prove which was correct, and the matter remained thoroughly confused. However, over the years those who advocated a seven-temple configuration had outnumbered those favoring four temples, and the strong points of the former group seemed obvious. He explained that the seven-temple configuration had been interpreted by most commentators as referring to rooms for six ancestors represented by *chao* and *mu* tablets, plus a room dedicated to the Great Ancestor. The Chin dynasty and southern regimes of Sung, Ch'i, and Liang had all followed this system by establishing six temples. It was proper to have an ancestral ritual which distinguished between high and low, and exalted the position of the emperor. "Ritual derives from human emotions and does not drop from Heaven", he reminded T'ai-tsung. Since a four-temple system did not confer sufficient honor on an emperor, he advocated adopting a six-temple system in accordance with both past dynastic ritual and classical practice embodied in the ancient records. T'ai-tsung accepted this plan. Thereupon, the ancestral temples were expanded to six by moving the tablet of Kao-tsu's fifth-generation ancestor, Li Ch'ung-erh (d. 423), and also that of Kao-tsu, into the two new rooms.[34]

In the last month of the same year in which it was decided to expand

the T'ang ancestral temple, T'ai-tsung raised the possibility of establishing
an additional temple dedicated to his father in special recognition of Kao-
tsu's heroic feat of founding the dynasty and restoring order to the country. It was to be located in T'ai-yüan, scene of the original T'ang uprising
against the Sui. Noting that Kao-tsu had cautioned that frugality had to be
observed in such matters, T'ai-tsung asked his officials to deliberate the
plan in detail.[35] The director of the imperial library, Yen Shih-ku, bitterly
opposed the plan. He maintained that according to the classics ancestral
temples were to be located in the capital and were not to be established
elsewhere. The policy of constructing ancestral temples in the commande-
ries and principalities at the beginning of the Han dynasty was in violation
of ancient regulations. Thus, after the Confucians discussed it (in 40 B.C.)
they decided to abolish the practice. From that time onward down to the
present ancestral temples were not separately established. To do so now,
he concluded, could challenge the regulations of old.[36] T'ai-tsung thereupon abandoned his plan.

With T'ai-tsung's own death in 649, and the six rooms of the imperial
ancestral temple already completely occupied, some decision had to be
reached as to what policy would prevail regarding the ancestral tablets.
According to one account, T'ai-tsung's successor, Kao-tsung, came up
with the novel idea of placing his father's tablet in his own bedchamber,
where it would be displayed and honored. But some of the most respected
statesmen of the age, including Li Chi, recoiled at this unorthodox suggestion, which had no classical precedent, and so Kao-tsung was forced to
relent.[37] Nevertheless, the problem of what to do with T'ai-tsung's tablet
had to be solved some way or another. Thus, late in the eighth month of
649, the president of the Board of Rites, Hsü Ching-tsung, memorialized
advocating that the tablet of Li Ch'ung-erh, the most remote ancestor kept
at the ancestral temple, which had been placed in the expanded ancestral
temple only a little more than a decade earlier, now be removed. But what
to do with his tablet? Hsü dismissed the suggestions of scholars of earlier
ages that tablets removed from the ancestral temple either be buried or
stored in a separate temple. Contemporary ancestral temples were different from those of old, he observed; they were comprised of several rooms
sharing a common foundation, with the western part of the building regarded as most sacred. Tablets stored in a storeroom in the western portion of the building would thus still occupy a respected place and might
be prayed to and sacrificed to as before. Hsü proposed that the old tablet
of Li Ch'ung-erh be so disposed. His advice was followed and, on the

twenty-eighth day of the eighth month, T'ai-tsung's tablet joined those of his father and his more remote ancestors inside the ancestral temple, while that of Li Ch'ung-erh was moved to the storeroom.[38]

Upon Kao-tsung's own death in the eighth month of 684, his spirit-tablet was routinely placed in the T'ang ancestral temple, displacing the tablet of Kao-tsu's great-great-grandfather.[39] By no means did this mean that the basic features of the T'ang ancestral temple system had been resolved, however. Throughout the dynasty the court repeatedly debated such questions as the appropriate number of rooms in the temple, who was to be designated Great Ancestor or First Ancestor, which ancestors were to have a temple dedicated to them in perpetuity and which were to have their temple "destroyed," how to reckon the number of spirit-tablets allowed to remain in the temple when brothers succeeded one another, and so forth.[40] It is apparent that the early T'ang ritualists were confused in their deliberations on the ancestral temple system by a lack of clear classical authority as well as by the opposing arguments presented centuries earlier by exegetes like Cheng Hsüan and Wang Su, arguments which over time had assumed the authority of canon. When reading through the early T'ang debates, one is struck by how alike they all sound; indeed, they are hardly different at all from similar debates that took place during the Period of Disunion. It is almost as if no progress had been made by the ritualists, as if each dynasty, each generation, were condemned to attack the same ritual problems with the same limited number of solutions. Were the discussants merely trapped in a conceptual straitjacket? Or, more likely, had the litany of argumentation itself become fixed, forming an integral and indispensable part of the ritual process?[41]

It was essential, no matter what side of the argument ritualists took, for them to have either ample classical authority or the interpretation of "canonical" commentators to back them up. In this respect, during the early T'ang, as in many other matters of ritual importance, the views of Cheng Hsüan gave way to those of Wang Su. But it also appears that the traditional notion that ritual was ultimately based on human feelings rather than on divine authority lent a certain degree of flexibility to the ancestral temple system during the early T'ang. Appeals could be made both to scripture/exegesis *and* practicality, and by no means were these viewed as mutually exclusive. Temples could be four or six in number and paradoxically still be both ritually correct and emotionally satisfying. Perhaps what was just as important as the determination of the precise number of rooms in the ancestral temple or the content of the sacrifices offered there were periodic demonstrations by the dynasty that it exerted complete control over its ancestral destiny. Not only was this ritually necessary; such control over its own past both symbolized and helped generate the political power that enabled the dynasty to order the present.

THE EARLY T'ANG ANCESTRAL RITES

Only two motives, observed the Han philosopher Wang Ch'ung, under-lay all Chinese sacrifice: gratitude for received benefits and ancestral worship.[42] The major sacrifices undertaken at the T'ang ancestral temple were the seasonal sacrifices (*ssu-shih chih chi shih-hsiang*) and the Ti and Hsia. The seasonal sacrifices were offered four times a year, in the first, fourth, seventh, and tenth months (five times if we include the La rite of the twelfth month). Because of their frequency, they were considered less important than the Ti and Hsia. The Ti and Hsia were performed only once every five and three years, respectively.[43] Whereas in the seasonal rites a sacrifice was made to each ancestor in the ancestor's individual room of the ancestral temple, in the Ti and Hsia all the ancestors were sacrificed to en masse in the temple of the Great Ancestor (*t'ai-tsu miao*).[44] During the T'ang there were thus five or six ancestral temple rites in a typical year. The emperor did not personally perform all of them, how-ever, and officials often substituted for him.

The solution to an enduring problem concerning the Ti and Hsia ear-ly in the T'ang illustrates the ability of ritualists of the time to achieve solutions based on "human feelings" as a complement to purely classical orthodoxy, or even recent historical precedent. According to classical tradition, at the Ti and Hsia rites the spirit-tablet of the Great Ancestor was to occupy a privileged position in the western portion of his temple facing the spirit-tablets of his descendants, which were arrayed toward the east. Even the tablets of the spirits of "destroyed temples" were to be displayed and arranged among the *chao* and *mu* for the occasion; in this way they could all be "fed" together with the Great Ancestor. In the early dynasties of Shang and Chou, when the Great Ancestor was chosen from a mythological hero–figure many generations back in time from the actual dynastic founder, even at the beginning of a dynasty the Great Ancestor was able to occupy the seat facing the tablets of his descendants. With the fall of the Han and the onset of the Period of Disunion, a problem arose. Regimes rose and fell so rapidly, and ancestors suitable for worship at the ancestral temple were in such short supply, that dynastic founders were often themselves designated as Great Ancestor. Since in these instances tablets from "destroyed temples" all represented the ancestors rather than the descendants of the Great Ancestors, they were not arranged among the *chao* and *mu* and thus they could not "eat" with the Great Ancestor as at the Ti and Hsia rites of old. The early T'ang ritualists thus tried a new tack. At the beginning of the T'ang, when Li Hu was designated Great Ancestor, his recent ancestors were placed among the *chao* and *mu*. At Ti and Hsia rites, out of respect for them, the seat facing east was left vacant and the Great Ancestor's tablet was simply placed among those of his ancestors and descendants. Only in 764, soon after the emperor Tai-tsung came to power, and the tablets of Li Hu's father and grandfather were finally returned to the storeroom, could the Great Ancestor claim his traditionally sanctioned seat facing east toward the tablets of his descendants at the Ti and Hsia rites.[45]

The T'ang ancestral temple rites were not dissimilar in form from those at the suburban altars, except that they took place in an enclosed space and were dedicated primarily not to Hao-t'ien shang-ti but to designated lineal ancestors of the imperial house. According to the *K'ai-yüan li*, again our most important source for the rites (and again reflecting the practice at high T'ang), the emperor was to observe seven days of seclusion prior to the beginning of the ceremonies, four days of relaxed seclusion and three days of strict seclusion.[46] Three days before the rites, positions were marked off for the participants and invited audience, including the lineal descendants of the objects of sacrifice, foreign dignitaries, and military and civil officials, as well as for all the ritual vessels, miscellaneous paraphernalia, and members of the imperial orchestra. Shortly before the ceremonies began, the sacrificial victims were examined and butchered, and platters containing their hide, blood, and liver laid out, intended for use at the spirit-thrones of the ancestral spirits. Finally, the imperial carriages were made ready.

The two major steps of the seasonal sacrifices as well as of the La rite consisted of a sunrise libation of wine immediately followed by an offering of food. About one hour before dawn on the day of the sacrifice, ritual officials donned their ceremonial costume, entered the temple precincts, and made ready the drinking vessels and food platters and baskets that were to be employed. Three-quarters of an hour before dawn, the presiding ritual officials as well as those bearing the platters, baskets, and wine vessels took their places at the stairways leading up to the temple proper. Some officials now mounted the stairs and swept the temple clean. One-half hour before dawn the presiding ritual officials mounted the temple by the eastern stairs and went to the rooms of each of the ancestral spirits, in order of rank from the highest on down, and removed his spirit-tablet, placing each on its spirit-throne. Shortly before the arrival of the emperor's carriage, ritual officials charged with making the secondary and tertiary offerings, the descendants of the ancestors, foreign dignitaries, and so forth, were led to positions at the outer gates of the temple. The emperor could now make his entrance. Dismounting from his carriage, he was borne by sedan chair to the great canopy. The temple was swept once more. Then all the participants and spectators entered the temple precincts and took their assigned places.

Led to a washstand inside the temple precincts, the emperor laved his hands and the sacrificial wine cup. He was then led to the room of the highest (most remote) ancestor, where, facing north and kneeling, he poured out a libation of wine on the ground, prostrated himself, and rose, before being led out of the room. Outside, facing north once again, as a subject to a master, he made a double obeisance. This process was repeated all down the line, in the rooms of each of his ancestors. While the emperor was performing these libations, the vessels and platters containing the hide, blood, and liver of the sacrificial victims had been brought to the outside of the eastern gate of the temple; they were now brought inside, up the stairs, and placed in front of each spirit-tablet. Charcoal braziers and glutinous panicled millet mixed with fragrant artemisia were also brought up and placed outside each of the rooms. Both millet and liver were then roasted on the braziers.

The offering of food to the ancestors could now be made. Following another ritual washing of hands and winecup, and another offering of wine by the emperor, a sacrificial prayer addressed from the emperor to his highest ancestor was read and deposited at the latter's spirit-throne. This procedure was repeated for each of the ancestors in turn. The emperor was then led to the eastern section of the temple, where he stood facing west. Just before, the ritual wine at the spirit-throne of each of the ancestors had been combined and poured into a single cup. Accepting this cup with a double obeisance, the emperor collectively sacrificed the wine to all his ancestors by sipping it. Lastly, offerings of sacrifical meat and rice, which had been handled personally by the emperor, were laid out for the ancestors. The emperor now drained the last dregs of wine, and the winecup was returned to its stand. Prostrating himself, rising, and performing a double obeisance, the emperor descended the stairs. After the secondary and tertiary offerings were performed by his officials and the ritual proceedings declared over, the emperor returned to his palace.

No record survives of any personal sacrifices made at the ancestral temple by Kao-tsu after he founded his dynasty. Whether this reflects the actual case or merely the failure of the historians to note the fact is impossible to say. The first time a T'ang emperor is recorded as having personally sacrificed at the ancestral temple is the first month of 629, on which occasion T'ai-tsung is said to have been especially moved on seeing the spirit-tablet of his mother.[47] T'ai-tsung made another personal sacrifice in 643, when he visited the ancestral temple to beg forgiveness for the actions of his errant son, whom he had just sacked as heir. His successor, Kao-tsung, made a total of four personal sacrifices, in 652, 666, 668, and 677.[48] One account of his first visit describes, in a somewhat formulaic manner, how the emperor was overwhelmed with emotion as he lay prostrate before his late father's tablet.[49]

Given that the first ancestral sacrifice personally performed by both T'ai-tsung and Kao-tsung occurred after their first suburban altar rites, and given the lack of any record whatsoever of personal sacrifice by Kao-tsu, it is doubtful that these rites were viewed during the early T'ang as the primary means of legitimating imperial power—as they had once been during the Han. Yet only two of twenty-one successors to Kao-tsu failed to make at least one personal ancestral sacrifice during their reigns, and in both of these cases they rule for only a short period.[50] Moreover, whether personal ancestral sacrifices were made soon after their accession or not, T'ang emperors often established the spirit-tablets of their deceased predecessors in the ancestral temple in a rite of ancestral veneration prior to their personal performance of any altar rites.[51] Kao-tsu, as we saw, deposited the spirit-tablets of his ancestors in the ancestral temple even before his accession. Kao-tsung had the spirit-tablet of his father deposited less than three months following his assumption of power and some thirty months prior to his first performance of the altar rites. Announcements of momentous events affecting the state or the imperial family were still routinely made in the presence of the ancestors in a rite called kao-miao.[52] Thus, even though the power of ancestors to legitimate and bless their descendants with good fortune may have been reduced by T'ang times, it had by no means become negligible.

THE CULT OF POLITICAL ANCESTORS

In the autumn of 1980 I had the good fortune to visit the People's Republic of China and tour some of its major historical sites. One of my stops while in Beijing was the mausoleum containing the embalmed body of Chairman Mao. To pay respects to the Great Helmsman one had to register some days in advance, appear at the tomb at the assigned time, and take one's place in a long, solemn line winding slowly toward the interior of the building, watched over by armed guards at strategic intervals. Those on line were silent and respectful, and most of the Chinese I observed were greatly moved when in the presence of Mao's corpse, which was halfdraped in a red flag and enclosed in a glass case. It was obvious that these people were deeply responding to Mao as a father figure, an "ancestor" of them all. It was also obvious that by associating itself so closely with this dominant political symbol, by identifying itself as both the provider of the memorial which housed him and as chief caretaker of his corpse, the state was milking the feelings of political obligation engendered among the pilgrims. It was, in other words, reaping political benefits by means of its power to control access to a dead national ancestor.[53] We can see the same process at work in the ability of the T'ang imperial house to control and manipulate the trappings of the cult of its own political ancestors.

In addition to presiding over a cult of their own forebears, T'ang monarchs were also caretakers of rites dedicated to previous Chinese rulers. Such rulers collectively constituted what I call the "political ancestors" as opposed to the biological ancestors of the T'ang dynasts. As identification with lineal ancestors could generate diffuse support for a dynastic house and the regime it represented, so might the identification of incumbent rulers with their political ancestors. By portraying themselves symbolically as the end-points on a long line of heroic monarchs, T'ang rulers could share in their charisma, could, loosely speaking, inherit that charisma. Moreover, the mere act of honoring former imperial houses, which by T'ang times was an age-old tradition, was itself legitimating, as the T'ang were seen as conservers of a hallowed rite. Their ability to choose which among several former imperial houses were to be honored with special rites implied that they had the authority to do so. By honoring the descendants of other dynastic houses, and through them their dynastic founders, the T'ang identified itself with the hallowed notion that the empire was not the perpetual monopoly of one house only, itself a legitimating ideology. The cult of political ancestors thus legitimated T'ang authority in at least three complementary ways: through tradition (Weber), facticity (Berger), and ideology (Easton).

Rulers of past dynasties could be honored by venerating their living descendants, who were seen as stand-ins for the founders of these dynasties, and also by offering sacrifices to them directly.

The *locus classicus* of the tradition of honoring descendants of royal houses is the "Single Victim at the Border Sacrifices" (*Chiao t'e sheng*) chapter of the *Book of Rites*: "The Son of Heaven preserved the descendants of [the sovereigns] of the two [previous] dynasties, still honoring the worth [of their founders]. But this honoring the [ancient] worthies did not extend beyond the two dynasties."[54] Here, the Son of Heaven is a dynastic founder, such as the Chou dynasty founder who generously enfeoffed descendants of the Hsia and Shang as representatives of their defunct royal houses.[55] From Chou times onward it was the practice of dynastic founders to "resurrect what had been destroyed and continue what had been interrupted" by honoring the descendants of two earlier dynastic founders, who became known as the Descendants of the Two Kings (*erh-wang hou*).[56] The selection of the Descendants of the Two Kings, moreover, generally took place soon after the establishment of a new dynasty, usually within a year or two at most, underlining the importance of the rite.[57] The T'ang was no exception to this tradition. A mere two days after ascending the throne, on the twenty-second day of the fifth month, 618, Kao-tsu issued an edict proclaiming the former Sui puppet emperor, along with a descendant of the Northern Chou house, as Descendants of the Two Kings, keepers of the rites of the two former dynastic houses. Echoing the "Charge to Viscount Wei" of the *Book of History*, which established the Viscount as conserver of Shang royal ceremonies, Kao-tsu pledged that the Sui puppet emperor, whom he now enfeoffed as Duke of Hsi, would forever be a "guest" of the T'ang. (How sincere Kao-tsu was in his pledge is doubtful, for just a year later the Duke of Hsi lay dead.) The heir of the Northern Chou house was enfeoffed as the Duke of Chieh principality (*Chieh-kuo kung*).[58] The *erh-wang hou* occupied the rank of third degree, first class, and participated in all the major T'ang imperial sacrifices, including the round altar sacrifice, the ancestral temple sacrifice, rites at the Ming-t'ang, and the Feng and Shan sacrifices. At such times they were physically situated between the descendants of T'ang royal ancestors in collateral lines and lower-ranking civil and military officials, an indication of their relative standing in the rites.[59] T'ai-tsung, in his turn, also contributed to the tradition of the Descendants of the Two Kings. Noting that there were no ancestral temples dedicated to the Sui and Northern Chou, and that thus there were no places at which the rulers of these defunct dynasties could be venerated, in 628 he ordered local officials to erect shrines to Sui and Northern Chou ancestors in their government offices.[60] In 682 Kao-tsung changed the dynastic houses of the Two Kings to those of the original Chou and the Han. But in 705 the T'ang returned to the earlier practice of honoring the descendants of the Northern Chou and Sui.[61]

The political dimension of the tradition of the Descendants of the Two Kings did not go unrecognized by the great T'ang poet Po Chü-i. In a "New Yüeh-fu" poem entitled "The Descendants of the Two Kings" (*Erh-wang hou*), composed in 809, Po wrote:

Who are the Descendants of the Two Kings?	*Erh wang hou pi ho jen*
The Duke of Chieh and the Duke of Hsi are the dynasty's guests;	*Chieh kung Hsi kung wei kuo pin*
They are the descendants of Chou Wu[-wang] and Sui Wen[-ti].	*Chou Wu Sui Wen chih tzu sun*
The ancients had a saying: *The empire Is not one man's empire.*	*Ku jen yu yen t'ien hsia che Fei shih i jen chih t'ien hsia*
When the [Northern] Chou was destroyed the empire passed on to the Sui.	*Chou wang t'ien hsia chuan yu Sui*
When the Sui people lost it the T'ang gained it.	*Sui jen shih chih T'ang te chih*
T'ang has flourished for ten generations and two hundred years;	*T'ang hsing shih yeh sui erh pai*
The Duke of Chieh and the Duke of Hsi have always been its guests.	*Chieh kung Hsi kung shih wei k'o*
At times of ancestral sacrifice at the Ming-t'ang and ancestral temple,	*Ming t'ang ta miao ch'ao hsiang shih*
They are led in to occupy the guest positions to serve as [the dynasty's] retainers.	*Yin chü pin wei pei wei i*
Serving as retainers they assist at the state sacrifices,	*Pei wei i chu chiao chi*
[According with] the regulations left behind by Kao-tsu and T'ai-tsung.	*Kao tsu T'ai tsung chih i chih*
Not only have [Kao-tsu and T'ai-tsung] resurrected destroyed dynasties;	*Pu tu hsing mieh kuo*

Not only have they continued inter- rupted generations;	*Pu tu chi chüeh shih*
They have made their successors pre- serve the descendants of	*Yü ling ssu wei shou Wen chün*
The destroyed dynasty of Emperor [Sui] Wen and take them as a warning.	*Wang kuo tzu sun ch'ü wei chieh*[62]

Here Po points out that in the tradition of the Descendants of the Two Kings, which he traces to the Chou founding, the early T'ang rulers provided strong political lessons to their successors in the persons of the unfortunate heirs of destroyed regimes. But Po saw yet another political benefit that the rite furnished. By honoring the heirs of destroyed dynasties the T'ang rulers had embraced on yet another level the doctrine of *t'ien-hsia wei kung*, that the empire was not the property of one man or one house only. As we have seen this doctrine provided a powerful legitimating ideology that helped to overcome the moral limitations inherent in the concept of hereditary succession.

The practice of sacrificing to previous rulers is narrated in "The Law of Sacrifices" (*Chi-fa*) chapter of the *Book of Rites*. According to this practice, which is traced back to "the sage-kings" of old,

> sacrifice should be offered to him who had given [good] laws to the people; to him who had laboured to the death in the discharge of his duties; to him who had strengthened the state by his laborious toil; to him who had boldly and successfully met great calamities; and to him who had warded off great evils.[63]

The text lists a long series of heroic rulers who had been honored by sacrifice, including Yao, Shun, Yü, T'ang of the Shang, and Chou Wen-wang and Wu-wang. In post-Chou times down to the T'ang the list of former rulers receiving sacrifice varied widely, ranging from one person to several.[64] The Sui dynasty rites to political ancestors largely mirrored the practice described in the *Book of Rites*, with the addition of Han Kao-tsu as a sacrificial object.

At the beginning of the T'ang, sacrificial rites to former rulers were not carried out. But in 657 Chang-sun Wu-chi and Hsü Ching-tsung recommended that the ceremonies be reinstituted, and that in addition to those rulers cited in the *Book of Rites*, Han Kao-tsu also be so honored. They made no reference to the recent Sui example, but provided a rationale of their own to support the additional sacrifice. Although both the Ch'in and Han had provided the institutions and practices of later ages, they explained, Ch'in Shih-huang-ti had been tyrannical and therefore had to be rejected as an object of sacrifice. But Han Kao-tsu deserved a special place, even though there was no classical precedent for sacrificing to him. They proposed that rites be dedicated to Yao, Shun, Yü, T'ang, Chou Wen-wang and Wu-wang, and Han Kao-tsu once every three years in a geographical location, such as a tomb, associated with each. Their plan was accepted, thus inaugurating the T'ang sacrifices to political ancestors.[65] In the *K'ai-yüan li* the sacrifice to rulers of previous ages (*hsien-tai ti-wang*) was considered an intermediate sacrifice, normally performed by officials rather than the emperor.[66]

It is noteworthy that rites to a much larger number of political ancestors were introduced by the T'ang emperor Hsüan-tsung. In 748, at the peak of T'ang power, and just a few years before the twin military setbacks provided by Arab forces at Talas and armies of rebellion led by An Lu-shan and Shih Ssu-ming, Hsüan-tsung added the names of Ch'in Shih-huang-ti, Han Kuang-wu-ti, Wei Wu-ti, Chin Wu-ti, Tao-wu-ti of the Later Wei, Chou Wu-ti, and Sui Wen-ti to the list of former rulers to whom sacrifices were to be dedicated. The rites were to be performed in the places in which the rulers first arose or in the capitals they founded.[67]

The importance to early T'ang rulers of the cult of lineal ancestors and the cult of political ancestors cannot, of course, be equated. Because the spirits of political ancestors were never considered as having the ability to exert any direct power over their political descendants, they were never courted like those of lineal ancestors. In terms of frequency of performance, lavishness, the personal participation of the emperor, and the intensity of emotions generated among the participants, rites to political ancestors could not compete with rites to lineal ancestors. But the cult of political ancestors served the requirements of *t'ien-hsia wei kung* doctrine the way the cult of lineal ancestors served the requirements of *t'ien-hsia wei chia*. Emperors needed the political legitimation conferred by their ritual association with epic rulers of the past and with the symbolism of the throne being "open to all."

At this point it may be useful to recapitulate our earlier discussion regarding the native Chinese notion of legitimation, or *cheng-t'ung*. The original meaning of *cheng-t'ung* concerned lineal relationships within the family, or *chia*: It concerned the line of orthodox succession within a royal house or any family. This is the way it was understood, for example, during the Han. By Sung times at latest, perhaps already in the T'ang, *cheng-t'ung* had become a political more than a familial notion, signifying the line of orthodox *political* succession from remote times to present. We might say that *cheng-t'ung* embodied the notion of political ancestry the way the earlier concept of *cheng-t'ung* had embodied the notion of lineal ancestry. The power of lineal ancestors to legitimate had been displaced, in this respect, by the power of political ancestors to legitimate. It is in this context that the early T'ang cult of political ancestors should be understood.

CHAPTER 7

The Imperial Tombs and the Cult of the Political Family

The funeral rites have no other purpose than this: to make clear the principle of life and death, to send the dead man away with grief and reverence, and to lay him at last in the ground. At the interment one reverently lays his form away; at the sacrifices one reverently serves his spirit; and by means of inscriptions, eulogies, and genealogical records one reverently hands down his name to posterity. In serving the living, one ornaments the beginning; in sending off the dead, one ornaments the end. When beginning and end are fully attended to, then the duties of a filial son are complete and the way of the sage has reached its fulfillment.

Hsün-tzu

THE ANCESTRAL TEMPLE WAS NOT THE ONLY PLACE THE DISEMBODIED SPIRITS of the dynastic ancestors resided, according to Chinese belief. Another was the graveyard, the repository of their physical remains. During the earliest historical dynasty of Shang, royal tombs of great size were cut into the ground and then refilled with pounded earth after the corpse had been deposited. Such pit burials gave way during the late Spring and Autumn period (eighth–fifth century B.C.)—a time of great social transformation—to burials in tumuli.[1] Confucius is said to have buried his parents under a modest mound only four feet high.[2] But aristocratic burials were more elaborate. A grave mound dating to the fifth century B.C. discovered in Honan province is about 23 feet (7 meters) high, with a diameter of 180 feet (55 meters). By Warring States time (fifth–third century B.C.) the practice of building tumuli with square or rectangular bases had become general among the ruling class, ranging in height from about 30 to 50 feet (10–15 meters) and from 130 to 165 feet (40–50 meters) per side.[3] In Ch'in times the tombs of rulers were referred to as "mountains" (*shan*) because of the great height of the mounds raised over them. In later ages imperial tombs were called "mountain tombs" (*shan-ling*).[4] The custom of raised burials continued, with minor lapses, down through the T'ang and afterward.[5]

The construction of imperial tombs dramatically demonstrated the power of a regime by harnessing the labor of thousands to create impressive and enduring monuments, palpable symbols of the glory and achievements of great men. Imperial tombs helped to legitimate past regimes or rulers in the minds of posterity through the mere quality of their being. But such constructions also served to legitimate contemporary authority. When emperors constructed tombs in honor of deceased predecessors they ostensibly demonstrated filial piety or fraternal love in conformance with the prevailing Confucian ideology. When emperors built tombs intended to house their own remains they were perceived as carrying out a royal prerogative long sanctioned by tradition. Tomb-building thus embraced both a Confucian devotion to the family and the emulation of ritual forms associated with political ancestors. The construction of imperial tombs also provided ample opportunities to reward favored officials by granting them permission to be buried with the prince they had faithfully served in their lifetimes. Such "accompanying burials" of meritorious ministers generated gratitude among the families and descendants of these men, and, along with that gratitude, political support. Emperors could reward faithful officials not only by granting them a treasured final resting place near the imperial remains but also by composing panegyrics and, even, in special cases, personally providing the calligraphy for the inscriptions on their grave steles, permanent testimony of the imperial regard. Such favors could be pointed to with pride by family members and serve to bind them more closely to the regime. In the form of the imperial tomb and its associated ritual trappings, then, an emperor's control over the institutions of death was perhaps even more dramatic and wide-ranging than at the ancestral temple.

As in life, so in death were Chinese rulers differentiated from other social classes. Almost every aspect of the funeral rites—the number, thickness, and materials of the coffins, the funeral garments worn by the deceased, the tomb furniture and decoration, and so on—was minutely graded from ruler on down to lower levels of society.[6] A weft text, the *Li wei han wen chia*, provides an ideal model for some of the gradations that were thought necessary to differentiate the royal tomb from tombs of other social classes:

The grave-mound of the Son of Heaven is thirty feet high[7] with a pine-tree planted on it; that of a Feudal Lord is half that height with a cypress planted on it; that of a great officer is eight feet high with a *luan*-tree planted on it; that of a common officer four feet with an acacia planted on it; the common man has no grave-mound, but a willow is planted on the grave.[8]

Beginning in Han times the characteristics of mounds for various social strata, from feudal lords on down, appear to have been regulated by law.[9] In the T'ang code we find minutely prescribed regulations for the official class and those below concerning such matters as the size of the parcel of land on which the tomb was to be situated, the height of the burial mound, the decoration of the grave stele, what might be written on it, the number of decorative stone statues, and other matters.[10] There were no similar restrictions governing imperial tombs, however, other than the usual canonical, historical, or dynastic precedents. In the early T'ang there was not even dynastic precedent to serve as a model, leading to numerous arguments over the form the imperial burials should take.

The tombs of the Han rulers provided a general model for those of the T'ang.[11] Han tombs were usually constructed during the lifetime of the emperors whose bodies they were to house, often beginning in the second year of a reign. Such tombs were called *ch'u-ling* (tombs at the beginning [of a reign]) or *shou-ling* (long-life tombs). Nine of the eleven tombs of Former Han dynasts were situated north of the Wei River near the capital, Ch'ang-an; the other two were located south of it. Tombs of Later Han emperors were built near the capital at Lo-yang. Chinese imperial tombs always lay outside the capital, for the city was a place not of death but of life. Han tombs were surrounded by a rectangular wall with a gate in each side. The area inside the wall was called a *ling-yüan*, or tomb park. At the center of the park was a rectangular pyramid called the square center (*fang-chung*).[12] The recorded height of Former Han imperial mounds ranged from about 90 feet (12 *chang*) to somewhat more than 150 feet (20 *chang*) in one case.[13] The crest of these mounds was level, and upon them, or to the side, was built a "dwelling hall" (*ch'in-tien*), which contained clothing and other articles used by the deceased in daily life. At the dwelling hall, harem women were assigned to serve the spirit of the deceased as they had served him in real life: They arranged his bedding, prepared his bath water, and laid out his toilet articles all according to a precise schedule. The dwelling hall was thus an architectural and ritual analogue of the imperial palace. Here, daily sacrifices to the spirit of the deceased were also conducted. Located within a few hundred meters of the dwelling hall was a temple (*miao*) dedicated to the dead emperor, in which sacrifices were conducted twice a month; on these days the emperor's clothing was brought from the dwelling hall and paraded inside the temple. The temple was thus an analogue of the ancestral temple (*tsung-miao*) at the capital. During the Later Han the dwelling hall also became the focus of the bimonthly sacrifices previously performed at the temple.[14]

The building and maintenance of the tombs and their associated structures entailed an enormous expenditure of money and manpower. Of the total annual income of the Han, it was said, probably with exaggeration, that fully one-third was used for the imperial tombs.[15] In the cases of seven of the eleven Former Han tombs, counties (*hsien*) were established out of the tomb districts and inhabitants forcibly moved there to provide for their upkeep and protection. By the end of the Former Han these *hsien* had become extremely populous, sometimes numbering fifty or sixty thousand households. Those who had been moved to the tomb districts were not just commoners, they were also the wealthy and powerful, a way for the dynasty to "strengthen the trunk while weakening the branches," that is, to increase centralized power at the expense of entrenched local elites. Beginning with the Later Han, tomb districts were no longer employed.[16]

The largest and grandest of the Han tombs is the Mao-ling, burial place of Han Wu-ti, situated about 25 miles (40 kilometers) northwest of the capital of Shensi province, Sian. The earthen pyramidal mound is 153 feet (46.5 meters) high, 129.4 by 116.5 feet (39.5 by 35.5 meters) at the top, and 758 by 768 feet (231 by 234 meters) at the base. It was originally surrounded by a wall 1414 feet (430.87 meters) from east to west and 1361 feet (414.87 meters) from north to south. The site covers about 13.5 acres (54,054 square meters). Twenty-one satellite tombs of favored officials and imperial family members are scattered on the east, west, and north sides of the tumulus, of which five have been identified. The most famous of these is the tomb of the general Huo Ch'ü-ping (140–117 B.C.), whose stone animal sculptures, averaging about 5 feet (1.5 meters) in height, prefigure the much larger paired stone guardian sculptures facing one another along the "spirit road" (*shen-tao*) of the tombs of later ages.[17] Construction of the Mao-ling was begun in the second year of Wu-ti's reign (139 B.C.) and was finished fifty-three years later, at the time of his death. The tomb contents were sumptuous, reflecting the great length and enormous success of his rule.[18]

It was this very tendency toward extravagance in imperial burials that, from Han times onward, caused voices to be raised against the practice. Perhaps one of the best-known personal crusades against lavish imperial tombs was undertaken by the famous Former Han scholar-official, Liu Hsiang (79–8 B.C.). Emperor Ch'eng, whom Liu served, had begun construction of one tomb only to abandon work on it after several years and begin work on another. Liu condemned this waste in a long memorial filled with historical allusions, the major theme of which was that those rulers who spent vast resources in money and manpower on grandiose mausolea were doomed to failure.[19] In his memorial Liu recounted the story of the Han emperor Wen-ti (rg. 179–156 B.C.), who when visiting his tomb heaved a deep sigh, wondering how he might protect its contents from bandits. He speculated that if his coffin were to be cut from stone and properly sealed, it would be impregnable. Hearing this, his official Chang Shih-chih came forward to say: "If you were to make its contents desirable, although [your coffin] were solid as the Southern Mountains it would still be as if it had fissures. If you were to make none of its contents desirable, even if you did not use stone, what would there be to grieve about?" Liu greatly praised Chang's words, noting that Han Wen-ti had been enlightened by them, so that when he died a high burial mound was not raised. Liu ended his long memorial with the observation that when his own sovereign, Emperor Ch'eng, had first begun his reign, his policies had been frugal. Even his first tomb had been modest in scale. But construction of the second tomb had been costly beyond measure: Earth had been piled up as if it were a mountain, thousands of laborers had been assembled, and they had been worked oppressively. "If the dead have consciousness, when men's tombs are opened the harm would be great. If they have no consciousness, why bother with great expense?" he demanded. Emperor Ch'eng should therefore reduce the scale of his tomb, Liu respectfully suggested. Although the emperor was said to have been moved by Liu's words, he could not bring himself to change his policies.

Closer to the T'ang, the Sui philosopher Wang T'ung had also spoken out against excesses connected with interment. When asked by a disciple about the practice, Wang dourly replied: "The poor [merely] arranged the hands and feet; the rich prepared coffins. The mound area was not extensive nor did they use arable land. The ancients did not use death to injure the living, did not employ prodigality for [their burial] rites."[20] Such Confucian injunctions as those of Liu Hsiang and Wang T'ung naturally ran counter to the desires of most Chinese emperors to build impressive physical monuments to themselves or to their fathers, and to follow in the footsteps of other political ancestors who had similarly required appropriate symbolic vehicles by which to express extraordinary political achievements.

Although the contents of T'ang imperial tombs may in general have been less costly than those of Han burials, by early Five Dynasties (907–60) times almost all of them had been broken into and looted, testimony to the impressive treasure they had once contained.[21] Eighteen of the twenty T'ang emperors, all except the last two, were buried north of the Wei River in the vicinity of the T'ang capital, Ch'ang-an. T'ang imperial tombs were of two types: the artificial raised mound on a Ch'in-Han model and tombs which were situated atop natural mountains. Of the eighteen T'ang tombs near Ch'ang-an, only four were of the raised-mound type. These mounds were 50 or more feet high and were situated on plateaus ranging from about 1,640 to 2,625 feet (500–800 meters) above sea level. Mountain tombs varied in height between 3,940 and 5,250 feet (1,200–1,600 meters), but were always cut into the south face of the mountain.[22] The emperor, normally facing south in life, faced south in death as well.

The central focus of a T'ang imperial tomb was the funeral vault (ling-ch'in), a chamber where the emperor's remains reposed. The vault consisted of a main room (cheng-ch'in) and two side-rooms (hsiang) east and west. These structures were surrounded on the surface by a protective rectangular wall, at the four corners of which stood guard towers. Each side of the wall contained a gate. Inside the southern gate was usually an "offering hall" (hsien-tien, successor to the Han ch'in-tien), where sacrifices were periodically offered to the spirit of the deceased. The southern gate also opened onto the so-called imperial road (yü-tao), stretching southward from the vault for some distance, which was traversed at the time of interment. Often the first section of this road was punctuated by paired stone monumental sculptures of animals, birds, human figures, and ornamental pillars. This was the spirit road.[23]

Mountain tombs afforded certain advantages over artificially raised mounds: (1) Manpower expenditures could be reduced; (2) they were much more imposing; (3) the job of protecting their contents theoretically was made easier.[24] The T'ang did not adopt the Former Han practice of establishing special counties for the tomb districts, nor their coercive policy of moving large numbers of inhabitants there to provide for the upkeep and protection of the tombs. Instead, tomb families (*ling-hu*) were established to provide the usual maintenance services and also to perform daily and seasonal sacrifices at the tombs.[25]

The regulations for visits by emperors to the tombs of their fathers are contained in the *K'ai-yüan li*, a summary of which follows.[26] Two days before a visit, the impending ritual is announced at the ancestral temple, a detached palace is established about ten *li* from the tomb site, and a sacrifice consisting of a bull, a ram, and a pig is prepared. One day before, the emperor travels to the detached palace, where he begins his seclusion. Stations are marked out for the audience along the spirit road leading to the tomb and in front of the entrance to the offering hall compound, where the emperor's great canopy is placed. Before dawn on the day of the visit, yellow banners are arrayed around the hall, outside of which high-ranking spectators—officials of various ranks, imperial family members, and foreign dignitaries—take their assigned places according to rank. At dawn the emperor arrives on horseback wearing white mourning, dismounts at the small canopy located southwest of the tomb, and performs a series of double obeisances. He then remounts his horse, arriving at the great canopy in front of the offering hall. Dismounting, he is led through the southern gate of the complex as far as the southwest corner of the eastern stairway leading up to the offering hall. He mounts the stairs to stand in front of the spirit-thrones of his father and mother, where he performs double obeisances before making an offering of sacrificial meat. While this ritual is being performed, offerings are also made, below the eastern verandah (*lang*) of the hall, to the spirits of the other occupants of the tomb complex. The emperor then makes an offerings of wine to the spirits of his parents. A message to his parents, inscribed on jade tablets, is read, following which the emperor performs more double obeisances before their spirit-thrones. The ritual now concluded, the emperor is led back to the great canopy, where he mounts his horse for the short ride back to the detached palace.

KAO-TSU'S TOMB, THE HSIEN-LING

Kao-tsu made no preparations for a tomb during his own lifetime. But he did address himself to the question of the style of burial he desired. Once, while passing the tomb of the Ch'in founder, Shih-huang-ti, he commented negatively on the extravagance of raising high burial mounds. His attending official, Feng Lun (Te-i), agreed, observing that from the time of Ch'in and Han everyone from rulers down to commoners had tried to imitate the First Emperor's model. Moreover, the policy of filling the tombs with precious articles was also mistaken, since these tombs were always looted. Echoing the words of Liu Hsiang, Feng said: "If there is no consciousness after death, then expensive burials are a terrible waste; if the soul has consciousness and [the tomb] is broken into, how could it not be pained?" Upon hearing this, Kao-tsu pledged that from this time forward all burials from the emperor's on down would be carried out frugally.[27]

Since Kao-tsu had not begun construction of his own tomb during the period he was in power, T'ai-tsung may have felt that it was unfilial to begin one for him after his abdication, while he was still alive. Thus, it was only upon the T'ang founder's death following a long illness in the fifth month of 635 that T'ai-tsung ordered work begun on a tomb for his father on the model of that of the Han founder, Kao-tsu. The Hsien-ling, as it was named, was located some forty miles northeast of the T'ang capital. The architect Yen Li-te was placed in charge of the project.[28] Unfortunately, even though the model for the Hsien-ling was appropriate enough, given Kao-tsu's position as the founder of the dynasty, its scale and cost also exceeded his express wishes in the matter.

Because Kao-tsu's tomb had to be constructed rapidly, the tomb laborers were worked mercilessly. The formidable expense devoted to the project, along with the oppressive treatment accorded the workers, prompted a long and angry memorial from the director of the Imperial Library, Yü Shih-nan. Yü used illustration after illustration to drive home his point that when tombs were filled with treasure they were bound to be looted. Taking a leaf from Liu Hsiang's book, he repeated the story of Chang Shih-chih's warning to Han Wen-ti. He further observed that when the Red Eyebrows rebel band had brought down the Han usurper, Wang Mang, they had looted the richest of all the tombs of the Former Han, that of Wu-ti, carrying away treasure as if there were no end to it. Thus, the Han had oppressively taxed the people to pay for the contents of Wu-ti's tomb, only to have them fall into the hands of bandits! Wei Wen-ti (rg. 220–27), Yü approvingly pointed out, had adopted a policy of frugality for his own tomb. This policy was based on the examples of the legendary sage-kings of old as well as on the knowledge that all of the Han imperial tombs had been looted, from their jade suits with metallic threads down even to the imperial skeletons. "From ancient times to the present", Wen-ti observed, "there was never a dynasty that did not perish nor a tomb that was not opened." Yü's final point concerned the raising of a burial mound. Even if T'ai-tsung did not bury rare and valuable articles in his father's tomb yet raised a high mound, people of later ages would surely think that precious objects were stored inside and would loot it. He thus advised T'ai-tsung to adopt the Chou method, described in the *Po Hu T'ung*, of erecting mounds only twenty-four feet high and installing grave articles of clay and wood. Such would be an intelligent policy indeed![29] When the emperor did not immediately respond to his memorial, Yü dashed off another, virtually an addendum to the first. In it he observed that the Han tombs had taken many years to complete, but that now in the space of months the T'ang was completing a monument of comparable size. Moreover, the Han (with their tomb districts) had more manpower at their disposal to devote to work on the tombs than had the T'ang. These two factors had served greatly to overwork the people.[30]

T'ai-tsung handed Yü's memorials over to his officials, ordering them to devise a proper policy to follow. In the end, Fang Hsüan-ling and others suggested a compromise: a burial mound lower than that of Han Kao-tsu but higher than Yü Shih-nan's proposed twenty-four feet. They suggested taking the six-*chang* tumulus of Han Kuang-wu-ti as a model.[31] T'ai-tsung responded with a pledge that he would employ great economy for his father's tomb.[32] This he appears to have done. The Hsien-ling is about 69 feet (21 meters) high and rectangular at the base, 492 by 394 feet (150 by 120 meters).[33] It was therefore smaller than the tomb of Han Kao-tsu, which is about 90 feet high in a rectangle roughly 554 by 485 feet.[34] The entire site of the Hsien-ling is about 6.2 miles in circumference, compared to the 37-mile (60-kilometer) circumference of T'ai-tsung's tomb, the Chao-ling.[35] The decoration seems also to have been relatively unpretentious by later T'ang standards: A pair of stone tigers situated on the spirit road south of the tomb is only seven feet high. But columns further south are over thirty feet in height, suggesting that such modesty in ornamentation did not go to the extreme. Kao-tsu was buried in the Hsien-ling on the twenty-seventh day of the tenth month (December 12), 635.[36] His wife's remains were at this time transferred from her own temporary tomb to his. It was just a little over five months from Kao-tsu's death to his interment; it may well be that upon his burial some work had yet to be completed on his tomb. In the following year imperial permission was granted for military and civil officials who had played key roles in the founding of the dynasty and close relatives of Kao-tsu to be buried along with him at the Hsien-ling. According to the edict, on the day an official died his death was to be announced at court. Land for a tomb at the Hsien-ling and a special coffin were thereupon to be provided him.[37] Eventually, according to the records, some twenty-five accompanying burials were made.[38] However, by 1980 archaeologists had discovered a total of sixty-seven burial mounds in the vicinity of the Hsien-ling.[39]

Not until the first day of the first month of 639 did T'ai-tsung pay his personal respects at his father's tomb. Descending from his palanquin (not a horse, as in the *K'ai-yüan li* regulations), he entered the compound of the offering hall on foot. The hall had been completely encircled the previous day by banners of yellow. At the entranceway the emperor wept profusely and made a double obeisance. He then entered the hall, where he personally attended to the sacrificial offerings of meat and wine. He also examined the clothing and objects personally used by Kao-tsu and his mother the empress, which were stored there. So moved was he, it is said, that he fell prostrate before them.[40] Before returning to Ch'ang-an, T'ai-tsung took advantage of the occasion to grant pardons to the residents of the county in which the Hsien-ling was situated and to remit them one year's *tsu* tax. Presents were distributed to various enumerated classes of people. Finally, those charged with the protection and management of the tomb were promoted one honorary grade.[41]

A story, perhaps apocryphal, provides a touching finale to T'ai-tsung's visit to his father's tomb. The night before the ceremony a great storm had blown in, dumping much rain and snow on the site. When T'ai-tsung had entered the courtyard of the offering hall, and he and those assembled had begun to wail loudly, the snow increased in intensity and the wind grew even more violent. Suddenly a great dark cloud rose from atop the burial mound and darkness fell over everything. Upon completing the sacrifices T'ai-tsung had to walk back to his palanquin through several hundred feet of mud. Now, the wind subsided, the snow stopped, and the sky cleared. All those who had witnessed the event believed that the sudden improvement in the weather occurred because the emperor had demonstrated such sincere feelings of filial piety.[42]

T'AI-TSUNG'S TOMB, THE CHAO-LING

T'ai-tsung's tomb, the Chao-ling, is located atop Chiu-tsung Mountain, some thirty-seven miles northwest of Ch'ang-an and fifteen miles northeast of the modern prefectural capital of Li-ch'uan.[43] The mountain, 3,564 feet (1,188 meters) above sea level, towers majestically over the surrounding plain, a fitting place of repose for an extraordinarily successful ruler.

The architect of the site was again Yen Li-te, designer of Kao-tsu's tomb.[44] The tomb consists not just of T'ai-tsung's funeral vault, but a complex of 167 known satellite tombs situated both on the mountain and spread out on the plain below it; the total number may actually be around two hundred. The site occupies an astounding 45,000 acres (300,000 *mou*), enough to supply three thousand peasants with land under the T'ang equal field system, or six thousand, figuring that farmers in the crowded capital region were only receiving about one-half the normal allotment of one hundred *mou*. It was largest tomb in all of Chinese history, dwarfing anything that came before or would come after, and set the pattern for the other T'ang mountain tombs. T'ai-tsung was interred there on the eighteenth day of the eighth month (September 29), 649.

Work on the site had actually begun many years earlier, in 636, following the death of T'ai-tsung's consort, the Wen-te Empress, who was the first to be buried on Chiu-tsung Mountain. At the time, T'ai-tsung personally wrote a eulogy for his beloved wife, which was inscribed on stone. In the text the emperor praised her great frugality and also her last wish that she be given a modest burial. He recorded her exact words: "The desire of thieves is only to obtain valuables. If there are no valuables, what can they obtain?" T'ai-tsung paid lip service to her view. Since rulers consider the whole empire their property (*t'ien-hsia wei chia*), he said, surely it was not merely by placing articles in tombs that they became imperial possessions. Because Chiu-tsung Mountain comprised the empress's tomb, he maintained, the work of cutting the stone had only involved some hundred or so men, and was therefore completed in a short time. The simple grave furniture made of clay and wood would not entice robbers. The empress's burial was thus a model that could be passed down to all their descendants.[45] In this manner, he threw the best possible light on the undertaking.

The following year, T'ai-tsung issued an edict publicly confirming Chiu-tsung Mountain as the site of his own tomb.[46] The emperor claimed he was afraid that after his death his descendants would give him an elaborate burial. By selecting a mountain for his tomb (and thus eliminating the need to pile up a large earthen mound), his burial would be economical, he maintained. He attributed the practice to ancient times: "The ancients relied on the mountains for their tombs. That truly was advantageous." He specified that only one coffin was to be employed for his remains, and that wooden horses, plaster carriages, and the like were to be used, all in conformance with the ancient idea that the grave furniture was not to consist of articles used in real life.[47] Citing earlier precedents, he ordered that provision was also to be made for the burial at the site of loyal officials, close relatives, or anyone who had made an extraordinary contribution to the age, as a way of rewarding them. They were to be granted a plot of land as well as a coffin, and at the time of their interment nothing was to be lacking in the proper observance of the funeral rites. Later, the invitation was extended to cover the descendants of meritorious officials, who, if they desired, might be buried along with their eminent ancestors.[48] Wives could be buried with their husbands, but it appears that special imperial permission had to be obtained.[49]

T'ai-tsung's funeral vault was chiseled out of stone to make it as impregnable as possible. Indeed, a tenth-century grave robber found it the most formidable of all the T'ang imperial tombs.[50] On the east and west sides of the vault two side-chambers were hollowed out to house stone boxes filled with treasure. The surface structures surrounding T'ai-tsung's vault were laid out on a north-south axis. To the north was a prayer altar (chi-t'an), measuring 175.5 feet (53.5 meters) from east to west and 284 feet (86.5 meters) from north to south. The prayer altar is a special feature of the Chao-ling not found at the other T'ang imperial tombs. Because the topography of Chiu-tsung Mountain forced the architects to locate the offering hall some distance from the funeral vault, the prayer altar appears to have replaced the offering hall as the site of the main sacrificial rites.[51] Beyond the prayer altar was the northern or Ssu-ma (also called Hsüan-wu) Gate. Inside the gate were stone statues of fourteen "barbarian" chieftains who had submitted to T'ang overlordship during T'ai-tsung's reign.[52] They were placed there at T'ai-tsung's express order, to follow, he claimed, the "admirable practice of former emperors," but actually in imitation of the Turkish burial custom of placing at the tomb statues of the slain enemies of the deceased.[53] Also inside this gate were bas-reliefs of six of the emperor's favorite horses.[54] The concentration of stone monuments to the north of the funeral vault is unique to the Chao-ling, another result of its peculiar topography.[55] Directly to the south of T'ai-tsung's funeral vault was the offering hall, and beyond this building was the southern gate, the Gate of the Vermilion Bird (chu-ch'iao men). A reconstruction of the site shows the offering hall approached by a triple staircase similar to those now seen at the Forbidden City in Beijing.[56]

About 1,300 feet (400 meters) to the southwest of the tomb wall was the largest complex of surface structures at the site, stretching 778 feet (237 meters) from east to west and 1,096 feet (334 meters) from north to south;

the foundations of its walls were 11.5 feet (3.5 meters) thick. The complex was known in T'ang times as the imperial city (*huang-ch'eng*); it was also called the nether palace (*hsia-kung*). It was the place where T'ai-tsung's spirit was supposed to eat, drink, and live daily life. The imperial city probably housed officials responsible for maintenance of the tomb, and also harem women whose duty it was to serve the dead emperor's spirit.[57] Thus, in T'ang times, unlike the Han, the place where sacrificial offerings were made to the tomb spirit was completely separated from the place where it was supposed to live its daily life. Not much of these buildings remains today, but a tile "owl's tail" acroterion, a decorative element curving inward at either end of the main ridge of the roof of T'ang buildings, which was excavated in 1964 at the site of the offering hall, is almost 5 feet (1.5 meters) tall and weighs 330 pounds (150 kilograms), giving some idea of the impressive scale of construction.[58]

In a status-conscious society like that of the T'ang, differences could be manifested among the satellite tombs by their size and shape, the number, size, and type of associated stone decorations, and the funerary articles deposited in them.[59] Satellite tombs at the Chao-ling took various forms. Some were situated atop their own breast-shaped peaks, which were lower than Chiu-tsung Mountain but still impressive in height. Others were made of heaped-up earth in various forms: square pyramids, with earthen towers at the four corners; "mountain" tumuli, consisting of a central peak flanked by two lower, flatter mounds; or single "round awl" mounds, the most typical example. At one grave no mound at all appears to have been raised. Large stone animal and human sculptures in various configurations were often associated with the burials. Each tomb was marked by a tall, rectangular stone stele (*pei*), inscribed with calligraphy by some of the finest masters of the age, such as Ou-yang Hsün and Ch'u Sui-liang.[60]

The pattern of burial at the Chao-ling was generally from north to south, with northern burials being earlier and southern burials later. Status was thus reflected more by whether a tomb had its own mountain or by the height and shape of its artificial mound than by how close it was to T'ai-tsung's funeral vault. At the Chao-ling, status was less a function of blood relationship or social position than of political power or imperial favor. For example, high ministers often had tumuli greater in height than those of members of the imperial family. The eminent minister, Wei Cheng, was buried on his own peak 2,953 feet (900 meters) above sea level, a sign of his special esteem in the emperor's eyes.[61] One imperial daughter, the Hsin-ch'eng Princess, for reasons unknown, was also accorded this distinction. Her mountain is 3,281 feet (1,000 meters) tall, surpassing, in this respect, the burial of all her brothers. According to the T'ang statutes, the mounds of the highest-ranking officials were to be between three and four *chang* tall.[62] But it is apparent that these regulations were ignored in certain cases. The central peak of the "mountain" tumulus of the great T'ang general Li Chi is about 66 feet (20 meters) tall, or almost seven *chang* by T'ang reckoning. According to these same regulations, the tombs of civil and military officials were to be separately arrayed east and west below T'ai-tsung's tomb. But this was not followed in practice, and much mixing and overlapping of statuses is evident.[63] Excavated satellite tombs at the Chao-ling have yielded, among other things, three-color pottery vessels and human and animal figurines, articles of clothing, as well as some fascinating murals of life among the ruling elite. Archaeologists have yet to open T'ai-tsung's tomb.

It should be apparent by now that although T'ai-tsung portrayed the selection of a mountain for his tomb as a revival of an ancient Chinese tradition, the Chao-ling was actually a near-revolutionary development in Chinese imperial mausolea that provided a model for the rest of the T'ang as well as for other imperial ages, most notably the Ming dynasty. Far greater in conception than any previous imperial burial, the Chao-ling astonishes the viewer by the magnificence of Chiu-tsung Mountain, its monumental scale, and the sheer abundance of its satellite tombs. T'ai-tsung's selection of the site was carefully calculated to impress not only posterity but also contemporary men. When emperors visited the tombs of their fathers, their retinues included hundreds of court and diplomatic personnel, and thousands of military retainers, a captive audience for whatever magic these grandiose constructions might exert over them. Moreover, in clear weather Chiu-tsung Mountain was visible from Ch'ang-an.[64] It therefore served as a daily reminder to all the inhabitants of the capital region of T'ai-tsung's relationship to other great emperors of the past who had erected tumuli for themselves on the plains north of the capital. In forging a mental link between the Chao-ling and the enduring monuments of China's other great dynasts—his political ancestors—T'ai-tsung gained legitimation through association. If he had exceeded the norms of his political ancestors in terms of the scale of his tomb, perhaps his subjects might reason that this was because he had also surpassed their heroic deeds.

Yet T'ai-tsung's audacity put him at risk. Poor handling of imperial burials might work not to legitimate a regime but to alienate its subjects. This had been amply demonstrated in the case of Ch'in Shih-huang-ti and, much more recently, in the case of his own father's tomb. Although he had claimed that using a mountain for his tomb would be economical, thus bowing to the prevailing Confucian notion of moderation and frugality, was anyone really fooled by this? The conclusion must be reached from the number and scale of the surface buildings surrounding the emperor's vault, and the roads and other supporting infrastructure which were built on the mountain to permit its excavation, that the Chao-ling was an expensive undertaking, indeed. Moreover, the Chao-ling, which so dwarfed the Hsien-ling, was the ultimate symbol of T'ai-tsung's lack of filial piety: He had reserved the best not for his father but for himself and his consort. Soon after the empress's burial on Chiu-tsung Mountain, T'ai-tsung built a lookout tower in the imperial park from which to view her tomb. One day he invited his counselor Wei Cheng to accompany him in ascending the tower. The crusty minister could not resist criticizing his prince for lavishing more attention—both material and emotional—on the memory of his wife and on his own final resting place than on his father. Upon reaching the top of the tower, Wei Cheng pretended that he could not see the Chao-ling because of weak eyesight. In exasperation, the emperor finally pointed out the imposing tomb to him. At this point, Wei Cheng said: "I thought Your Majesty was looking at the Hsien-ling. If that is the Chao-ling, I certainly can see it!" The implication was, of course, that the Hsien-ling should have been the greater of the two tombs. Upon hearing his words, T'ai-tsung shed tears, and had the lookout tower destroyed.[65]

Surprisingly, however, there was no outburst of criticism at court concerning the Chao-ling the way there had been over the construction of the much more modest Hsien-ling. For one thing, the Chao-ling was built over a period of more than ten years. The work was not rushed and, presumably, the gangs of laborers were not unduly oppressed. For another, the lure of a burial at the Chao-ling accompanying that of the emperor, and of sharing in his glory, must have served to blunt any outrage that may have been generated among many court officials. Such a lure was made even more tempting by the fact that at the Chao-ling the accompanying tombs of officials were permitted to have higher burial mounds than those set by law in normal circumstances.[66] Such a reward would endure down the ages: like T'ai-tsung, his meritorious officials would also be permanently impressed on the memory of posterity. Moreover, not only would officials be immortalized in this way, but their descendants as well. It was a plum greatly to be sought after, and probably none were willing to undermine their resting place near the Son of Heaven by criticizing the Chao-ling.

On the first day of 655 Kao-tsung paid a personal visit to the Chao-ling, observing substantially the same sacrificial rites to his father that T'ai-tsung had observed exactly sixteen years earlier to Kao-tsu. This time, however, Kao-tsung shared the important responsibility of handling the sacrificial meat dishes and wine vessels with some of the great men of the age—eminent statesmen like Chang-sun Wu-chi and Li Chi, three princes of the blood, and the commander of an imperial guard.[67] The significant participation of these figures in the ceremonies symbolized the collective nature of the Chao-ling. The tomb complex commemorated not just the emperor and his family but all those who had contributed in some special way to the age, even those foreign chieftains who had had the wisdom to declare themselves vassals of the T'ang. It was a recognition that the Chao-ling was as much a political space as an imperial necropolis, designed not merely to provide for the dead but also to impress and seduce the living.

KAO-TSUNG'S TOMB, THE CH'IEN-LING

Like T'ai-tsung's tomb, that of Kao-tsung also employed a mountain to house the imperial remains. Kao-tsung's final resting place, called the Ch'ien-ling, is situated atop Liang-shan, 3,438 feet (1,047.9 meters) above sea level. Liang-shan was located more than 50 miles (85 kilometers) northwest of T'ang Ch'ang-an, and is 6 kilometers north of the modern administrative capital of Ch'ien county in southern Shensi province. The Ch'ien-ling is a joint tomb: Interred there is not only the third T'ang emperor but also his consort, Empress Wu, who usurped power, founded her own regime, and ruled as "emperor" of the Chou dynasty between 690 and 705. Kao-tsung was buried at the Ch'ien-ling on the tenth day of the eighth month (September 25), 684, having died the twelfth month of the previous year.[68] His consort's remains, after some heated debate among the T'ang courtiers, joined his in the fifth month of 705.[69] The Ch'ien-ling is the best-preserved and most beautiful of the eighteen T'ang imperial tombs, and, largely because of the spectacular stone sculptures comprising its spirit road and the restored wall-paintings of some of its satellite tombs, has become one of China's major tourist attractions.[70]

Liang-shan is actually composed of three peaks. The highest one, of "round awl" shape, is in the north; its southern flank is the site of the imperial mausoleum proper. The pair of lower hills to the south form a kind of natural gateway to the mausoleum; atop their crests tall earthen towers were built almost 50 feet (15 meters) tall. The mausoleum was originally surrounded by a double wall 4,757 by 5,190 feet (1,450 by 1,582 meters), with the usual four gates. Outside each of the gates was a pair of large stone lions. The spirit road extended about a kilometer from the two southern hills to the south gate of the mausoleum, the Gate of the Vermilion Bird.[71] It has been called "perhaps the largest and most splendid of its kind."[72] Enumerating from south to north, the stone monuments of the spirit road consist of one pair each of octagonal stone pillars, winged horses, and vermilion birds (i.e., ostriches, these in bas-relief), as well as five pairs of horses and ten pairs of generals in armor each holding a sword in their two hands. These beautifully wrought forms, ranging from about 6 to 15 feet high for the animals and human sculptures and more than 25 feet high in the case of the octagonal pillars, may be compared with those of the spirit road leading to the thirteen Ming tombs.[73] Slightly to the left and right of the northern section of the spirit road lie the "Stele Narrating the Wise Deeds (of Emperor Kao-tsung)" (*Shu sheng chi pei*) and the "Stele with No Inscription" (*Wu-tzu pei*), the latter symbolizing that words alone were insufficient to praise Kao-tsung's achievements, both of which date from the time of Empress Wu. North of these originally stood sixty-one stone sculptures representing "barbarian" chieftains who had attended Kao-tsung's funeral ceremony; they were erected in honor of her husband by Empress Wu. Today they are either partially or completely headless. Just inside the Gate of the Vermilion Bird there originally stood a shrine containing the portraits of sixty great officials of the age.[74] In T'ang times buildings containing three hundred and seventy-eight rooms were constructed at the site. These were restored during the Chin dynasty in 1135, but have since disappeared. Compared to the Chao-ling, the satellite tombs of the Ch'ien-ling are relatively few in number. According to written accounts, there were seventeen, divided about evenly between royal relatives and eminent officials.[75] However, up to the present twenty-three associated burials have actually been identified at the Ch'ien-ling and more may well be discovered in the future.[76] Since 1960 five of these tombs have been opened.[77]

At the time of his death, it is said that Kao-tsung made the formulaic but by now entirely hollow request that he be given a "frugal" burial in accordance with the "T'ang practice regarding tombs."[78] It is clear, however, that notions of what was appropriate regarding imperial mausolea had swelled mightily following T'ai-tsung' example, and it may have been difficult for his successors to return to the more modest scale of the Hsien-ling. Although he did not attempt entirely to model his own tomb on the Chao-ling, Kao-tsung (as well as, perhaps, his co-ruler, Empress Wu) was clearly influenced by it. Second only to the Chao-ling in scale among T'ang tombs (its circumference being 40 kilometers to the Chao-ling's 60),[79] it was a grandiose conception, worthy of a son of T'ai-tsung. Its significant use of accompanying burials and the presence of a temple dedicated to the great statesmen of the age again proclaimed it a political as well as sacred space. Beyond its calculated celebration of officialdom, the Ch'ien-ling's magnificent spirit road, surface structures, and overall design were intended to inspire awe and compel admiration among contemporaries as well as posterity. Like the other T'ang imperial tombs, the Ch'ien-ling mausoleum was a permanent monument, contrasting starkly with the more evanescent secular forms of Chinese architecture constructed with wood and tile. Its construction perpetuated the traditions of both the lineal and political ancestors of the T'ang, yet in some respects, most notably its spirit road, it exceeded them all.

THE CULT OF THE POLITICAL FAMILY

The practice of accompanying burials (*p'ei-ling*) at imperial tombs can be traced back in Chinese literature to a passage in the *Chou-li*, which describes the interment of rulers in the company of their relatives, feudal lords, great statesmen, and meritorious officials.[80] During the Former Han, emperors sometimes granted plots of land located inside the park of their tombs to their favorite ministers or generals.[81] This practice persisted to some extent during the post-Han period as well.[82]

At the beginning of the T'ang, however, a veritable explosion of accompanying burials appears to have taken place: perhaps some sixty-seven at Kao-tsu's tomb, somewhere around two hundred at T'ai-tsung's, and twenty-three or more at the joint tomb of Kao-tsung and Empress Wu. Burials at the imperial mausolea were routinely granted not only to imperial family members but to meritorious ministers and successful generals, their descendants, and even, by special permission, their wives. An accompanying burial was a much-coveted honor, ardently sought after by courtiers to help ensure their posthumous reputations and the con-

tinued prominence of their families. It was made even more alluring by the
knowledge that the spirits of all those buried at the imperial tombs, not
just those of the emperor and his consort, would receive sacrificial offerings there on a periodic basis. Accompanying burials were prestige symbols, manipulated, as Etzioni would say, as part of the normative power of
rulers, designed to generate enhanced support for the regime among
various segments of the elite. Indeed, at the Chao-ling, there are more
meritorious officials represented among the accompanying burials than
imperial family members.[83] Early T'ang emperors thus made extraordinary use of this power. By so doing, they expanded the concept of "family"
beyond mere sanguinary or marriage ties, creating a far more inclusive,
politically oriented collectivity, which, for lack of a better term, I shall call
the "political family." Membership in the political family was based on
the political power and prestige a member had possessed while alive, and
also on the imperial favor he had enjoyed. Judging by what we know
about T'ai-tsung's Chao-ling, relative standing in the political family was
manifested by the size, shape, and siting of an individual's grave. The
imperial tomb complexes can thus be conceived of as three-dimensional
"political maps" of the early T'ang courts. In such a setting, a minister like
Wei Cheng, a general like Li Chi, or an imperial daughter like the Hsin-
ch'eng Princess might surpass others in relative status.

The political family was a symbolic vehicle designed to emphasize the
ties that bound the imperial house to other elite families in the state, and
vice versa, rather than the differences that separated them. It was a demonstration, in the physical realm of death, that political power was not the
monopoly of one house or one ruler only but was shared to a significant
degree with others. Its ground of being was not *t'ien-hsia wei chia* but
rather *t'ien-hsia wei kung*. The early T'ang imperial tomb complexes were
nothing less than spectacular material expressions of this latter doctrine.

CHAPTER 8

The Imperial Tour of Inspection

Now he is making a tour through the States, May Heaven accept him as
its Son!

Shih-ching

HERETOFORE, ALL THE IMPERIAL RITUALS WE HAVE DISCUSSED TOOK PLACE
inside the imperial capital or in its immediate environs. But emperors
could roam far from their palaces in the performance of important ceremonies of state. One of these was an ancient rite known as *hsün-shou*,
which we translate as tour of inspection.[1] According to one widely
accepted interpretation, *hsün* means "to follow a road," and *shou* means
"to shepherd." Thus, on behalf of Heaven, the king goes along the roads
to guard and shepherd his people. His personal performance of the task of
inspection is the highest expression of his care and esteem for the masses.[2]
The tour of inspection may also have had important political functions.
First, it seems to have been a means whereby a new king tested the acceptance of his sovereignty throughout the land, and his acknowledgment as
ruler by Heaven, the spirits, and all the people.[3] Second, it also appears to
have been designed as a technique of royal control over feudal domains.[4]
On his tours of inspection the king met in audience with his feudal lords,
examined their administration, and held them accountable for their
administrative performance. He punished those who were remiss and
rewarded those who had governed well.[5]

Even in imperial times, after China had been unified under a single
monarch, the rite of *hsün-shou* continued to be a useful political tool. On
tours of inspection, emperors who lived in relative political isolation could
gauge firsthand the quality of local government and popular sentiments
toward the dynasty. By personally visiting outlying areas they demonstrated a tender, Confucian concern for the masses. Inquiring into govern-

ment, they might ameliorate the most intolerable of local economic or social ills. Traveling with great numbers of courtiers and military escorts, they could capitalize on resplendent demonstrations of power to persuade local dissidents of the folly of challenging central control. Old personal contacts with members of local elites might be renewed and new loyalties forged. Emperors routinely used the occasion of circuits of their empire to distribute rewards, remit taxes, and reduce sentences for crimes, all measures designed to win political support among the populace. Since the *hsün-shou* was regarded as having been created by the sage-rulers of ancient China, emperors who carried out such tours were seen as part of an age-old tradition, conformance to which helped to justify their exercise of authority in the eyes of the people.[6]

The *Book of Poetry*, *Record of Rites*, *Rites of Chou*, *Tso-chuan*, and many other early sources all speak of the tour of inspection, if in a somewhat idealized manner. In the *Book of History* we read:

> In the second month of the year, [Shun] made a tour of inspection [*hsün-shou*] eastwards, as far as Mount T'ai, where he presented a burnt-offering to Heaven, and sacrificed in order to the hills and rivers. Thereafter, he gave audience to the nobles of the East, putting in accord their seasons and months, and rectifying the days; he made uniform the standard tubes, the measures of length and of capacity, and the steelyards; he regulated the five [classes of] ceremonies.... In the fifth month, he made a similar tour to the south, as far as the southern mountain, observing the same ceremonies as at T'ai. In the same way, in the eighth month, he travelled westwards, as far as the western mountain; and in the eleventh month he travelled northwards, as far as the northern mountain. When he returned [to the capital], he went to the [temple of the] Cultivated ancestor, and offered a single bullock. In five years there was one tour of inspection, and four appearances of the nobles at court.[7]

According to this account, the culture-hero Shun embarked on almost a year-long tour of inspection. Beginning with the east and following the route of the sun, he visited the four "sacred" mountains of T'ai, Heng, Hua, and Heng (a different Chinese character than the first Heng) consecutively, before returning to his capital to announce the completion of his circuit with a sacrifice at the ancestral temple. At each of his halting places he performed a sacrifice to Heaven by burning an animal victim on a large woodpile.[8] Then he conducted an audience for his nobles, corrected their calendars, standardized their musical scales, weights, and measures, and regulated their ritual ceremonial. Because travel was difficult and his tasks onerous, Shun decreed that tours of inspection were to be carried out only once every five years.

The sacred destinations and religious content of the ancient tours of inspection lead us to compare them with the religious pilgrimage, an enduring institution in both East and West. In their study of pilgrimage as a liminoid phenomenon, Victor and Edith Turner propose that pilgrimages possess some of the same attributes as liminal phases in rites of passage. In the tour of inspection we can observe some correspondences with the pilgrimage as characterized by the Turners: The ruler is released from mundane structure; the rigors of travel allow a greater homogenization of status among ruler and members of his entourage—such as reflected in costume and travel conveyance—than is normally the case; there is time for him to reflect on the meaning contained in the basic religious and cultural values of society; he moves from a mundane center to a sacred periphery, which suddenly and temporarily becomes a spiritual center to him, and so forth. The Turners view the pilgrim as a kind of initiate, who, traversing a mystical path, is entering into a new and deeper level of existence than he knew in his normal, everyday life.[9]

Two commentaries on a passage about the *hsün-shou* contained in the *Mencius* further clarify the rite as traditional Chinese understood it, especially its political dimension. The early T'ang commentator K'ung Ying-ta observes that the ancient kings were too busy always to think about their far-off subjects. Their fedual nobles sometimes took advantage of their power to oppress the weak or to invade the territories of others, but the kings might not hear of the matter because it was kept concealed from them. Thus, the kings developed the tour of inspection (presumably to ascertain local conditions and thus to deter popular rebellion or the aggrandizement of power by the fedual lords).[10] Lü Tsu-ch'ien of the Sung dynasty sees the *hsün-shou* as a political instrument designed to reinvigorate sentiments of loyalty among the people and to improve government. The ancient sage-kings made circuits of their realms, he says, because after a long period of time people tended to become alienated and local government to grow remiss. With the stimulative properties of tours of inspection, the people's loyalty and the quality of government might be "continually renewed" (*hsin-hsin pu i*).[11] Thus, Lü sees the tour of inspection in modern terms, as a means by which monarchs rejuvenated their political support among the people, support that was ever in danger of atrophying. The element of "inspection" was therefore only secondary to the primary aim of shoring up flagging loyalties or establishing them anew.

From Ch'in times onward emperors periodically went out on tour, but these are not always identified in the sources as true *hsün-shou*.[12] The "Monograph on Suburban Sacrifices" (*Chiao-ssu chih*) of the *History of the Former Han Dynasty* records that in the third year of his reign Ch'in Shih-huang-ti made a *hsün-shou* eastward, on his way to T'ai-shan.[13] The same history records that in 134 B.C. Emperor Wu of the Han traveled to Yung and there performed the suburban sacrifices at the five altars, but the trip is not called a *hsün-shou*.[14] Only in 110 B.C. did Wu-ti apparently first make a regular tour of inspection of his realm in conjunction with his performance of the Feng and Shan rites at T'ai-shan.[15] On the other hand, in A.D. 14 the usurper Wang Mang made elaborate plans for carrying out a *hsün-shou* of his domains before being persuaded by his courtiers to drop the plan because it would have been too taxing of his energies.[16] For the Later Han period, records of *hsün-shou* become more common. Whether this is because instances of the practice occurred more regularly, because the sources recorded them more routinely, or merely because the historians broadened the term to include other forms of imperial travel, is not clear.[17] During the two Han dynasties and the Period of Disunion emperors carrying out tours of inspection sometimes made inquiries concerning the aged and infirm, distributed presents, and remitted taxes for specified periods in the districts through which they passed.[18] Except for such epic figures as Ch'in Shih-huang-ti and Han Wu-ti, emperors were rather "un-ambitious in their travels" and their tours were limited in territorial scope.[19]

In a period closer to the T'ang, Sui Yang-ti appears to have been a particularly peripatetic ruler.[20] On his frequent travels across his realm it is said that he was often accompanied by retinues of more than one hundred thousand men.[21] According to the Sui regulations, when an emperor was personally leading troops in battle or conducting a tour of inspection, he would first offer a special *lei* sacrifice to Shang-ti and then sacrifice both at the altar of earth (*she*) and at the ancestral temple. When he returned from his travels he would again carry out the identical ritual.[22] The practice was based on the regulations contained in the *Record of Rites*.[23]

Sources for the T'ang, like those for other periods, do not clearly discriminate between *hsün-shou* and other types of imperial travel. The tours of the T'ang founder at any rate, were more limited in extent than those of his immediate predecessor, a function of his advanced age and also the necessity of limiting his travels only to those areas that had been pacified and made safe by T'ang forces. In the tenth month of 619 Kao-tsu visited Hua-yin, located northeast of Ch'ang-an, in modern Shansi province. There he pardoned military deserters from their crimes. Later in the same month he visited Hua Mountain, northwest of the capital, where, on a *chia-tzu* day, he sacrificed to the mountain god.[24] In the first month of the following year, the emperor traveled to P'u-chou, east of the capital, and ordered a sacrifice performed at the temple dedicated to the culture-hero Shun.[25] The sacrifice takes on added significance given the role of the Yao-Shun myth in Kao-tsu's accession rites and the fact that the emperor made the journey to P'u-chou just as soon as it had been liberated by T'ang forces from the grip of the rebel Liu Wu-chou. In the fourth month Kao-tsu once again sacrificed at Hua-shan.[26] Although he made other excursions from the imperial palace, these were largely in the immediate capital region and of short duration.[27]

The first *hsün-shou* of T'ai-tsung's reign, as classified by the Ch'ing scholar Ch'in Hui-t'ien, began in the ninth month of 630.[28] On the seventeenth day of this month T'ai-tsung arrived in Lung-chou, to the northwest of the T'ang capital, in modern Shensi province, where he prohibited the grazing of animals on the graves of ancient rulers, eminent officials, and other notables. On the first day of the following month he issued a general amnesty for Lung-chou and a nearby prefecture, and remitted their *tsu* tax for that year. He also reduced criminal penalties imposed on Hsien-yang, Shih-p'ing, and Wu-kung counties, all located in the general capital region. Later in the month he remitted the current year's *tsu* tax for Wu-kung. He returned to the capital early in the eleventh month.[29] When T'ai-tsung traveled to Lo-yang and through its surrounding region in 637 and 638, he bestowed similar dispensations on the fortunate districts he visited.[30] On a second trip to Lo-yang in 641, T'ai-tsung decreed that all those troops in his retinue whose families were poor or whose parents were old might return to their homes to care for them, and he feasted representatives of the aged of Lo-yang and of families in the region bearing the imperial surname. The common people were also T'ai-tsung's beneficiaries when, in a fit of fury over the siting of the Hsiang-ch'eng Palace to the southwest of Lo-yang, he ordered the palace razed and its materials distributed among the local populace. The emperor returned to Ch'ang-an at the end of 642.[31] Again in Lo-yang in 644, on his way to wage war against Korea, the emperor reduced the sentences of convicted criminals

and appointed emissaries to visit four prefectures to inquire after the welfare of the aged. He himself personally feasted one hundred and ninety old
people at the imperial palace and distributed gifts to them according to
their station.[32] On a visit to two prefectures in western Shensi and eastern
Kansu provinces in 646, T'ai-tsung distributed grain and silk to the elder-
ly, widowers, widows, orphans, and the childless.[33]

Kao-tsung practiced much the same policies as his two predecessors
while touring his realm: selectively remitting taxes; reducing penal sentences or pardoning crimes outright; granting grain and silk to the disadvantaged; making personal calls on the very aged; appointing envoys to
inquire about local conditions; and so forth.[34] In addition, he took special
precautions not to overburden the regions hosting his massive entourages.
When journeying to Lo-yang in 657, he decreed that local preparations
were to be made with economy and that the roads were not to be specially
repaired in his honor.[35] In 660, on a trip from Lo-yang to central Shansi
province, he called on the prefectures and counties through which he
passed to observe frugality in making preparations for his arrival.[36]
When preparing for a journey from Ch'ang-an to Lo-yang in 670, he
ordered that imperial needs that arose en route were to be furnished by
official sources and that no burdens were to be placed on the local populace.
Construction of bridges, way-stations, and the like were to be kept to a
minimum. People were not recklessly to present him with gifts.[37]

The excesses local officials were nevertheless capable of in preparing
for the emperor's visit—and the havoc they sometimes wreaked on the
people—is well illustrated by the following story. In 679 Kao-tsung was
scheduled to visit Ping prefecture, near T'ai-yüan in modern Shansi province. The road on which the emperor was to travel was situated close to a
shrine dedicated to a deity known as the Jealous Female (*Tu-nü*), whose
wrath was easily incurred. Thus, the administrator-in-chief (*ch'ang-shih*) of
the prefecture sent out tens of thousands of soldier-laborers to construct an
alternate imperial highway. He was finally stopped by one of Kao-tsung's
envoys who had learned of the project.[38]

Because of problems like these, the emperor and his officials were
occasionally at odds concerning the wisdom of carrying out a tour of inspection at a particular time. If Kao-tsung was intent on making a grand
show of his journeys, his bureaucrats were more concerned about the
massive logistical problems such spectacles generated and the consequent
economic pressures placed on the host localities. In 669 Kao-tsung made
preparations to visit Liang prefecture, located in modern Kansu province

near the Great Wall. The region had recently suffered from poor harvests, and discussants at court were unanimous in agreeing that an autumn tour of inspection to the west would not be appropriate. Upon hearing this, the emperor testily summoned his high officials to confront them on the matter. He began by citing a passage in the *Book of History* substantiating his right to carry out such a tour:

> In five years there was one tour of inspection for rulers and four appearances of the nobles at court. This was the normal rite. I want to make a short journey to Liang prefecture, [but] now I hear that all those outside [the palace] say that it is inappropriate. Why is this?

None of the officials dared to reply. Finally, one of them, Lai Kung-min, stepped forward to argue that T'ang campaigns against northern Korea had only recently ended and conditions were still greatly unsettled. If Kao-tsung were to make a western tour, his soldiers (who would serve as guards) would again have no rest. Moreover, the population of the Kansu region was especially small, and it would be a great burden on the people to furnish the necessary provisions for the imperial entourage. Lai concluded his argument by noting that he was not alone in thinking that a tour at this time would be unwise. Kao-tsung was thus persuaded to scale down his trip substantially: He would only inquire after the aged and do a little hunting in the Kansu region before returning to the capital. He then issued an edict calling off a full-scale western tour of inspection and rewarded Lai for his frank words.[39]

Perhaps Kao-tsung's most important *hsün-shou* took place in 665–66, when he journeyed first from Ch'ang-an to Lo-yang and then proceeded from the Eastern Capital to T'ai-shan, where he performed the Feng and Shan sacrifices to Heaven and Earth. (See the following chapter.) On the same trip he visited the nearby Confucian Temple, where he sacrificed to the Great Sage, and then went southward to northern Anhui province to pay his respects at the Taoist temple dedicated to the T'ang ancestor, Lao-tzu, before returning first to Lo-yang and then to Ch'ang-an.[40] The journey took more than a year in all and, in terms of the sacred sites visited and the sacrifices performed, was as close an approximation as possible to the tours of inspection of the ancient sage-kings.

The *K'ai-yüan li* contains an idealized description of the T'ang *hsün-shou* ritual.[41] It assumes that the emperor first visits the eastern peak of T'ai-shan and then, as in ancient times, follows a year-long route leading him to the other sacred mountains of the south, west, and north. The

emperor's safety on the journey is ensured by his offering a sacrifice, prior
to his departure, to the gods of all the mountains and streams in the regions he will transit. As a further precaution, in the localities to be visited
sacrifices are offered to all former rulers, famous officials, and other
notables who are buried there. At T'ai-shan a round altar is constructed,
where a burnt-offering is made to Hao-t'ien shang-ti to announce the
emperor's arrival. Prior to the announcement, the emperor, the ritual
officiants, and his other officials all observe a period of seclusion of
varying lengths. The sacrifice itself is conducted much like that at the
round altar at the winter solstice, with the spirit-thrones of Hao-t'ien
shang-ti and Kao-tsu (who is *p'ei*) arranged similarly. At the end of the
ceremony, the emperor's carriage returns to his detached palace. The day
after the announcement to Hao-t'ien shang-ti, another sacrifice is performed to China's hills and streams (*wang chih yü shan-ch'uan*). The term
wang, "to gaze at, look toward," derives from the fact that the offerer
performs the sacrifice at a distance from the actual sacrificial objects. In
this case, the sacrifice is performed not by the emperor but by his ritual
officials. The following day the emperor conducts an audience for his
Eastern Nobles (*ssu-chin tung-hou*), actually those local officials whose areas
of jurisdiction lay in the eastern region. Finally, one day later, the emperor
sends his highest officials to enquire into local administration and conditions among the people and report their findings back to him. Good government is rewarded and misgovernment punished. The same process is
repeated when the emperor visits south, west, and north. All these elements derive from the "Canon of Shun" of the *Book of History*. Except
possibly for the occasion of Kao-tsung's trip to T'ai-shan for the Feng and
Shan sacrifice, however, it is unlikely that during the early T'ang the *hsün-
shou* ritual was actually performed as it was recorded in the *K'ai-yüan li*.

The formal tour of inspection, in which emperor, court, and army
traveled en masse, had, by its very nature, to be used sparingly by any
regime. The recent excesses of Sui Yang-ti in this regard must have provided a good warning for the early T'ang emperors. Kao-tsu, at any rate,
was prevented by age and the limited area under secure T'ang control
from roaming widely from the capital during his reign. His son, T'ai-
tsung, was able to embark upon travels of wider scope, especially to the
Lo-yang region on China's eastern plain. Lo-yang had provided a strong
base of support for T'ai-tsung during his struggle with his brothers over the
succession, and he must have felt comfortable there.[42] The gradual consolidation of T'ang military power and improved economic conditions

among the people also must have allowed him freedom to choose destinations of greater remoteness from Ch'ang-an. Yet, all in all, T'ai-tsung's travels outside of the capital region were modest in number and limited in reach. Of the first three T'ang emperors, Kao-tsung perhaps made the fullest use of the *hsün-shou*. Kao-tsung roamed farther afield and for longer periods of time than either of his predecessors, a not surprising fact given his long reign and conditions of relative peace and plenty over most of the empire. But much of his traveling, especially to Lo-yang and the eastern peak of T'ai-shan, probably owed more to the emotional and political needs of his consort, Empress Wu, than to his own.[43] At any rate, *hsün-shou* were not lightly embarked upon, and the early T'ang emperors cannot be said overall to have exceeded the ancient rule, recorded in the *Book of History*, of one tour every five years.

Such tours, while costly of money and manpower, probably yielded sufficient political returns on their investment. Since an imperial visit might be scheduled at any time, local officials were encouraged to maintain minimum standards of government lest they be sacked or punished. Emperors could display a showy concern toward the masses and carry out policies of generosity aimed at specific localities. Not surprisingly, then, tours of inspection during the early T'ang were largely confined to regions of greatest population density—around the great metropolitan districts of Ch'ang-an and Lo-yang and the corridor in between.[44] Here the greatest numbers of persons could directly view, or at least hear about, the glorious transit of the Son of Heaven, in magnificient train, making solicitous inquiries about the disadvantaged or freely dispensing largesse, and evoking potent images of and identification with revered political ancestors, who, in the course of performing similar rituals, had also passed this way so long ago.

CHAPTER 9

The Feng and Shan Sacrifices

Among the emperors and kings who from ancient times have received the mandate of Heaven to rule, why are there some who did not perform the Feng and Shan sacrifices? For all who were blessed with the heavenly omens signifying their worthiness to perform these rites hastened without fail to Mount T'ai to carry them out, and even some who had not received such signs took it upon themselves to perform them. Yet others, though they enjoyed the mandate to rule, felt that their merit was not yet sufficient; or, though their merit was sufficient, they felt that their virtue had not been fully manifested to all creatures; or again, though their virtue had been fully manifested, they felt that they could not spare the time to carry them out. This is the reason that these rites have seldom been performed!

Ssu-ma Ch'ien, *Records of the Grand Historian*

THE FENG AND SHAN SACRIFICES DEDICATED TO HEAVEN AND EARTH WERE YET other rites carried out by rulers far from their capitals, traditionally at Mount T'ai and the nearby hill of Liang-fu in central Shantung province in eastern China. The Feng and Shan are considered by some scholars to have been perhaps the most solemn and important of any rites that could be performed by a Chinese ruler.[1] They were for this reason rarely carried out, by six men at most in all of Chinese history: Ch'in Shih-huang-ti, Han Wu-ti, Han Kuang-wu-ti, T'ang Kao-tsung, T'ang Hsüan-tsung, and Sung Jen-tsung. They were last performed in the year 1008. In Confucian tradition the rites had several interrelated purposes. They were an expression of the ruler's receipt of the Mandate of Heaven. They symbolized that he legitimately bore Heaven's appointment. They acknowledged and gave thanks for the blessings of Heaven and Earth. They were an announcement to Heaven and Earth that the ruler had unified the empire and brought peace to the world, that is, that the divine charge had been fulfilled.[2] The sacrifices thus bore strong political as well as religious overtones.

Beyond the immediate political statement that the sacrifices made, they could be politically exploited in other ways. Beginning with Han Wu-ti, rulers often changed reign-names to commemorate their performance of the Feng and Shan, usually incorporating into them the character *feng* or some allusion to the circumstances surrounding the rites, such as the appearance of auspicious omens. Such reign-periods were suffused with reflected glory from the rites. From the time of Han Kuang-wu-ti general amnesties were always issued upon the performance of the Feng and Shan, thereby publicizing the event over the entire empire.[3] The Feng and Shan were also the occasion of rewards bestowed by the throne to a grateful populace. For example, when Han Wu-ti performed the Feng and Shan in 110 B.C. he granted one ox and ten piculs of wine to every one hundred households, and two bolts of silk cloth to those over eighty, orphans, and widows. Selected districts were exempted from corvée labor and taxes for the year.[4]

The origins of the Feng and Shan are unclear. The earliest notice of the sacrifices appears in the late-Chou–early-Han work *Kuan-tzu*, where the minister Kuan Chung speaks of seventy-two rulers of remote antiquity who had performed them.[5] But the section on the Feng and Shan seems to have been an interpolation of later date, probably taken from Ssu-ma Ch'ien's *Records of the Historian* of the first century B.C.[6] There is no mention, at any rate, of the Feng and Shan anywhere in the Confucian classics, including the *Book of Rites*, a fact which suggests that the sacrifices were not originally part of Confucian legitimation theory.[7] Traditional Chinese opinion has been divided on the antiquity of the Feng and Shan.[8] Ssu-ma Ch'ien stated that the tradition had begun in ancient times, but because the rites were performed so rarely their details had become completely cost.[9] Ssu-ma Ch'ien's views influenced the Han commentator Cheng Hsüan to accept the early origins of the ceremonies.[10] But during the Period of Disunion, some scholars were beginning to observe that the Feng and Shan had not appeared in the orthodox canon.[11] The Sui Confucian philosopher Wang T'ung went so far as boldly to assert that the Feng and Shan were not ancient rites but originated only during the Ch'in and Han dynasties.[12] Yet the early T'ang compilers of the *Sui History*, and the early T'ang classical exegete K'ung Ying-ta, all apparently influenced by Cheng Hsüan, upheld the archaic origins of the rites.[13]

The thrust of much modern scholarship has been to discount the early origins of the Feng and Shan and to treat them as a ritual innovation in response to the institutionalization of empire and centralized government, to the peculiar psychological and emotional needs of certain heroic rulers, usually Ch'in Shih-huang-ti or Han Wu-ti, and to their personal quest for immortality.[14] But some modern scholars trace the beginnings of the Feng and Shan back to pre-Ch'in times. They view the rites as an evolution from simple and primitive mountain sacrifices centered on T'ai-shan. It was only much later, according to this view, that they became sacrifices dedicated to Heaven and Earth.[15] The employment of fire in a high place in the Feng sacrifice may link it to similar rituals dating as far back as the Shang dynasty.[16] One hypothesis is that the Feng and Shan entered China from the West, since in ancient times the use of burnt-offerings in sacrifice was common to many peoples between India and East Asia.[17] The altars on which the sacrifices were offered may have been influenced, according to one view, by Babylonian architecture.[18]

By Han times there already was confusion over the precise meaning of the terms *feng* and *shan*. The character *feng* has often been interpreted in traditional Chinese scholarship as a piling up of earth in order to make a grave mound, thus the employment of earth to construct a raised altar; and *shan* as a sweeping away of earth or the clearing of an area to make a flat altar.[19] *Feng* and *shan* thus may have signified the preparation of a place for sacrifice, the place of sacrifice itself, or else generalized terms for sacrifice.[20] Another line of interpretation is contained in the *Po Hu T'ung* of the first century A.D., which records that at the Feng sacrifice golden mortar was used to cover silver bindings, or stone mortar to cover gold bindings, and that they were sealed (*feng*) with a seal.[21] The character *feng* in this case seems to refer to the "sealing up" of a stone coffer containing jade tablets inscribed with an announcement to Heaven concerning the success of the dynasty, apparently a contemporary practice.[22] Since the "sealing up" was an activity performed on an earthen altar, since the meaning of *feng* is also "to pile up earth" to make an altar, and since the sacrifices were performed atop earthen altars, eventually, according to this reasoning, the T'ai-shan rites came especially to be designated as *feng*.

It appears originally that *feng-shan* was not a two-character phrase, as it later was treated by the Chinese, and that the sacrifices had no intrinsic relationship to one another.[23] Nor were the primitive *feng* and *shan* rites exclusively dedicated, as they later were, to Heaven and Earth; rather they seem to have been generalized sacrifices to mountains, streams, and various spirits and deities, as well as to Heaven and Earth.[24] Neither were they performed solely on Mount T'ai, but could be carried out on other peaks as well.[25] It was probably during the Ch'in and early Han period that the Feng and Shan were first combined, linked primarily to Heaven and Earth, and centered on Mount T'ai. How did this come about?

Mount T'ai, or T'ai-shan, is situated due north of the town of T'ai-an in central Shantung province. It is the single tallest peak in the region, rising 4,992 feet (1,545 meters) above sea level, affording a commanding view of the surrounding plain. As in many other societies, mountains have played a powerful secular and religious role in China. During the chaotic Spring and Autumn and Warring States periods of the Chou dynasty, T'ai-shan became an object of both awe and armed contention. Its sheer size also made it an object of superstition and religious veneration: A belief existed that all those who passed by it had to sacrifice to its spirit-god or incur his wrath.[26] The *Analects* of Confucius mentions a sacrifice performed on the mountain, which was likely made to this spirit.[27] At the same time, Shantung and the region northwest of it, modern Hopei, comprising the old feudal states of Yen and Ch'i, had long been the home of native cults and shamanistic practices that treated T'ai-shan as a sacred mountain. The region became a center of arcane practices promising a prolongation of life which were manipulated by a class of wizards called *fang-shih*.[28] It is probably no accident that the famous islands of the immortals, known as P'eng-lai, were supposedly located somewhere off the Shantung peninsula, in the Eastern Sea. By traveling to P'eng-lai it was believed that one could obtain the elixir of immortality and become an immortal (*shen-hsien*). To the *fang-shih* T'ai-shan was the continental equivalent of P'eng-lai; it too was a mountain of immortals.[29]

T'ai-shan was thus conceived of by the *fang-shih* as an object of sacrifice, a place of sacrifice, and the habitation of spirits. It was also the place where spirits descended from Heaven. It has long been pointed out that sacred mountains are cosmic axes, places where Heaven and Earth meet, and thus paths that lead to and from Heaven. By ascending a mountain, the pilgrim reaches the Center of the world; he transcends a profane plane to enter a sacred region.[30] "The sumit of a cosmic mountain," Eliade says, "is not only the highest point of the earth, it is also the earth's navel, the point at which Creation began."[31] Paradise (immortality) lies at the navel of the earth and the Center of the cosmos. For the *fang-shih*, this place was T'ai-shan. Climbing the mountain and sacrificing on its peak were acts that brought perpetual life. Since the generalized and primitive *feng* and *shan* both were linked to the concepts of "altar" and "sacrifice," and both were prayers to gods and spirits for blessings, it may have been relatively easy for the *fang-shih* to combine them into a single practice and, further, to appropriate them as royal supplications for a particular type of divine blessing—immortality. As Han Wu-ti was promised by one of his magicians, "perform the Feng and Shan sacrifices, (and) you will never die."[32] Under the influence of the *fang-shih*, many of whom were men of the Shantung region, it is not surprising that T'ai-shan, home of immortals, should have become the locus of Feng and Shan activity.[33]

The Shantung region was not only the home of the *fang-shih* wizards but also of Confucian scholars from the old feudal states of Ch'i and Lu, the latter being the birthplace of Confucius. The *Records of the Historian* states that three years after coming to the throne Ch'in Shih-huang-ti summoned seventy Confucian scholars from the old states of Ch'i and Lu in Shantung to meet with him at the foot of Mount T'ai to debate the proper ritual procedures for carrying out the Feng and Shan. Tired of their incessant wrangling, he eventually dismissed them.[34] Confucians nevertheless continued to influence the determination of state ritual in the Ch'in and, especially, the Han. In certain respects, the goals of Confucians and *fang-shih* were not dissimilar. Each group sought a privileged position at court and the creation of policies favorable to its interests. Each was willing to exploit the hopes and fears of rulers and to pander to their desire for increased grandeur in return for various concessions. *Fang-shih* and Confucian alike thus seized upon the ancient religious reverence for T'ai-shan in order to flatter the throne and exalt the newly centralized dynastic power. They linked T'ai-shan, the supreme peak in Eastern China, to the absolutist monarch—he who was highest. T'ai-shan thus became the symbol of kings. As we saw in the last chapter, T'ai-shan was the first destination of rulers performing a tour of inspection. Literary tradition also had it that Chou Wu-wang traveled to T'ai-shan to announce to Heaven his conquest of the Shang. Although the historical reliability of the story is doubtful, "going to T'ai-shan" assumed a powerful political meaning: It signified gaining possession over the empire.[35] The Feng and Shan sacrifices performed at T'ai-shan were thus fashioned into a momentous religious and political ceremony, a potent symbolic vehicle for expressing the ruler's supreme position as the "one man" under Heaven, as well as his acknowledgment of Heaven's Mandate.

As T'ai-shan became the primary geographical locus of sacrifices expressing the king's legitimate position, Heaven and Earth grew in importance as the chief objects of worship in the ceremonies performed there.[36] We noted earlier that in the primitive stage of their development, the Feng and Shan appear to have been generalized sacrifices made to several deities,

including those of Heaven, Earth, mountains, streams, and various ancestors. But when the Feng and Shan were adopted as important rites of the
state cult it became necessary to adopt sacrificial objects reflecting the ruler's dominant political position. Up to the early Han little or no evidence
exists that any sacrifices exclusively dedicated to Heaven and Earth were
performed, or that rulers took any personal role in them. From the time of
Han Wu-ti in the first century B.C., however, the Feng and Shan were
increasingly viewed by rulers, in addition to a means of seeking immortality, as an announcement to Heaven and Earth of a change in dynasties and
of their personal achievements, what is called *shou-ming kao t'ien*. By the
time of Han Kuang-wu-ti's performance of the rites in the first century
A.D., as the search for immortality declined, *shou-ming kao t'ien* became a
predominant motive for the rites.[37] With this came a sharper focus on their
sacrifical objects, so that the Ch'ing ritual commentator Ch'in Hui-t'ien
might conclude simply that "the Feng and Shan are nothing more than
sacrificial rites dedicated to Heaven and Earth."[38]

After the Later Han dynasty, the Feng and Shan ceremonies were not
performed for over half a millennium. Rulers of the relatively short-lived
Northern and Southern Dynasties appear to have been too timorous to
perform rituals designed to announce their successes to Heaven, especially
the establishment of a Great Peace and plenty throughout the land. Nevertheless, in discussions at court in both northern and southern regimes, the
Later Han view generally prevailed that the Feng and Shan were rites of
shou-ming kao t'ien which were to be performed at T'ai-shan.

The Sui dynasts, rulers of a revivified empire and seeking ways of
symbolizing their impressive achievements, made genuine efforts to restore the Feng and Shan tradition. But in the end even they appear to have
been intimidated by the weighty political symbolism of the rites and the
possible consequences of hubris. In 589, the year in which he reunited
China, Wen-ti shrugged off requests by his officials that he perform the
sacrifices.[39] But in 594, after consolidating his conquest of the South, he
was persuaded to go so far as to order a compilation of regulations governing the Feng and Shan. When they were completed and presented to
him, however, he once again "shrank back" from the question, saying:
"This is a great matter. What virtues do I possess to be worthy of it?"
Instead, he decided simply to make a tour of inspection eastward to T'ai-
shan in order to sacrifice at the mountain itself.[40] Wen-ti arrived at T'ai-
shan in the spring of 595. There he had an altar built at the foot of the
mountain, and performed a rite modeled on the southern suburban sac-

rifice, and also a special sacrifice dedicated to one of the Five Emperors.[41] But, as Arthur Wright notes, "Wen-ti's observance fell short of the full ritual performance, either out of fear of the consequences of presumption or out of concern that the famine conditions in the country he had just passed through cast a shadow on his own stewardship of the realm."[42]

Wen-ti's successor similarly failed to perform a full Feng and Shan sacrifice. In 608 Yang-ti made a progress to Mount Heng in modern Hopei province, northernmost of China's five sacred mountains. There he performed a sacrifice almost identical to that made by his father at T'ai-shan years earlier, which was witnessed by local officials of the region north of the Yellow River as well as by several foreign dignitaries.[43] When journeying to his eastern capital at Lo-yang in 614, Yang-ti passed by and sacrificed at Mount Hua, yet another sacred mountain that was a frequent destination of ancient rulers performing tours of inspection. But, notes the *Sui History*, because the proper form of the Feng and Shan could not be determined, they too remained incomplete.[44]

THE T'ANG RITES—T'AI-TSUNG

The T'ang dynasty continued the Later Han view of the Feng and Shan as a politico-religious statement in which the receipt of Heaven's Mandate was appropriately acknowledged in a ritual act of the utmost gravity. This is reflected in the opening passage on the Feng and Shan in the *Sui History*, compiled early in the T'ang, in which the compilers quote (without attribution) the Later Han work, *Po Hu T'ung*:[45]

> Whenever different surnames arise and a Great Peace is achieved, [rulers] make a Feng on T'ai-shan to announce their successes. When the Feng is completed they perform a Shan on Liang-fu.... The Feng and Shan are like [acts] of heightening and thickening. "Heaven is honored for its height; Earth owes its positive qualities to its thickness. The height of Mount T'ai is increased [by an earthen altar] that thanks may be rendered to Heaven. The base of Liang-fu is made thicker [by an earthen altar] that thanks may be rendered to Earth. This means that since what Heaven has commanded [has enabled the ruler] to accomplish his aims and bring his tasks to a successful conclusion, he increases [the greatness] of Heaven and Earth by adding to their height and thickness."[46]

Thus, during the early T'ang the Feng and Shan were conceived of as a means of acknowledging Heaven and Earth for the blessings they had bestowed on the ruler, and of "repaying" them for their kindness.

Although the Feng and Shan were first performed during the reign of the third emperor, Kao-tsung, T'ang officials began clamoring for them almost from the beginning of the dynasty. Sometime during Kao-tsu's reign, a prefect in the region around T'ai-shan, thinking that a Great Peace had been brought about, and that under such circumstances rulers of old had performed the Feng and Shan, sent a scholar to climb the mountain and view the ancient traces of rulers who had sacrificed there. He then compiled a work called *Feng and Shan Diagrams and Ceremonial (Feng-shan t'u chi i)* and sent it to the throne. But because of Kao-tsu's modesty, it is said, he did not assent to performing the exalted ceremonial.[47]

Similar proposals were made near the beginning of T'ai-tsung's reign. Early in 631 some of T'ai-tsung's officials requested that since the empire was united and the Four Barbarians had declared themselves subjects of China, it was appropriate that he perform the Feng and Shan. Another entreaty was made at the close of the year. The emperor refused both requests outright.[48] But in the first month of the following year a group of high-powered officials, including Fang Hsüan-ling and Wang Kuei, resumed their pleas. T'ai-tsung professed to have no interest in performing the ceremonies, rhetorically inquiring whether a ruler like Han Wen-ti, who had not offered the sacrifices, was not to be preferred to Ch'in Shih-huang-ti, who had. Moreover, Heaven could be acknowledged by sweeping away earth to prepare an altar, as in the suburban altar rites. What need was there to climb Mount T'ai and pile up an earthen mound several feet high to display the proper reverence?[49] Court officials, however, continued without cease to call for the sacrifices, and T'ai-tsung appears eventually to have become seduced by the notion of becoming the first ruler since Han Kuang-wu-ti to revive the Feng and Shan tradition.[50]

A dramatic exchange at court between T'ai-tsung and Wei Cheng provides much insight into the conditions deemed necessary during the early T'ang for a ruler to carry out the Feng and Shan. According to a near-contemporary source, when Wei Cheng, of all the court ministers, opposed T'ai-tsung's intention to perform the sacrifices in 632, the emperor angrily confronted him, saying:

> "I want your straightforward opinion, without hiding anything. Is not my merit [*kung*] high?" [Wei] replied, "Your merit is indeed high." "Has not my virtue [*te*] become substantial?" [Wei] replied, "Your virtue has indeed become substantial." "Has not China become peaceful?" [Wei] replied, "It is peaceful." "Do not far-off barbarians emulate us?" [Wei] replied, "They emulate us." "Have not auspicious omens arrived?" [Wei] replied, "They

have arrived." "Have not the yearly harvests increased?" [Wei] replied, "They have increased." "Then why do you think it improper for me [to perform the rites]?"[51]

Wei then acknowledged a great improvement in conditions since the establishment of the dynasty but questioned whether, with the economy still shaky, it would be wise for the state to carry out such elaborate ceremonies that would burden the people. He compared China to a man who had just suffered a ten-year-long disease, and who, although much recovered, was still not well enough to perform feats of strength or endurance.[52] What is important to note in this context is that all or at least some of the following conditions were thought necessary by both emperor and official before the Feng and Shan could be undertaken: general domestic peace; the submission of China's border neighbors; the appearance of auspicious omens; abundant harvests; generally favorable economic conditions; and a demonstration of both the personal merit and virtue of the ruler.

T'ai-tsung is said to have greatly appreciated Wei Cheng's advice. But continued entreaties from his officials prompted him at least to make inquiries among his ritual experts concerning the Feng and Shan as they had been performed during the two Han dynasties. He even dispatched an envoy to journey to T'ai-shan to survey the traces of the seventy-two rulers said to have made the sacrifices there in ancient times. Only widespread flooding on the northeastern plain caused him to abandon his plans to journey to Mount T'ai in order to duplicate their feats, it is said.[53]

Although temporarily frustrated, when in 637 T'ai-tsung's officials again urgently requested him to carry out the ceremonies, he allowed them to discuss the sacrifices with the intention of settling once and for all the precise form of the ritual.[54] It may well have been around this time that Wei Cheng once again strongly stated his opposition to the rites:

> [The success of] rulers lies in their virtue and not in [their performance of] the Feng and Shan. From the time of the [Sui] disorders, the prefectures and counties surrounding T'ai-shan have been exhausted and injured most severely. If the imperial carriages were to travel there, you could not entirely avoid causing [the people] to serve you. This would then be making the common people render you toilsome service because of the Feng and Shan.[55]

T'ai-tsung, who by now appears to have come fully to appreciate the political advantages to be gained by performing the rites, denied precisely this point. Performance of the Feng and Shan, he argued, was not an act that would confer any personal merit on himself. Rather, the rites would merely give him the means to acknowledge Heaven for all that it had allowed him to accomplish. "It is like Fang Hsüan-ling and the other meritorious officials, who, although they aid the dynasty, are able humbly to concede [the ultimate merit] as mine. Now, when I travel to T'ai-shan, I will be conceding the merit as Heaven's in the same way."[56] The emperor thereby attempted to fend off any criticism that his performance of the sacrifices was an act of political aggrandizement.

As the court debated the Feng and Shan ritual, there was much wrangling over minutiae, and wide agreement that the commentary on the ceremonies contained in the recently published *Chen-kuan li* was deficient in detail. The emperor therefore appointed "several tens" of eminent Confucians from across the country to determine the ritual, the most important among them being his courtiers Yen Shih-ku and Chu Tzu-she. In the end, however, this group also failed to reach a consensus. Thus, the ministers Fang Hsüan-ling, Yang Shih-tao, and (ironically) Wei Cheng were assigned to hammer out a compromise package by selecting the most practical of the conflicting views. For the most part, it is said, they adopted the interpretations of Yen Shih-ku. T'ai-tsung then ordered that their conclusions be appended to the *Chen-kuan li*.[57]

These regulations survive in surprising detail, insofar as they were never actually put into practice during T'ai-tsung's reign.[58] According to the regulations, when the emperor arrived at T'ai-shan he first was to make a sacrifice to inform the spirits of the forthcoming ritual and to demonstrate the purity of his intentions. The altar for this preliminary sacrifice was to be situated at the foot of the mountain, and constructed 120 feet in diameter and 12 feet high. The principal object of the sacrifice was to be Hao-t'ien shang-ti; Li Hu, the dynastic ancestor, was to be *p'ei*. Only when this ceremony had been completed was the emperor to begin his ascent of T'ai-shan. The altar where the Feng ceremony proper was carried out was to be located on the peak of the mountain, built round in shape, 50 feet in diameter and 9 feet high. It was to have four paths radiating from it in the four directions, and four stairways leading up the altar. The emperor was to ascend the altar by the southern stairway to perform the rite. When T'ai-tsung descended the mountain he was to perform the Shan ceremony at an altar also situated at the foot of the mountain, which was to be square in shape, 81 feet on a side, and 3 feet high, with stairways facing the four directions.

It is clear from a reading of the other regulations that the early T'ang understanding of the character *feng* embraced both the "sealing up" of jade tablets and the "piling up" of earth around them. The announcement of the emperor's achievements was to be inscribed on five tablets of jade (*tieh*), each measuring one foot three inches long by five inches wide by two inches thick. After being placed one atop another the stack of tablets was to be enclosed by two jade covers (*chien*), each two inches thick, which had the same dimensions as the tablets and which thus fit precisely over and under the stack. Gold cord was to be wrapped around the stack five times to secure it tightly. It was then to be placed in a stone coffer (*han*) comprising three slabs. In the center of the middle slab was a cutout whose dimensions exactly matched those of the jade stack. The stack was to be placed inside the cutout, then covered top and bottom with the other two slabs, forming a solid mass. In order to prevent any movement of the slabs, they were to be fastened by ten narrow stone bars which were to be slipped into notches carved into the four vertical faces of the stack. They were to be further secured by gold cords that were sealed (*feng*) by reinforced clay in which tiny bits of stone were embedded (*shih-ni*). All of this was in accordance with procedures devised during the Han dynasty.[59] The clay was then to be sealed with an imperial seal. Here, the character *feng* obviously refers to the sealing up of the stone coffer containing the jade tablets. But another regulation governs the way earth was to be piled up at the round altar on the summit of T'ai-shan. As the early T'ang commentator Yen Shih-ku explains: "Whenever we say *feng*, it is always a term referring to the piling up of earth." The square stone coffer was to be placed atop the round altar. The emperor was to mount the altar via the southern stairway to seal the coffer and stamp it with his seal. Then, five-colored earth was to be piled around the coffer to form a mound twelve feet high and twenty feet in diameter, thus burying it completely. Since the piled-up earth firmly held the stone coffer, it was not necessary, as in Later Han times, further to support the coffer with stone buttresses, it was explained. When the Shan ceremony and the inaugural sacrifice at the foot of T'ai-shan were performed, the identical procedure was to be followed.

At the preliminary Feng sacrifice made at the foot of T'ai-shan, inscribed jade slips (*ts'e*) were to be employed instead of jade tablets. The slips, measuring one foot three inches long by one and one-half inches wide by one-half inch thick, were secured by gold threads into four bundles of five.[60] Each bundle was to be accomodated in a small gold coffer (*kuei*), which was wrapped in gold cord, sealed with clay reinforced with gold dust (*chin-ni*), and stamped with the emperor's *shou-ming* seal. Each coffer was to be placed at the spirit-throne of one of the four objects of the sacrifice: Shang-ti and his *p'ei*, the dynastic ancestor, Li Hu; and the God of Earth and his *p'ei*, the T'ang founder, Kao-tsu.

At the end of his text, Yen reminded T'ai-tsung that traces of the Feng and Shan were absent from the classics, and that even for the Ch'in and Han period the evidence was fragmentary and difficult to trace. Much of the exegesis written on the ritual over the centuries therefore consisted of "empty words" and was worthless. From the records it was clear that the Feng and Shan ritual of each dynasty was different. The present age, moreover, far surpassed the achievements of those earlier times. Thus, Yen urged T'ai-tsung not blindly to follow past precedent merely for the sake of conformity, but to select from among the suggestions of his wise ministers and put them into practice.

By 641 T'ai-tsung had once again deemed it a suitable time to carry out the Feng and Shan, which was officially scheduled for the second month of the following year. In his edict announcing the event, he was careful to enumerate the conditions justifying his performance of such weighty rites: He had brought order out of chaos and restored peace throughout the empire; the harvests were good; foreign lands were coming to court in token of their submission to China; and auspicious omens from Heaven had appeared (for example, a rare purple fungus symbolizing long life and prosperity had recently been reported growing widely across a prefecture in modern Kansu province). Although he appointed high court officials to settle the final form of the ceremonies, the discussants again stubbornly clung to their individual positions, and in the end T'ai-tsung decided to adhere to the interpretations presented to him four years previous. With everything in readiness, the emperor set out for Lo-yang on his way to T'ai-shan. But when a comet was sighted crossing the constellation known to the Chinese as the *T'ai-wei kung*, the sovereign's southern palace, it was interpreted as an unpropitious omen directed against the emperor, forcing him to cancel the rites.[61]

The next wave of official exhortations that T'ai-tsung perform the Feng and Shan came late in 646, with the influential Chang-sun Wu-chi leading the pack. Although T'ai-tsung demurred on the ground that recent foreign military campaigns had left the people in need of rest, he held out the hope that once they had recovered, discussions on the rites could be resumed.[62] Encouraged by this opening, Chang-sun Wu-chi wasted little time in renewing his campaign. Scarcely a month later he sent a memorial to the throne in which he listed a variety of reasons why T'ai-tsung should announce his great accomplishments to Heaven. But perhaps the most important one was left unstated. T'ai-tsung had never fully recovered from an illness he had contracted on the Liao-tung campaign of 645, and his condition had worsened during 646. Just recently he had turned over much of the day-to-day affairs of government to his son, the future Kao-tsung.[63] There was not much time remaining if he was to carry out the sacrifices. Perhaps the emperor, too, had read the handwriting on the wall, for he now ordered experts on ritual affairs summoned to court in order speedily to settle the final form of the rites.[64]

A new date was set for the sacrifices, the second month of 648. Inasmuch as he was soon to take the grave step of formally announcing his achievements to Heaven, he ordered all the officials of the empire, great and small, to take special precautions that the quality of government not decline and that their administrative duties be performed with the utmost reverence. He also ordered the most learned men in the land in the literary and political arts, as well as those of outstanding abilities, to proceed to T'ai-shan to witness the ceremonies.[65] Upon the deliberations of Fang Hsüan-ling and others, it was decided that the ailing monarch would perform the Shan ceremony not at Liang-fu, which was about twenty-three miles distant from T'ai-shan, but at a hill less than two miles away, called She-shou, reputedly the site of the Chou dynasty Shan ceremony.[66] With this exception, all the regulations of the Feng and Shan were to accord with those adopted by the court in 641.[67]

But even this carefully planned and much-hoped-for ceremony was not to be. Citing a number of reasons—the need to consolidate the recent T'ang victory over the Hsüeh-yen-t'o, a Turkish people living in modern Sinkiang province; large-scale and costly construction projects, first the poorly sited Ts'ui-wei Palace and then its replacement, the Yü-hua Palace; and recent flooding on the northeastern plain, all of which had taken a great toll on the people's strength—in the eighth month of 647 T'ai-tsung canceled the Feng and Shan sacrifices scheduled for the following year.[68] In his edict announcing the cancellation, the emperor once more enumerated the presence of a host of conditions that normally would have served to endorse a ruler's performance of the Feng and Shan, among them the conquest of the "barbarians" and the appearance of auspicious omens. It was truly fitting, he observed, that he, who had received Heavenly blessings greater than those bestowed on all the kings of ancient times, should perform such august rites. But as "father and mother of the people," he was concerned above all else with their welfare, and had no other choice than to stop the proceedings, he explained.[69]

It is perhaps ironic that one of the greatest monarchs in all Chinese history was in this manner frustrated in announcing his accomplishments to Heaven and Earth. After all, who but T'ai-tsung, who had conquered the Eastern and Western Turks, subdued the T'u-yü-hun and Hsüeh-yen-t'o, brought to heel the several oases of Central Asia, and had given China a measure of peace, stability, and economic prosperity unknown since the halcyon days of the Han, really deserved such an honor? Was he too incapacitated to undertake the long journey eastward to T'ai-shan? Was the second T'ang campaign against Koguryŏ, which had begun early in 647 and had so far yielded only inconclusive results, sapping too much of the energy and resources of China? Only a month after canceling the sacrifices, T'ai-tsung was compelled to take the step of ordering the construction of an armada of several hundred ships with which to invade the Korean kingdom. The cost of such an enormous project must have been staggering.[70] Or had T'ai-tsung lost his taste for a ritual act that surely would have invited the charge from historians of later times that he had committed hubris? We may never know the answers to these questions. But at least one Ch'ing commentator warmly praised T'ai-tsung for not having been seduced, as had Han Kuang-wu-ti, by the grandeur of the ceremonies. Surely it was not comets or flooding which in the end prevented T'ai-tsung from performing the Feng and Shan, he concluded. Rather, it was because of the prudent advice of men like Wei Cheng and the emperor's own good sense in avoiding the pitfalls associated with such a difficult enterprise.[71] In this manner, T'ai-tsung avoided the condemnation of later generations.

KAO-TSUNG'S RITES

Just as T'ai-tsung's successive campaigns to conquer the Korean kingdoms had provided a powerfully impelling legacy for his son, so too had his repeated attempts to perform the Feng and Shan. In the sixth month of 659, exactly ten years after Kao-tsung ascended the throne, he appointed the chief minister Hsü Ching-tsung to conduct discussions on the rites. Not much more came of them, however, until the tenth month of 662, when a formal date for their performance was set: the first month of 664. The timing was significant. By the early 660s the T'ang had subjugated the Western Turks in the region of the Ili Valley and Issyk-Kul, as well as the peoples formerly subject to them in western Sinkiang province, Russian Turkestan, and the Oxus Valley. The borders of China now stretched from the Sea of China all the way to Persia, an expanse unprecedented in all Chinese history. The empire was also enjoying a healthy economy. Performance of the Feng and Shan by Kao-tsung would have provided a fitting reflection in ritual of the world-wide imperium he had established and of the great age of peace and prosperity he had brought his people.

Yet a new and significant factor also entered the picture at this time— Kao-tsung's consort, Empress Wu. According to the "Monograph on Ritual" of the *Old T'ang History*, shortly after her elevation as empress, Wu had secretly suggested to her husband that he perform the Feng and Shan. By the late 650s Hsü Ching-tsung had become the chief spokesman at court for the empress, and it is more than likely that she had something to do with his appointment in 659 to discuss the ceremonies. Moreover, Kao-tsung had suffered what seems to have been a stroke late in 660, which periodically rendered him at least partially paralyzed, with impaired vision, and subject to frequent relapses. The empress took easily to administering affairs of state during these periods of incapacity, and soon became co-ruler of the empire in fact if not in name. By the end of 662 her power had become firmly consolidated, as her supporters, among them Hsü Ching-tsung, established themselves at the highest levels of government.[72] The empress's dominant position at court, however, ran counter to Confucian notions of conduct appropriate to females in general and wives in particular, and her power was ever being challenged, in ways both open and covert, by various court officials. Wu saw the Feng and Shan, in which she planned to play a major role, as a way of lending support to her status as equal partner with her husband and of silencing her critics.

Nevertheless, only two months after the date for Kao-tsung's Feng and Shan were announced, they were abruptly canceled, a decision that was officially blamed on the continuing T'ang campaigns against Koguryŏ and Paekche, and the heavy military burdens suffered by the people of the northeastern plain.[73] Since the renewed Korean campaigns had begun years before, this pretext may have been formulated to veil other factors— perhaps the worsened physical condition of the emperor, or else some other pressing court problem.[74] The rites were once again scheduled in the seventh month of 664 for the first month of 666.[75] This time Kao-tsung became the first ruler in more than six centuries to ascend T'ai-shan and perform the august ceremonies. But without the empress's pressing need for additional legitimation to support her role as co-ruler, it is perhaps doubtful that they would have been successfully completed during the reign of her sickly and timid husband.[76]

The edict of 664 announcing the Feng and Shan also ordered that all local officials of the rank of governor-general (*tu-tu*) and prefect (*tz'u-shih*) were to attend the ceremonies and assemble below T'ai-shan in the twelfth month of 665. The imperial princes (*wang*) were to gather in Lo-yang in the tenth month of the same year, where they would link up with the emperor's party. Various classes of talented persons were also summoned to appear below the mountain to witness the momentous event. Another edict issued a short time thereafter specified that those areas through which the imperial entourage passed were not to make any elaborate preparations. No bridges were to be erected over shallow water that was easily forded, and no roads were to be cut into passable terrain. Nor were the prefectures, Buddhist and Taoist temples, or common people to supply the imperial party with food.[77] The court apparently hoped by such means to reduce local burdens and generate as little resistance to the rites as possible.

The imperial carriages left Ch'ang-an for Lo-yang on the first leg of the journey to Mount T'ai in the second month of 665. At this time, ritual officials and scholars were ordered to complete the regulations governing the ceremonies. According to their deliberations, the rites were to be carried out beginning the first day of 666, a year that was officially designated *Ch'ien-feng*, or Supernal Feng. The emperor was to observe four days of relaxed seclusion at a detached palace in the immediate vicinity of Mount T'ai, followed by three more days of intense seclusion just prior to the rites.[78] Other participants were to observe much shorter periods of seclusion. Slightly more than a mile south of T'ai-shan a round altar was to be constructed on the model of the southern suburban altar at the capital, consisting of three tiers with four stairways each, for the total of twelve. This was the site of the preliminary Feng sacrifice. The top of the altar was to be painted green, and the side of each quadrant was to be painted a color governing its respective direction. An altar for burnt-offerings was also to be constructed.[79]

The regulations governing the implements used in the ceremonies generally adhered to those devised during T'ai-tsung's time, with some exceptions.[80] One of these was the use of thin jade slips (*ts'e*) instead of the thicker jade tablets (*tieh*) at all the altars of the ceremonies.[81] Another was the use of small jade as well as gold coffers (*kuei*) to contain the slips; the jade coffer was for use at the spirit-throne of Hao-t'ien shang-ti, and the gold at the spirit-thrones of the *p'ei*. These coffers were to be placed in larger coffers made of stone, which in turn were to be secured by stone buttresses, a Han practice that had been rejected earlier in the T'ang but had now been revived.[82]

The round altar at the summit of T'ai-shan, where the Feng ceremony was performed, was to have the same dimensions as those prescribed by Yen Shih-ku: 50 feet in diameter and 9 feet high, with stairways facing each of the four cardinal directions. Like the altar for the preliminary Feng sacrifice at the base of the mountain, its top was to be painted green and its sides painted with colors appropriate to their respective directions. The jade slips, stone coffers, buttresses, and so on, were also to be like those employed at the preliminary Feng sacrifice. The Shan altar at She-shou mountain was to be a one-tiered octagonal structure, with one staircase abutting each side, thus conforming to the regulations governing the northern suburban square altar at the capital. The top of the Shan altar was to be painted yellow, and its sides painted with colors harmonizing with their respective directions. All the ritual implements were to be the same as those used at the Feng sacrifice.[83] Such were the main elements of the regulations determined by the discussants for the ceremonies of 666, which were also largely followed in the Feng and Shan ritual carried out during the reigns of Empress Wu and Hsüan-tsung.[84]

The imperial party, having enjoyed a lengthy interlude in Lo-yang, during which time its number had been augmented by the addition of imperial princes and other personnel, departed for Mount T'ai in the tenth month. It must have presented a magnificient spectacle. The line of civil and military officials and those bearing insignia traditionally carried in front of an emperor is said to have stretched without break for several hundred *li*. Their camps and tents filled the entire northeastern plain. Also represented in the ranks were the chiefs or representatives of a number of foreign countries and tribes, among them the Turks, the kingdoms of Khotan, Persia, India, and Japan, and the Korean states of Silla, Paekche, and even Koguryŏ, all of whom led large bands of followers. The latter, in turn, had brought along with them their herds of cows, sheep, camels, and horses, which clogged the highways.[85]

The emperor's carriages arrived on schedule below T'ai-shan in the twelfth month of 665. According to the deliberations of the ritualists, the spirits of Kao-tsu and T'ai-tsung were both to be *p'ei* at the Feng ceremony, while those of their respective wives were to share the same status at the Shan, according with a precedent established by the Later Han founder, Kuang-wu-ti.[86] Following the personal performance of the Feng and Shan by the emperor, the secondary and tertiary offerings were to be made by the highest officials of the empire. Empress Wu, who had counted on her personal participation in the rites to enhance her prestige at court, strongly objected to this last point. She argued that it was quite inappropriate for male officials to offer sacrifice at the altar of the God of Earth, whose associated ancestral deities were female. As Heaven and Earth had their fixed places, the qualities of masculine and feminine were also distinct. The classics had made it clear that male and female ceremonies were to be kept separate. The *p'ei* deities of the Shan altar were feminine, in conformance with the sex of the God of Earth. How, then, could male officials properly participate in this kind of undertaking? Hoping to fend off any criticism that her advocacy of female participation in the ceremonies was unprecedented, Wu observed that the ancient regulations for the Feng and Shan were disordered, and that rulers had utilized the ceremonies for selfish motives. Since Kao-tsung's merit had far surpassed those of former kings, why need he adhere to outworn regulations and miss the opportunity of creating a new and more perfect ritual? In the end, Kao-tsung relented, ordering that at the Shan ceremony the empress was to make the secondary offering, while the wives of the imperial princes were to make the tertiary offering.[87]

With these and several other thorny ritual questions finally settled, the ceremonies moved forward as planned. On the first day of 666 Kao-tsung personally sacrificed to Hao-t'ien shang-ti on the altar of the preliminary Feng sacrifice below T'ai-shan. When the sacrifice was concluded, the emperor sealed up the jade slips and set up the stone buttresses, then piled up five-colored earth to cover them completely. That same day he led his officials in climbing up to the peak of T'ai-shan, where, the next day, he again performed the ceremony of sealing up the jade slips. Afterward, he descended the mountain and returned to his detached palace. On the third day he performed the Shan sacrifice to the God of Earth at She-shou. It is said that when the emperor finished making his offering, all the supervising ritual officials hurried down from the altar. Then, eunuchs bearing curtains and canopies made of multicolored embroidered silk, and the empress, leading the other ladies of the harem, ascended in their place to carry out the ceremony for which Wu had so strenuously fought. The ladling out of wine, the filling of the food dishes, and the singing were handled by the harem ladies. The officials all witnessed the spectacle from afar at their assigned places; some reportedly could not refrain from secretly ridiculing the proceedings, in which women were participating for the first time in Chinese history. Adhering to ancient precedent, on the fourth day Kao-tsung held an audience for his officials at yet another altar, designated the altar of audiences (*ch'ao-chin t'an*). Here, he received their enthusiastic congratulations.[88] At the audience Kao-tsung claimed, like his father before him, that in performing the Feng and Shan he had sought no merit for himself, but was only returning the credit to his ancestors. His acts were merely in response to Heaven's will and the expectations of all the people.[89]

After the audience was concluded, Kao-tsung ordered the altar converted to a place for feasting, and there banqueted his civil and military officials. Those of the third rank and higher sat atop the altar, whereas those of the fourth rank and lower sat below it, according to rank. The wine flowed freely, music was played, and the many officials approached the emperor to wish him long life. The banquet went on for an entire day before ending. Kao-tsung rewarded his officials with promotions in honorary rank. At the same time, he declared a general amnesty for the empire and officially designated the new reign-name of *Ch'ien-feng* in honor of the ceremonies.[90] On the tenth day of the month, the emperor ordered that three Taoist and three Buddhist temples were to be established in Yen prefecture, site of T'ai-shan, a generous gift to the area that had served as host to the enormous imperial entourage these last several weeks. One Taoist and one Buddhist temple were to be established at state expense in each of the rest of the empire's prefectures.[91] Before quitting the sacred mountain later in the first month, the emperor commanded that stone stelae were to be erected at the various altars on the mountain to commemorate the momentous ritual events just concluded. The altars themselves were to be given new names reflecting the auspicious omens that were said to have appeared in conjunction with the ceremonies.[92]

The history of the Feng and Shan during Kao-tsung's long reign does not end with the performance of 666. On several occasions afterward plans were made to repeat the sacrifices, but without any success. Early in 676 an imperial edict was issued that the Feng and Shan would be performed in the winter of that year on Sung-shan, the "central" sacred mountain, located just south of Lo-yang in modern Ho nan province.[93] The plan for the ceremonies is said to have been conceived by Empress Wu. Soon afterward, however, they were canceled owing to Tibetan incursions of the T'ang western frontier.[94] Another sacrifice on Sung-shan was announced for the winter of 679, but it too was quickly called off because of troubles with the Western Turks.[95]

Preparations reached the most advanced stage for the Feng and Shan at Sung-shan scheduled for the eleventh month of 683. A new palace, known as the Feng-t'ien (Serve Heaven), was constructed to the south of Sung-shan, for which the emperor set out at the beginning of the year. Since the Feng and Shan were being carried out not on T'ai-shan but on another mountain, the form of the ritual once again had to be discussed by court officials, and new regulations issued.[96] These were generally similar to those of 666, but with some variations. For example, different dimensions were specified for some of the altars, and they were sometimes to be painted different colors.[97] In the tenth month the imperial party reached Feng-t'ien Palace, but because of the emperor's failing health, the ceremonies had been postponed to the first month of 684.[98] At the beginning of the eleventh month of 683 Kao-tsung issued what was to be his final edict regarding the ceremonies. His ritual at Sung-shan, he explained, had been intended to announce the dynasty's achievements to Heaven rather than to confer any personal honor on himself. Because the harvests had been plentiful, he had planned to repeat a ritual on Sung-shan that had been performed by successive sage-rulers of the past. But recently there had been widespread drought in the regions of Hopei and Honan, compounded by "barbarian" incursions of the border north of the capital, which had caused serious damage. Because of these unsettling conditions, it was fitting that he cancel next year's planned Feng and Shan ceremonies on Sung-shan.[99]

About this time, a children's ballad arose belittling Kao-tsung's efforts regarding the Feng and Shan on Mount Sung, and predicting his failure ever to complete the cermonies.:

How many peaks has Sung-shan?	*Sung-shan fan-chi ts'eng*
Do not fear not reaching the top;	*Pu wei teng pu te*
Only fear not getting the chance to climb it.	*Tan k'ung pu te teng*
Soldiers and horses three times summoned;	*San-tu cheng ping ma*
Going round and round on the side roads.	*Pang-tao ta t'eng-t'eng*[100]

Kao-tsung died in the twelfth month of 683 without achieving his goal of climbing Sung-shan and carrying out the Feng and Shan, just as the song had predicted.

CONCLUSIONS

Previously, in the chapter on the suburban altar rites, we spoke of the act of sacrifice as a crossing of metaphysical space and time. The altar is a sacred area which serves to connect the world of men with the world of gods. The time in which the sacrifice is performed is a sacred non-time, a time of the gods not normally experienced by men, in which past, present, and future are fused together. The rites of T'ai-shan can also be examined in this light.

In the course of making a sacrifice at each of the three altars on the mountain, the ruler crosses the boundary of sacred space and time, enters a marginal state, then recrosses the boundary to re-emerge in profane space and time. Interestingly, during the Feng and Shan this three-stage process takes place not only at each of the three altars on T'ai-shan, it is also replicated in the domain of the mountain taken as a whole. Thus, the preliminary sacrifice at the base of T'ai-shan, in which the emperor announces his intention to perform the Feng and Shan, represents the rite of separation, in which the initiate is removed from normal existence and becomes temporarily an abnormal person existing in abnormal time. The ascent of T'ai-shan and the Feng ceremony performed at its summit represent the marginal (or liminal) state, in which the initiate is usually kept physically apart from most normal people, operates in a sacred timelessness, and may gain knowledge or power beyond the range of ordinary men. The descent from the peak and the performance of the Shan ceremony at the base of T'ai-shan represent the phase in which the initiate is brought back into normal society and integrated into his new role or status. The emperor's audience for and banqueting of officials symbolizes this re-entrance into the profane world; it is thus characterized by the opposite of the seclusion and fasting which preceded the commencement of the ceremonies.[101] The emperor's activities as a whole at T'ai-shan may thus be seen as bringing about a transition from normal space and time at the beginning of the rites and another transition from abnormal space and time at the end.

Although by early T'ang times the Feng and Shan had lost much of their magical character, especially related to the pursuit of immortality, we can nevertheless still discern certain symbolic meanings and elements associated with their original form. T'ai-shan, the Cosmic Mountain, sustains the planes of the cosmos and is at the same time the axis connecting them. The ruler's ascent to its summit is a movement toward the Center, where the three planes of Heaven, Earth, and Man intersect. At the summit of the Cosmic Mountain, the highest place on earth, communication is possible between men and gods. Here the ruler experiences a breakthrough to another state, either of immortality or grace. Ritual approaches to the Center, notes Eliade, are equivalent to the conquest of immortality. The sovereign is thus reborn, transcends the human condition, becomes a "new" man.[102] The descent of the mountain brings the ruler back to the profane world. The concepts of ascent and descent, and by implication their symbolic meanings, are encompassed in the very names given to the Feng and Shan altars during the T'ang: the *teng feng t'an* (altar for performing the Feng upon ascending the mountain) at the summit, and the *chiang shan t'an* (altar for performing the Shan upon descending the mountain) at the base. Of course, the ruler also approaches the sacred Center in the course of sacrificing at each of the altars of T'ai-shan. Every time he piles up earth over the coffers holding the jade tablets or slips, he is, in effect, recreating the world.[103] The re-creation of the world likewise implies his transcendence over death. The symbolism of immortality is carried over even to the materials employed for the announcement to Heaven: gold and, especially, jade. As Yen Shih-ku observed in his regulations for the Feng and Shan of T'ai-tsung's time, the jade tablets were so durable, they would last forever.[104]

Given the overall history of the Feng and Shan, one might well ask the following question: If the sacrifices indeed were such important vehicles serving to legitimate imperial power, why were they not performed more often? One line of explanation might go as follows. We observed in the chapter on the suburban altar rites that one way a sacrifice may be viewed is as an act of purification, wherein the animal victim becomes identified with the donor of the sacrifice and substitutes for him. When the animal is killed and sacrificed, the soul of the donor, by vicarious association, is first purified and then integrated into his new ritual status. According to ancient Chinese belief, in coming to power the sovereign commits acts that pollute him, and therefore he must expiate his triumph. The Feng and Shan can thus be regarded not only as an announcement to Heaven about the success of the dynasty but also as an expiatory rite in which the sovereign offers himself to the gods to atone for his crimes. Naturally, he must, at the same time, be certain that Heaven will accept a sacrificial victim as a substitute for himself. Since the Feng and Shan could only be justified by a concatenation of special conditions—the arrival of a Great Peace, auspicious omens, and so forth—the ruler had to be certain that the animal victim would actually be accepted. He was thus in great dread of the rites.[105] From this we can see that performing the Feng and Shan, because of the possible implication of hubris, was reserved for supremely confident monarchs, or else those with political, religious, or personal needs so pressing as to sweep away any reservations they may have had about performing them.

A second reason may be that the value of the Feng and Shan was at least partly a function of the rarity of their performance. Their ability to legitimate may have stemmed not solely from their actualization but also from the mere promise of their actualization. In this way, every official exhortation that the ruler perform them, every imperial command that officials discuss and determine their form, every announcement of a time-table for them, that is, every act which linked the sovereign however tenta-tively to the Feng and Shan, served nevertheless to enhance his prestige and increase his political capital among court and empire. That the Feng and Shan may have conferred legitimacy on rulers merely by virtue of association is suggested by the generous amount of material in the official sources relating to the sacrifices even for emperors, such as T'ai-tsung, who never completed them.

Yet during the T'ang dynasty the Feng and Shan ritual was, in fact, not as rare a phenomenon as it had been during the preceding several cen-turies. Kao-tsung and Hsüan-tsung (in 725) both carried out the rites at T'ai-shan, and Empress Wu, as ruler of her own dynasty, performed them at Sung-shan in 696.[106] How are we to explain this? Was it perhaps that the monarchs of an expanded world-wide imperium required ritual statements commensurate with their newly exalted status, and that no other altar rituals could serve this function so well? Could this have also been the basis for T'ai-tsung's urgent desire to perform the Feng and Shan after he had conquered the Turks and brought to heel most of the oases of Central Asia? Or was it an increased willingness by the T'ang rulers, in a world grown more secular and less superstitious, to utilize the sacrifices more for political than personal ends?

The last point raises the question of "audience," which for the Feng and Shan was potentially quite large. This was well understood by the early T'ang emperors, who were sensitive to the benefits to be reaped by exploiting popular sentiment. The Feng and Shan journeys of T'ai-tsung and Kao-tsung were leisurely affairs that took them through the most populous portions of their empire. All along the way countless numbers of people must have watched with excitement and awe the progress of the imperial parties. The two emperors had, moreover, ensured large audiences of spectators for their Feng and Shan by commanding various classes—imperial princes, local officials, erudites, commoners of special skills and talents, and so on—to assemble below T'ai-shan as witnesses to the momentous proceedings. In modern parlance we would call these kind of people "opinion makers," and their presence at the rites was calculated to reap the greatest political benefits for the throne. Finally, the favors Kao-tsung bestowed upon the empire at the time of his Feng and Shan allowed his subjects, near and far, to share with him, in some manner, however small, his great moment of triumph.

Another point in this regard is that a fundamental change seems to have taken place in the rites between Ch'in–early Han times and the T'ang dynasty. In the former period the Feng and Shan were essentially private rites performed for the personal benefit of the ruler with little or no thought of the people; they were simultaneously an expression of the ruler's receipt of the Mandate and a vehicle for his attainment of immortality.[107] Lest the mystery of immortality be revealed to others, the ceremonies were kept almost totally secret. This was particularly true of the Feng ceremony at the summit of T'ai-shan, by which means the sovereign was to meet the immortal genies (*shen-hsien*) and become one of them, and which was, consequently, especially shielded from public view. The jade tablets on which the announcement to Heaven was inscribed were first encased in coffers, reinforced by stone buttresses, and then buried, not only to protect them but also to guarantee that their messages would forever remain concealed. When Han Wu-ti ascended to the summit of T'ai-shan he was accompanied only by a single attendant, who died under mysterious circumstances a short time afterward, forever ensuring the secrecy of the rites.[108] Increasingly, however, the Feng and Shan came to be seen as rites performed for the sake of the people as well as the ruler, and took on a public as well as a private character.

Precisely when this change occurred is difficult to say, but it may well have taken place around the time of Han Kuang-wu-ti in the first century A.D.[109] Whereas rites designed to obtain immortality had to be kept secret, rites announcing a new dynasty to Heaven, *shou-ming kao t'ien*, or praying for Heavenly blessings, did not. Thus Han Wu-ti's Feng ceremony at the summit of T'ai-shan, the purpose of which was to gain immortality, had to be kept secret. But Kuang-wu's ceremonies, essentially of the *shou-ming kao t'ien* variety, with a more political purpose, did not have to be so hidden. We know, for example, that Kuang-wu-ti was accompanied on his ascent of T'ai-shan by officials, courtiers, and attendants in waiting, all of whom witnessed his Feng ceremony at the peak.[110] However, even in Kuang-wu-ti's rites, the announcement to Heaven was kept strictly secret.[111]

The T'ang Feng and Shan, as we have seen, continued the *shou-ming kao t'ien* character of Kuang-wu-ti's ceremonies, but carried their public character even further.[112] Those witnessing Kao-tsung's inaugural Feng sacrifice below T'ai-shan—including even dignitaries from foreign lands—must have comprised a sizable mass of people. On his ascent of the mountain, Kao-tsung was accompanied by "attending officials and those ranked below them,"—another numerous group.[113] Participating in the ceremonies at every altar, in addition to the emperor, were ritual officials. Lastly, his consort and concubines also played prominent roles in the Shan ceremony at She-shou mountain. The Feng and Shan thus had clearly opened up and out to embrace large numbers of people, either as participants or as eyewitnesses. Their public nature is further underlined in a document related to the abortive Feng and Shan scheduled for Mount Sung in the year of the emperor's death, 683. In his last edict on the matter, Kao-tsung stated that the purposes of the ceremonies were "to venerate the great accomplishments of successive worthies, and to pray for the protection of the people."[114]

The trend toward public disclosure reached a peak during the rites conducted by Hsüan-tsung in 725. The emperor rode a horse up the mountain, followed by his attendant officials and military guards. It is said that because he felt that a holy mountain should remain undefiled, the emperor limited the numbers of people ascending with him, ordering that his high officials would participate only in those sacrifices conducted at the foot of T'ai-shan.[115] But, unlike his predecessors, Hsüan-tsung saw no reason to protect the secrecy of his announcement to Heaven inscribed on the jade tablets buried at the altars. Secrecy had been maintained, he was informed by a ritual expert, because the ceremonies had previously been carried out for the selfish motives of rulers—such as their search for long life and immortality. Hsüan-tsung replied: "Because [the rites] We are performing today are all prayers for the sake of the people, there is much less [reason] for Us to desire secrecy. Let the jade tablets be taken out and shown to all the officials to let them know Our intent." In the announcement Hsüan-tsung thanked Heaven for the success he and his house had achieved, and prayed for prosperity for his descendants and blessings for his people.[116]

The T'ang Feng and Shan rites thus very much fit the trend we have been observing in other key ritual and symbolic acts of the period toward more openness, greater inclusivity of participants, and the seeking of ends that are more public and political than personal and private.

CHAPTER 10

The Ming-t'ang

The cosmic temple is much older than Pythagoras; it never began, but gradually grew out of something that was there before.

Hocart, *Kings and Councillors*

"HAIL RESPLENDENT MING T'ANG! MING T'ANG OF (HEAVENLY) RADIANCE!"[1] So wrote the Later Han dynasty historian and poet Pan Ku (32–92) in a composition celebrating the many sights of the dynastic capital. From the time of Pan Ku, the Ming-t'ang fired the imaginations of successive generations of literati. One of the greatest of all Chinese poets, Li Po of the T'ang, is said to have written his first datable composition on it.[2] An architectural symbol of virtuous government, the Ming-t'ang exerted a powerful spell over Chinese rulers, who were drawn to it in the hope of benefiting from its legendary association with China's epic heroes.[3] Both Wang Mang and Empress Wu depended on it to help legitimate their usurpations of the throne. Even a thoroughly legitimate ruler like Ming-ti (rg. 58–75) of the Later Han appears to have substantially profited from its construction.[4] Wen-ti and Yang-ti of the Sui as well as T'ang T'ai-tsung and Kao-tsung all made plans to build a Ming-t'ang. The values associated with the structure were so great that any Chinese ruler would have benefited from one. But there were so many obstacles—textual, ritual, and political—preventing its completion, that few ever did.

Called variously a sacred house, a magic building, a house of the calendar, and a model of the universe, the Ming-t'ang has both fascinated and deeply confounded scholars, past and present, who have been able to reach little agreement regarding some of its most fundamental characteristics. Much of the confusion has been a product of the extant sources, which are dated, by their own accounts, hundreds of years after the inception of the Ming-t'ang and contain much mutually contradictory or even self-contradictory information. Direct references to the Ming-t'ang in the ancient literature are relatively few; it is mentioned not at all in such revered texts as the *Book of Changes*, *Book of Poetry*, *Book of History*, and the *Analects* of Confucius. The most important early canonical sources are the *Rites of Chou*, the *Book of Rites*, especially the "Monthly Instructions" (*Yüeh-ling*) chapter, the *Tso-chuan*, the *Book of Filial Piety*, and the *Mencius*, all variously dating from the third to first centuries B.C. It is also mentioned or discussed in a number of non-canonical works of the third to second centuries B.C., including the *Kuan-tzu*, *Huai-nan-tzu*, and *Lü-shih ch'un-ch'iu*.

Traditional sources have traced the creation of the Ming-t'ang variously to three culture-heroes of the third millennium B.C., Fu Hsi, Shen Nung, and Huang-ti (the Yellow Emperor), or alternately to the founders of the Western Chou dynasty, especially the Duke of Chou. In our own century it became fashionable to debunk the ancient origins of the Ming-t'ang and to assign it to a far later period, such as the Eastern Chou or Ch'in-Han times.[5] But as we shall see, there is evidence to suggest that the Ming-t'ang, at least as a body of ritual practice, may have originated in an earlier age.

How did the ancient Ming-t'ang function? The old texts have depicted the Ming-t'ang, variously and sometimes contradictorily, as a center of government; an audience hall where the Son of Heaven received his Feudal Princes; a place where the aged were fed and the worthy rewarded; a hall where the seasons were announced and the calendar conferred; a temple for sacrifices to the deities; an ancestral temple of the royal family; and a royal residence.[6] The Ming-t'ang thus appears to have been a center of politico-religious and politico-ceremonial activities. Beyond these mundane functions, the Ming-t'ang also seems to have served as an abode in which the ruler's potency was constantly revitalized. According to the "Monthly Instructions" chapter of the *Book of Rites*, while in the Ming-t'ang the ancient kings adjusted their activities, clothing, food, and ritual to harmonize with the twelve months and the five seasons (as the Chinese calculated them) of the year.

> In the first month of spring ... the Son of Heaven occupies the apartment on the left of the Ch'ing-yang [hall]; rides in the carriage with the phoenix [bells] drawn by the azure-dragon [horses] and carrying the green flag; wears the green robes, and the [pieces of] green jade [on his cap and at his girdle pendant]. He eats wheat and mutton. The vessels which he uses are slightly carved, [to resemble] the shooting forth [of plants]. . . . The canons of sacrifice

are examined and set forth, and orders are given to sacrifice to the hills and forests, the streams and lakes.... In the first month of summer ... the Son of Heaven occupies the apartment on the left of the Ming-t'ang [Great Hall]; rides in the vermilion carriage, drawn by the red horses with black tails and bearing the red flag. He is dressed in the red robes, and wears the carnation jade. He eats beans and fowls. The vessels which he uses are tall, [to resemble] the large growth [of things]. In this month the Son of Heaven [entertains his ministers and princes] with strong drink and with [much] observance of ceremony and with music.[7]

Additional regulations governed the three other seasons and the remaining ten months. The ruler's circumambulation of the Ming-t'ang in the course of the year served, thus, to order space and time, and to maintain an exact correspondence between the seasons and the points of the compass.[8] Harmonizing his movements with the motions of Heaven, and thereby successfully demonstrating his virtue, appears to have enabled the ruler to resonate with the rhythms of the universe and to absorb cosmic energy, thereby augmenting his temporal powers.

What does Ming-t'ang mean? Scholars have used various renderings depending on their understanding of the functions of the Ming-t'ang or of the Chinese character *ming*: Hall of Distinction, based on a section of the *Book of Rites* which says that the Ming-t'ang was so called "because in it the rank of the princes was clearly shown as high or low";[9] Hall of Illumination or Hall of Light, because in it "things were made clear";[10] Hall of Enlightenment, since in the Ming-t'ang the ruler was to "proclaim or make clear his general policy goals as well as to proclaim the calendar for the following year";[11] Hall of Spirits, in honor of the objects of the sacrifices that were performed there;[12] Bright Hall, in the sense that *ming* may signify "the brightness of the sun, or of imperial prestige, or of sage-like intelligence, or of widely influential moral excellence";[13] Hall of Heaven, equating *ming* with "sky," and taking Ming-t'ang to refer to a place in which to sacrifice to the sky or Heaven.[14] Adopting another approach, some scholars are convinced that the term Ming-t'ang has nothing to do with any functions that may have been carried out in the structure at a relatively late stage of its evolution, such as the Chou dynasty. They believe the *ming* refers simply to light, that the Ming-t'ang originally derived its name from a subterranean courtyard receiving the direct rays of the sun, and that when it became a structure above the ground and was roofed over, it retained its old name.[15] Another view is that the Ming-t'ang may originally have referred to a single room exposed to the sun.[16]

   That the term Ming-t'ang may have originally referred only to a single room rather than to a whole building is suggested by the "Monthly
Instructions," which gives the names of the five *shih*, or rooms, of the
structure: *ch'ing-yang*, *ming-t'ang*, *t'ai-shih* (*t'ai-miao*), *tsung-chang*, and
hsüan-t'ang. The five rooms appear to have been arranged according to the
points of the compass, with the *t'ai-miao* in the center and the other four
around it. The *ming-t'ang*, naturally, was situated in the southern quarter,
the quarter of light. Some scholars have hypothesized that these five terms
may actually refer to the names of five different structures existing during
successive periods of Chinese history, each of which should be considered
a kind of Ming-t'ang.[17]

   The association of the number five (as in five *shih*) with the Ming-
t'ang raises the question of the extent to which Ming-t'ang thought was
influenced by Five Element theory and, therefore, the possibility that it
was a product of only the late Chou or Ch'in-Han period. For the Han
interpreters of the structure, almost all its measurements have cosmological significance deriving from Five Element and yin-yang speculations.
The Later Han scholar, Ts'ai Yung, maintained that

> all the numbers of measurements of the Ming-t'ang are symbolic. The struc-
> ture situated on the terrace is square, 144 feet [per side], the number of the
> trigram K'un [Earth]. The round tower, diameter 216 feet, is the number [of
> the trigram] Ch'ien [Heaven].... There are 8 corridors to symbolize the 8
> trigrams, 9 rooms [*shih*] to symbolize the 9 provinces, 12 halls [*t'ang*] to cor-
> respond to the signs of the zodiac....[18]

Ts'ai's contemporary, Ying Shao, added that the thirty-six doors of the
Ming-t'ang were modeled on the thirty-six rains, and its seventy-two
windows on the seventy-two winds.[19] It might be noted that the Chinese
year is formed by thirty-six periods of ten days each, or by seventy-two
periods of five days each.[20] Such cosmological interpretations of the
Ming-t'ang structure continued down to T'ang times.[21]

   Despite its association with cosmological speculations of relatively
late date, there is a growing body of opinion among contemporary scholars that the Ming-t'ang owed its inception to religious belief and practice
which may be datable to quite early times. One view is that the Ming-
t'ang arose out of Chinese prayers to Heaven for good crops and to the
gods of nature to avoid natural catastrophe. The Ming-t'ang was a specially designated place for the carrying out of this ceremonial, and the form it
took was an earthen altar (*t'an*). Only later, perhaps in order to cope with

the elements, might a wooden structure have been built.[22] Another view is
that the Ming-t'ang arose from ritual sacrifice employing fire, which took
place on a mountain or high plateau, and whose purpose was to seek rain
for crops, long life, good health, victory in war, and so forth. Thus, the
Ming-t'ang, Feng and Shan sacrifices, and sacrificial altars of all kinds
shared the same origins—the employment of fire in ritual—which may be
dated as far back as Shang times.[23] Archaeological investigations in Honan
province have confirmed, furthermore, that five-*shih* structures were
already known during Shang dynasty times of the second millennium
B.C., and that these complexes, because of the remains of burnt-offerings,
appear to have been used as sacrificial altars, or *t'an*.[24] Both of these characteristics, as we have seen, were associated with the ancient Ming-t'ang.

What did the Ming-t'ang look like?[25] Disagreement arose from early
times concerning whether the Ming-t'ang was square or cross-shaped;
how many rooms or halls it contained, the numbers five, nine and twelve
being the most oft-cited; how these rooms or halls were arranged; whether
they were fully attached to one another, connected at the corners, or completely separated; whether they were under a single roof or several; how
they were subdivided into yet smaller units; what their measurements
were; whether the architectural proportions cited in the sources reflected
actual practice or only ideal models; how the thirty-six doors and seventy-
two windows mentioned in some texts were distributed; how certain
vague architectural terms were to be interpreted. Much of the discussion
has revolved around the question of whether the Ming-t'ang resembled
two other early Chinese structures, the royal palace (*ch'in* or *lu-ch'in*) and
the ancestral temple,[26] or two other structures often associated with it, the
pi-yung "jade-ring moat," and the *ling-t'ai* "spirit tower." Blueprints have
been drafted of a score or more hypothetical Ming-t'ang configurations,
all based either on information derived from the original texts or on their
traditional Chinese commentaries.[27]

In ancient times Ming-t'ang appear to have been established in at least
three separate locations. In the *Mencius* King Hsüan speaks of a Ming-t'ang
located in his state of Ch'i.[28] Many scholars have concluded that this structure must have been situated at the foot of T'ai-shan in modern Shantung
province, which was located in the heart of the Ch'i state. Later, Han
Wu-ti's Ming-t'ang was also situated in the same general vicinity.[29] A
second location for the Ming-t'ang is "south of the capital" (*kuo-nan*), or in
the "near suburbs" (*chin-chiao*), at a distance variously placed at three,
seven, or thirty *li*.[30] Yet another location is "beyond the frontiers" (*sai-*

wai), which is given in the *Hsün-tzu*.[31] From this we can see that whereas sacrifices at the ancestral temple, or at the altars of state (*she-chi*), could only be performed inside the capital, those at the Ming-t'ang, like the Feng and Shan sacrifices, could be performed even in remote regions far from the royal city.

It has been suggested that Ming-t'ang at different locations may have functioned along somewhat different lines. This would provide a possible reason for some of the contradictions contained in the old texts. According to this view, the structure established at the foot of T'ai-shan, in a region that since olden times had been linked to notions of longevity and immortality, may have been more oriented toward mysticism and magic. This T'ai-shan Ming-t'ang functioned analogously to the Feng and Shan sacrifices and suburban altar rites. On the other hand, the Ming-t'ang located in the suburbs of the capital may have been oriented more toward governmental administration and the demonstration of what was commonly associated with Confucian values—moral government, filial piety, ancestor worship, and the like. It functioned analogously to a ceremonial hall and ancestral temple. In short, whereas the T'ai-shan Ming-t'ang was more "Taoist' in nature, the suburban Ming-t'ang represented a more "Confucian" dimension of the structure.[32]

THE MING-T'ANG AND IMMORTALITY

We have seen that T'ai-shan was worshiped by the populace in the surrounding region as a *shen-hsien* mountain, and that it had associations with longevity and immortality.[33] It is likely, therefore, that Han Wu-ti's construction of a sacred edifice at the foot of the mountain was motivated by a desire to communicate with genies and obtain immortality, the same goals he hoped to attain by performing the Feng and Shan rites.[34] Wu-ti built his Ming-t'ang at T'ai-shan during a trip whose purpose was to view the P'eng-lai Mountains from a selected spot on the Shantung peninsula. It appears that in some manner Wu-ti equated T'ai-shan with the magical mountains of P'eng-lai, home of immortals. By sacrificing at his T'ai-shan Ming-t'ang, Wu-ti may have hoped to contact these transcendent beings and learn their secrets.[35] It is well known that when Wu-ti announced his desire to erect a Ming-t'ang, the blueprints he followed were presented to him by Kung-yü Tai, a native of the Shantung region, center of Chinese wizardry. These blueprints were purported to represent the Ming-t'ang of the mythological culture-hero Huang-ti, the Yellow Emperor. The build-

ing was of two stories, the bottom square and the top round. It had no
walls, and the roof was made of thatch. It was surrounded by an earthen
ditch. There was a covered passageway named the K'un-lun Way (*K'un-
lun tao*) leading into the building from the southwest, which the emperor
traversed when performing a sacrifice.[36]

The inclusion of a K'un-lun Way in Wu-ti's Ming-t'ang has generated
quite a bit of speculation among scholars about the origins and nature of
the building. The term K'un-lun began appearing in Chinese texts during
the Warring States period of the late Chou.[37] Scholars have argued with
one another over whether K'un-lun is a foreign or Chinese term, and have
attempted to link it with different foreign peoples and places, including the
"ziggurat culture" of ancient Babylonia.[38] In the largely Taoist texts *Huai-
nan-tzu* and *Shan-hai-ching* of the Han, K'un-lun typically appears as a
mountain of immortals, a paradise, a final goal. In the *Chuang-tzu* it is
depicted as the resting place of the Yellow Emperor, who supposedly
ascended to Heaven. The most persuasive hypothesis, it seems to me, is
that, whatever the actual origins of K'un-lun, it represents in the last
analysis a sacred archetype common to many of the world's ancient
cultures—a cosmic mountain soaring above the center of the world which
provides a bridge between Heaven and Earth. This mountain symbolizes
the original cosmos, and also the place where Creation began.[39] By means
of the cosmic mountain K'un-lun, communication was made with the
Chinese god-on-high, Shang-ti. Passing over the K'un-lun Way was the
same as climbing K'un-lun Mountain: those who ascended to its summit
gained everlasting life. The Ming-t'ang was thus located, in a religious
sense, at the Center of the world, and was a bridgeway to Heaven.[40] In
this respect the T'ai-shan Ming-t'ang was far more representative of
theurgy than of any Confucian notions of kingship or ritual.

Yet even the more "Confucian" suburban Ming-t'ang seems to have
had the power of conferring a kind of immortality. The suburban Ming-
t'ang was lunar-oriented in its division into twelve compartments, which
the sovereign traversed according to the phases of the moon. Eliade believes that the moon's phases reveal what he calls the "Eternal Return," a
paradigmatic concept existing in many ancient or primitive cultures.
Eliade sees in the lunar rhythm the archetype of a cycle of waxing and
waning that mirrors the birth of humanity, its growth, decrepitude, and
disappearance. But "just as the disappearance of the moon is never final,
since it is necessarily followed by a new moon, the disappearance of man is
not final either...." The death of an individual and of humanity is neces-

sary for their regeneration, as the death of the moon is a necessary prelude
to its rebirth. Thus, the circular movement within the Ming-t'ang of time
and man is projected upon three planes—cosmic, biological, and historical. It is a circular movement going nowhere, only returning to the point of
departure once the lunar phases have run their course. It is an affirmation
that "everything begins over again at its commencement every instant."
As such, time becomes suspended, or, at least, its effect is diminished.[41]

THE MING-T'ANG AND GNOSIS

In this section we must return to van Gennep's notion that rites of passage
are characterized by three stages—preliminal, liminal, and postliminal—
by which ritual subjects are symbolically separated from and reincorporated into society. Here, we are especially concerned with liminal rites, or
rites of transition. Van Gennep likened such transitions to the spatial
crossing of frontiers or architectural thresholds: Limens are literally
"thresholds." "When one passes from one [frontier] to the other he finds
himself physically and magico-religiously in a special situation for a certain length of time: he wavers between two worlds. . . . This symbolic and
spatial area of transition may be found in more or less pronounced form in
all ceremonies which accompany the passage from one social and magico-
religious position to another."[42] The portal itself, therefore, was a sacred
object.[43] By crossing the threshold a person left one world behind and
entered a new one. Van Gennep noted that passage from one social position to another was often identified among peoples with a territorial passage, such as entering a village or house, moving from one room to
another, or crossing streets or squares. He observed that human transitions were, among some peoples, linked to the celestial passages, the
revolution of the planets, and the phases of the moon. This cosmic conception, he said, "relates the stages of human existence to those of plant
and animal life and by a sort of prescientific divination, joins them to the
great rhythms of the universe."[44]

Victor Turner has expanded our understanding of the state which
ritual subjects enter when they undergo a rite of transition, which he calls
"liminality."[45] For Turner a subject in a state of liminality is in an ambi-
guous position, "neither here nor there, betwixt and between the positions
assigned and arranged by law, convention and ceremonial." Rites of liminality characteristically begin with the symbolic killing of the subject or
his separation from ordinary secular or profane relationships, and con-

clude with his symbolic birth or reincorporation into society. Liminality, Turner notes, "is frequently likened to death, to being in the womb, to invisibility, to darkness, to bisexuality, to the wilderness, and to an eclipse of the sun and moon." In liminality, subjects are stripped of all symbols of rank or role; they have no status, property, or insignia. Particularly germane to our argument are three observations by Turner. First, liminality "often draws on poverty for its repertoire of symbols." Second, "since liminality represents ... 'a leveling and stripping' of structural status, an important component of the liminal situation is ... an enhanced stress on nature at the expense of culture." Third, gnosis or "deep knowledge" is highly characteristic of liminality; new knowledge is imparted, new power absorbed, power that will become active in the subject's postliminal life when he has been reincorporated into society.[46]

If we recall descriptions of the Ming-t'ang provided earlier in this chapter, some correspondences should become apparent in the light of the theories of van Gennep and Turner. First, the Ming-t'ang was a structure of several rooms—five, nine, or twelve—each containing doors and windows. It lacked ornamentation and was topped by a humble thatch roof—symbols of poverty. According to the "Monthly Instructions" chapter of the *Book of Rites*, the sovereign was supposed to pass through these rooms and establish residence in them one by one according to the months or seasons of the year. His territorial passage from room to room was made possible, presumably, by proceeding through the doors and crossing their thresholds—as many as thirty-six of them. He thus circumambulated the structure once each year. In the Ming-t'ang time was circular, as it was also circular in the Chinese method of reckoning with branches and stems. By moving the proper spatial distance, as well as by changing his clothing, food, music, ritual behavior, royal administrative practice, and so on, he was able to harmonize his behavior with the seasons and governing lunar phases. All this suggests that the circumambulation of the Ming-t'ang by the sovereign was both figuratively and literally a rite of passage, a passage linked to "the great rhythms of the universe."

It is also clear from the "Monthly Instructions" that while in transit through the five seasons the sovereign entered states of liminality marked in part by the doffing of clothing and insignia appropriate to one season and assuming those appropriate to the next one. He was thus stripped for a time of distinctions of rank and role. At this moment he was "neither here nor there, betwixt and between" his usual position in society. At this moment nature prevailed over culture. The ruler passed through a state of darkness or invisibility before emerging into the light (provided by the windows) of the next room, a figurative eclipse of the sun and moon before their re-emergence (sun plus moon = *ming*) in the next temporal phase. He was in effect, passing through life and being reborn.

At the same time, circumambulation of the Ming-t'ang seems to have been a territorial passage designed to achieve gnosis, or deep knowledge. As Eliade points out in his study of initiatory rites, initiatory death is indispensable to the beginning of spiritual life.[47] First comes a return to the womb, darkness, then re-emergence (thus paralleling van Gennep's pre-liminal, liminal, and postliminal stages). In this respect, the re-emergence of the Chinese sovereign from the darkness of the threshold to the light of the room reflected his new, transcendant mode of existence, a spiritual rebirth.[48] This rebirth was based on new knowledge, the knowledge of an initiate. The *ming* of Ming-t'ang, whatever source it may have originally been derived from, or whatever else it may connote, should in this respect be understood as sacred knowledge.

In a review of the newly discovered silk manuscripts at Ma-wang-tui, Tu Wei-ming has pointed out elements of Huang-Lao thought which may tell us something about the early Taoist approach to *ming*. Tu notes that a Huang-Lao sage-ruler was ideally expected to possess a quality known as *kuan*, or "penetrating insight." *Kuan* is "the ability to observe things as they really are; this ability can best be cultivated by distancing oneself from the immediate demands of politics so that one can see objectively the 'timeliness' [*shih*] of the interpenetration of heaven and earth, the evolution of the four seasons, and the alternation of the yin and yang forces." Tu goes on to observe that "a most eloquent symbol of the perception required of the ruler is the statue which is alleged to be the Yellow Emperor's self-portrait. It is a square statue with four similar faces pointing out from the center so that he can see all twelve directions."[49] When we remember that the T'ai-shan Ming-t'ang, which was supposedly modeled on that of the Yellow Emperor, was square in shape and open on four sides so that vision in all directions was unobstructed, the correspondence is suggestive. Might it be possible in this context to understand the *ming* of Ming-t'ang as the unobstructed or unhindered (i.e., lucid) vision of the sovereign, which he hoped to attain by sojourning in his cosmic house?

At a certain level, then, wherever its location or whatever governing ideas it was based upon, the Ming-t'ang was a place where the sovereign's vision was made lucid and deep knowledge was obtained, each a form of *ming*. At the T'ai-shan Ming-t'ang, the elements of centrality, *k'un-lun*, ascension, and so forth, underlined the characteristics of *ming*. Built at the base of a sacred mountain, the T'ai-shan Ming-t'ang was itself a cosmic mountain, the "ascension" of which brought the ruler into communication with the *hsien* deities and the gods. His enlightenment derived from his contact with the "other world" and its spiritual denizens. Alternately, as suggested by the statue of the Yellow Emperor, *ming* may have constituted unobstructed or unhindered vision which all sage-rulers were believed to possess, and which later sovereigns hoped to attain for themselves by circulating in their Ming-t'ang. At the suburban Ming-t'ang enlightenment was achieved in the form of deep knowledge, gnosis, symbolized by the light pouring through the seventy-two windows. Similarly, both Ming-t'ang had the power to confer immortality on a sovereign, either a *hsien* immortality in the case of the T'ai-shan structure, or a repetitive, cyclic rebirth, perhaps more spiritual than physical, in the case of the suburban Ming-t'ang.

EARLY T'ANG EFFORTS TO RESTORE THE MING-T'ANG

Whether or not the ancient Ming-t'ang, as some of the early sources suggest, ever served as a center of government, during Han times most of its alleged functions came to be exercised by other units of government.[50] Thereafter, it became primarily a place for performing sacrifices to various deities, especially the Five Emperors and the dynastic ancestors.[51] This situation continued in the Period of Disunion as well. Except for the Northern Wei dynasty, Ming-t'ang practice appears to have declined in the North. In the South, the sacred edifice was constructed more often. But here, many of the Ming-t'ang ceremonies were carried out at the same time as the suburban altar rites, somewhat negating their singularity and, consequently, lowering their status.[52] The Northern Ch'i and Northern Chou dynasties had no Ming-t'ang, although plans were made for them.[53] When dynasties had no formal Ming-t'ang, the sacrifices normally performed there were held in a room of the palace or at the suburban altars.

Both Sui rulers considered establishing Ming-t'ang. In 593 the dynastic founder, Wen-ti, ordered his courtiers to discuss the project.[54] The president of the Board of Rites, Niu Hung, depending for much of his data on the interpretations of Cheng Hsüan, envisaged a five-room structure, with the top round and the bottom square, surrounded by a moat.[55] The emperor's master architect, Yü-wen K'ai, made a wooden model of a Ming-t'ang and presented it to the throne. The lower storey consisted of a square hall divided into five rooms, and the upper storey of a round tower, with gates oriented to the four directions.[56] Wen-ti then appointed officials to survey the land in the vicinity of the capital as the location for the structure. But wrangling among the Confucian ritualists, who could not agree on a suitable blueprint, caused the eventual cancellation of the project.[57] Yü-wen K'ai again presented his wooden model to the throne during Yang-ti's time. But again on this occasion no Ming-t'ang was built, owing variously, it is said, to Sui military campaigns in Liao-tung and Yang-ti's construction of a new capital on the Yangtze River, Chiang-tu.[58]

Of the early T'ang rulers, Kao-tsu is portrayed as having had no time to consider establishing a Ming-t'ang.[59] But shortly after ascending the throne, his son, T'ai-tsung, ordered his officials to discuss the matter. What followed was the usual Confucian wrangling over just about every detail of Ming-t'ang practice.[60] In 631 it was suggested by the president of the Board of Rites and another official that the Ming-t'ang should be a two-storey structure. The top storey, access to which was to be by means of a K'un-lun Way, was to be devoted to sacrifices to Heaven. The bottom storey was to be devoted to conducting court affairs. However, K'ung Ying-ta bitterly denounced the plan as sanctioned neither by the Confucian classics nor by ancient historical precedent. Attacking Han Wu-ti, who, he said, had been seduced by his *fang-shih* wizards into creating an unorthodox and unnecessarily elaborate structure, he advocated a far simpler building on the model of the sage-rulers of old. In response to K'ung's plan, the president of the Chancellery, Wei Cheng, advocated that the T'ang construct a Ming-t'ang of five rooms, round on top and square below. Agreeing with the earlier proposal of the president of the Board of Rites, he specified that the sacrifices to Heaven were to be performed on the upper storey, and court audiences were to conducted on the lower. In this way, he explained, what pertained to men and what pertained to the gods would be kept distinct. As for the rules regarding the height, width, size of the mats for the rooms, and so forth, all could be determined according to contemporary taste rather than by slavishly relying on past practice.[61] In the end, however, the discussants could not come to any decision on what the structure should look like.

Later in T'ai-tsung's reign, in 643, the Ming-t'ang issue was again addressed by the president of the Imperial Library, Yen Shih-ku. The documents for the Ming-t'ang were in such disarray, he observed, that not even the most erudite of Confucians could claim a full understanding of them. All the evidence, however, pointed to the fact that the Ming-t'ang was the formal residence of the ancient kings. He disagreed with those, such as Cheng Hsüan, who claimed that the structure should be located south of the capital—for how could the royal residence be in the suburbs? He suggested, therefore, that the Ming-t'ang be constructed close to the palace. Moreover, as the times changed, so did the ritual and music that men created; it was thus proper, he concluded, to make decisions regarding the Ming-t'ang ritual on the basis of contemporary tastes.[62] On another occasion Yen counseled T'ai-tsung that the most important thing was for him simply to build a Ming-t'ang, and not waste time fretting over the number of windows or doors or the measurements of its rooms. "If you allow the Confucians to hold different views without quickly arriving at a solution, it will only delay [the performance of] your rites." He advocated that the emperor adopt his own blueprint for a Ming-t'ang, much as Han Wu-ti had made his own decision when faced with disagreement among his ritualists over the Feng and Shan rites.[63] Whether or not in the end T'ai-tsung would have heeded such advice is debatable, for all plans to build a Ming-t'ang had to be postponed upon the commencement of the T'ang military campaigns against Korea, which occupied the final years of his reign.[64]

The Ming-t'ang debate of Kao-tsung's period, like many other ritual issues of the time, pitted supporters of the doctrines of Cheng Hsüan against those of other classical exegetes. In 651, just two years after coming to power, Kao-tsung issued an edict inaugurating discussions on the sacred edifice among his officials and ritual experts. Thereupon, the followers of Cheng Hsüan upheld the view that the Ming-t'ang was a structure of five rooms; their opponents held to a view of nine rooms, based on the opinions of the Later Han scholars Lu Chih and Ts'ai Yung. Each side drafted blueprints of their models and stubbornly stood their ground. At first, Kao-tsung leaned toward the nine-room model and, with this as a starting point, ordered his officials to settle and details. But the following year more wrangling broke out among the discussants, and Kao-tsung was moved to order a public debate between the two camps. This time, under the influence of the master architect, Yen Li-te, the emperor opted for a five-room design. Nevertheless, no permanent agreement was reached.[65]

In 656 yet another Ming-t'ang controversy involving the views of Cheng Hsüan erupted at court. In order to understand it more fully, we need once more to discuss briefly the deities known as the Five Emperors

(*Wu-ti*).[66] The Five Emperors took various forms: the Five Heavenly Emperors (*Wu t'ien-ti*), the Five Human (i.e. "historical") Emperors (*Wu jen-ti*), and the Spirits of the Five Elements (*Wu-hsing chih shen*). The Five Heavenly Emperors, we saw earlier, were associated both with the five colors and the five cardinal directions. Along with Hao-t'ien shang-ti they comprised the Six Heavens of Cheng Hsüan's theory. Cheng viewed the Six Heavens as the same as Heaven (*t'ien*) but also identified them with stars—the Northern Chronogram/Radiant Moon-Soul Gem in the case of Hao-t'ien shang-ti, and five other stars in the case of the Five Heavenly Emperors. Wang Su opposed Cheng's view that the Five Heavenly Emperors, as mere stars, could be equated with Heaven.[67] The Five Human Emperors were believed to be human embodiments of the essence of the Five Elements; although identified variously, they often included culture-heroes like the Yellow Emperor, Yao, and Shun.[68] When the Five Heavenly Emperors were worshiped, the Five Human Emperors frequently served as *p'ei*.

In Kao-tsu's time, under the influence of Cheng Hsüan's ritual interpretations, the Five Emperors were worshiped at the four suburban altars and at the Ming-t'ang. At the Ming-t'ang rites, the dynastic ancestor, Li Ping, was designated associated ancestral deity. Because by the end of T'ai-tsung's reign no formal Ming-t'ang had yet been built, these sacrifices actually came to be performed at the round altar, where Kao-tsu was designated *p'ei*.[69] But in 651, the same year in which Kao-tsung first decided to construct a Ming-t'ang, T'ai-tsung was also designated *p'ei* for the sacrifices performed there: Kao-tsu was to be *p'ei* in relation to the Five Heavenly Emperors, whereas T'ai-tsung was to be *p'ei* in relation to the Five Human Emperors.[70]

In 656, as part of the general turning away from Cheng Hsüan's ritual theories at the T'ang court, Chang-sun Wu-chi and other ritual officials protested T'ai-tsung's designation as *p'ei*. The issue revolved around the interpretation of a passage in the *Book of Filial Piety*:

> In reverencing one's father, nothing is greater than making him *p'ei* to Heaven. The Duke of Chou did this. Formerly, the Duke of Chou sacrificed to [his ancestor] Hou Chi as the *p'ei* to Heaven [*t'ien*], and sacrificed to his ancestor King Wen in the Ming-t'ang as the *p'ei* to Shang-ti.[71]

On the basis of this passage, and also the well-known section of the *Book of Rites* which recorded that the Chou sovereigns sacrificed to King Wen as their *tsu* and King Wu as their *tsung* (both ancestral designations), Cheng

Hsüan had upheld the concept of joint *p'ei* at the Ming-t'ang.[72] Wang Su, on the other hand, believed that the terms *tsu* and *tsung* referred to the fact that, because of their virtue and merit, the spirit-tablets of the two kings at the ancestral temple were never to be destroyed. They were thus merely terms of veneration, having nothing to do with the designation of *p'ei* at the Ming-t'ang. The T'ang memorialists upheld Wang Su's views against those of Cheng Hsüan. In earlier times, they pointed out, dynastic founders were always made *p'ei* to Heaven in state sacrifices. In conformance to this tradition, they requested that Kao-tsu be made *p'ei* to Hao-t'ien shang-ti at the round altar. T'ai-tsung, who had also made essential contributions to the founding of the dynasty, should be made *p'ei* to Shang-ti at the Ming-t'ang. In this way both could jointly be honored as *p'ei* to Heaven.[73] The emperor acceded to their request.

The opposition to Cheng Hsüan's ideas as the basis of Ming-t'ang practice accelerated during the following year with the campaign of Chang-sun Wu-chi, Hsü Ching-tsung, and other ritualists to overturn the supremacy of Cheng's theory of the Six Heavens.[74] In their memorial to Kao-tsung they pointed out that Cheng, influenced by the weft texts, had viewed the Six Heavens as nothing more than celestial bodies—stars and constellations. But it was clear from the classics, they maintained, that stars were not the same as Heaven, nor did they occupy its exalted status. Since, according to the *Book of Filial Piety*, the ancestral objects of sacrifice at the Ming-t'ang were to be *p'ei* to Heaven, it was improper to make them *p'ei* to mere stars. They therefore requested that the sacrifices to the Five Emperors at the Ming-t'ang be terminated, and that Hao-t'ien shang-ti be treated as the principal object of worship in their place. The emperor followed their advice.[75] The new regulations were incorporated into the *Hsien-ch'ing li* of 658.

This state of affairs lasted until 666, when worship of the Five Emperors at the Ming-t'ang was restored. The next year, Hao-t'ien shang-ti was made a sacrificial object at the Ming-t'ang along with the Five Emperors; Kao-tsu and T'ai-tsung were again, as in 651, designated joint *p'ei*.[76] In the midst of great indecisiveness among the emperor and his officials, Cheng Hsüan's views thus seemed to have held a tenuous sway. But in 677, with the order that the regulations incorporated into both the *Chen-kuan li* and *Hsien-ch'ing li* were to be followed in determining ritual practice, Wang Su's ideas appeared to triumph overall as the basis of Ming-t'ang practice.[77] In the end, however, Kao-tsung never did succeed in erecting his cosmic house.

Despite this fact, he sought to milk every possible political advantage from his association with the projected structure. In 668, he changed his reign-name to *Tsung-chang*, supposedly the name of the Ming-t'ang of the culture-hero Shun. At the same time, he renamed the Wan-nien district of the capital Ming-t'ang *hsien*, a designation which lasted throughout the period of Empress Wu's domination of government.[78]

When a Ming-t'ang was finally constructed by Empress Wu in 688 in her capital at Lo-yang, it was largely because she ran roughshod over her Confucian ritualists in her desperate need to obtain additional legitimation for her usurpation.[79] Instead of the Confucians, she relied on the services of a Buddhist monk, Hsüeh Huai-i, and her Ming-t'ang consequently had a flavor as much Buddhist as Confucian.[80] At any rate, in 695 Hsüeh burned to the ground, in a fit of jealousy, the building whose construction he had supervised less than ten years before. The empress rebuilt her Ming-t'ang on a somewhat smaller scale, and it was again constructed in Hsüan-tsung's time. Afterward, it lapsed into disuse.[81]

Empress Wu's Ming-t'ang is said to have been a huge building, some 294 feet high, 300 feet square, and on three levels, the bottom two rectangular and the top one round.[82] Upon its completion she carried out in it some of the functions said to have been characteristic of the ancient Ming-t'ang: promulgation of edicts, nourishing of the aged, banqueting of officials, rewarding of the meritorious, and the reception of emissaries.[83] But these activities were on the whole one-shot affairs, not routine performances. Nowhere is there any indication that Wu ever ritually circumambulated the structure, according to the "Monthly Instructions," in order to produce a cosmic harmony. Her Ming-t'ang, moreover, was decorated in grandiose style, with much gold, pearl, and jade, and an ornate roof made of wood carved to resemble tile. In no sense did it suggest the simplicity or rusticity associated with the ancient Ming-t'ang, or with any symbols of liminality. It was not a structure designed to achieve any kind of clarity of vision or deep knowledge, but rather to overwhelm the senses by virtue of its sheer size and extravagant ornamentation. Its purpose was patently political and propagandistic, a device by which to enhance the empress's legitimacy and to bolster her authority. Even in this ritually imperfect state, Wu's Ming-t'ang appears to have worked some of its ancient magic. Within three years following its completion, she felt confident enough of her power to put to death members of the T'ang royal house and to announce her own dynasty.

It has been pointed out that basically there were two forms of worshiping Heaven in China, represented by the Feng and Shan rites on platforms located in the open air, and the Ming-t'ang ceremonies which took place in roofed-in halls. In Sung times, according to James T. C. Liu, Ming-t'ang worship followed the hall form, but the hall was brought inside the imperial palace, where, in effect, Heaven was worshiped as an ancestor. Such a practice served, Liu concludes, to elevate the emperor's position relative to Heaven, consequently increasing his absolutist power.[84] Ming-t'ang practice appears to have been viewed in a different light by the early T'ang rulers. For them, recreating a Ming-t'ang that was structurally independent from the imperial palace was the best means of enhancing their political position. As we have seen, in the early T'ang the power of ancestors to legitimate seems to have declined in relation of the power of Heaven to legitimate imperial authority. Hao-t'ien shang-ti emerged as the dominant sacrificial object at the altar rites and also at the Ming-t'ang. By making successive plans to construct formal Ming-t'ang outside of the palace, early T'ang emperors sought to forge more intimate links not with Hao-t'ien shang-ti as an ancestor but as a powerful religious entity in his own right. He was treated, then, not as a lineal ancestor of the dynastic house, of which there were many, but as a uniquely potent universal god of the whole empire. At the Ming-t'ang, as at the suburban altar rites, the concept of "there is only one Heaven" ruled the day.

CHAPTER 11

Promulgation of the Calendar

The founder of a new Chinese dynasty had to demonstrate the transition of legitimacy, after his victory, partly by his performance of certain imperial rituals and partly by reforming certain institutions which were closely related to the imperial charisma. One such practice was "correcting the beginning of years and months"—that is, calendar reform.

Kiyosi Yabuuti, "Chinese Astronomy"

STUDENTS OF THE CHINESE CALENDAR HAVE TENDED TO TRACE ITS ORIGIN TO one or the other of two basic needs. The first was the need of an agrarian people to know when to sow, reap, and perform a variety of other agricultural tasks.[1] The second was the need of a sacrally oriented elite to perform ritual and managerial functions at precisely prescribed times of the year. Supporters of this second position assume that the calendar was not primarily concerned with the needs of the farmer, since he might regulate his activities well enough merely by observing the signs of nature, but rather with those of the monarch.[2] Indeed, as we shall see, the fact that rulers felt compelled to continue to increase the precision of their calendars, long after all mundane needs had been satisfied, suggests that the calendar was not primarily a practical but rather a ritual vehicle, reflecting more the sovereign's cosmic identity than his stewardship of an agriculturally oriented realm.

In any case, the promulgation of a calendar was a major step in dynastic legitimation. Its acceptance by the sovereign's vassals, the common people, and even foreign tributaries was considered a demonstration of their loyalty to the throne.[3] The fixing of the calendar was a monopoly of the sovereign and his court, and from early times in China astronomical observation was wedded to state power and benefited from state support.

The royal relationship to astronomical duties is depicted in the very first passages of the *Book of History*, the "Canon of Yao," where Yao in-

structs two of his assistants, Hsi and Ho, and their deputies, on fixing the
agricultural year, determining the year's exact length, and introducing the
intercalary month, regulating, thereby, all human activities.[4] The "Monograph on Literature" of the *History of the Former Han Dynasty* relates
calendar-making to a variety of royal needs:

> Calendars arrange the four seasons in due sequence, adjust the equinoxes and
> solstices, and calculate the solar, lunar, and planetary concordances, so as to
> examine into the actualities of cold and heat, life and death. Therefore the
> Sage-kings had to correct their calendars in order to settle the clothing and
> color correspondences of the Three Sequences [*san-t'ung*, i.e., the sequence by
> which the governing colors of the Hsia, Shang, and Chou dynasties were
> supposed to have replaced one another]. By their investigations they knew
> the time of the conjunctions of the sun, moon, and planets. The misery of
> calamity and the happiness of prosperity were all made manifest through their
> [calendrical] arts. It was by these arts that the Sages came to know the Man-
> date [of Heaven].[5]

Since the sovereign came to be envisaged as an axis between Heaven and
Earth, it was his role to maintain a harmonious resonance between the
forces of nature and of mankind. As we saw in the preceding chapter, the
ruler moved through the rooms of the Ming-t'ang according to the seasons of the year so as to maintain a concordance between the realms of
chronology and ritual activity. The object of the Chinese calendar was
essentially the same.

Because of the calendar's weighty symbolic meaning there was an
"insatiable demand" by Chinese monarchs "for increased precision" in
calendrical calculations, far in excess of normal agricultural, bureaucratic,
or economic needs.[6] In his role as Grand Harmonizer, a new sovereign had
to deliver to his people calendars of ever greater accuracy. He had to calcu-
late with increasing success all known astronomical regularities, such as
eclipses of the sun and moon and the positions of the planets, in order
constantly to expand "the demonstrable order of the sky while reducing
the irregular and the ominous."[7] The great stress placed on astronomical
observation in traditional China was primarily for calendrical purposes,
and to facilitate the prediction of future events or the interpretation of
current events by the reading of Heavenly signs and portents.[8] Any empir-
ical evidence appearing in the cosmos that the ruler's calculations were
incorrect, such as an untimely eclipse or solstice, threatened the idea that
he retained Heaven's Mandate. Conversely, a demonstrated correspond-

ence between computed ephemerides and celestial phenomena was taken as a sign that his Mandate endured.[9] Thus, between the years 370 B.C. and A.D. 1742 it is estimated that the Chinese compiled no fewer than one hundred calendars or sets of astronomical tables (li).[10] Not only did new dynasties recalculate the calendar, but later in Chinese history, during the T'ang period, for example, the calendar was recalculated several times within a single dynasty. Not all of these calendars, of course, were actually improvements over their predecessors, but each was nevertheless a statement designed to enhance the authority of the sovereign under whose aegis it was calculated.

Every calendar faces the same problem: how to bring consonance between solar years (365.2422 days) and synodic months (29.53059 days), and what to do with the extra days contained in the solar year. The Chinese developed a number of systems to deal with this problem. According to modern scholars, these, like other features of their ephemerides, seem to have been arrived at largely independently of solutions reached in other world cultures. Early on, the Chinese realized that the excess accumulated in each solar year, approximately eleven days, added up to almost precisely seven months every nineteen years; that is, nineteen was the smallest number of years which equaled a whole number of months. (This method, also used in Greece, was called the cycle of Meton.) The year and month could start together only once every nineteen years of 235 months, a unit the Chinese called a *chang*. The seven extra months were inserted between months at two- or three-year intervals for a total of seven intercalations every nineteen years. The intercalated months were inserted in such a way as to ensure that the winter solstice always arrived in the eleventh month. Thus, the spring equinox fell in the second month, the summer solstice in the fifth, and the autumn equinox in the eighth.

By similar mathematical computations, Chinese astronomers were able to construct longer and longer cycles that harmonized wider numbers of celestial motions, not only of the sun and moon but also of the known planets, the Chinese sexagenary day and year cycles, and other variables, by employing the lowest common multiples of all their periods. The longest of these cosmo-numerological cycles lasted more than twenty-three million years, at which time another great epoch commenced.[11] By using these cycles the Chinese were able to determine lunations and years, along with the necessary intercalations, and so on, by calculating the *mean* motions of the sun, moon, and planets. But this method could achieve only limited accuracy in the prediction of eclipses or major planetary phenomena. Despite gradual progress, it was not until the eighth century, when Indian and Islamic advances were incorporated into Chinese astronomy, that astronomers were able to abandon the mean motions computed on the basis of cycles and employ more complex models.[12] But this development lies beyond the scope of our study.

THE PRE-T'ANG CALENDARS

Despite our knowledge of the existence of calendars in China as far back as about the fifth century B.C., details of the science of time measurement are available to us only from the Han period.[13] Until the reign of Emperor Wu, the Han dynasty employed the Ch'in calendar, whose year began in the tenth month. But, by this time, the old calendar's accuracy had declined and a new one was needed. Thus, at the time of his sacrifice to Shang-ti at the Ming-t'ang situated at the foot of T'ai-shan, the same spot the Yellow Emperor was said to have built his sacred edifice, Emperor Wu announced his new calendar. The epoch of this calendar, named Grand Inception (*T'ai-ch'u*), was December 24, 105 B.C.[14] It was simultaneously the winter solstice, a new moon, the dawn of the first day of the eleventh month, and a *chia-tzu* day. It was also the moment, according to the "Monograph on the Calendar" of the *History of the Former Han Dynasty*, when the sun and moon rose together and the planets were all lined up "like strung pearls," although, as Nathan Sivin has shown, they were actually fairly widely scattered across the sky.[15] The calendar was said to have originated with the Yellow Emperor, whose Grand Inception had taken place one great cycle, or 4,617 years, earlier.[16] The beginning of the year was now changed from the tenth month to the first month of spring, following a tradition begun, it was believed, during the Hsia dynasty. The first month has continued, with only minor interruptions, as the beginning of the Chinese year in the lunisolar calendar down to our own age. At the same time, the dynastic color was changed to yellow.[17] The promulgation of the Grand Inception Calendar was part of a ceremonial reform that linked the Former Han to the legendary dynasty of Hsia and also to the Yellow Emperor of an even more ancient age.[18]

The next major calendrical reform took place around A.D. 6, when Liu Hsin produced the Triple Concordance (*San-t'ung*) Calendar, probably in preparation for the usurpation of power by Wang Mang.[19] It was essentially a universal system of ephemeris calculation employing a much higher number of constants than the Grand Inception system. Two of the new constants were the 135-month lunar eclipse period and the synodic period of the planets.[20] According to Wolfram Eberhard, the numerical harmonies established in the Triple Concordance system also

> extended to comprise *I-ching* numbers, old historical dates, the doctrine of the five elements, the *Yin Yang* speculations, the length of tubes to produce musical notes, the units of length and volume, the standards for religious buildings [e.g., the *Ming-t'ang*], and for court ceremonies and attire. Thus, the *San-t'ung* calendar established more than a calendar system; it created a world-concept such as has been approximated only by that of Pythagoras.[21]

Probably for political reasons, the system did not much outlast the period of Wang Mang (rg. A.D. 9–23), who had overthrown the Han and founded his own dynasty.

Yet another calendar, developed toward the end of the first century A.D., was the Quarter Day (*Ssu-fen*).[22] Here, the solar year was measured as exactly 365.2500 days (thus lending the calendar its name) as opposed to the 365.2502 days of the Triple Concordance Calendar. It is therefore closer to the modern value of 365.2422, its excess amounting to one day about every 128 years. Nevertheless, because the concept of precession of the equinoxes (produced by the gyrating motion of the earth, which causes the equinox points to perform a slow clockwise movement on the ecliptic) was still unknown, and because of other factors, the Quarter Day Calendar was frequently in need of correction during the Later Han.[23]

A number of advances in astronomy and calendrical methods were made from the Later Han dynasty down to the Sui. For example, by the second century A.D. the fact that the plane of the equator is inclined to the earth's orbit, which accounts for the existence of the equinoxes and solstices, had been discovered, and the obliquity measured in degrees. In the fourth century Yü Hsi discovered that there was a difference between the length of the tropical and sidereal year. Called the "annual difference" (*sui-ch'a*), and equivalent to precession of the equinoxes, it was employed in a calendar for the first time by the Southern Sung mathematician and calendrical expert Tsu Ch'ung-chih (fl. 430–510).[24] Although some phenomena were more easily predicted than before, the accuracy of eclipse prediction was still a relative matter. The *Old T'ang History* "Monograph on the Calendar" (*Li-chih*) speaks of an incident during the 550–59 reign-period of the Northern Ch'i emperor, Wen-hsüan, when all three predictions of a solar eclipse by royal astronomers proved wrong.[25]

When the Sui first came to power, it employed a calendar of the Northern Chou that had been in effect since 580. But in 584 it issued a new calendar, called the *K'ai-huang li* after the current reign-name of Sui Wen-ti. Chang Pin, the compiler of the new calendar, seems not to have been a specialist in calendrical calculations but had some knowledge of astronomy and was well versed in *ch'an-wei* thought. Chang Pin's calendar in turn was largely modeled on one fashioned by Ho Ch'eng-t'ien of the Southern Sung dynasty (420–79), which had served as the basis for southern calendars down to the Southern Ch'i dynasty in the early sixth century.[26] One of the features of Northern Dynasties calendars since the Northern Wei was that they did away with the so-called "rule-cycle" method (*chang-fa*) of intercalation, by which the Chinese since ancient times had intercalated seven months every nineteen years. Instead, they employed a new system in which 221 months were intercalated every 600 years, aptly named the "broken rule-cycle method" (*p'o-chang fa*). The Southern Dynasties, on the contrary, had continued to use the rule-cycle method, a fact reflected in Ho Ch'eng-t'ien's calendar, and now also in Chang Pin's. Since the rule-cycle method was somewhat coarser than the broken rule-cycle method, and since Chang Pin's calendar also failed to take into consideration the annual difference, another astronomical advance, it received a rather critical reception from certain of Wen-ti's officials. But because Chang Pin was one of his favorites, the emperor remained adamant about retaining the *K'ai-huang li*, and it therefore continued in use for thirteen years, until 596.[27]

One of the most vociferous critics of Chang Pin's calendar was the scholar Liu Ch'o, who in A.D. 600 was summoned to the Eastern Palace to serve as a calendrical expert to the Sui heir, the future Yang-ti. Sometime afterward, Liu presented the future emperor a new calendar, called the *Huang-chi li*. The *Huang-chi li* represented a notable advance over previous calendars. For example, following the ideas of the Southern Sung calendrical expert Ho Ch'eng-t'ien, whom we have already met, it employed a method known as the true lunation (*ting-shuo*), in which the length of the month corresponded to the actual interval between conjunctions rather than mean months. This is a method used in our own modern calendars. Following Southern Dynasties tradition, it also recognized the annual difference, employing an even more accurate value than previously calculated. A further refinement was made in the area of lunar intercalation, which, in a return to the broken rule-cycle method of the Northern Dynasties, was fixed at 249 intercalations every 676 years. The *Huang-chi li* thus unified the divergent calendrical methodologies of North and South China, and at the same time represented a great improvement in calendar making. Although the Huang-chi Calendar was never put into practice, it nevertheless served, as we shall soon see, as the basis for the great calendars of the first half of the T'ang especially the Lin-te Calendar of Kao-tsung's period.[28]

From 597 to the beginning of the T'ang, the Sui employed a calendar fashioned by Chang Chou-hsüan. Chang's calendar had been strongly criticized at court. But Wen-ti had received a memorial noting that the great calendrical expert of the Han, Lo-hsia Hung, had claimed that his calendar, the Grand Inception calendar, would err one day every 800 years. It was 710 years since that prediction was made, and thus time to change the calendar, the memorial observed. Wen-ti, who was fond of *ch'an-wei* thought and, especially, its emphasis on prediction, thus accepted Chang Chou-hsüan's calendar, promoted him to the post of Grand Astrologer (*t'ai-shih ling*), and demoted his opponents. Almost immediately, Liu Ch'o found serious errors in Chang's calendar, but it was not until Liu's death in 608 that any corrections were made, probably along the lines of his original recommendations.[29]

In the almost two-hundred and ninety years of the T'ang dynasty the calendar was reformed a total of nine times.[30] That a single dynasty should have had so many calendars was previously unheard of. In early times, according to Yabuuchi Kiyoshi, the establishment of a dynastic calendar was considered a weighty ritual act, one that was never casually embarked upon. In the two Han dynasties, for example, where the principle of "upon receipt of the Mandate, there is a change of institutions" (*shou-ming kai chih*) operated, only one calendar was formally adopted per dynasty: the Grand Inception Calendar of the Former Han and the Quarter Day Calendar of the Later Han. The Triple Concordance Calendar seems originally to have been designed for use by the Han usurper Wang Mang. From Wei and Chin times onward, this tradition was preserved among the Southern Dynasties. Sometimes, even when there was a change of dynasty, there were cases in which the calendar was not changed. A completely different attitude prevailed, on the other hand, among the Northern Dynasties. In the Northern Wei the calendar was reformed three times, in the Northern Chou twice, and in the Sui twice. Yabuuchi suggests that the Northern Dynasties' reliance on *ch'an-wei* thought may have had something to do with this. Thus, by T'ang times the old idea that a calendar was a basic law of the state and therefore inviolable had declined, replaced by the concept that calendars could rather easily be altered for the political advantage of the ruler.[31]

THE WU-YIN CALENDAR (619–64)

Some months after ascending the throne, T'ang Kao-tsu ordered a new calendar compiled to symbolize his receipt of the Mandate. Upon the recommendation of the Grand Astrologer, Yü Chien, and the Assistant Grand Astrologer, Fu I, he appointed a Taoist monk from Lo-yang, Fu Jen-chün, to oversee the project. Fu Jen-chün took for the name of his calendar the stem and branch designation of the sexagenal year in which the T'ang came to power, Wu-yin. It was formally promulgated in the seventh month of 618 and put into effect at the beginning of 619.[32] Perhaps the most special feature of the Wu-yin Calendar was its employment for the first time in an official Chinese calendar of the true lunation method of calculation, ting-shuo fa, in which the lunar conjunction was calculated using not mean motion, which might throw it into the wrong day, but the actual positions of the sun and moon.[33] As we saw, this had been a feature of Liu Ch'o's calendar in the Sui, but it had never officially been put into practice. As Fu boasted, by using the true lunation method he avoided having the final crescent visible on the last day of the month or the new crescent visible on the first.[34] But the basic accuracy of a calendar is only slightly improved by using the ting-shuo method, and the Wu-yin Calendar was unfortunately still beset by problems of forecasting solar eclipses.[35] In 620 it was reported to the throne that eclipses predicted for the first, second, and eighth months had proved inaccurate.[36]

By 623 court opposition had begun to grow against Fu Jen-chün. Although Fu offered a spirited defense on his own behalf, his detractors succeeded in effecting a general disenchantment with his calendar.[37] Thus, in the middle of 626, the Wu-yin Calendar was emended in "several tens" of its sections by Ts'ui Shan-wei and Wang Hsiao-t'ung.[38] The changes were minor, for the most part returning to the Sui-period calculations of Chang Chou-hsüan. At the beginning of T'ai-tsung's reign, more criticism was heaped on the Wu-yin Calendar. The T'ang mathematician Li Shun-feng advocated that eighteen changes be made in Fu Jen-chün's calculations, seven of which were adopted by the court. In this manner the calendar was repeatedly modified, although it was not ritually renamed.[39]

Still, it was apparent that even the revised Wu-yin Calendar was deficient. In 640 T'ai-tsung was planning personally to perform the round altar sacrifice in the southern suburbs. According to the Wu-yin Calendar, the winter solstice was to fall on a *chia-tzu* day, which was to be the second day of the eleventh month. But Li Shun-feng had calculated that the winter solstice would fall on a *chia-tzu* day that would be on the first day of the month, the new moon, cosmologically a much more sastisfying configuration and a replication of the epoch of the Han dynasty Grand Inception Calendar. After a court discussion on the matter, Li Shun-feng's calculations were accepted as correct.[40] Five years afterward, in 645, it was discovered that because of Fu Jen-chün's true lunation method of calculation, four great months in a row were to occur from the ninth month onward, despite Fu's original promise that three great months of thirty days would be followed by three short months of twenty-nine days when he established his calendar at the beginning of Kao-tsu's reign.[41] On this pretext it was decided to abolish the most radical feature of the Wu-yin Calendar, the true lunation method, and substitute for it an older and simpler system of calculation using the mean synodic month, the *ching-shuo fa* or *p'ing-shuo fa*. In the *ching-shuo* system the average month is taken to be 29.5306 days long, and great months and small months alternate, except occasionally, when two great months follow each other successively.[42] According to Yabuuchi, the true lunation method had never been favored by conservative Confucians who blindly adhered to the ancient classics. This was because the *Spring and Autumn Annals* records solar eclipses as occurring anywhere from the last day of a month through the second day of the following month, and they therefore did not see any necessity for eclipses rigidly to coincide with certain days of the month. Moreover, the *ching-shuo* method had been used since ancient times, and they did not appreciate the practical advance the true lunation method represented.[43] Despite the problems with the Wu-yin Calendar, T'ai-tsung decided to continue it in its revised version, and it was not replaced until his son's time.[44]

THE LIN-TE CALENDAR (665–728)

By Kao-tsung's reign it had become apparent that a basic calendrical reform was in order, and so a new calendar was promulgated on the twentieth day of the first month of the second year of Lin-te (665), Unicorn Virtue, from which it took its name.[45] In his edict announcing the calendar, Kao-tsung praised its virtues. The year in which it began was designated *chia-tzu*, which, he said, was indeed the beginning of Heaven.[46]

Alluding to the propitious cosmological conditions supposedly attending the inauguration of the Grand Inception Calendar of Former Han times, Kao-tsung observed that the five planets were lined up like strung pearls, and the two luminaries of sun and moon rose together.[47] The emperor expressed the pious hope that the use of the Lin-te Calendar would usher in a great age of peace. He also referred to the prediction by Lo-hsia Hung that eight hundred years from the time of the Grand Inception Calendar there would be a wise man who would rectify it. From Lo-hsia Hung's time to his own, Kao-tsung reckoned, was about eight hundred years. His new calendar had thus fulfilled that ancient prediction.[48] The compiler of the Lin-te Calendar was the astronomer-mathematician Li Shun-feng (602–70), whose father had been a Taoist and noted scholar.[49] Earlier, Li had built a celebrated armillary sphere for T'ai-tsung and wrote a work on its theory. He had also compiled the astronomical chapters of the Chin and Sui Standard Histories. By the end of T'ai-tsung's reign he had risen to the post of Grand Astrologer. Along with Fu Jen-chün, he was considered the pre-eminent calendar maker of the early T'ang.[50]

Having been such an insistent critic of the Wu-yin Calendar, which had essentially been based on the calculations of Chang Chou-hsüan of the Sui, for his own calendar Li Shun-feng reached back to the unpromulgated Sui dynasty Huang-chi Calendar of Liu Ch'o. Li's admiration for the Huang-chi Calendar is almost certainly the reason it is treated so generously, despite the fact it was never formally put into practice, in his "Monograph on the Calendar" of the *Sui History*. Although the Lin-te Calendar was much praised in its time, Yabuuchi feels that generally its strengths stemmed more from Liu Ch'o's calculations than from those of Li Shun-feng, and that it did not contribute much to the progress of Chinese astronomy. Moreover, from all the available evidence it appears that the Lin-te Calendar did not employ the concept of annual difference, a thoroughly baffling point given its clear advantage in making accurate calendrical calculations.[51]

Like the original Wu-yin Calendar, and the Huang-chi before it, Li Shun-feng employed the true lunation method of calculating the lunar conjunction. But in order to avoid the pitfalls associated with a return to this system, Li stipulated that if the excess associated with the day of the new moon was more than three-fourths of a day, the new moon was to be advanced to the following day. He thus created the "advance the conjunction" method of calculation (*chin-shuo fa*), a system by which the occurrence of four successive great months was avoided. The *chin-shuo* method introduced by Li continued to be employed in later T'ang calendars and in those of the Sung as well. A second reform of Li's was to do away with the great conjunction cycles, such as the rule-cycle of 235 lunations every 19 years, that Chinese astronomers had long employed.[52] Until this time the years, months, and other constants had always been expressed in numbers of days whose fractions had different denominators. Now Li employed a master number, 1340, that served as the common denominator for all the different values, greatly simplifying calculations. Although these two reforms were mathematically trivial, they were clearly reforms in the art of calendrical calculation, which had important repercussions for later Chinese calendars.[53] The Lin-te Calendar remained in operation except for a short interregnum during Empress Wu's time, until 728, marking it as the longest lived of all the T'ang calendars.

CONCLUSIONS

We know very little about the ceremonial surrounding the promulgation of a new calendar during the T'ang. Such an irregular event, like royal accessions, was not considered as belonging to any of the five classes of rites (wu-li), and consequently was not included in the K'ai-yüan li. It is nevertheless apparent that, like many of the other rituals and symbolic acts treated in the present volume, promulgating a new calendar meant the inauguration of a new beginning.

By Han times and later, the establishment of a calendar was seen as part of the larger operation of altering the institutions of a predecessor when a new dynasty came to power in response to the Mandate of Heaven, called in Chinese shou-ming kai chih.[54] According to this idea, when the Hsia, Shang, and Chou dynasties had arisen in turn, they each had altered the designated first month of the year. A passage from the Po Hu T'ung explains the practice this way:

> Why is it that a King, having received his mandate [from Heaven], must alter the first month of the year? It means that he has changed the [dynastic] name, and indicates that he has not inherited [his kingship]. It means that he has received [his kingship] from Heaven and not from man. By this [measure] he changes the people's hearts and renovates their ears and eyes, as an aid in the [process of their] reform. Therefore the Ta Chuan says: "When a King ascends the throne he rectifies the first month of the year, he changes the colour of his equipage, he transforms the emblems of the standards, he alters the vessels and instruments, and he modifies the clothing".[55]

Although in the post-Han era only the usurper Empress Wu fell back on the old practice of actually changing the designated first month, for her new dynasty of Chou, the promulgation of a new calendar nevertheless symbolized a new regime and a new beinning.[56]

On another level, a new calendar served not simply to symbolize a new beginning. By changing the first month, *kai-shuo*, the emperor ritually regenerated time. As the *Po Hu T'ung* says, "*shuo* 'first month' means *su* 'to revive', *ke* 'to renovate'; it means that the ten thousand things are renovated at this [moment], and so will receive their [further] regulation by it."[57] Eliade believes that in many societies the New Year, and all the rituals associated with it, served not only as a means of purification from sin but also as a means of returning to the beginning of things and effecting a new birth. The effort to expel sins, diseases, and demons commonly associated with the New Year "is a resumption of time from the beginning, that is, a repetition of the cosmogony."[58] By determining the *shuo*, then, the Chinese sovereign, whose sole prerogative it was, both revived and renovated time. He put an end to the calendar of a defunct dynasty or a concluded reign and began the regeneration of time in his own.

Just as every New Year, *cheng-shuo*, serves to regenerate time, so there are no theoretical limits on the numbers of new beginnings that are possible. But through Han times the doctrine of one dynasty, one calendar seems to have prevailed. Only later, especially in the North, did regimes come to see the opportunities afforded by the creation of more than just one calendar and the inauguration of more than one beginning during their duration. Announcing new reign-names was one symbolic way of recommencing time. But these, with their carefully selected titles, represented not much more than the apotheosis of some fortunate contemporary event or the formulaic expression of optimistic hopes for the future. The promulgation of a new calendar was a far more ritually and politically potent act. It was yet one more demonstration of the sovereign's special relationship with the cosmos. It linked him to the sage-rulers of a remote golden age, his political ancestors, who had also rectified and renovated time. Finally, it demonstrated his sincere concern for the masses. His willingness to turn his back on the calendars of his lineal ancestors and to recompute the motions of the heavens was proof of his commitment to have time "work" for all his people.

CHAPTER 12

The Politics of Jade and Silk: Conclusions

We began this study by stating several by now rather commonly accepted propositions regarding the exercise of power by any regime and its authorities:

- coercion alone is not an effective long-term means of exercising and maintaining power
- the authorities therefore seek to control subordinates by other methods
- they may attempt to obtain short-term *specific support* as a quid pro quo for enacting various policies that benefit subordinates; often such policies involve the granting of material rewards
- they may also seek to obtain longer-term *diffuse support* that is not linked to the granting of any specific material benefits but which creates a reservoir of generalized good will toward the regime and its authorities
- such diffuse support may derive either from the arousal in subordinates of a profound belief in the legitimacy of the authorities and the regime, that is, that it is right and proper for them to rule; it may also derive from the employment of rites and symbols that rouse a deep sense of identification with the regime and the authorities, causing subordinates to evaluate them positively
- conceived alternately, the authorities may seek to gain *compliance* from subordinates by employing various modes of power; following the establishment of a regime compliance structures may shift so that *coercive* power is transformed into *remunerative* and *normative* power, involving the manipulation of both material rewards and also esteem, prestige, and ritual symbols.

Men of the early T'ang well understood that it was impossible for regimes to employ force alone for any length of time in maintaining their power, and that they therefore required legitimation. For them legitimation derived, first, from *t'ien-ming*, the Mandate of Heaven, by which Heaven vested authority in a supremely virtuous founding ruler and his descendants. It derived, second, from the correct performance of traditional forms of state ritual by the ruler or his designated officials. In a universe in which the realms of Heaven and Earth were believed to be mutually interrelated, harmony between the two could be preserved by punctilious attention to the ceremonies of state. Rituals properly performed by a ruler were not only a manifestation of Heaven's grace, they were also a means of ensuring the perpetuation of that grace. Ritual had, furthermore, been viewed since classical times as one of the most effective ways of cultivating moral values and regulating human emotions. It was therefore seen as one of the best means of facilitating social control and fostering popular acquiescence to the exercise of authority.

By T'ang times the mechanisms by which rulers legitimated their power and secured diffuse support or, alternately, remunerative and normative compliance, already had long traditions of their own. As we have seen, the T'ang did not invent new mechanisms so much as creatively manipulate tried and true ones, refining them further to serve their particular needs or shifting their reliance to one over the other. Nevertheless, in reviewing the ritual and symbolic acts carried out at the state level which we treated in previous chapters, certain new patterns begin to emerge. It is clear that by the early T'ang rulers had substantially moved away from a reliance on lineal ancestors to legitimate their regimes and more toward entities both consanguineously and affinally unrelated to the dynastic house. Ritual and symbolic vehicles, participation in which had previously been largely limited to members of the dynastic family, their relatives by marriage, or to just a few favored non-relatives, were now expanded beyond former bounds to encompass greater numbers and variety of participants. Rites that had previously been carried out entirely in secret were now more open to public scrutiny. Rituals and symbols that had formerly been immutably linked to the dynastic house now became less inviolable, more manipulated for political ends; political expediency thus came to prevail over blind loyalty to family tradition. In figurative terms, all this represented the ascendancy of the concept of *t'ien-hsia wei kung* over *t'ien-hsia wei chia*. It will be recalled that the quality of *kung* in this context is equated with a spirit of generosity and cooperation trans-

cending the parochialism of family ties; it connotes inclusivity as opposed
to exclusivity, social bonding as opposed to social separation, public property as opposed to private property. *Chia* in this context is equated with
selfishness and partiality toward family; it connotes an emphasis on "we"
at the expense of "they," and private over public. In the ritual and symbolic acts performed by early T'ang emperors to gain acquiescence for
their power, the idea of *kung* seems largely to have prevailed over *chia*,
and symbols of inclusivity largely to have prevailed over symbols of
exclusivity.

By the early T'ang the power of lineal ancestors to legitimate political
power had declined compared, for example, with the Han dynasty. In Han
times a ritual visit was made to the ancestral temple soon after an emperor's accession to seek the blessing of the ancestors and to repay their
kindness. In Later Han the practice was intensified by requiring all newly enthroned rulers to perform the *yeh-miao* ceremony even if they had
previously done so as crown princes. In the post-Han period, by means
of the altar rites, rulers had increasingly established a more direct relationship with Heaven unmediated by the intervention of lineal ancestors. At
the same time, the practice of *yeh-miao* declined. There is no record of any
personal sacrifice performed by the T'ang founder in the ancestral temple
related to his accession. T'ai-tsung performed his first sacrifice one and a
half years after his enthronement; Kao-tsung more than two and a half
years afterward. It is unlikely, therefore, that during the early T'ang these
rites were conceived of as a powerful legitimating device.

On the other hand, the importance of the altar rites seems to have
increased proportionately. Whereas in the Han dynasty no altar rites had
been associated with the emperor's accession, by T'ang times the suburban
altar rites had come to play a central role in confirming imperial authority.
Ancestral temple rites dedicated to lineal ancestors were essentially the
private rites of the imperial family. But the suburban altar rites were primarily dedicated not to the lineal ancestors of the dynastic founder but to
Heaven in the form of Hao-t'ien shang-ti, and also to the god of Earth,
deities belonging to no specific family or class but to all the people. In
contrast to rites at the ancestral temple, which were performed in an
enclosed structure located in or around the imperial compound, the
suburban altar rites were carried out in the open air, outside the capital,
on grounds not exclusively associated with any one house. Although the
suburban rites were also dedicated, secondarily, to the imperial ancestors
in the form of *p'ei*, associated ancestral deities, on such occasions these

ancestors were figuratively removed from their private havens in the ancestral temple and exposed on a public altar, thus symbolically serving as the ancestors of all the people. Anthropologists have pointed out that in many African societies whereas ancestral shrines are located within settlements, earth shrines are set up outside settlements. Furthermore, whereas ancestral cults represent power divisions and classificatory distinctions in society, earth cults represent ritual bonding between groups. The former stresses exclusiveness, the latter inclusiveness.[1] The Chinese suburban altar rites dedicated to Heaven and Earth appear to have functioned analogously to this second category.[2] They represented *kung*-ness as opposed to *chia*-ness, their sacrificial objects belonging to all the people rather than to a single family.

A similar development is apparent in the evolution of the Feng and Shan rites to Heaven and Earth at T'ai-shan in eastern China. Since their creation in Ch'in and Han times, the Feng and Shan had constituted perhaps the most solemn and important of all ceremonies performed by a ruler, and thus represented the highest demonstration of his legitimacy. In practice the Feng and Shan originally had two basic functions. They were announcements to Heaven and Earth that the ruler had successfully carried out the divine charge, and that peace and plenty had been brought to the world. They were also designed to provide for the personal salvation of the ruler by allowing him to meet with the immortal denizens of T'ai-shan and thus to attain eternal life. A fundamental change in the function of the Feng and Shan seems to have taken place between Ch'in-Han times and the T'ang dynasty. In the former period the Feng sacrifice, in which the ruler ascended to the summit of T'ai-shan to meet with the immortals, was carried out in the strictest of secrecy. The jade tablets on which the announcement to Heaven was inscribed were hidden from public scrutiny by a series of caskets and coffers, which were then buried, guaranteeing that their messages would forever remain a mystery. Gradually, however, the Feng and Shan came to be viewed as political rites performed for the sake of all the people, not just for the ruler, and thus there was no reason for such secrecy. During Kao-tsung's ascent of T'ai-shan, for example, he was accompanied by numerous attending officials and military guards. Other ritual officials participated in the Feng sacrifice at the summit. Led by his consort, Empress Wu, women of the harem played prominent roles in the Shan ceremony at the base of the mountain. From written records concerning Kao-tsung's Feng and Shan, including the preserved "Announcement to Heaven," it is clear that the ceremonies had come to be conceived not exclusively as the personal vehicles of the ruler but as political rituals carried out in the name of all the people. One of Kao-tsung's successors, Hsüan-tsung, even made a special point of displaying the jade tablets to all his officials, since, as he said, his performance of the rites was intended to bring prosperity to his people, and therefore there was nothing to hide.

Not only did the scale of participation in the Feng and Shan become greater and its ceremonies more public, during the early T'ang the sites deemed appropriate for the ceremonies were also expanded to include, for the first time, the central peak of Sung-shan. By this means the rites were removed from an exclusive link, long sanctioned by historical practice, to a single site in the northeastern corner of China. In a newly recentralized imperium perhaps there was a greater need to demonstrate that no one region of China was more important than another and to stress the emperor's identification with all his people rather than with just a part of them.

If such early T'ang ceremonies as the suburban altar rites and the Feng and Shan represented inclusivity over exclusivity and the ascendancy of what was public over what was private, a parallel process was taking place in the burial practices associated with rulers. T'ang tombs were on a scale unprecedented in Chinese history. Although the practice of burying loyal servitors with their lords had long been a tradition in China, the T'ang carried it beyond anything known previously. The largest tomb preceding that of T'ang T'ai-tsung was the Mao-ling of Han Wu-ti, which contained twenty-one satellite tombs of imperial family members and favored officials and generals. Its scale, however, was dwarfed by T'ai-tsung's Chao-ling, which was situated atop majestic Chiu-tsung Mountain, contained perhaps two hundred satellite tombs, and covered an astounding forty-five thousand acres. Kao-tsung's Ch'ien-ling, constructed on a somewhat more modest scale, nevertheless contained at least twenty-three associated burials, and probably more will be discovered there in the future. Even Kao-tsu's final resting place, the Hsien-ling, the smallest of the early T'ang mausolea, had sixty-seven associated burials. During the early T'ang, burial plots in the imperial tombs were generously granted to meritorious ministers and successful generals, their descendants, and even, by special permission, their wives. Such burials were prestige symbols manipulated as part of the normative power of a ruler. The early T'ang emperors seem to have made extraordinary use of this power by expanding the concept of family far beyond biological or even marriage ties and creating a more extended and more politically oriented collectivity, which I have called the "political family." The political family emphasized the ties that bound the imperial house to other elite families in the state rather than the differences that separated them, and thus represented inclusivity over exclusivity.

If there was such an entity as the political family, might there not also be "political ancestors" as differentiated from lineal ancestors? I think there were. Political ancestors were not related by consanguinity to the imperial house, but the latter nevertheless considered itself as having special ties to them that were manifested both ritually and symbolically. For example, rulers of previous dynasties were sacrificed to in ceremonies that were ranked during the T'ang among the intermediate sacrifices (*chung-ssu*), just below the most important category of rites. In Kao-tsung's reign, following a precedent first established in the Sui, the list of former rulers was expanded: To Yao, Shun, Yü, T'ang, Wen-wang and Wu-wang was added Han Kao-tsu, despite, it was admitted, the lack of classical precedent. This list was expanded on an even larger scale during Hsüan-tsung's time—not coincidentally at the very peak of T'ang power in Asia. Rulers of previous ages were revered in yet another way—by honoring their living heirs with the special designation "Descendants of the Two Kings" (*erh-wang hou*). A mere two days after his accession, Kao-tsu proclaimed heirs of the Sui and Northern Chou houses as the Descendants of the Two Kings. During most of the dynasty the representatives of these two houses occupied the noble rank of third degree, first class, and were present among the ritual audience at virtually all important sacrifices, such as the suburban altars, the ancestral temple, and the Ming-t'ang. By sacrificing to previous rulers and by dignifying the position of the heirs of previous dynasties, the T'ang embraced on yet one more level the notion that the empire was not the property of one man or one house only. In this respect political ancestors also functioned like the political family, performing an important legitimating function that derived from the *t'ien-hsia wei kung* concept.

Indeed, it was the concept of political ancestry, not lineal, which lay at the heart of the Chinese native notion of legitimation, *cheng-t'ung*. The original meaning of the term was the orthodox line of succession within a family or a dynastic house. Perhaps already by T'ang times, and certainly by the Sung, *cheng-t'ung* had become a corollary of the notion of political ancestry. It had come to signify the line of orthodox *political* succession, which the Chinese saw as beginning in mythological times and leading to the present. It embodied the notion of political ancestry the way the original notion of *cheng-t'ung* had embodied the notion of lineal ancestry.

Thus, we know from various indicators that the T'ang traced their political ancestry back to the Han and beyond through the Sui, Northern Chou, and other northern regimes. Legitimation in this case was conferred on the T'ang by virtue of its position as the end-point on a line of regimes related not by consanguinity but by means of virtue (*te*), a charismatic quality that was regarded as transmissible. In this respect, *cheng-t'ung* implies the power of political ancestors rather than lineal ancestors to legitimate.

A point worth observing in relation to the passage of imperial power in general during the T'ang was that, at least symbolically speaking, exclusivity had also given way to inclusivity. Since the time of the culture-heroes Yao and Shun, the ideal form of political transition was conceived of as a voluntary cession of the throne, or *shan-jang*. In *shan-jang*, power was transmitted on the basis of moral virtue rather than family ties. Beginning with the usurper Wang Mang in the first century A.D., founding rulers often attempted to create an aura of *shan-jang* around their seizures of power in order to confer great legitimacy on their regimes. In the post-Han period, in the pursuit of these goals rulers often employed instruments called *chao* and *ts'e*, testimonial edicts from emperors of defunct dynasties claiming that their successors had rightfully inherited the Mandate of Heaven owing to their superior moral virtues and accomplishments. The *chao* and *ts'e* were thus symbolic affirmations that the empire belonged to the most worthy rather than to members of one house only. We would not expect that in cases of political succession within a dynastic house, where power was routinely passed on from father to son, that the criteria of moral virtue and merit would have played much of a role. But during the Period of Disunion *chao* and *ts'e* were sometimes employed in cases when rulers abdicated in favor of lineal heirs. By T'ang times the use of *chao* and *ts'e* in same surname succession appears to have become expanded and regularized. Their promulation served to disguise the *t'ien-hsia wei chia* aspect of inherited power, to make it appear that political succession was being carried out more openly, more in accord with the more ideologically legitimating doctrine of *t'ien-hsia wei kung*. If the imperial position was to be inherited by a son (or brother), according to the rationale behind the *chao* and *ts'e* he nevertheless had to be capable, worthy, and virtuous. The *chao* and *ts'e* not only guaranteed the qualities of political successors, they also appear to have served as mechanisms by which the virtue or charisma of T'ang ancestors could be passed on to their descendants, a kind of routinization of charisma in the Weberian sense.

As time wore on, yet one more symbolic vehicle that became less bound up with a given dynastic house was the calendar. In the Han the promulgation of a calendar was already considered part of an extensive process of renovation of a predecessor's institutions when a new regime came to power, *shou-ming kai chih*. In the Han the calendar was dynasty-specific: The concept of one dynasty, one calendar appears to have prevailed. In the post-Han era this tradition was preserved among the regimes of the South. But in the North calendars could be reformed multiple times within a dynasty. During the T'ang the idea that the calendar was a basic law of a dynastic house was abandoned in favor of the concept of the calendar as primarily a political instrument, to be tinkered with at will. The T'ang calendar was reformed an impressive total of nine times, under the apparent assumption that calendrical reform served the ruler by linking him to increasingly accurate calculations of the movements of the cosmos. It is clear that by this time the calendar had come to be conceived of as a flexible political document rather than as a rigid monument preserved out of loyalty to family tradition.

We said at the beginning of this chapter that in seeking to gain *acquiescence* for their exercise of power, the early T'ang emperors in their ritual and symbolic acts tended to stress inclusivity over exclusivity. However, at first glance, in terms of the use of ritual and symbol as a means of *explaining* the nature of the ruler's power, the general trend during the early T'ang seems to have moved in the opposite direction, toward the ascendancy of the one over the many and exclusivity over inclusivity. With the victory of Wang Su's ideas over those of Cheng Hsüan during Kao-tsung's time, not only was the number of suburban altars reduced from four to two, but the sacrifices to Kan-sheng ti and Shen-chou were discontinued, leaving Hao-t'ien shang-ti as the chief deity at the round altar, and the god of Earth as the chief object of sacrifice at the square altar. Sacrifices to the Five Emperors at the suburban altars and at the Ming-t'ang were also terminated; thus at the Ming-t'ang Hao-t'ien shang-ti was also triumphant. The overall trend during the T'ang, despite some vicissitudes, was for Hao-t'ien shang-ti to remain the chief object of sacrifice. Yet to the extent that Hao-t'ien shang-ti represented an all-embracing, universal deity, a unity comprising elements of Heaven that had previously been conceived of as disparate, here, too, we can observe a movement in ritual toward inclusivity over exclusivity.

The intensified worship of Hao-t'ien shang-ti reflected a cosmological view that was increasingly being articulated during the time as part of the attack on Cheng Hsüan's ideas, especially his theory of the Six Heavens.

This view was embodied in the phrase *t'ien-shang wu erh*, "there is only one Heaven," which we find in various contemporary utterances. Among a people who believed that earthly states were merely reflections of a Heavenly pattern, the concept of a single supreme deity naturally had powerful political implications. The emperor's worship of and identification with an all-powerful Heaven strengthened his political status as the "one man" (*i-jen*) in relation to the rest of the empire, and thus helped establish the cosmological grounds for an intensified absolutism. Although such a political trend reached its height only in later times in China, in this respect it can be said that the seeds were largely sown during the early T'ang.

How might we account for the trends outlined above? One possible answer is that new conceptions of both religious and secular power had arisen in China during the years preceding the T'ang. It has been pointed out, for example, that the establishment of Hao-t'ien shang-ti early in the T'ang as a supreme sacrificial deity was preceded during the Period of Disunion by the evolution in Taoist religion of successive universal deities, such as T'ien-huang ta-ti and Yüan-shih t'ien-tsun.[3] The ascendance of Hao-t'ien shang-ti in state sacrifice may merely have paralleled the rise of other universal deities in religious ritual. Buddhism, too, provided its own model of universal deity, as well as of universal monarch: the Ćakravartin king, turner of the Wheel of Law and temporal sovereign of a universal Buddhist dominion.[4]

That new ideas regarding the nature of temporal power were current during the period is supported by a revealing development in the dynasty's foreign relations. Early in 630, T'ai-tsung succeeded in conquering an old "barbarian" nemesis, the Eastern Turks of what is now Outer Mongolia. Shortly afterward, the leaders of the tribes came to court "requesting" that T'ai-tsung assume a new title that had never been employed before, Heavenly Qaghan (*t'ien k'o-han*). T'ai-tsung thereupon agreed, declaiming, "I who am the Son of Heaven of the Great T'ang will also deign to carry out the duties of the qaghans!"[5] According to Lo Hsiang-lin, the title Heavenly Qaghan was equivalent to a supreme suzerain, a qaghan of qaghans. It carried the right to bestow patents of authority on submissive tribal chiefs and to mediate disputes between them, as well as the obligation to protect them in case of attack by other parties. In Kao-tsung's time the jurisdiction of Heavenly Qaghan was extended to include the newly conquered Western Turks and all the territories formerly under their control. The practice lasted about a century, until the time of Hsüan-tsung. Lo believes that some sort of formal system of international cooperation, especially against the spread of Arab power in Central Asia, arose between China and the tribes, as a result of the Heavenly Qaghan designation. Whatever the case, for our purposes it is sufficient to note that the new title paralleled the contemporary T'ang practice of symbolically extending the notion of family beyond traditional bounds. T'ang vassals in the Heavenly Qaghan organization addressed the Chinese emperor as "qaghan," signifying that he was as much their ruler as he was the ruler of all Chinese, a father to them all.[6] Heavenly Qaghan can be seen, furthermore, as a natural conceptual extension of the implications of universal sovereignty implicit in the heightened worship of Hao-t'ien shang-ti.

Perhaps not coincidentally, the word "Heaven" was also employed in titles adopted in 674 by Kao-tsung and Empress Wu: Heavenly Emperor (t'ien-huang) and Heavenly Empress (t'ien-hou).[7] These titles were unprecedented and, it is said, designed to set the emperor and his consort apart from all previous Chinese monarchs.[8] Although we know very little about the titles, it seems likely, given T'ai-tsung's particular use of "Heaven" some years previous, that they were meant to signify an overlordship on a scale beyond anything previously known, a universal dominion. The enormous expansion of territory during Kao-tsung's time, and the creation of a truly international order under Chinese suzerainty stretching from the Sea of China to the borders of Persia, suggests that the symbolism they were intended to convey was not so overblown.[9] In a universe where Heaven, Earth, and Man were conceived of as virtual mirror images of one another, we would expect to see a certain congruency between cosmologico-religious and politico-institutional conceptualizations. This would go far toward explaining the trend toward a more embracing inclusivity in state ritual and symbol during the early T'ang, where the notion of family was expanded to include not only persons unrelated to the dynastic house but also foreign peoples, just as the notion of deity was being amplified beyond previous images to universal proportions.

A completely different approach to the question revolves around the process of legitimation. With regard to legitimation in capitalist societies, the Frankfurt School theorist, Jürgen Habermas, has written:

> the expansion of state activity produces the side effect of a disproportionate increase in the need for legitimation. I consider a disproportionate increase probable, not only because the expansion of administratively processed matters makes necessary mass loyalty for new functions of state activity, but

because the boundaries of the political system vis-à-vis the cultural system shift as a result of this expansion. In this situation, cultural affairs that were taken for granted, and that were previously boundary conditions for the political system, fall into the administrative planning area.[10]

According to this view, a regime must not only legitimate itself. It must also legitimate all the new activities it undertakes which previously had been self-legitimating elements of the traditional cultural system, and thus not in any need of further legitimation. For example, when a state introduces a written legal code to replace or complement unwritten tribal- or clan-based law, or when it establishes as state-controlled system of land allocation to replace what heretofore had been free-market distribution, these additional activities require additional, but disproportionate, legitimation. As regimes increasingly co-opt activities formerly performed by traditional sectors of society, legitimation needs greatly expand.

It can be argued along these lines that the expansion of governmental activities in China from the Han dynasty through the T'ang—not only in the area of state legal codes and land tenure systems, but also in the establishment of universal military conscription systems, state supported and directed educational systems, state supported and controlled religious institutions, various state economic monopolies, and the like—may have required additional legitimation of unprecedented dimensions. Rulers of the early T'ang appear to have attempted to generate additional legitimation in a variety of ways. First, they drew upon the newer legitimating values of Buddhism and Taoism in order to expand the conventional body of philosophico-religious legitimation that had previously been centered on Confucianism. Second, they undertook to mask the proprietary aspects of family-based power by stressing in a variety of ways the ideologically more legitimating *t'ien-hsia wei kung* aspects of their rule. Third, by means of what I have called the political family and the cult of political ancestors, they shifted the emphasis of legitimating rituals and symbols away from the dynastic family and its lineal ancestors. By symbolically embracing wider groups of the populace in an extended dynastic family, they sought to render them more amenable to the state's expanded activities. Fourth, at the expense of his divine rivals, they promoted the ritual ascendancy of the universal deity Hao-t'ien shang-ti, which in turn served to enhance the "one man" aspect of imperial authority and provide a more convincing explanation for the basis of its augmented powers.

If an expanded imperium, both territorially and in terms of the activities routinely undertaken by government, requires disproportionate additional legitimation, I suggest that in early T'ang times it is to the ritual and symbolic activities carried out at the state level, simultaneously embodying the doctrine of *t'ien-hsia wei kung*, an expanded concept of dynastic family, and the dominance of a universal deity, that we must look for the most important sources of this legitimation.

Notes

PREFACE

1 For a good treatment of *chia* and *kung* as antipodes, see Ogata Isamu, *Chūgoku kodai no 'ie' to kokka—kōtei shihaika no chitsujo kōzō* (Tokyo, 1979), pp. 198–205.

INTRODUCTION

1 *CCC* 3.38–39; *CTS* 1.6; *HTS* 1.6; *TCTC* 185.5791.
2 *CHC* 3:160.
3 C. E. Merriam, quoted in Harold D. Lasswell and Abraham Kaplan, *Power and Society: A Framework for Political Inquiry* (New Haven, 1950), p. 121.
4 Talcott Parsons, "On the Concept of Political Power," *Proceedings of the American Philosophical Society* 107 (1963):240.
5 Marc J. Swartz, Victor W. Turner, and Arthur Tuden, eds., *Political Anthropology* (Chicago, 1966), editors' introduction, pp. 9–10.
6 Max Weber, *The Theory of Social and Economic Organization*, trans. A. M. Henderson and Talcott Parsons (1947; New York, 1964), p. 125.
7 David Easton, *A Systems Analysis of Political Life* (Chicago, 1965), p. 159. The support that members are willing to give a political system constitutes one of two basic inputs into that system, according to Easton. The other basic input is called demands, an expression of an opinion by members that the responsible authorities should or should not make some type of allocation, material or otherwise (p. 38). Easton views political systems as open, self-regulating, and self-transforming. They function by processing the inputs of demands and support to produce outputs, or political behavior on the part of authorities. These outputs provide informational feedback which influences the kinds of further demands members make on the system—and generates further sup-

port. In this manner a political system is able to adapt to or cope with stress (pp. 29–31). A political organization must generate at least a minimal level of support among its members to survive. Since it is possible that members will simultaneously favor, disapprove, or be indifferent to a political organization, or at least different aspects of it, support is conceived as "the net balance of support, opposition, and indifference of a member or group" (pp. 168–69).

8 Easton, *Systems Analysis*, pp. 268, 273; Swartz, Turner, and Tuden, *Political Anthropology*, pp. 23, 25.

9 Easton, *Systems Analysis*, pp. 278, 293. See chap. 13 on the concept of authorities.

10 Easton, *Systems Analysis*, p. 277; Swartz, Turner, and Tuden, *Political Anthropology*, p. 25.

11 Power is defined variously. Two definitions will be offered here. Power is the capacity of one actor or group of actors to modify the conduct of other actors or groups in a manner intended by the former. (See Lasswell and Kaplan, *Power and Society*, p. 75, quoting from R. H. Tawney; Amitai Etzioni, *A Comparative Analysis of Complex Organizations: On Power, Involvement and Their Correlates* rev. ed. [New York, 1975], p. 4; H. Goldhamer and Edward Shils, "Types of Power and Status," *American Journal of Sociology* 45 [1939]:171.) Although defined relationally in this way, power may also be seen interpersonally as participation in the making of decisions, as in the case A has power over B if A participates in decision-making affecting B in terms of such-and-such particulars. (Lasswell and Kaplan, *Power and Society*, p. 75.) The second definition is offered by Parsons: Power is the capacity to secure the performance of binding obligations by the use of negative sanctions. Parsons introduces the concepts of generalization and legitimacy to his definition. Power is a generalized capacity that is not limited merely to a single act that A is in a position to impose. It is legitimated by expectations of B that, having performed the obligation, he might in other contexts and on other occasions invoke obligations on the part of others. Parsons's idea is that obedience to the leader is conditional upon his undertaking, tacitly or explicitly, to reciprocate later on with beneficial actions. Power for Parsons is thus a symbolic medium lacking any intrinsic effectiveness, gaining efficacy only from the expectations of those who comply with it. (Parsons, "Concept of Political Power," 237–38; Swartz, Turner, and Tuden, *Political Anthropology*, pp. 17–18.

12 Etzioni, *Comparative Analysis*, pp. 5–6.

13 Etzioni, *Comparative Analysis*, p. xv. This orientation can take three forms. The first is called alienative (intensely negative, such as among conquest peoples, prisoners, or slaves). The second is called calculative (a negative or positive orientation of low intensity, such as among factory workers, and between merchants and customers). The third is called moral (high intensity, such as among devoted political party members and loyal followers) (p. 10). Given the three types of power and three types of compliance, there are nine possible compliance relationships, three of which are "congruent" because, simply, they are more organizationally effective (p. 14):

power	compliance	=	compliance relationship
coercive	alienative	=	coercive compliance
remunerative	calculative	=	utilitarian compliance
normative	moral	=	normative compliance

This means that coercive power works best with actors who are highly alienated, but less well with other types of actors; that normative power works best with morally committed actors, not others; and that remunerative power is largely ineffective when actors are already highly committed or alienated (pp. 13, 109).

14 Etzioni, *Comparative Analysis*, pp. 14, 119–20.

15 Burton Watson, trans., *Records of the Grand Historian of China, Translated from the Shih-chi of Ssu-ma Ch'ien*, 2 vols. (New York, 1961), 1:277–78.

16 *HTS* 107.4060.

17 For briefer treatments of the ritual and symbolic acts carried out by two earlier dynastic founders, see Hans Bielenstein, *The Restoration of the Han Dynasty*, vol. 4, *The Government, Bulletin of the Museum of Far Eastern Antiquities* 51 (1979), chap. 6; Arthur F. Wright, *The Sui Dynasty: Unification of China, A.D. 581–617* (New York, 1978), pp. 110–16.

18 Derk Bodde, *Festivals in Classical China: New Year and Other Annual Observances during the Han Dynasty 206 B.C.–A.D. 220* (Princeton, 1975), pp. 389–90.

19 Abner Cohen, *Two-Dimensional Man: An Essay on the Anthropology of Power and Symbolism in Complex Society* (Berkeley and Los Angeles, 1976), preface.

20 Lasswell and Kaplan, *Power and Society*, p. 119.

CHAPTER 1

1 For an extensive examination of this theme, see the twelve papers offered by participants in the Conference on Legitimation of Chinese Regimes, sponsored by the Committee on the Study of Chinese Civilization of the American Council of Learned Societies, Asilomar, Monterey, California, 15–24 June 1975.

2 Dolf Sternberger, "Legitimacy," in *International Encyclopedia of the Social Sciences*, ed. David L. Sills, 17 vols. (New York, 1968), 9:244.

3 Max Weber, *Theory*, p. 325.

4 David Easton, *Systems Analysis*, p. 278; Sternberger, "Legitmacy," p. 244.

5 Talcott Parsons, "Concept of Political Power," 238; also quoted in Swartz, Turner, and Tuden, *Political Anthropology*, introduction, p. 11.

6 Sternberger is critical of Weber's use of tradition as a basis of legitimation since, as he points out, tradition plays a part in almost every kind of legitimacy, ranging from the rational to the charismatic; "Legitimacy," pp. 244–45, 247.

7 Weber, *Theory*, pp. 328, 366.

8 Easton, *Systems Analysis*, pp. 278–303. The ideology of a system, according to Easton, is "an articulated set of ideals, ends, and purposes which help the

members of the system to interpret the past, explain the present, and offer a vision of the future." It describes the aims for which some members feel political power ought to be used. It lends the authorities the moral right to rule. Structural legitimacy arises from the perception that the authorities conform to established structural arrangements and practices, e.g., they are perceived as occupying valid roles in the structure, as having been recruited in accordance with prescribed procedures, as wielding power correctly, and so on, without any necessary reference to whether they conform to the members' ideology. Structural legitimacy thus works independently of ideological legitimacy. Personal legitimacy rests on the members' perception, for whatever reason, that those who fill authority roles are moral. Here the personal merit and behavior of the authorities outweigh any considerations about their conformance to structural arrangements and norms or any ideological principles.

9 Easton, *Systems Analysis*, pp. 309.

10 Peter L. Berger, *The Sacred Canopy: Elements of a Sociological Theory of Religion* (Garden City, N.Y., 1967), pp. 29–34.

11 Easton, *Systems Analysis*, p. 306.

12 Easton, *Systems Analysis*, pp. 306–08.

13 Timoteus Pokora, "Pre-Han Literature," in *Essays on the Sources for Chinese History*, ed. Donald D. Leslie, Colin Mackerras, and Wang Gungwu (Canberra, 1973), p. 24. These appear among its authentic early Chou-time chapters, and thus appear to be an accurate reflection of early Chou political ideas and ideals; Burton Watson, *Early Chinese Literature* (New York, 1962), p. 26.

14 Fung Yu-lan, *A History of Chinese Philosophy*, trans. Derk Bodde, 2 vols. (Princeton, 1952), 1:400–02.

15 Herrlee Glessner Greel, *The Birth of China: A Study of the Formative Period of Chinese Civilization* (New York, 1937), p. 367.

16 James Legge, trans., *The Shoo King*, pp. 453–64. For the notion that the Mandate of Heaven had its origin in pre-Chou times, see David Keightley, review of Herrlee G. Creel, *The Origins of Statecraft in China*, *Journal of Asian Studies* 30 (1971):658.

17 Legge, *Shoo King*, pp. 15–27; Watson, *Chinese Literature*, pp. 31–32.

18 Quoted in Kung-chuan Hsiao, *A History of Chinese Political Thought*, vol. 1: *From the Beginnings to the Sixth Century A.D.*, trans. F. W. Mote (Princeton, 1979), p. 496.

19 See Fung, *Chinese Philosophy*, 1:22–42; Hsiao, *Political Thought*, pp. 484ff.

20 Quoted in Fung, *Chinese Philosophy*, 1:161–62.

21 See Fung, *Chinese Philosophy*, 1:162–63. An alternative sequence, in which the Five Elements generated rather than overcame one another, was also used; see Joseph Needham, *Science and Civilisation in China*, vol. 2, *History of Scientific Thought* (Cambridge, 1956), pp. 255ff.

22 Chao Ling-yang, *Kuan-yü li-tai cheng-t'ung wen-t'i chih cheng-lun*, (Hong Kong, 1976), p. 4.

23 *SC* 8.394; *HS* 1B.82; Chao, *Cheng-t'ung wen-t'i*, pp. 5–6.

24 *HS* 25B.1248; Chao, *Cheng-t'ung wen-t'i*, p. 6.

25 *HS* 86.3506, biography of Shih Tan; *CWTTT* 5:7576.340.

26 *CS* 7.119.

27 T'ao Hsi-sheng, "K'ung-tzu miao-t'ing chung Han-ju chi Sung-ju ti wei-tz'u (I)," *Shih-huo yüeh-k'an* 2 (1972):29n49.

28 See Fung, *Chinese Philosophy*, 2:410.

29 Kanai Yukitada, "Bunchūshi Chūsetsu no seitōron ni tsuite," *Bunka* 3 (1936):971. The problem developed when the Eastern Chin dynasty scholar Hsi Tso-ch'ih (d. 384) wrote his *Chronicle of Han and Chin* (*Han-Chin ch'un-ch'iu*), in which he disputed the assessment made a century earlier by the Chin dynasty historian Ch'en Shou (233–97), in his *History of the Three Kingdoms* (*San-kuo chih*), that the Wei dynasty was the legitimate successor of Han; Hsi instead championed Shu as legitimate. See also *DJ* 6:6383.352.

30 Kanai, "Bunchūshi Chūsetsu," 971.

31 See Howard J. Wechsler, "The Confucian Teacher Wang T'ung: One Thousand years of Controversy," *T'oung Pao* 63 (1977):225–72.

32 *WCTCS* 8.85.

33 *WCTCS* 10.106.

34 *WCTCS* 8.85, annotation of Juan I; Yoshikawa Sadao, "Bunchūshi kō," *Shirin* 53:2 (1970):246. Cf. Kanai, "Bunchūshi Chūsetsu," 975.

35 Yoshikawa, "Bunchūshi kō,' 246–47.

36 See Ch'en Yin-k'o, *Sui-T'ang chih-tu yüan-yüan lüeh-lun kao* (1944; Shanghai, 1946); Yoshikawa, "Bunchūshi kō," 247.

37 Based on the *Book of Poetry*; James Legge, trans., *The She King or the Book of Poetry*, p. 357.

38 *WCTCS* 7.73.

39 See *DJ* 6:6383.350.

40 Kanai, "Bunchūshi Chūsetsu," 977–78; Chang Ch'ün, "Wang T'ung chih ssu-hsiang chi ch'i ying-hsiang," *Chung-hua wen-hua fu-hsing yüeh-k'an* 10:2 (1977):82.

41 Howard J. Wechsler, *Mirror to the Son of Heaven: Wei Cheng at the Court of T'ang T'ai-tsung* (New Haven, 1974), pp. 37–42; idem, "Wang T'ung," 265–66.

42 Ozaki Yasushi, "Gu Seinan no Tei-ō ryaku ni tsuite," *Shidō Bunko ronshū* 5 (July 1967):185–86. The work was originally in five *chüan* but was later lost. Considerable sections have been pieced together in this century, however, from a Tunhuang manuscript brought back to France by Paul Pelliot, a Japanese manuscript dating from the Kamakura period (1185–1333), now in the Tōyō Bunko, and quotations from the text in various Chinese sources of the T'ang and later periods.

43 Ozaki, "Gu Seinan," 207, 209.

44 Ozaki, "Gu Seinan," 202.

45 See, for example, Arthur Waley, trans., *The Analects of Confucius* (IX.1), (London, 1938) p. 138. Wing-tsit Chan, *A Source Book in Chinese Philosophy* (Princeton, 1963), pp. 78–79, lists five ancient theories about destiny in the Mandate of Heaven concept.

46 C. K. Yang, "The Functional Relationship between Confucian Thought and

Chinese Religion," in *Chinese Thought and Religion*, ed. John K. Fairbank (Chicago, 1957), pp. 272–74; Hsiao, *Political Thought*, pp. 179–80.

47 Ozaki, "Gu Seinan," 218.

48 Such a view must be contrasted with that of the mid-T'ang historical commentator, Liu Chih-chi (661–721), who once criticized a similar notion expressed by the great Han historian Ssu-ma Ch'ien regarding the Ch'in conquest of the small state of Wei, which Ssu-ma believed was Heaven-ordained and therefore inevitable. Liu sarcastically observed that when success and failure are being measured, human affairs, not Heaven's Mandate or fate, must be considered as primary. To do otherwise would be a dereliction of the historian's duty to criticize human errors and provide a warning to future generations. Ozaki, "Gu Seinan," 218–19; Burton Watson, *Ssu-ma Ch'ien: Grand Historian of China* (New York, 1958), pp. 186–87, 238n14. The passage comes from Liu's *Generalities on History (Shih-t'ung)*.

49 SS 2.55.

50 Jack Goody, "Religion and Ritual: The Definitional Problem," *British Journal of Sociology* 12 (1961):159.

51 Goody, "Religion and Ritual," 159–60.

52 Edmund Leach, *Political Systems of Highland Burma* (1954; Boston, 1965), p. 14; Raymond Firth, *Elements of Social Organization* (Boston, 1963), p. 222; John Beattie, "Ritual and Social Change," *Man* 2 (1966): passim.

53 See Emile Durkheim, *The Elementary Forms of the Religious Life: A Study in Religious Sociology*, trans. Joseph Ward Swain (London, n.d.).

54 See, for example, Max Gluckman, *Order and Rebellion in Tribal Africa* (New York, 1963), pp. 19, 127; Victor Turner, *Schism and Continuity in an African Society: A Study of Ndembu Village Life* (Manchester, 1957), p. 289; idem, *The Forest of Symbols: Aspects of Ndembu Ritual* (Ithaca, N.Y., 1967), pp. 360, 392.

55 Edmund R. Leach, "Ritual," in the *International Encyclopedia of the Social Sciences*, 13:524; idem, *Culture and Communication: The Logic by Which Symbols Are Connected* (Cambridge, 1976), p. 53; Firth, *Elements*, pp. 224–25; Terrence Turner, "Transformation, Hierarchy and Transcendence: A Reformulation of van Gennep's Model of the Structure of Rites de Passage," in *Secular Ritual*, ed. Sally F. Moore and Barbara G. Myerhoff (Amsterdam, 1977), pp. 59, 61; Moore and Myerhoff, *Secular Ritual*, introduction, pp. 3–4.

56 Abner Cohen *Two-Dimensional Man*, p. 77.

57 Meyer Fortes and E. E. Evans-Pritchard, eds., *African Political Systems* (London, 1948), pp. 17–18

58 Robert G. Wesson, *The Imperial Order* (Berkeley and Los Angeles, 1967), pp. 79, 221.

59 Mary Douglas, *Natural Symbols: Explorations in Cosmology* (New York, 1970), pp. 20–36.

60 Maurice Bloch, "Symbols, Song, Dance and Features of Articulation: Is Religion an Extreme Form of Traditional Authority?" *Archives Européenes de Sociologie* 15 (1974):55–81: idem, *Political Language and Oratory in Traditional Society* (New York, 1975), pp. 19, 25–26.

61 Bloch, *Political Language*, p. 24.

62 Moore and Myerhoff, *Secular Ritual*, introduction, p. 18.

63 See Bloch, *Political Language*, p. 16; and Abner Cohen, "Political Symbolism," *Annual Review of Anthropology* 8 (1979):98.

64 In his *International Encyclopedia of the Social Sciences* article entitled "Ritual" (p. 523), the anthropologist Edmund Leach underlines a heightened appreciation for the expressive dimension of ritual by observing, "in those types of behavior labeled ritual, the aesthetic, communicative aspect is particularly prominent, but a technical (instrumental) aspect is never entirely absent." For a recent study of ritual by an anthropologist that seeks to avoid making a false distinction between its expressive and instrumental qualities, see Clifford Geertz, *Negara: The Theatre State in Nineteenth-Century Bali* (Princeton, 1980).

65 See S. P. Nagendra, *The Concept of Ritual in Modern Sociological Theory* (New Delhi, 1971), chap. 7; Susanne Katherina Langer, *Philosophy in a New Key; A Study in the Symbolism of Reason, Rite, and Art* (New York, 1962).

66 See Moore and Myerhoff, *Secular Ritual*, introduction, pp. 7–8; Firth, *Symbols: Public and Private* (Ithaca, N.Y., 1973), p. 176; Orin E. Klapp. *Ritual and Cult: A Sociological Interpretation* (Washington, D.C., 1956), pp. 10–13; Nagendra, *Concept of Ritual*, pp. 9–10; Turner, "Transformation," 61.

67 A vivid examination of ritual as theatre is Geertz's *Negara*.

68 Leach, *Culture and Communication*, p. 44.

69 Barth, *Ritual and Knowledge among the Baktaman of New Guinea* (New Haven, 1975), p. 225.

70 Noah Edward Fehl, *Li: Rites and Propriety in Literature and Life: A Perspective for a Cultural History of Ancient China* (Hong Kong, 1971), p. 4.

71 Fehl, *Li*, p. 81.

72 Fehl, *Li*, chaps. 3–4; Ch'u Chai and Winberg Chai, "Introduction," in James Legge, trans., *Li Chi, Book of Rites*, 2 vols. (New Hyde Park, N.Y., 1967), 1:xxxiii–xxxiv; Waley, *Analects*, pp. 54–69.

73 Legge, *Li Chi*, 1:390.

74 Fung Yu-lan, *Chinese Philosophy*, 1:337; Waley, *Analects*, pp. 54–55.

75 Legge, *Li Chi*, 2:236.

76 Legge, *Li Chi*, 1:367; Fung, *Chinese Philosophy*, 1:338.

77 William Theodore de Bary et al., *Sources of Chinese Tradition* (New York, 1960), p. 192; Legge, *Li Chi*, 1:366. See also Lester James Bilsky, *The State Religion of Ancient China*, 2 vols. (Taipei, 1975), 2:202.

78 Fung, *Chinese Philosophy*, 1:339; Burton Watson, trans., *Hsün Tzu: Basic Writings* (New York, 1963), p. 91.

79 Waley, *Analects* (II.3), p. 88; (XIII.4), p. 172; (XIV.44), p. 191.

80 Legge, *Li Chi*, 2:352. See also Bilsky, *State Religion*, 2:200.

81 *SC* 99.2722–23; Burton Watson, *Records*, 1:293–95; *HS* 43.2126–28. See also Benjamin Wallacker, "Han Confucianism and Confucius in Han," in *Ancient China: Studies in Early Civilization*, ed. David T. Roy and Tsuen-hsuin Tsien (Hong Kong, 1978), pp. 223–24.

82 Waley, *Analects* (XIII.12), pp. 97 and 97n2–3; Bilsky, *State Religion*, 1:197.

83 See, for example, Legge, *Li Chi*, 2:236.

84 Watson, *Hsün Tzu*, p. 89.

85 Watson, *Hsün Tzu*, pp. 109–10. On this theme, see also Fehl, *Li*, p. 118; Waley, *Analects*, p. 97n3.

86 Watson, *Hsün Tzu*, p. 89. It should be noted that Hsün-tzu, while affirming the expressive functions of ritual, also had a healthy appreciation of its instrumental dimensions. By means of rites, he observed, "those below are obedient, those above are enlightened; all things change but do not become disordered; only he who turns his back upon rites will be destroyed. Are they not wonderful, indeed?" *Hsün Tzu*, p. 94.

87 On this theme, see Fehl, *Li*, p. 157; Ho Ping-ti, *The Cradle of the East: An Inquiry into the Indigenous Origins of Techniques and Ideas of Neolithic and Early Historic China, 5000–1000 B.C.* (Hong Kong, 1975), p. 325.

88 Watson, *Hsün Tzu*, p. 110.

89 Alfred Forke, trans., *Lun-Heng*, 2d ed., 2 vols. (New York, 1962), 1:523, 2:397.

90 C. K. Yang, *Religion in Chinese Society* (Berkeley and Los Angeles, 1970), pp. 254–55; Bilsky, *State Religion*, 1:221.

91 Donald Holzman, *Poetry and Politics: The Life and Works of Juan Chi (A.D. 210–263)* (Cambridge, 1976), chap. 4.

92 *WCTCS* 6.62.

93 *WCTCS* 8.86.

94 *WCTCS* 10.107–08. See Waley, *Analects*, p. 162; Ichikawa Mototarō, *Bunchūshi* (Tokyo, 1970), pp. 230–31.

95 *WCTCS* 6.64. This passage echoes *LC* 15.2b; Legge, *Li Chi*, 2.259.

96 *WCTCS* 7.74.

97 Chang Ch'ün, "Wang T'ung," 81–82. Chang makes a serious error, however, in attributing to Wang T'ung remarks actually made by his Sung dynasty annotator, Juan I: "When China had no rulers, legitimacy [*cheng-t'ung*] resided in Chin and [Southern] Sung; when China had rulers, legitimacy resided in Wei and [Northern] Chou"; *WCTCS* 6.66.

98 *WCTCS* 8.86.

99 *WCTCS* 3.24.

100 *WCTCS* 2.18. On Wang's *Continued Classics*, see Wechsler, "Wang T'ung," 237, 270.

101 *CKCY* 7.234. See also the memorial of Ts'en Wen-pen, *CTW* 150.15b.

102 *CTS* 24.912.

103 See, for example, the cases of Yen Shih-ku, *CTW* 147.19a–22b; and *TCTC* 194.6116; of Fang Hsüan-ling, *CTS* 21.817; *CTW* 137.5a; and of Ch'u Sui-liang, *CTW* 149.16b.

104 See, for example, *CKCY* 5.153.

105 *T'ang-shih chi-shih* (*SPTK* ed.), 4.9b.

106 Legge, *Li Chi*, 2:258; *Hsiao-ching* (*SPTK* ed.), 12a.

107 *TTCLC* 105.537, 81.465, and in a *fu* of Li Pai-yao, *CKCY* 4.117.

108 *CKCY* 7.238; *THY* 32.588.

109 *SS* 39.1691.

110 Legge, *Li Chi*, 2:93.

111 Edward Sapir, "Symbolism," in *Encyclopedia of the Social Sciences*, ed. Edwin R. A. Seligman, 15 vols. (New York, 1930), 14:498–93.

112 On this theme, see Firth, *Symbols*, p. 15; Langer, *Philosophy*, pp. 27–28; Mircea Eliade, *Mephistopheles and the Androgyne: Studies in Religious Myth and Symbol*, trans. J. M. Cohen (New York, 1965), p. 190.

113 Firth, *Symbols*, pp. 60, 111; Clifford Geertz, *The Interpretation of Cultures: Selected Essays by Clifford Geertz* (New York, 1973), p. 89; Cohen, *Two-Dimensional Man*, p. 85.

114 *OED* compact ed. (New York, 1971), 2:3206.

115 Philip Wheelwright, *The Burning Fountain: A Study of the Language of Symbolism* (Bloomington, Ind., 1968), pp. 18–19.

116 Murray Edelman, *The Symbolic Uses of Politics* (Urbana, Ill., 1964), p. 117; see also Thurman W. Arnold, *The Symbols of Government* (New York, 1962), p. 10.

117 Firth, *Symbols*, p. 86.

118 Michael Walzer, "On the Role of Symbolism in Political Thought," *Political Science Quarterly* 82 (June 1967):194–95.

119 Victor Turner, "Symbolic Studies," *Annual Review of Anthropology* 4 (1975):155.

120 Cohen, *Two-Dimensional Man*, p. 24.

121 Firth, *Symbols*, pp. 64–65.

122 Turner, "Symbolic Studies," 155; idem, *Dramas, Fields, and Metaphors: Symbolic Action in Human Society* (Ithaca, N.Y., 1974), pp. 55–56.

123 For a good background treatment of the Ho-t'u and Lo-shu, see Anna Seidel, "Dynastic Treasures and Taoist *lu* Registers" (an unpublished paper presented at the Conference on the Legitimation of Chinese Regimes, Asilomar, Monterey, California, 15–24 June 1975), 19ff.

124 Edelman, *Symbolic Uses of Politics*, p. 38.

125 Walzer, "Role of Symbolism," p. 196.

126 Firth, *Symbols*, p. 52; Paul Tillich, "Theology and Symbolism," in *Religious Symbolism*, ed. F. Ernest Johnson (Port Washington, N.Y., 1969), pp. 109–10. See also Roger Grainger, *The Language of the Rite* (London, 1974), pp. 15–16.

127 Geertz, *Interpretation of Cultures*, p. 112. In this way symbol differs from art, notes Geertz.

128 Langer, *Philosophy*, p. 151.

129 Fung, *Chinese Philosophy*, 2:88, 91–93. Apocrypha were not limited to commentaries on the *Book of Changes* but were written on other Confucian classics as well. For a full-length treatment of the apocrypha, see Jack Dull, "A Historical Introduction to the Apocryphal (ch'an-wei) Texts of the Han Dynasty" (Ph.D. dissertation, University of Washington, 1966).

130 Bernhard Karlgren, *Grammata Serica Recensa* (Stockholm, 1957), p. 193.

131 Legge, *Shoo King*, p. 80; Schuyler Cammann, "Types of Symbols in Chinese Art," in *Studies in Chinese Thought*, ed. Arthur F. Wright (Chicago, 1953), p. 204.

132 *LC* 8.5b; Legge, *Li Chi*, 1:429–30.

133 *CTS* 45.1947; also discussed in Cammann, "Types of Symbols," p. 206. Cammann notes that whereas in earlier times the twelve symbols partook of a cosmological quality, they now were explained merely as symbols of the emperor's superior qualities, thus reflecting a growing trend away from cosmic speculation toward materialism; pp. 205–06. Although his point is well made, the cosmological aspects of ritual and the objects employed therein were by no means forgotton by the early T'ang. See, for example, the memorial dated 656 by Chang-sun Wu-chi, Yü Chih-ning, Hsü Ching-tsung, and others, where reference is made to the number twelve being associated with the emperor because the number was "modeled on" (*fa*) Heaven; *CTS* 45.1939.

134 *CWTTT* 1:515.521. The *Tso-chuan*, under the year 709 B.C., records a speech in which it is mentioned that when King Wu of Chou had subdued the Shang, he removed the nine caldrons to his own capital at Lo; James Legge, trans., *The Ch'un Ts'ew with the Tso Chuen*, p. 40.

135 *CWTTT* 1:521.653.

136 See the tables in Wang Shou-nan, *Chung-kuo li-tai ch'uang-yeh ti-wang* (n.p., 1964), pp. 168–79.

137 Legge, *Li Chi*, 1:416–17. Legge notes (p. 417*n*1) that commentators explained that a calf was used because of its "guileless simplicity."

138 Watson, *Hsün Tzu*, p. 103.

139 Walzer, "Role of Symbolism," 196.

140 Edelman, *Symbolic Uses of Politics*, p. 20.

141 For a useful discussion of the question of audience in the process of legitimation in traditional China, see Arthur F. Wright, "Some Preliminary Reflections on Legitimation in Chinese History," pp. 2–4 (unpublished paper offered at the Conference on Legitimation of Chinese Regimes, Asilomar, Monterey, California, 15–24 June 1975).

142 Easton, *Systems Analysis*, p. 401.

143 Leach, *Culture and Communication*, p. 45.

CHAPTER 2

1 Arthur F. Wright and Denis Twitchett, eds., *Perspectives on the T'ang* (New Haven, 1973), introduction, p. 1.

2 Denis C. Twitchett, "The Sui (589–618) and T'ang (618–907) Dynasties: An Introduction," in *Essays on T'ang Society*, ed. John Curtis Perry and Bardwell L. Smith (Leiden, 1976), p. 6. On the first three reigns of the T'ang, see *CHC* 3:150–289.

3 On the Hsüan-wu Gate Incident, see *CHC* 3:182–87.

4 *SS* 14.345.

5 Waley, *Analects* (XVII.11), p. 212, slightly emended.

6 See, for example, the discussion of Li Pai-yao, *CKCY* 4.117, and that of Wei Cheng, *CKCY* 7.238; *THY* 32.589.

7   *TTCLC* 81.465.

8   *SS* 6.105; *CTS* 21.826, quoting from an edict of 667. In his edict ordering the compilation of a ritual commentary sometime before the year 640, T'ai-tsung routinely referred to the fact that the ritual texts had become disordered; *CTW* 9.3a; *THY* 36.651.

9   *SS* 6.105–07.

10   Ch'ien Mu, "Lüeh-lun Wei-Chin Nan-Pei-ch'ao hsüeh-shu wen-hua yü tang-shih men-ti chih kuan-hsi," *Hsin-ya hsüeh-pao* 5:2 (1963):26–27; Étienne Balazs, *Le traité économique du "Souei-chou"* (Leiden, 1953), p. 305.

11   T'ao, "K'ung-tzu miao-t'ing (I)," 24.

12   Ch'ien, "Wei-Chin Nan-Pei-ch'ao hsüeh-shu," 27–28; Wright, *Sui Dynasty*, pp. 36–37.

13   See Yamazaki Hiroshi, "Zuidai no gakkai no kenkyū," *Risshō Daigaku Bunga-kubu ronsō* 37 (1970):29–78; Wright, *Sui Dynasty*, p. 115. A list of the major compilers of the Sui code is found in *SS* 2.48.

14   Ch'en, *Sui-T'ang chih-tu*, pp. 8–40.

15   *CTS* 21.816–17; *HTS* 11.308; *THY* 37.669; *TT* 41. 233c; Ch'en, *Sui-t'ang chih-tu*, pp. 41–42.

16   *CTW* 161.5b–7b.

17   On the problem of Wang T'ung's discipleship, see Wechsler, "Wang T'ung," 261–66.

18   T'ao, "K'ung-tzu miao-t'ing (I)," 27.

19   *CTS* 21.818–19; *HTS* 11.308–09; *THY* 37.670; *TT* 41.233c.

20   Biography: *HHS* 35.1206–13. See also Jerzy Mieczyslaw Künstler, "Deux biographies de Tcheng Hiuan," *Rocznik Orientalistyczny* 26:1 (1962):23–64; Kao Ming, *Li-hsüeh hsin-t'an* (Hong Kong, 1963), pp. 231–44; T'ao, "K'ung-tzu miao-t'ing (I)," 19–20; Dull, "Apocryphal Texts," p. 393–95.

21   Herbert A. Giles, *A Chinese Biographical Dictionary* (1898, reprint ed., Taipei, n.d.), p. 113.

22   Kao, *Li-hsüeh hsin-t'an*, p. 273.

23   P'i Hsi-jui, *Ching-hsüeh li-shih* (1924; reprint ed., Hong Kong, 1961), pp. 142–55; T'ao, "K'ung-tzu miao-t'ing (I)," 20; Dull, "Apocryphal Texts," p. 395.

24   Dull, "Apocryphal Texts," pp. 109, 216.

25   For a good discussion of the nature of the dispute between the New Text and Old Text schools, see Dull, "Apocryphal Texts," pp. 374ff.

26   Biography: *SKC* 13.414–23. For a translation of Wang's biography and a discussion of his official career and scholarship, see R. P. Kramers, trans., *K'ung Tzu Chia Yü: The School Sayings of Confucius* (Leiden, 1950), chap. 3. For two other studies in which Wang also figures prominently, see T'ang Yung-t'ung (Walter Liebenthal, trans.), "Wang Pi's New Interpretation of the *I Ching* and *Lun-yü*," *Harvard Journal of Asiatic Studies* 10 (1947):124–61, and Yoav Ariel, "K'ung-Ts'ung-Tzu and the Polemical Tradition in Chinese Philosophy," (Ph.D. dissertation, University of Tel-Aviv, 1981), esp. pp. 105–31.

27   *SKC* 13.419; P'i, *Ching-hsüeh li-shih*, p. 156. Kramers, *K'ung Tzu Chia Yü*,

pp. 81–82, believes that instead of having been written by Wang Su, the *Sheng-cheng lun* is actually a recorded dispute between Cheng and Wang's followers.

28 *SKCSTMTY* 3:1874–75; P'i, *Ching-hsüeh li-shih*, pp. 155–56.

29 P'i, *Ching-hsüeh li-shih*, p. 160; Fujikawa Masakazu, *Kandai ni okeru reigaku no kenkyū* (Tokyo, 1968), pp. 256–57; T'ao, "K'ung-tzu miao-t'ing (I)," 22.

30 P'i, *Ching-hsüeh li-shih*, p. 170; T'ao, "K'ung-tzu miao-t'ing (I)," 26.

31 P'an Chung-kuei, "Wu-ching cheng-i t'an-yüan," *Hua-kang hsüeh-pao* 1 (1965):13–15, quoting the prefaces to individual classics in the *Sui History* 'Monograph on Literature," and also Lu Te-ming's *Ching-tien shih-wen*; T'ao, "K'ung-tzu miao-t'ing (I)," 25–26.

32 *THY* 77.1405.

33 On the dating of the *Wu-ching cheng-i*, see Su Ying-hui, "Ts'ung Tun-huang-pen hsien-ming-yeh lun Wu-ching cheng-i chih k'an-ting," *K'ung Meng hsüeh-pao*, 16 (Sept. 1968):181–93; *idem*, "Wu-ching cheng-i ti-i-tz'u p'an-hsing yü Chen-kuan nien-chung shuo," *Kuo-li Chung-yang t'u-shu-kuan kuan-k'an* n.s. 2:2 (1968):29–33.

34 Chien Po-hsien, "K'ung Ying-ta Ch'un-ch'iu Tso-chuan cheng-i p'ing-i," *K'ung Meng hsüeh-pao* 20 (Sept. 1970):65.

35 P'an, "Wu-ching cheng-i," 15, 19–20.

36 P'i, *Ching-hsüeh li-shih*, p. 196.

37 Chien, "K'ung Ying-ta Ch'un-ch'iu Tso-chuan," 55–57.

38 T'ao, "K'ung-tzu miao-t'ing (I)," 27. For the view that Wang Pi's *I-ching* commentary may have substantially reflected the teachings of Wang Su, see T'ang, "Wang Pi," 133.

39 Ch'ien Po-hsien, "K'ung Ying-ta Shang-shu cheng-i pu-cheng," *K'ung Meng hsüeh-pao* 19 (1960):156; T'ao, "K'ung-tzu miao-t'ing (I)," 27.

40 P'an, "Wu-ching cheng-i," 15.

41 Quoted in Kao, *Li-hsüeh hsin-t'an*, p. 273.

42 *CTS* 21.818.

43 Kaneko Shūichi, "Gi-Shin yori Zui-Tō ni itaru kōshi sōbyō no seido ni tsuite," *Shigaku zasshi* 88 (1979):1529.

44 Kaneko, "Gi-Shin yori," 1522; Fukunaga Mitsushi, "Kōten jōtei to Tennō daitei to Genshi tenson—Jukyō no saikōshin to Dōkyō no saikōshin," *Chūtetsu bungakkai hō* 2 (June 1976):12.

45 *HTS* 46.1194–96; Robert des Rotours, *Traité des fonctionnaires et traité de l'armée*, 2 vols. (Leiden, 1947), 1:80–96. See also *TTLT* ch. 4.

46 *HTS* 46.1194; des Rotours, *Traité des fonctionnaires*, 1:81–82. For a complete listing of the ceremonies, see *TTLT* 4.9a–14b.

47 *TTLT* 4.9a.

48 *THY* 37.671.

49 See the list of compilers in *THY* 37.670.

50 *THY* 37.669.

51 Biographies: *CTS* 73.2601–03; *HTS* 198.5643–45.

52 Biographies: *CTS* 73.2594–95; *HTS* 198.5641–42.

53 Biographies: *CTS* 65.2446–56; *HTS* 105.4017–22.

54 Biographies: *CTS* 66.2459–67; *HTS* 96.3853–57.
55 See Wechsler, *Mirror*, for his biography.
56 On Wei Cheng's *Lei-li*, see R. P. Kramers, "Conservatism and the Transmission of the Confucian Canon: A T'ang Scholar's Complaint," *Journal of Oriental Studies* (Hong Kong) 2 (1955):121.
57 Biographies: *CTS* 82.2761–65; *HTS* 223A.6335–39.
58 On the topic of political alignments in the early T'ang, see the author's "Factionalism in Early T'ang Government," in *Perspectives on the T'ang*, ed. Arthur F. Wright and Denis Twitchett (New Haven, 1973), pp. 87–120, and the articles cited therein.

CHAPTER 3

1 James Legge, trans., *The Doctrine of the Mean*, p. 417; idem, *Li Chi*, 2:320.
2 Quoted in Fung, *Chinese Philosophy*, 1:161.
3 Hsiao, *Political Thought*, pp. 514–30. See, for example, "The Destiny of Kings" (*Wang-ming lun*), by the Han historian Pan Piao (A.D. 3–54), who counted auspicious omens among the five signs that Han Kao-tsu would govern the empire; de Bary et al., *Sources*, p. 195.
4 Miyakawa Hisayuki, *Rikuchōshi kenkyū (seiji shakai hen)*, (Tokyo, 1956), p. 160.
5 Jack Goody, ed., *Succession to High Office* (Cambridge, 1966), editor's introduction, p. 22.
6 On this latter category, see Edward H. Schafer, *Pacing the Void: T'ang Approaches to the Stars* (Berkeley and Los Angeles, 1977), chap. 6.
7 Ogata Isamu, "Chūgoku kodai ni okeru teii no keishō—sono seitōka no katei to ronri," *Shigaku zasshi* 85 (1976):319–20.
8 See *HFHD* 3:249ff.; Hsiao, *Political Thought*, pp. 514–17; de Bary, *Sources*, pp. 196–98. For a study of Wang Mang's overall efforts at legitimation, see Jack L. Dull, "Kao-tsu's Founding and Wang Mang's Failure: Studies in Han Time Legitimation" (an unpublished paper presented to the Conference on the Legitimation of Chinese Regimes, Asilomar, Monterey, California, 15–24 June 1975), 39ff.
9 See the chart in Ogata, "Teii no keishō," 311.
10 *SS* 6.117.
11 *SS* 9.174.
12 *SS* 69.1608; Wright, *Sui Dynasty*, p. 114.
13 See Edward H. Schafer, "The Auspices of T'ang," *Journal of the American Oriental Society* 83 (1963):200. Ho Peng-yoke, *The Astronomical Chapters of the Chin Shu. With Amendments, Full Translation and Annotations* (Paris, 1966), p. 21, notes that the *Chin-shu* lists twice as many bad omens as good omens.
14 See the "Monograph on the Five Elements" of the Sui and T'ang Standard Histories; Schafer, "Auspices," 200–01.
15 *TTLT* 4.18a–20b; *HTS* 46.1194; des Rotours, *Traité des fonctionnaires*, 1:84–85.

16 *SS* 22.617–18.

17 Ozaki, "Gu Seinan," 219.

18 *CKCY* 10.298–99; *CTS* 72.2567. On another occasion during the same year, Yü maintained that omens of misfortune were not as strong as the ruler's virtue, and that if T'ai-tsung cultivated virtue, the omens could be made to disappear; CKCY 10.297–98; CTS 37.1249, 72.2566–67.

19 *CKCY* 10.299; *WCKCL* 3.21b–22a.

20 *CCC* z.17.

21 *HTS* 1.7. Obviously, Kao-tsu's decree had no influence on the writing of Wen Ta-ya's *Diary*.

22 *CTS* 37.1368; *THY* 28.532; Schafer, "Auspices," 205.

23 *THY* 28.531; *TTCLC* 114.594. See also the expression of similar sentiments by T'ai-tsung in the year 644; *THY* 28.532.

24 *THY* 28.531; *TTCLC* 114.594.

25 See *CTS* 37.1351; *THY* 28.532.

26 *TTCLC* 30.115.

27 On Wen Ta-ya's *Diary*, see Wechsler, *Mirror*, pp. 19–21.

28 *CCC* 1.1.

29 *CCC* 1.2.

30 *CCC* 1.3.

31 *CCC* 1.4.

32 *CCC* 1.4.

33 See Schafer, *Pacing the Void*, pp. 47–53.

34 *CCC* 1.4. Hearing of the Son of Heaven vapor's link with Lou-fan prompted Sui Yang-ti to build a palace there. By linking himself with the region and its imperial symbols in this way, Yang-ti hoped thereby to counteract the prophecy that the next Son of Heaven would arise in T'ai-yüan.

35 *CCC* 1.8.

36 On Taotistic omens, see pp. 69–72. Just as before, when Yang-ti constructed a palace at Lou-fan, he also attempted to accord his behavior with this prophecy. He now always wore white, and every time he traveled to his "river capital" at Chiang-tu, on China's eastern coast, he would compare it with the Eastern Sea: *CCC* 1.8.

37 *CCC* 1.8.

38 Woodbridge Bingham, "The Rise of Li in a Ballad Prophecy," *Journal of the American Oriental Society* 61 (1941):274–75. The writer of the "Treatise on the Five Elements" (*Wu-hsing chih*) of the *Sui History*, compiled early in the T'ang, viewed the line "Be not extravagant in speech" as indicating Li Mi, whose given name means "secret"; *ChTS* 875.9900. According to Wen Ta-ya's *Diary*, Sui Yang-ti also took the ballad to refer to Li Mi; *CCC* 2.17. On the other hand, there is much in the ballad to point to Li Hung. Li Hung called himself King of T'ang, the same T'ang as that of Kao-tsu and T'ao-T'ang. In one version of the "Peach-plum Li" ballad there is the line "As a great heron [*hung-ku*] you fly round the Yang Mountain." The *hung* of this versions replaces the *huang* ("yellow") in the third line of Wen Ta-ya's ver-

sion, and is homonymous with the *hung* of Li Hung. It is possible, Bingham notes (p. 275), that the *huang* was also at that time pronounced *hung*.

39 Anna Seidel, "The Image of the Perfect Ruler in Early Taoist Messianism: Lao-tzu and Li Hung," *History of Religions* 9 (1969–70):235–47.

40 *SS* 37.1121. Li Hun is also called Li Chin-ts'ai; see *CTS* 37.1375.

41 *SS* 37.1124; see also Bingham, "Balled Prophecy," 273, 275. On the possibility of T'ang Kao-tsu also being linked to this water symbolism, see below, p. 67.

42 *CCC* 1.9.

43 *CCC* 1.10.

44 *DJ* 8.8139.43, 8154.557; Schafer, "Auspices," 199.

45 Schafer, "Auspices," 198.

46 *CCC* 1.10.

47 See Forke, *Lun-Heng*, 1:178; Cammann, "Types of Symbols," p. 210.

48 *CCC* 1.10.

49 *CCC* 2.19. Basically the same story is told in *HYSC* 8.3a–b, and other Taoist sources.

50 *CCC* 2.22.

51 *CWTTT* 2.2722.21. During the time of Han Kuang-wu-ti, an auspicious blade of grain was discovered that had three roots, one stalk, nine ears, and was two feet higher than usual; Forke, *Lun-Heng*, 1:180.

52 *CCC* 2.22–23.

53 *CCC* 2.24.

54 See *HHS* 1A.12.

55 *CCC* 2.25.

56 *CCC* 2.27.

57 *CCC* 3.37.

58 *CCC* 3.37.

59 *CCC* 3.38.

60 Bingham, "Ballad Prophecy," 278–79.

61 Quotes in *ChTS* 875.9900. There is always the possibility that this source interpreted *yüan* after the fact, with Li Yüan in mind. Bingham in his interpretation of the poem, seems to have overlooked this work; "Ballad Prophecy," 278.

62 "Ballad Prophecy," 279.

63 See pp. 92–98.

64 *HTS* 33.851; Schafer, *Pacing the Void*, p. 214. According to the note of Hu San-hsing, *TCTC* 191.6003, Venus' appearance in the daytime might have been interpreted in a variety of ways: as armies come to grief, someone not being a loyal vassal, a change of rulers, a strong country becoming weak, or a small country becoming strong.

65 *THY* 28.531.

66 *TFYK* 24.1a.

67 See *TFYK* 24.1a–2b, 37.11a; *THY* 28.531. On the significance of red birds, see Schafer, "Auspices," 199.

68 See Miyakawa Hisayuki, *Rikuchōshi kenkyū (shūkyō hen)* (Tokyo, 1964), pp. 176–85; Charles D. Benn, "Taoism as Ideology in the Reign of Emperor Hsüan-tsung" (Ph.D. dissertation, University of Michigan, 1977), 14–35; and Stephen Bokenkamp, "Taoist Millenarianism and the Founding of the T'ang" (unpublished paper presented at the Conference on the Nature of State and Society in Medieval China, Stanford University, 16–18 August 1980).

69 *HYSC* 8.2b.

70 *CCC* 2.21.

71 Miyakawa, *Rikuchōshi kenkyū (shūkyō)*, p. 180.

72 *CTS* 192.5125; *HTS* 204.5804; *LTCTC* 5a–b. For a study of Mao-shan, a center of Shang-ch'ing ("Highest Clarity") Taoism, see Edward H. Schafer, *Mao Shan in T'ang T'imes* (Society for the Study of Chinese Religions Monograph no. 1, 1980). Wang Yüan-chih is discussed on pp. 45–46.

73 *HYSC* 8.2b–3a.

74 *HYSC* 8.3a. The Sui capital was taken on the ninth day of the eleventh month; *CHC* 3:160.

75 *HYSC* 8.2b.

76 *HYSC* 8.4a–6b; *LTCTC* 4a–5a; *THY* 50.865; Miyakawa, *Rikuchōshi kenkyū (shūkyō)*, p. 181.

77 See *THY* 50.865.

78 On problems concerning the dates given in this passage not jibing with historical events, see Miyakawa, *Rikuchōshi kenkyū (shūkyō)*, p. 186n8. Other versions, such as *HYSC* 8.7b–8, seem to accord more closely with fact.

79 *HYSC* 8.6a; Chang Tsun-liu, "Sui-T'ang Wu-tai fo-chiao ta-shih nien-piao," in Fan Wen-lan, *T'ang-tai fo-chiao* (Peking, 1979), p. 117. Accounts of this episode vary; see Benn, "Taoism as Ideology," pp. 329–30n18.

80 *HYSC* 8.6a; *CSTP* 41.8a–11a; Chang, "Fo-chiao ta-shih nien-piao," pp. 117–18.

81 On this theme, see Benn, "Taoism as Ideology," p. 330n18.

82 *HYSC* 8.8a; Miyakawa, *Rikuchōshi kenkyū (shūkyō)*, p. 182; cf. Benn, "Taoism as Ideology," pp. 31–33.

83 *HTS* 1.18; *TFYK* 113.9b; *HYSC* 8.8a; *CSTP* 41.14b–15a. Chang, "Fo-chiao ta-shih nien-piao," p. 120, says that this was a "second visit." He is evidently following the account of *HYSC* 8.6a, which records that Kao-tsu's first visit to Lou-kuan was in 620, when he had halls of worship built there, but this is a point not corroborated in other texts.

84 *CCC* 2.17.

85 Benn, "Taoism as Ideology," p. 35.

86 On T'ai-tsung's relationship with Buddhism, see Arthur F. Wright, "T'ai-tsung and Buddhism," in *Perspectives on the T'ang*, ed. Arthur F. Wright and Denis Twitchett (New Haven, 1973), pp. 239–63; and Moroto Tatsuo, "Tō Taisō no Bukkyō shinkō ni tsuite," *Akidai shigaku* 27 (1980):1–17.

87 Tao-hsüan, *Hsü Kao-seng chuan*. 30 *chüan*. Ca. 645. *T* vol. 50, 26.671b; *CTS* 101.3158–59.

88 From *Lo chung chi-i lu* (*Shuo-fu* ed., Taipei, 1972), 20.21b–22a; quoted in Li Shu-t'ung, *T'ang-shih hsin-lun* (Taipei, 1972), pp. 166–67.

89 *CTS* 2.21.

90 *CTS* 2.21; *HTS* 2.23.

91 *CTS* 192.5125; *HTS* 204.5804; Li Shu-t'ung, *T'ang-shih k'ao-pien*, p. 132; Benn, "Taoism as Ideology," pp. 42.

92 *CTS* 192.5125; *HTS* 204.5804; *LTCTC* 5a–b.

93 *CTS* 191.5089; *HTS* 204.5804; Li, *T'ang-shih k'ao-pien*, p. 130; Benn, "Taoism as Ideology," pp. 42–43.

94 *CSTP* 41.7a–b; *CTW* 146.25a–b; Wright, "T'ai-tsung and Buddhism," p. 260; Chang, "Fo-chiao ta-shih nien-piao," p. 118.

95 *TTCLC* 30.115–16.

96 *HTS* 34.881.

97 *THY* 28.532.

98 *THY* 28.533.

99 *THY* 38.533.

100 *CCC* 1.10; Fan Tsu-yü, *T'ang-chien* (1086; Shanghai, 1980), 1.1b.

101 *ChTS* 874.9895.

102 Michel Strickmann, "The Mao Shan Revelations; Taoism and the Aristocracy," *T'oung Pao* 63 (1977):1–64.

CHAPTER 4

1   Robert S. Ellwood, *The Feast of Kingship: Accession Ceremonies in Ancient Japan* (Tokyo, 1973), pp. 3–7; A. M. Hocart, *Kingship* (London, 1927), pp. 189–90, 201–02.

2   Mircea Eliade, *The Myth of the Eternal Return or, Cosmos and History*, trans. Willard R. Trask (Princeton, 1974), p. 80.

3   Arnold van Gennep, *The Rites of Passage*, trans. Monika B. Vizedom and Gabrielle L. Caffee (Chicago, 1960), p. 3.

4   Van Gennep, *Rites of Passage*, pp. 10–11.

5   Turner, *Dramas, Fields, and Metaphors*, p. 53. See also Leach, *Culture and Communication*, pp. 78–79; Hocart, *Kingship*, p. 70 and chap. 7, passim.

6   See chap. 1, n. 7.

7   Easton, *Systems Analysis*, pp. 301, 308–09.

8   Meyer Fortes, "Ritual and Office in Tribal Society," in *Essays on the Ritual of Social Relations*, ed. Max Gluckman (Manchester, 1962), p. 86.

9   Fortes, "Ritual and Office," p. 83. Fortes here expands upon an idea of Robert Redfield.

10 See Nishijima Sadao, "Kandai ni okeru sokui girei—toku ni teii keishō no ba'ai ni tsuite," in *Enoki Hakase kanreki kinen Tōyōshi ronsō* (Tokyo, 1975) p. 404; Ogata Isamu, "Teii no keishō," 308; idem, *Chūgoku kodai no 'ie'*, pp. 297–98.

11 On the distinction between accession and enthronement, see D. C. Holtom,

The Japanese Enthronement Ceremonies with an Account of the Imperial Regalia (1928; reprint ed., Tokyo, 1972), pp. 46–47. In contrast to Holtom, in this study we employ the more generalized term "accession ceremonies" to include the rites surrounding both accession and enthronement.

12 See Ku Chieh-kang, "Shan-jang chuan-shuo chi yü Mo-chia k'ao," *Shih-hsüeh chi-k'an* 1 (1936):163–230, for the theory that the *shan-jang* ideal originally derived from Mohist thought and was later seized upon and expanded by the Confucians to include the story of Shun's cession of the throne to Yü. The "Yao-tien" chapter of the *Book of History* is, according to Ku, a relatively late narration of the myth, probably dating to Former Han times; 220–21.

13 For an interesting study of the use of *shan-jang* in the Han-Wei transition, see Carl Leban, "Managing Heaven's Mandate: Coded Communications in the Accession of Ts'ao P'ei, A.D. 220," in *Ancient China: Studies in Early Civilization*, ed. Roy and Tsien, pp. 315–41. Chao I, *Nien-erh-shih cha-chi*, 36 *chüan* (1795; Taipei, 1965), 7.87, notes that the Chin, Sung, Southern Ch'i, Liang, Ch'en, Northern Ch'i, Northern Chou, and Sui dynasties all employed the *shan-jang* procedure.

14 Sarah Allan, *The Heir and the Sage: Dynastic Legends in Early China* (San Francisco, 1981), p. 142.

15 De Bary, *Sources*, p. 192. See also Legge, *Li Chi* 1:364, 366.

16 See preface, n. 1.

17 Ellwood, *Feast of Kingship*, p. 19.

18 Legge, *Shoo King*, pp. 32, 64; *WLTK* 128.2a, b.

19 Legge, *Shoo King*, p. 191; *WLTK* 128.3a–b, 5a.

20 Legge, *Shoo King*, pp. 544–61; *WLTK* 128.10b–13a, commentary of compiler.

21 Legge, *Shoo King*, pp. 562–68; *WLTK* 128.13a; cf. *HFHD* 1:303n1.2.

22 *WLTK* 128.11b, 16a–b, 21b, commentary of compiler.

23 *SC* 10.415–18; Watson, *Records*, 1:344–46; *HS* 4.108–10; *HFHD* 1:228–31.

24 Six of a total of twelve Later Han emperors who followed the founder assumed the imperial position on the day of their predecessor's death. In other cases, for various reasons, including the lack of an immediate heir, succession took place later; Nishijima, "Kandai ni okeru sokui girei," 406–07.

25 Nishijima, "Kandai ni okeru sokui girei," 407; Bielenstein, *Restoration of the Han Dynasty*, 4:182–83. For the case of Ching-ti, whose accession came after the interment of the previous emperor, see Nishijima, "Kandai ni okeru sokui girei," p. 411; *HFHD* 1:303n1.2.

26 *Kung-yang chuan* (*SPTK* ed.) 11.2a. The accession of Chao-ti would have been the first opportunity for the new procedure to be implemented; Nishijima, "Kandai ni okeru sokui girei," 419–20; cf. *HFHD* 1:303n1.2.

27 Nishijima, "Kandai ni okeru sokui girei," 419.

28 Ogata, "Teii no keishō," 320.

29 *Chao* and *ts'e* were instrumental in the change of dynasties from the Later Han down through the Sui-T'ang transition; see Ogata's chart in "Teii no keishō," 311; idem, *Chūgoku kodai no 'ie,'* p. 301.

30 Ogata, "Teii no keishō," 309–10; idem, *Chūgoku kodai no 'ie,'* pp. 300–01.

31 Ogata, "Teii no keishō," 312.

32 *CS* 7.118–19; Ogata, "Teii no keishō," 312–13.

33 Ogata, "Teii no keishō," 312.

34 *HHS* "Monograph on Ritual and Ceremonial," p. 3143; Nishijima, "Kandai ni okeru sokui girei," 413–17.

35 Nishijima, "Kōtei shihai no seiritsu," in *Iwanami Kōza Sekai rekishi, vol.* 4 (*Kodai*), 218–48.

36 Nishijima, "Kōtei shihai no seiritsu," 244–49; Ogawa, *Chūgoku kodai no 'ie,'* pp. 131–32, 291–96.

37 Ogata Isamu, "Kōtei no jishō keishiki to sokui girei," *Yamanashi Daigaku Kyōikugakubu kenkyū hōkoku* 28 (1977):100–08. Ogata uses the accession of Wei Wen-ti at the time of the Later Han-Wei transition as his model.

38 Nishijima, "Kandai ni okeru sokui girei," 417–18; he uses the accession of Han Wen-ti as his model. See also Ogata, "Kōtei no jishō keishiki," 106. In the Former Han the duration of this two-stage sequence was one or two days; in the Later Han it was always one day. In same surname succession, assumption of *huang-ti* status usually took place before the coffin of the deceased ruler, but the assumption of *t'ien-tzu* status took place at the suburban altar or in more mundane locations.

39 See Holtom, *Japanese Enthronement Ceremonies*, pp. 3–5, 45.

40 Goody, *Succession to High Office*, editor's introduction, p. 12.

41 Nishijima, "Kandai ni okeru sokui girei," 406; idem, "Kōtei shihai no seiritsu," 245.

42 Kurihara Tomonobu, *Shin-Kanshi no kenkyū* (Tokyo, 1970), p. 145; Nishijima, "Kōtei shihai no seiritsu," 245–48. Ogawa, *Chūgoku kodai no 'ie,'* pp. 131–32, 291–96, further refines our understanding of the basis of this division. According to Ogawa, the title *huang-ti* connoted the emperor's stewardship of a human realm; it was used, for example, when he sacrificed to the ancestral deities, who were, after all, originally human. Here the focus was on the emperor as head of his own dynastic house. The title *t'ien-tzu* connoted the emperor's role in a higher realm; it was used, for example, when he sacrificed to the spirits of Heaven and Earth. Here, he was head not merely of his own house but a "house" consisting of "all under Heaven," thus including foreign states recognizing China's suzerainty.

43 Kurihara, *Shin-Kanshi*, p. 150.

44 Kurihara, *Shin-Kanshi*, p. 135.

45 *HS* 98.4032. See also *HFHD* 3:260n2.

46 Kurihara, *Shin-Kanshi*, pp. 136–53. That the seal was a creation of Ch'in times was accepted by the T'ang; see *TTLT* 8.33a–35a.

47 For the history of the transmission, see Shen Ch'in-han, *Han-shu shu-cheng* (Che-chiang kuan-chü k'an-pen, 1900), 35.73b–75b; Chao I, "Yang Huan ch'uan-kuo-hsi k'ao chih wu," *Kai-yü ts'ung-k'ao* ed., 20.11b–12a; *CWTTT* 6:9702.320.

48 Chao I, "Yang Huan," 20.15a. Chao cites differing inscriptions on the seal as recorded in different ages to prove his point. Even by T'ang times the inscription appears to have been repeatedly altered; 20.15a–b. The practice of coun-

terfeiting seals during the Period of Disunion led to an increase in the number of imperial seals. In 394, under the Eastern Chin, a seal that was larger and of a different shape than the *ch'uan-kuo* seal, but similar to it in other respects, was "discovered" and presented to the throne. The Eastern Chin passed this seal on to the Liang, which called it the Seal That Wards Off Evil Influences (*chen-hsi*). The Northern Ch'i, which obtained it in turn, boasted that it was the *ch'uan-kuo* seal, and even announced its acquisition at the ancestral temple. After passing through the Northern Chou it was transferred to the Sui. Wen-ti, the Sui founder, at first mistakenly regarded it as the *ch'uan-kuo* seal. In 582 he changed its name to the Seal by Which the Mandate Is Received (*shou-ming hsi*). But in 589, when the Sui conquered the Ch'en and he obtained the "real" *ch'uan-kuo* seal, Wen-ti renamed the *shou-ming* seal the Divine Seal (*shen-hsi*). The Divine Seal, like the *ch'uan-kuo* seal, was not used for official business but served as an emblem of authority. When the Sui emperor was holding court, the Divine Seal was placed in front of his mat on the right and the *ch'uan-kuo* seal on the left. (*SS* 11.250) Thus by Sui times the total number of imperial seals had increased to eight. (*TTLT* 8.34b; Shen, *Han-shu shu-cheng*, 35.74a–75a.) According to the "Monograph on Carriages and Clothing" of the *New T'ang History*, *HTS* 24.524, there were nine imperial seals in the T'ang: the *ch'uan-kuo* and eight others, comprising the old six seals plus a *shou-ming* and a *shen* seal. However, most T'ang records usually speak of the "eight seals" or the "eight treasures" (*pa-pao*), as they were later called in the time of Empress Wu; see, for example, *TTLT* 8.30a.

49   *WHTK* 89.810; *WLTK* ch. 128–29.

50   The sacrifices are variously identified as *ch'ai-liao*, burnt-offerings, and *lei*. In ancient times the *lei* sacrifice, about which much is not known, was used by monarchs on such occasions as ascending the throne, marching off to war, and making tours of inspection (*hsün-shou*); *WLTK* 1.122a–b; Bilsky, *State Religion*, 1:54.

51   See the cases of the Han emperor Kuang-wu, *HHS* 1A.22–23, and of the first Wei dynasty ruler, Wen-ti, *SKC* 2.62.

52   *TCTC* 15.502; *WLTK* 128.21b.

53   Watson, *Records*, 2:43; *HFHD* 2:121; *WLTK* 128.22a.

54   Arthur F. Wright and Edward Fagan, "Era Names and Zeitgeist," *Études Asiatiques* 5 (1951):113–21; Edward H. Schafer, "Chinese Reign Names—Words or Nonsense Syllables?" *Wennti* (Yale University) 3 (July 1952):33–40; idem, "The Origin of an Era," *Journal of the American Oriental Society* 85 (1965):543–50.

55   *WLTK* 128.27b–28a. When Emperor Hui of the Chin dynasty succeeded to the throne in 290, he broke with custom by immediately inaugurating his first era-name. Soon afterward, however, he became convinced that his decision was in error, and so again changed his era-name the following year, hoping thereby to begin anew; *WLTK* 128.9a.

56   Miyakawa, *Rikuchōshi kenkyū (seiji shakai)*, pp. 77–78.

57   Marcel Granet, *Danses et légendes de la Chine ancienne*, 2 vols. (Paris, 1959), 1:212ff.; Kaltenmark, "Religion and Politics," 38. For an explanation of

how the victim is identified with the donor of a sacrifice, and the donor, by vicarious association, is purified, see Leach, *Culture and Communication*, pp. 83–84.

58 Kaltenmark, "Religion and Politics," 22, 38.

59 Brian E. McKnight, *The Quality of Mercy: Amnesties and Traditional Chinese Justice* (Honolulu, 1981), p. 4.

60 Michael Loewe, "The Orders of Aristocratic Rank of Han China," *T'oung Pao* 48:1–3 (1960):142.

61 In some cases the interment of the previous emperor preceded the visit to the ancestral temple, and in some cases it followed it; *WLTK* 128.26b, note of compiler; Nishijima, "Kandai ni okeru sokui girei," 407.

62 Nishijima, "Kandai ni okeru sokui girei," 408. The period between accession to the throne and visit to the ancestral temple was occasionally a fairly long one, in the case of Huan-ti of the Later Han, who became emperor in A.D. 147, comprising fifty-two days; *WLTK* 128.6a, note of compiler.

63 Nishijima, "Kandai ni okeru sokui girei," 421.

64 Nishijima, "Kandai ni okeru sokui girei," 408–10, 421.

65 *WHTK* 89.810; *WLTK* 128.30a–b.

66 *NCS* 9.135–36; *WLTK* 129.3a–b.

67 *CCC* 3.30.

68 On the nine gifts, see p. 34.

69 *CCC* 3.30–33. The *ts'e* issued in the name of the young Sui emperor was, like most of the other accession documents, actually written by Ch'en Shu-ta, a former Sui official now in the T'ang employ.

70 See, for example, the cases of the Han-Wei and the Northern Chou-Sui dynastic transitions; *SKC* 1.37–38; *SS* 1.7–11.

71 *CCC* 3.33–34.

72 *CCC* 3.34.

73 *CCC* 3.34.

74 *CCC* 3.35. There is no mention in either of the T'ang Standard Histories that Kao-tsu had any reservations about accepting the nine gifts, nor of his decision to distribute them among his subordinates.

75 *CCC* 3.35 gives a date of the fourth lunar month. I am here following the *SS*, *CTS*, and *HTS* chronology.

76 *CCC* 3.35–36; *SS* 5.101–02; *CTS* 1.5–6; *HTS* 1.6.

77 *CTS* 1.6; *HTS* 1.6.

78 *CCC* 3.37–38. For the speech of Han Kao-tsu, see Watson, *Records*, 1:106; *HFHD* 1:101–02.

79 *CCC* 3.38–39; *CTS* 1.6; *HTS* 1.6.

80 *CCC* 3.38–39; *CTW* 3.17a–18b.

81 *TTCLC* 2.5–6; *CTW* 1.7b–8b.

82 Miyakawa, *Rikuchōshi kenkyū (seiji shakai)*, pp. 159–61.

83 *CCC* 2.15.

84 *CWTTT* 5:7614.374.

85 *CTS* 1.4; *WCKCL* 2.28a.

86 Ellwood, *Feast of Kingship*, pp. 24–26.

87 *SS* 1.13.

88 *CCC* 3.39.

89 *SS* 5.101; *CTS* 1.6; *HTS* 1.6.

90 *CCC* 3.35.

91 *CTS* 54.2242; *HTS* 85.3703. See also *TTLT* 8.35a; *TPYL* 594.21a.

92 Chao I, "Yang Huan," 20.12a.

93 Quoted by Shen Ch'in-han, *Han-shu shu-cheng*, 35.75b.

94 *SS* 1.13.

95 Kaneko Shūchi, "Chūgoku kodai ni okeru kōtei saishi no ichi kōsatsu," *Shigaku zasshi* 87:2 (1978):186–92.

96 *WHTK* 99.906b; Kaneko, "Kōtei saishi," 175. Two months after his accession in 712, Hsüan-tsung paid a visit to the ancestral temple to perform a routine sacrifice, but no announcement of his accession was made at that time; *HTS* 5.121; *TFYK* 30.6b. Even in this special case during the T'ang, however, the sixty-day hiatus between the emperor's accession and his first visit to the ancestral temple suggests that the ceremony did not have the importance it had during the Han; Kaneko, "Kōtei saishi," 184.

97 *CTS* 25.941; *TCTC* 185.5794; *TFYK* 30.1a–b.

98 *CTS* 2.30; *HTS* 2.27.

99 This date is given in *HTS* 2.27; *THY* 1.2; and *TCTC* 191.6017. It is corroborated in T'ai-tsung's edict announcing a general amnesty, *CTW* 4.13a, and also in the *ts'e* at the time of his accession, *TTCLC* 1.1. *CTS* 2.30 mistakenly gives the eighth day of the eighth month, which was the day not of T'ai-tsung's accession but of his father's cession of the throne; see *THY* 1.2.

100 See the edict in *TTCLC* 2.2a–3a; *CTW* 4.12b–13b.

101 *CTW* 4.14a–b.

102 The edict is in *CTW* 4.17a–b.

103 *Chou-i* (*SPTK* ed.), 8.1b; cf. James Legge, trans., *I Ching: Book of Changes* (1899; reprint ed., Secaucus, N.J., 1964), p. 370.6. T'ai-tsung was the first to select Chen-kuan for an era-name. Later it was also used under the Sung and the Hsi-Hsia; *CWTTT* 8:13775.211.

104 *TTCLC* 3.115–16; *CTW* 3.9b–10b; *THY* 1.2.

105 Retired Emperor (*t'ai-shang huang*), the title adopted by Kao-tsu, already had a long history prior to the T'ang. Originally it was a posthumous name conferred on an emperor's father, and only later came to refer to an emperor who had abdicated in favor of a son. Ch'in Shih-huang-ti posthumously honored his father as *t'ai-shang huang*; *SC* 6.236; *CWTTT* 2:3414.51. Han Kao-tsu, as mentioned by T'ang Kao-tsu in his *ts'e*, treated his own father very respectfully, paying homage to him every fifth day beginning in 201 B.C. In the summer of that year, the Han founder, issuing an edict acknowledging that his merit in bringing peace to China sprang from the teachings of his father, granted him the title *t'ai-shang huang*, Grand Emperor, thus honoring for the first time the living father of an emperor. (*HFHD* 1:115; *WHTK* 251.1979) Annotators have suggested that the title lacks the character *ti* after the *huang* because otherwise it would have denoted that the bearer actually ruled as emperor. (*WLTK* 142.13a–b; *CWTTT* 2:3414.51) That this is so can

be seen in the cases of the Northern Wei emperor Hsien-wen and the Northern Ch'i emperor Wu-ch'eng. When they abdicated in favor of their sons in 471 and 565, respectively, they continued to control real power from behind the throne and so adopted the more "active" title of *t'ai-shang huang-ti*. (*WS* 6.132; *PCS* 7.94) A further twist to the practice was added by the Northern Chou emperor Hsüan, a devotee of Taoist quietism, who at the age of twenty voluntarily ceded power in 579 to his son. To symbolize that he was still in charge of government, he employed the title *t'ien-yüan huang-ti*, and to show that his position was superior to that of his son, he took twenty-four as his number, double the traditional number of an emperor. (*CS* 7.119; *WHTK* 251.1983; *WLTK* 142.14b–15a) Given this history of the title, T'ang Kao-tsu's adoption of *t'ai-shang huang* can be seen as a statement that he was going to be a retired emperor in fact as well as in name.

106   *TTCLC* 1.1–2; *CTW* 3.19a–20a.

107   Kaneko, "Kōtei saishi," 184, 185, believes that announcements to Heaven (*ch'ai-liao*) made by both T'ai-tsung and Su-tsung (rg. 756–62) may have been assoiated in some way with the cession of power to sons by still-living fathers. On Su-tsung's sacrifice, see *CTS* 10.242.

108   On this theme, see Ogata, "Teii no keishō," 314–16; idem, *Chūgoku kodai no 'ie,'* pp. 309–10.

109   Ogata, "Teii no keishō," 314–18; idem, *Chūgoku kodai no 'ie,'* pp. 309–13.

110   See *CTS* 4.66; *HTS* 3.51; *TCTC* 199.6267–68.

111   *TTCLC* 11.67; *CTW* 9.7a–8b.

112   *TCTC* 199.6268.

113   There was no *chia-tzu* day in the sixth lunar month of 649. Another one did not occur until the twentieth day of the seventh month (September 3).

114   See the edict in *CTS* 4.66; *CTW* 11.18b.

115   *CTS* 4.67; *HTS* 3.52; *CTW* 11.19b. The name appears to have no *locus classicus*, nor was it adopted for use by any emperor prior to or after Kao-tsung.

116   From *Tso-chuan*, Duke Hsi, ninth year; Legge, *The Ch'un Ts'ew with Tso Chuen*, p. 154.

117   *TTCLC* 11.67. T'ai-tsung had praised Kao-tsung's qualities in similar fashion in two edicts appointing him to oversee governmental affairs in the emperor's absence in 645 and 646; see *TTCLC* 30.111.

118   *HTS* 3.51; *TCTC* 199.6267.

119   *TCTC* 199.6267.

CHAPTER 5

1   *WLTK* 2.1a. Ch'in Hui-t'ien, a Ch'ing dynasty scholar, argues that, strictly speaking, there is only one sacrifice to Heaven per year—that at the round altar at the winter solstice. All others commonly regarded as such, i.e., the prayer for grain, or against drought, or at the Ming-t'ang, are prayers of supplication or of thanks, thus belonging to different categories of rites; *WLTK* 1.16a, 17a.

2   *HTS* 11.310.

3   Kaneko Shūichi, "Tōdai no daishi, chūshi, shōshi ni tsuite," *Kōchi Daigaku gakujutsu kenkyū hōkoku* 25:2 (1976):14. See the list of rites under these classifications in *HTS* 11.310.

4   Kaneko, "Tōdai no daishi," 15; Ogata Isamu, "Kandai ni okeru 'Shin bō' keishiki—kodai teikoku no kunshin kankei ni tsuite," *Shigaku zasshi* 76 (1967): 1159–1203.

5   *WLTK* 41.1a–b.

6   Kaneko, "Kōtei saishi," 194.

7   For a summary of the argumentation, see Utsugi Akira, "Raiki no kōrei ni tsuite no okusetsu," in *Wada Hakase koki kinen Tōyōshi ronsō* (Tokyo, 1961), 175–85.

8   Ishibashi Ushio, *Tendan* (Tokyo, 1975), pp. 82–86. On the inseparability of ancestral and altar rites, see also Kurihara, *Shin-Kanshi*, pp. 105–12.

9   According to the interpretation of Cheng Hsüan; Nishida Tai'ichirō, "Kōsai no taishō to sono jiki to ni tsuite," *Shinagaku* 8 (1935): 47–48; *Tso-chuan*, Duke Hsiang, seventh year, in Legge, *The Ch'un Tsew with the Tso Chuen*, pp. 430, 431.

10 Ishibashi, *Tendan*, p. 85; Schafer, *Pacing the Void*, pp. 45–46.

11 Ishibashi, *Tendan*, p. 77; Utsugi, "Raiki no kōrei," 176; Kurihara, *Shin-Kanshi*, pp. 92–105. For records regarding the suburban sacrifices from earliest times through the T'ang period, see *TT* chs. 42–43.

12 *Chou-li* (*SPTK* ed.) 6.4b.

13 *LC* 14.1a–b; Legge, *Li Chi*, 2:201–03.

14 Kaneko, "Kōtei saishi," 195n4; Michael Loewe, *Crisis and Conflict in Han China* (London, 1974), pp. 170–79. On the altar of Heaven rites of the Later Han, see Bielenstein, *Restoration of the Han Dynasty*, 4:166–67.

15 Utsugi, "Raiki no kōrei," 176.

16 Fukunaga, "Kōten jōtei," 8–10.

17 Kaneko, "Kōtei saishi," 190; idem, "Kōshi sōbyō no seido," 1529.

18 See Kaneko, "Kōtei saishi," 176; idem, "Kōshi sōbyō no seido," 1499–1519.

19 See Wang's annotation to the *K'ung-tzu chia-yü* (*SPTK* ed.), 7.4b–5a; Kramers, *K'ung Tzu Chia Yü*, pp. 85, 146.

20 *SS* 6.108, 111.

21 See Cheng's annotation of the *Chi-fa* chapter of the *LC*, 14.1a.

22 See Kramers, *K'ung Tzu Chia Yü*, p. 85 and 85n227; *CWTTT* 4:5382.10.

23 *HTS* 13.333; Schafer, *Pacing the Void*, p. 45.

24 On the Five Emperors, see *TCTC* 79.2495–96; *WLTK* ch. 31–32; Chin O, *Ch'iu-ku lu li-shuo* (*Huang-Ch'ing ching-chieh hsü-pien* ed., 1888), 10.24b–26a, 13.4b–8b; Kaneko, "Kōshi sōbyō no seido," 1525–28; Kramers, *K'ung Tzu Chia Yü*, pp. 85, 141–44. For a discussion of the origins of the sacrifices to the Five Emperors, see Kurihara, *Shin-Kanshi*, pp. 101–05; Loewe, *Crisis and Conflict*, pp. 167–68.

25 *Chou-li* 5.19b.

26 *SC* 27.1351; W. Allyn Rickett, *Kuan-tzu: A Repository of Early Chinese Thought* (Hong Kong, 1965), pp. 196, 196n37; *HTS* 13.333.

27   See, for example, *K'ung-tzu chia-yü*, 6.1a–b, commentary of Wang.
28   *Sung-shu*, comp. Shen Yüeh (Peking, 1974), 16.5b–6a; *TCTC* 79.2495; Kaneko, "Kōshi sōbyō no seido," 1525.
29   *SS* 7.128–29.
30   *SS* 6.113–16.
31   *SS* 6.116–17.
32   *SS* 6.119.
33   *CTS* 21.816
34   These measurements were also essentially the same as those for Hsüan-tsung's time; see *HTS* 12.325.
35   In T'ang sources Kan-sheng ti is often simply called Kan-ti.
36   *TCTC* 185.5794, note of Hu San-hsing.
37   On the early T'ang suburban sacrifices, see *THY* 9A.141, 10A.204, 211–12; *CTS* 21.820–21; *HTS* 13.333–34; *TCTC* 185.5794, 193.6059, note of Hu San-hsing; *TT* 43.247a.
38   *HTS* 1.13.
39   *TCTC* 193.6059; Kaneko, "Kōshi sōbyō no seido," 181. For other performances of suburban sacrifices by T'ai-tsung, see *THY* 9A.142–44; *WLTK* 9.2b.–5a.
40   See, for example, *TTCLC* 68.1b.
41   *CTS* 86.3718; *THY* 7A.142.
42   *CTS* 57.2288; *THY* 9A.142.
43   See *TCTC* 197.6206; *CHC* 3:236–39.
44   *THY* 9A.144–45; *TFYK* 33.4b–5b; *WLTK* 9.4a–5a.
45   *HTS* 3.53; *TCTC* 199.6276. This was two months prior to the time when Kao-tsung first visited the ancestral temple; Kaneko, "Kōtei saishi," 182.
46   *CTS* 21.823–25; *THY* 9A.145–46; *TT* 43.247a–b; *TCTC* 200.6304. The memorial is variously dated 651 and 657, and attributed either to Chang-sun Wu-chi or to Hsü Ching-tsung. The mistaken dating probably owes to the fact that Hsü served as president of the Board of Rites during both 651 and 657; Yen Keng-wang, *T'ang p'u-shang ch'eng-lang piao*, 4 vols. (Taipei, 1956), 1:89, 90.
47   See *CTS* 198.5654–55, biography of Hsiao Te-yen.
48   *CTS* 21.825.
49   *HTS* 13.334.
50   *CTS* 21.818.
51   *HTS* 13.334, 198.5665; *THY* 9A.148, 10A.201.
52   *THY* 10A.212.
53   *HTS* 13.334, 198.5655; *THY* 9A.148–49; *TT* 43.247c; *TTCLC* 67.376.
54   *CTS* 21.818.
55   *CTS* 21.818.
56   See *CTS* 21.833–36.
57   *CTS* 28.1040–42; *HTS* 21.460–61; *THY* 32.588–89; *TCTC* 192.6051, note of Hu San-hsing.
58   *TT* 109.573a–77b; *KYL* 4.1a–18b.
59   *HTS* 11.312 and *KYL* 4.2a list the restrictions associated with *san-chai* as they

applied to officials participating in the ritual. They could not do the following: condole with those in mourning or inquire after the sick, play music,
involve themselves in legal cases involving capital punishment, carry out
capital punishment, or engage in sexual debauchery. The restrictions on a Son
of Heaven presumably were similar.

60 In the rite described in the *K'ai-yüan li*, the burning of the offerings takes place
at the very end of the round altar ceremony, after the emperor has reassumed
his south-facing position. Early in Kao-tsung's time, however, a memorial
was sent to the throne by a group of ritual officials claiming that all the textual
evidence suggested that the burning of offerings (or, the burying of them)
should occur at the beginning of the ceremony, not at the end. They requested that the consigning to the flames at the end of the ceremony, which
was embodied in the *Chen-kuan li*, be ended in favor of more ancient practice.
Kao-tsung complied with their request; *THY* 9A.146–47; *TT* 43.247b–c. It
is clear that the ritual described in the *K'ai-yüan li* was a reversion to the
practice of Chen-kuan times.

61 Leach, *Culture and Communication*, pp. 81–84.

62 Victor Turner, "Variations on a Theme of Liminality," in *Secular Ritual*, ed.
Moore and Myerhoff (Amsterdam, 1977), pp. 38–39.

63 In addition to Chang-sun Wu-chi and Hsü Ching-tsung's memorial of 657,
cited in n. 46 of this chapter, see also an edict of Empress Wu's time (689) in
TTCLC 67.376.

CHAPTER 6

1   See, for example, Ho, *Cradle of the East*, p. 324.

2   Fehl, *Li*, p. 18.

3   Yang, *Religion in Chinese Society*, p. 255; idem, "Confucian Thought and
Chinese Religion," p. 278.

4   Turner, *Dramas, Fields, and Metaphors*, p. 185; Cohen, "Political Symbolism," 92.

5   Legge, *Li Chi*, 1:103–04.

6   Yang, *Religion in Chinese Society*, p. 107.

7   Quoted in Wang Yu-ch'üan, "An Outline of the Central Government of the
Former Han Dynasty," in *Studies of Governmental Institutions in Chinese History*, ed. John L. Bishop, Harvard-Yenching Institute Studies 23 (Cambridge,
1968), p. 140; *HS* 73.3116.

8   David N. Keightley, "The Religious Commitment: Shang Theology and the
Genesis of Chinese Political Culture," *History of Religions* 17:3–4 (1978): 213.

9   Waley, *Analects* (III.10), p. 96; see also p. 65.

10 Waley, *Analects* (III.11), p. 96.

11 Kaneko, "Kōtei saishi," 187–88, 192.

12 Kaneko, "Kōtei saishi," 194, 201n33. Sometimes emperors, at the time they
appointed sons as crown princes, would themselves personally visit the
ancestral temple to make the announcement; see the case of the Northern
Chou emperor, Wu-ti; *CS* 7.115.

13   *CTS* 6.127, 8.180.

14   *TT* 126.661b-c; *KYL* 110.12a-b; Kaneko, "Kōtei saishi," 202n34.

15   See Wang Kuo-wei, "Ming-t'ang miao ch'in t'ung-k'ao," in *Kuan-t'ang chi-lin*, 4 vols. (Peking, 1959), 1:123-44; Mikami Jun, "Shin, byō, meidō no kibo ni tsuite no ichi kōsatsu," *Hijiyama Joshi Tanki Daigaku kiyō* 6 (1972): 11-24.

16   Bilsky, *State Religion*, 1:34, 66; Creel, *Origins of Statecraft*, 1:383-84.

17   *SS* 7.138.

18   Ikeda Suetoshi, "Byōsei kō—seigen byōsū no mondai," *Nippon Chūgoku gakkaihō* 11 (Oct. 1959):14-17.

19   Uchino Tairei, "Tenshi shichibyōsetsu ni tsuite," *Daitō bunka* 17 (1937): 23-24.

20   *TT* 47.267a, note of Tu Yu; *WLTK* 58.21a; *SS* 7.137; Kramers, *K'ung Tzu Chia Yü*, pp. 140-41.

21   *CTS* 1.5; *HTS* 1.6; and *TFYK* 30.1a all give different days of the third month.

22   I am here following the dating of *CTS* 25.941, and Hsü Sung, *T'ang Liang-ching ch'eng-fang k'ao*, in Hiraoka Takeo, ed., *Chōan to Rakuyō (Shiryō)* (T'ang Civilization Reference Series no. 6, Tokyo, 1956), 4.5a. *HTS* 1.7, *TCTC* 185.5794, *THY* 1.1, and *TFYK* 30.1a all given the sixth month. For the location of the T'ang ancestral temple, see maps 2 and 18 of Hiraoka Takeo, ed., *Chōan to Rakuyō (Chizu)*, (T'ang Civilization Reference Series no. 7, Tokyo, 1956).

23   See, for example, the memorial of Chang Ch'i-hsien in 705; *CTS* 25.946. For a discussion of the *shih-tsu*, see Ikeda, "Byōsei kō," 19. The traditional Chinese practice of reducing ancestors to nominal categories such as Great Ancestor or First Ancestor may reflect what Mircea Eliade has described among ancient peoples as "the anhistorical character of popular memory, the inability of collective memory to retain historical events and individuals except so far as it transforms them into archetypes" (*Myth of the Eternal Return*, p. 46). When Li Hu became a Great Ancestor he lost his historical individuality and became simply an impersonal archetype, lumped together with all the other Great Ancestors of Chinese dynastic lineage. When a dead person becomes an "ancestor" in this way, he survives in the collective memory only by losing his individuality; his survival is as impersonal as it is permanent; *Myth of the Eternal Return*, pp. 46-48.

24   *HTS* 13.339.

25   *HTS* 70A.1957; *CHC* 3:150-51.

26   Legge, *Li Chi*, 2:42. The "Law of Sacrifices" (*Chi-fa*) chapter of the same text (2:201-02) also lists sacrifices to four objects performed during the time of the culture-hero Shun, and the Hsia, Shang, and Chou dynasties, but only two of the four were direct lineal ancestors.

27   *SS* 7.136.

28   *SS* 7.135.

29   For such a discussion during Sui Yang-ti's time, see *SS* 7.137-39.

30   *CTS* 78.2693-94.

31   The edict ordering the discussion is found in *TTCLC* 75.423.

32   See *TT* 47.267a-69c.

33 *CTs* 25.941–42; *HTS* 13.339; *CTW* 135.7a–8a; *TFYK* 585.3a–4a.

34 *CTS* 25.943.

35 The edict is in *TTCLC* 75.423–24.

36 *THY* 15.325; *TFYK* 585.7b–8a; *CTW* 147.19a–20a.

37 *THY* 12.294, note of compiler.

38 *CTS* 25.994; *TCTC* 199.6269; *THY* 12.293–94; *TFYK* 585.9b–10a.

39 *CTS* 25.944.

40 See *THY* chs. 12–16. Some of the major changes in the T'ang ancestral tem-
    ple system can be summarized as follows. In 688 the usurper Empress Wu
    established a temple dedicated to her own Wu family ancestors at her capital
    at Lo-yang. Soon afterward, certainly at Wu's urging, her underlings re-
    quested that she increase the number of rooms in the temple to seven, at the
    same time decreasing those in the Li-T'ang ancestral temple to five. Such a
    move would have symbolized the ascendancy of the Wu over the Li house,
    and therefore drew furious objections at court, compelling Wu temporarily to
    retreat from her plan. But in 691, shortly after she declared herself emperor of
    the Chou dynasty, she expanded the number of rooms at her Lo-yang ances-
    tral temple to seven. At the same time she downgraded the status of the
    Li-T'ang temple in Ch'ang-an by permitting seasonal sacrifices to be offered
    in only three of the rooms. (*CTS* 25.944–45) When the Li-T'ang house was
    restored in 705, the seven-room configuration was continued, this time in
    Ch'ang-an. (*THY* 12.294–97; *HTS* 13.339–40) In 723 the rooms of the ances-
    tral temple were expanded to nine. (*THY* 12.298; *HTS* 13.340) Much later in
    the dynasty, because of the intricacies of succession, the temple had eleven
    rooms—but these represented only nine generations of ancestors. (*HTS*
    13.341)

41 On the possibility that patterns of communication in traditional Chinese gov-
    ernment might themselves represent a form of ritual, see also Brian
    McKnight, "Patterns of Law and Patterns of Thought: Notes on the Spe-
    cifications (*shih*) of Sung China," *Journal of the American Oriental Society* 102:2
    (April–June 1982):323–31.

42 Forke, *Lun-Heng*, 1:521.

43 From T'ai-tsung's time onward, the T'ang adopted Cheng Hsüan's views
    concerning the frequency of the Ti and Hsia; *TT* 50.288a. Calculating the
    frequency of the rites was nevertheless troublesome; see the entry for 674 in
    HTS 30.343.

44 *WHTK* 97.883c; Kaneko, "Kōshi sōbyō no seido," 1499–1500.

45 *HTS* 13.344; *CTS* 25.945, memorial of Chang Ch'i-hsien; Ch'üan Te-yü,
    "Hsien I erh-tsu ch'ien-miao tsou-i," in *Ch'üan Tsai-chih wen-chi* (*SPTK* ed.),
    29.8b–9a.

46 See *TT* 114.597a–600c and *KYL* 37.1a–22a for a description of the ancestral
    rites.

47 *THY* 13.301; *TFYK* 27.12a. The charge made in 632 by the examining censor
    Ma Chou that T'ai-tsung had not made any personal sacrifices at the ancestral
    temple since coming to the throne challenges this date—if inexplicably; see
    the note of Su Mien, *THY* 13.301; also *WHTK* 97.885c.

48   *THY* 13.301.
49   *TFYK* 27.126a.
50   See *THY* 13.301–03.
51   Kaneko, "Kōtei saishi," 179.
52   For one of the T'ang *kao-miao* rituals as described in the *K'ai-yüan li*, see *KYL* 91.5b–8a.
53   On this theme, see Cohen, "Political Symbolism," 93–94.
54   *LC* 8.3a; Legge, *Li Chi*, 1:422–23.
55   See Legge, *Li Chi* 1:422*n*9; idem, *Shoo King*, pp. 376–77*n*.
56   For historical examples down to the T'ang, see *TFYK* 173.1a–13b; *WLTK* 225.1a–16a. A similar designation existed, known as the *san-k'o*, or Three Honored States, in which the descendants of the three former dynasties were so honored; its *locus classicus* was the *Tso-chuan*. (Duke Hsiang, 25th year, in Legge, *The Ch'un Ts'ew with the Tso Chuen*, pp. 512, 516.) There was disagreement among commentators whether the *san-k'o* included the *erh-wang hou* or were entirely separate from them. Cheng Hsüan supported the second position, whereas Wang Su and Tu Yü supported the first. The Han, Wei, and regimes of the Period of Disunion generally followed Cheng Hsüan's interpretation, whereas in T'ang times and afterward Wang Su's position found favor; *WLTK* 225.1a, 4a, 14b–15a.
57   See *WLTK* 225.10b–14b.
58   *THY* 24.461; *TFYK* 173.13b–14a; Legge, *Shoo King*, p. 376. Descendants of the Northern Chou and Sui were regarded as the *erh-wang hou* throughout the T'ang, with only minor lapses; *WLTK* 225.17b, note of the compiler.
59   See *HTS* 11.312, 313, 315; *TT* 114.597a, b; *KYL* 37.2b, 4a; des Rotours, *Traité des fonctionnaires*, 1:93*n*1.
60   *THY* 24.461; *CTW* 4.8b–9a.
61   *THY* 24.462.
62   *Po-shih ch'ang-ch'ing chi* (*SPTK* ed.), 3.5b–6a.
63   *LC* 14.3a–b; Legge, *Li Chi*, 2:207–08.
64   See *WHTK* 103.937c–38b; *TT* 53.304c–05a; also the discussion of T'ao Hsi-sheng, "K'ung-tzu miao-t'ing chung Han-ju chi Sung-ju ti wei-tz'u (II)," *Shih-huo yüeh-k'an* 2 (1972):83. The Ch'in worshiped the sage-rulers Shun and Yü. No former sovereigns were sacrificed to at the beginning of the Han, but Kao-tsu decreed that rites were to be dedicated to the Chou royal ancestor, Hou Chi; Watson, *Records*, 2:32. His successor, Wu-ti, is recorded as having ordered ceremonies dedicated to the legendary Yellow Emperor, Huang-ti; *TPYL* 557.2b. In Wang Mang's time (rg. A.D. 9–23) the culture-heroes Yao and Shun were worshiped; Loewe, *Crisis and Conflict*, pp. 181–82. The Later Han emperor, Ch'eng-ti (rg. 76–89) worshiped Yao. During the reign of Wen-ch'eng-ti (452–66) of the Later Wei, the Yellow Emperor again had rites dedicated to him. A successor, Hsiao-wen-ti (rg. 471–500), ordered the worship of Yao, Shun, Yü, and Chou Wu-wang.
65   *CTS* 24.915; *THY* 22.430; *WHTK* 103.938b; *TT* 53.305a.
66   See Kaneko, "Tōdai no daishi," table on p. 15.
67   *WHTK* 103.938c; T'ao, "K'ung-tzu miao-t'ing (II)," 83.

CHAPTER 7

1   Yang K'uan, *Chūgoku kōteiryō no kigen to hensen*, trans. Nishijima Sadao, Ogawa Isamu, and Ōta Yūko (Tokyo, 1981), pp. 16–18.

2   Legge, *Li Chi*, 1:123; Tjan Tjoe Som, trans., *Po Hu T'ung*, 2 vols. (Leiden, 1949), 2:651.

3   Yang, *Chūgoku kōteiryō*, pp. 18–19.

4   Yang, *Chūgoku kōteiryō*, pp. 26–27.

5   On the history of the imperial tombs during certain of the Northern Dynasties and the Mongol Yüan, when the practice of raised mounds was abandoned, see Yang, *Chūgoku kōteiryō*, pp. 67–68, 74.

6   See Legge, *Li Chi*, 2:173–200; Som, *Po Hu T'ung*, 2:634–51.

7   The text actually says "three *jen*," i.e., about 24 Chinese feet.

8   Quoted in Som, *Po Hu T'ung*, 2:651; *TPYL* 558.3b–4a, and other sources. On the association in other cultures of burial mounds with sacred trees, see Hocart, *Kingship*, chaps. 14–15.

9   Tsuruma Kazuyuki, "Kanritsu ni okeru funkyū kitei ni tsuite," *Tōyō bunka* 60 (Feb. 1980):1; Yang, *Chūgoku kōteiryō*, pp. 97–98.

10 Niida Noboru, *Tōryō shūi* (1933; reprint ed. Tokyo, 1964), pp. 806–41. For regulations in the *K'ai-yüan li* and *T'ang-lü shu-i*, see the discussion in Tsuruma, "Kanritsu ni okeru funkyū." 1–2.

11 On the Han imperial tombs, see Yang, *Chūgoku kōteiryō*, pp. 28–63; Mitsunaga Shunsuke, "Kan Rikuchō bosei ni okeru ryōbo no shūhen," *Tōhō kodai kenkyū* 9 (Nov. 1959):32–40; Kamada Shigeo, *Shin-Kan seiji seido no kenkyū* (Tokyo, 1962), pp. 517–36; Tu Pao-jen, "Hsi-Han chu-ling wei-chih k'ao," *K'ao-ku yü wen-wu* 1980 no. 1:29–33; Yoshinami Takashi, "Kandai kōtei shihai chitsujo no keisei—teiryō e no shisen to gōzoku—," *Tōyōshi kenkyū* 35 (1976):211–42; Adachi Kiroku, *Chōan shiseki no kenkyū* (Tokyo, 1933), pp. 79–108; Shih Chang-ju, "Han-T'ang ti kuo-tu ling-mu yü chiang-yü," *Ta-lu tsa-chih* 6 (1953):245–47; Bielenstein, *Restoration of the Han Dynasty*, 4:168–69, 171.

12 Cf. Ann Paludan, *The Imperial Ming Tombs* (New Haven, 1981), p. 47.

13 See the discussion in Yang, *Chūgoku kōteiryō*, pp. 98 and 137*n*14. The Han *chang* was 2.3 meters.

14 Yang, *Chūgoku kōteiryō*, pp. 28–34, 52–56.

15 See *Chin-shu* 60.1651, biography of So Lin; and the memorial of the T'ang official Yü Shih-nan, *THY* 20.393.

16 Mitsunaga, "Kan Rikuchō bosei," 39–40.

17 On the development of the spirit road, see Yang, *Chūgoku kōteiryō*, pp. 106–23. Yang traces the stone sculptures of the spirit road to the Former Han, but sees the practice as becoming widespread only in the Later Han (p. 110).

18 *HS* 72.3070–71, biography of Kung Yü; Shan-hsi sheng wen-wu kuan-li wei-yüan hui, "Shan-hsi Hsing-p'ing hsien Mao-ling k'an-ch'a," *K'ao-ku* 1964, no. 2:86–89; Adachi, *Chōan shiseki*, pp. 99–100; Shih, "Han-T'ang ti kuo-tu," 246–47; Shensi People's Arts Publishing Company, *Mao-ling Huo Ch'ü-ping mu chien-chieh* (n.p., n.d.); Yü Ying-shih, ed., *Early Chinese History*

in the People's Republic of China: The Report of the Han Dynasty Studies Delegation October-November 1978, Parerga, Occasional Papers on China 7 (Seattle, 1981), pp. 46–47.

19 *HS* 36.1950–57.

20 *WCTCS* 2.16; Ichikawa, *Bunchūshi,* 2.99.

21 *HWTS* 40.441.

22 Ho Tzu-ch'eng, "'Kuan-chung T'ang shih-pa ling' tiao-ch'a chi," *Wen-wu tzu-liao ts'ung-k'an* 3 (May 1980):139–40.

23 Ho, "T'ang shih-pa ling," 140.

24 Adachi, *Chōan shiseki,* pp. 272–74; Shih, "Han-T'ang ti kuo-tu," 247–48.

25 For Kao-tsu's tomb the *ling-hu* comprised a total of three hundred people, for T'ai-tsung and Kao-tsung's tomb, four hundred people; *TTLT* 14.28b.

26 *TT* 116.607a–b: *KYL* 45.1a–3b.

27 *CTS* 63.2396.

28 *CTS* 77.2679.

29 *CTW* 138.5a–7a; *THY* 20.393–94; *HTS* 102.3971–72.

30 *CTW* 138.7a; *HTS* 102.3972; *TCTC* 194.6114.

31 Although Han and T'ang measurements differed from one another, T'ang writers usually cite measurements recorded in Han sources without converting them. Thus, whereas the Han "foot" (*ch'ih*) is 7.6 inches (23 centimeters), and the Han *chang* is 7.6 feet (2.3 meters), the T'ang "foot" is equivalent to our foot, and the T'ang *chang* is equivalent to ten of our feet. See Adachi, *Chōan shiseki,* chap. 2, and Yang, *Chūgoku kōteiryō,* p. 137n12,14.

32 *THY* 20.394–95; *CTW* 137.4b; *TCTC* 194.6114.

33 Ho, "T'ang shih-pa ling," 140.

34 Yang, *Chūgoku kōteiryō,* p. 98; Adachi, *Chōan shiseki,* pp. 95–96; Shih, "Han-T'ang ti kuo-tu," 245.

35 Ho, "T'ang shih-pa ling," 140.

36 *CTS* 1.18.

37 *THY* 2.416; *TTCLC* 63.346.

38 *THY* 21.412; *WHTK* 125.1124b.

39 For a convenient guide to the recorded and actual accompanying burials at the T'ang imperial tombs, see Ho, "T'ang shih-pa ling," table 4, p. 151.

40 *CTS* 25.972–73; *THY* 20.400; *TCTC* 195.6134; *TT* 52.299c.

41 *CTS* 25.973.

42 *CTS* 25.973; *THY* 20.400; *TT* 52.299c. *TFYK* 26.9a gives the year as 636.

43 On the Chao-ling, see Yün Shih, "Chao-ling," *Wen-wu* 1977, no. 10:60–62; Chao-ling wen-wu kuan-li-so, "Chao-ling p'ei-tsang mu tiao-ch'a chi," *Wen-wu,* 1977, no. 10:33–40; Yang, *Chūgoku kōteiryō,* pp. 75–81; Nunome Chōfū, "Zui-Tō jidai no ketsusō to teiryō—Rakuyō kara Seian e—," *Tōyō gakujutsu kenkyū* 18:1 (1979):38–42; Ts'en Chung-mien, *Sui-T'ang shih* (Peking, 1957), pp. 237–42; Adachi, *Chōan shiseki,* pp. 249–55; Lin T'ung, *T'ang Chao-ling shih-chi k'ao-lüeh* (1697; *Ts'ung-shu chi-ch'eng* ed., Shanghai, 1960).

44 *CTS* 77.2679.

45 *TCTC* 194.6122; see also the biography of the empress, *HTS* 76.3471.

46 Conflicting dates exist in the sources for this edict. *CTS* 3.46–47, *TCTC*

194.6127, and *TTCLC* 76.431 all give the second month of 637. *THY* 20.395 gives the year 644, but part of the text it quotes from appears in *CTS* 21.416, dated 634. Here, I follow Nunome, "Zui-Tō jidai no ketsusō to teiryō," 41, who accepts 637 as accurate.

47   See Watson, *Hsün Tzu*, pp. 104–05.

48   THY 21.416 and *TTCLC* 63.346–47 provide dates of 8/649 (thus after T'ai-tsung's death) and 8/646, respectively, for this edict. On accompanying burials at the Chao-ling, see *THY* 21.412–14; Ts'en, *Sui-T'ang shih*, pp. 137–38; Chao-ling wen-wu kuan-li-so, "Chao-ling," 35–36.

49   Chao-ling wen-wu kuan-li-so, "Chao-ling," 39.

50   *HWTS* 40.441.

51   Ho, "T'ang shih-pa ling," 141.

52   *WHTK* 125.1124c. For a list of these, see *THY* 20.395–96.

53   Ts'en, *Sui-T'ang shih*, pp. 140, 142*n*4. This placement of stone sculptures behind the tomb rather than in front of it was unique; see Adachi, *Chōan shiseki*, p. 274; Ho, "T'ang shih-pa ling," 142.

54   Four of these are at the Shensi Provincial Museum; the other two are in the United States, at the University of Pennsylvania Museum, Philadelphia.

55   Ho, "T'ang shih-pa ling," 142.

56   This reconstruction, located at the Chao-ling Museum tomb of Li Chi, is unpublished.

57   Ho, "T'ang shih-pa ling," 141; Yang, *Chūgoku kōteiryō*, pp. 75–84. The complex was originally situated atop the crest of Chiu-tsung Mountain, but after burning down it was later moved to a location below the crest, thus giving rise to the name *hsia-kung*.

58   Yün, "Chao-ling," 60.

59   See the discussion in Yang, *Chūgoku kōteiryō*, p. 101; Chao-ling wen-wu kuan-li-so, "Chao-ling," 34ff.

60   Many examples of these can be viewed in the "Forest of Stelae" (*Pei-lin*) of the Chao-ling Museum; thirty-nine of them are listed in Nunome, "Zui-Tō jidai no ketsusō to teiryō,"45*n*43, and forty-one in Ho, "T'ang shih-pa ling," table 1, pp. 146–47.

61   Cf. the author's interpretation of the meaning of Wei Cheng's burial site before he had personally visited the Chao-ling, in his *Mirror*, p. 160.

62   *TTLT* 14.29a; *THY* 21.412.

63   Chao-ling wen-wu kuan-li-so, "Chao-ling," 40.

64   Adachi, *Chōan shiseki*, p. 249.

65   *HTS* 97.3871 *TCTC* 194.6123.

66   Yang, *Chūgoku kōteiryō* p. 105.

67   *THY* 20.401; *TFYK* 27.16a–b. *TT* 52.299c dates this event, erroneously, during T'ai-tsung's time.

68   *CTS* 5.112.

69   *CTS* 6.132; *THY* 20.396–97.

70   On the Ch'ien-ling, see Shan-hsi sheng wen-wu kuan-li wei-yüan hui, "T'ang Ch'ien-ling k'an-ch'a chi," *Wen-wu* 1960, no. 4:53–60; Iijima Taket-

sugu, "Tō Kōsō Kenryō," *Kodai bunka* 31:4 (1979):69–71; Adachi, *Chōan shiseki*, pp. 255–61; Ch'ien-ling Museum, *Ch'ien-ling* (n.p., n.d.); Shih, "Hang-T'ang ti kuo-tu," 247–48; Nunome, "Zui-Tō jidai no ketsusō to teiryō," 30–38.

71   Ho, "T'ang shih-pa ling," 140.
72   Paludan, *Imperial Ming Tombs*, p. 24.
73   See Paludan, *Imperial Ming Tombs*, chap. 3.
74   Adachi, *Chōan shiseki*, p. 256; Shan-hsi sheng wen-wu kuan-li wei-yüan hui, "T'ang Ch'ien-ling," 53.
75   *THY* 21.414; *WHTK* 125.1125c.
76   Nunome, "Zui-Tō jidai no ketsusō to teiryō," 33. Although the written sources at our disposal indicate that no T'ang imperial tomb built after the Ch'ien-ling contained so many associated burials, archaeologists have discovered otherwise. For example, according to Ho, "T'ang shih-pa ling," 144–45, a total of 43 large mounds have been discovered in the immediate vicinity of the Ch'ung-ling, the tomb of Te-tsung, although no accompanying burials are listed in the records. Similarly, 53 large mounds have been detected near the Kuang-ling, the tomb of Mu-tsung, but only two accompanying burials are listed.
77   The wall-paintings of some of these tombs have been published; see, for example, Shensi Provincial Museum, *T'ang Li Chung-jun mu-pi hua* (Peking, 1974); idem, *T'ang Li Hsien mu-pi hua* (Peking, 1974).
78   *CTS* 5.112.
79   Ho, "T'ang shih-pa ling," 140.
80   *Chou-li* 5.45b.
81   Yang, *Chūgoku kōteiryō*, pp. 100–01.
82   See *SKC* 1.51 *CWTTT* 9.15041.24.
83   Chao-ling wen-wu kuan-li-so, "Chao-ling," 39; Yang, *Chūgoku kōteiryō*, p. 101.

CHAPTER 8

1   On the practice, see *WLTK* chs. 178–79; *TT* 54.309a–10c; *THY* ch. 27; *WHTK* ch. 109; Som, *Po Hu T'ung* 2, chap. 19.
2   See Som, *Po Hu T'ung*, 2:495.
3   On this theme, see Legge, *She King*, p. 577n.
4   Creel, *Origins of Statecraft*, pp. 389–96.
5   See Som, *Po Hu T'ung*, 2:495–96.
6   Cf. Leban, "Managing Heaven's Mandate," pp. 323–24.
7   Legge, *Shoo King*, pp. 35–37. Cf. idem, *Li Chi*, 1:216–18.
8   From this account and others, it appears that on his tours of inspection the king always set fire to a large woodpile. For example, the *Record of Rites* (Legge, *Li Chi*, 1:426) says that "the son of Heaven in his tour [of Inspection] to the four quarters [of his kingdom] as the first thing [on his arrival at each]

reared the pile of wood [and set fire to it]." The significance of the rite has been interpreted variously, however; see *WLTK* 1.17b.

9 Victor and Edith Turner, *Image and Pilgrimage in Christian Culture: Anthropological Perspectives* (New York, 1978), editors' introduction.

10 Quoted in *WLTK* 178.2b.

11 Quoted in *WLTK* 178.2b–3a.

12 On the Ch'in and Han tours, see Bielenstein, *Restoration of the Han Dynasty*, 4:41–49.

13 *HS* 25A.1201. *WHTK* 109.984b gives the date as the twenty-eighth year of his reign.

14 *HS* 6.162; *HFHD* 2:38.

15 *TT* 54.310a erroneously gives a date of 119 B.C. See also *WHTK* 109.984c.

16 *HS* 99B.4133–34; *HFHD* 3:333–35.

17 See *WLTK* 179.4a–8b; *WHTK* 109.984c–85c; Bielenstein, *Restoration of the Han Dynasty*, 4:42.

18 *TT* 54.310a–b; *WHTK* 109.984c–86a; Bielenstein, *Restoration of the Han Dynasty*, 4:41–49.

19 Bielenstein, *Restoration of the Han Dynasty*, 4:47.

20 See Wright, *Sui Dynasty*, p. 165.

21 *TT* 54.310b. *WHTK* 189.986a–87b gives an account of Yang-ti's many travels.

22 *SS* 8.159–60.

23 See Legge, *Li Chi*, 1:218.

24 *CTS* 1.10; *HTS* 1.10; *TFYK* 33.3b.

25 *CTS* 1.10; *WLTK* 179.21a.

26 *HTS* 1.10; *TFYK* 33.3b.

27 See *TFYK* 113.9a–10a.

28 *WLTK* 179.21a.

29 *HTS* 2.31–32.

30 *HTS* 2.37–38.

31 *TFYK* 113.11a–b; Wechsler, *Mirror*, pp. 148–49.

32 *TFYK* 133.12a.

33 *HTS* 2.45.

34 See *WLTK* 179.22b–23b; *TFYK* 113.13a–17a; *WHTK* 109.987b; *CTS* 4.82.

35 *THY* 27.515.

36 *TFYK* 113.14a.

37 *TFYK* 113.15a–b.

38 The envoy was the famous Ti Jen-chieh of Robert van Gulik's "Judge Dee" novels; see *THY* 27.517; *HTS* 115.4208.

39 *THY* 27.517.

40 *TCTC* 210.6347; *TFYK* 113.14b–15a.

41 *TT* 118.617b–19c; *KYL* 62.1a–15b; *WHTK* 109.987b–89c.

42 See Wechsler, "Factionalism," pp. 106–07.

43 See *CHC* 3:257–58.

44 Cf. Bielenstein, *Restoration of the Han Dynasty*, 4:43.

CHAPTER 9

1 Kurihara, *Shin-Kanshi*, p. 34; Kushitani Michiko, "Hōzen ni mirareru futatsu no seikaku—shūkyōsei to seijisei," *Shisō* 14 (Mar. 1959):59.

2 Ishibashi, *Tendan*, p. 89; Kushitani, "Hōzen," 59; Tsuda Sōkichi, "Kandai seiji shisō no ichi men," in *Tsuda Sōkichi zenshū*, 28 vols. (Tokyo, 1963–66), 17:91; Takeuchi Hiroyuki, "Shiba Sen no Hōzenron—Shiki Hōzensho no rekishi kijutsu o megutte," *Tetsugaku nempō* 34 (1975):91; Fukunaga Mitsushi, "Hōzensetsu no keisei (I)," *Tōhō shūkyō* 6 (Oct. 1954):31; Kurihara, *Shin-Kanshi*, p. 31.

3 Ishibashi, *Tendan*, p. 95, table 5.

4 Watson, *Records*, 2:59–60.

5 *Kuan-tzu* (*SPTK* ed.), 16.5a–6a.

6 Fukunaga, "Hōzensetsu no keisei (I)," 33–34; Rickett, *Kuan-tzu*, p. 1. The section is in Watson, *Records*, 2:19–20.

7 Kimura Eiichi, "Hōzen shisō no seiritsu," *Shinagaku* (reprint ed.) 11:2 (1942–43):194–95; Tsuda, "Kandai seiji shisō," 17:91.

8 See the summary in Takeuchi, "Shiba Sen no Hōzenron," 92–95; Kushitani, "Hōzen," 59.

9 Watson, *Records*, 2:14.

10 Kushitani, "Hōzen," 59.

11 See, for example, the memorial of Hsü Mao, *LS* 40.577.

12 See *WLTK* 49.6b.

13 *SS* 7.139; Kushitani, "Hōzen," 59.

14 See, for example, the views of Fukunaga, "Hōzensetsu no keisei (I)"; idem, "Hōzensetsu no keisei (II)," *Tōhō shūkyō* 7 (Feb. 1955):59–60; Kushitani, "Hōzen," 59; Kimura, "Hōzen shisō no seiritsu," 205ff.; Takeuchi, "Shiba Sen no Hōzenron," 94; Tsuda, "Kandai seiji shisō," 90–91; Kanaya Osamu, "Shinsen no keisei," in *Chikuma Shobō Sekai no rekishi* (Tokyo, 1960), 3:247–48.

15 See Kanaya, "Shinsen no keisei," p. 247; Fukunaga, "Hōzensetsu no keisei (II)," 58n.

16 Hsü Chin-hsiung, "Liao-chi feng-shan yü ming-t'ang chien-chu," *Chung-kuo wen-tzu* 19 (Mar. 1966):1b.

17 Ishibashi, *Tendan*, p. 77.

18 Ling Shun-sheng, "Chung-kuo ti feng-shan yü Liang-ho-liu yü ti k'un-lun wen-hua," *Chung-yang yen-chiu-yüan min-tsu-hsüeh yen-chiu-so chi-k'an* 19 (Mar. 1965):1–38 (English summary, 39–51); idem, "Pei-p'ing ti feng-shan wen-hua," *Chung-yang yen-chiu-yüan min-tsu-hsüeh yen-chiu-so chi-k'an* 16 (Sept. 1963):1–82 (English summary, 83–97).

19 Fukunaga, "Hōzensetsu no keisei (I)," 52–53; Kushitani, "Hōzen," 67–78; Ishibashi, *Tendan*, p. 89.

20 Fukunaga, "Hōzensetsu no keisei (II)," 53; Kimura, "Hōzen shisō no seiritsu," 180–85.

21 *PHT* 5.1b; Som, *Po Hu T'ung*, 1:240.

22 Édouard Chavannes, *Le T'ai chan: Essai de monographie d'un culte Chinois* (1910; reprint ed. Taipei, 1970), pp. 22–24; Som, *Po Hu T'ung*, 1:240, 329n306; Kurihara, *Shin-Kanshi*, p. 39; Kushitani, "Hōzen," 67.

23 Fukunaga, "Hōzensetsu no keisei (II),", 58; Hattori Katsuhiko, "Kodai Chūgoku ni okeru Santō to shinsen shisō," *Ryūkoku Daigaku ronshū* 392 (Jan. 1970):77; Kimura, "Hōzen shisō no seiritsu," 185–86; Kushitani, "Hōzen," 59, 60, 67–68.

24 Fukunaga, "Hōzensetsu no keisei (I)," 30; idem, "Hōzensetsu no keisei (II)," 54; Kimura, "Hōzen shisō no seiritsu," 194; Kushitani, "Hōzen," 59.

25 Kimura, "Hōzen shisō no seiritsu," 196–98; Fukunaga, "Hōzensetsu no keisei (I)," 53; Kurihara, *Shin-Kanshi*, p. 35.

26 Fukunaga, "Hōzensetsu no keisei (II),"48–49.

27 Waley, *Analects* (III:6), p. 95; Fukunaga, "Hōzensetsu no keisei (II)," 46. The Kung-yang commentary to the *Tso-chuan* also mentions a sacrifice on T'ai-shan; Kimura, "Hōzen shisō no seiritsu," 204. On the theme of T'ai-shan as a holy mountain, see Takeuchi, "Shiba Sen no Hōzenron," 103; Kushitani, "Hōzen," 65–66; Kimura, "Hōzen shisō no seiritsu," 203ff.; Tu Erh-wei, *Chung-kuo ku-tai tsung-chiao hsi-t'ung* (Taipei, 1960), pp. 129–130, 162–163; Hattori, "Santō to shinsen shisō."

28 Fukunaga, "Hōzensetsu no keisei (I)," 51–57; Kushitani, "Hōzen," 62, 66. For a recent study of *fang-shih*, see Kenneth J. DeWoskin, trans., *Doctors, Diviners, and Magicians of Ancient China: Biographies of Fang-shih* (New York, 1983).

29 Hattori, "Santō to shinsen shisō," 86; Fukunaga, "Hōzensetsu no keisei (II)," 45.

30 Eliade, *Myth of the Eternal Return*, pp. 12–16; idem, *Images and Symbols: Studies in Religious Symbolism*, trans. Philip Mairet (New York, 1961), pp. 42–45.

31 Eliade, *Myth of the Eternal Return*, p. 16.

32 Watson, *Records*, 2:39.

33 Fukunaga, "Hōzensetsu no keisei (II)," 49–50, 58.

34 Watson, *Records*, 2:23.

35 Fukunaga, "Hōzensetsu no keisei (II)," 55n; Kushitani, "Hōzen," 66.

36 On this theme, see Fukunaga, "Hōzensetsu no keisei (II)," 58; Kimura, "Hōzen shisō no seiritsu," 194, 200ff,; Kurihara, *Shin-Kanshi*, pp. 31ff.; Loewe, *Crisis and Conflict*, pp. 182–86.

37 Bielenstein, *Restoration of the Han Dynasty*, 4:179–80; Loewe, *Crisis and Conflict*, pp. 182ff.

38 *WLTK* 49.1a–b.

39 *SS* 2.33.

40 *SS* 7.140; *TFYK* 35.18a.

41 *SS* 7.140; *CTS* 23.881; *TFYK* 35.18a.

42 Wright, *Sui Dynasty*, p. 125.

43 *SS* 7.140; Wright, *Sui Dynasty*, pp. 165, 174.

44 *SS* 7.140.

45 *SS* 7.139.

46 *PHT* 5.1a–b; Som, *Po Hu T'ung*, 1:239–40.

47 *THY* 7.79.
48 *TCTC* 193.6086, 6090; *TFYK* 35.18b–19a.
49 *TCTC* 194.6093; *CTS* 23.881–82; Chavannes, *Le T'ai chan*, pp. 169–70.
50 There is disagreement over whether T'ai-tsung really wanted to perform the
    rites at this time; see *TCTC* 194.6093–94; *k'ao-i*; *CTS* 25.881–82. In a pas-
    sage dated 632, he appears to have strongly rejected the entreaties of his
    officials, *THY* 7.81–82; *TFYK* 35.19b–20a.
51 *WCKCL* 2.17a–b. For similar passages, see *TCTC* 194.6093–94; *THY*
    7.80–81.
52 See the passage translated in the author's *Mirror*, p. 124.
53 *CTS* 23.882; Chavannes, *Le T'ai chan*, p. 171; *TFYK* 7.80.
54 *CTS* 23.882; *TCTC* 194.6093.
55 *WCKCL* 4.19a–b; *THY* 7.81.
56 *WCKCL* 4.19a–20a.
57 *CTS* 23.882; Chavannes, *Le T'ai chan*, pp. 171–72; *THY* 7.83.
58 See *CTS* 23.882–83; Chavannes, *Le T'ai chan*, pp. 172–79; *HTS* 14.350;
    THY 7.82–83; *TFYK* 35.20a–22a; *CTW* 147.5b–8a.
59 See Wang Kuo-wei, "Chien tu chien shu k'ao" (*Wang Kuan-t'ang hsien-sheng
    ch'üan-chi* ed.), 6.2349–50.
60 According to Chavannes, *Le T'ai chan*, p. 174n4, the dimensions of each slip
    allowed only one line of writing.
61 *CTS* 23.884; *THY* 7.87–89, 95; *TFYK* 35.24a–26b; *TTCLC* 66.367–68;
    Schafer, *Pacing the Void*, p. 111.
62 *THY* 7.89; *TFYK* 35.26b–27a.
63 *TCTC* 198.6241–42.
64 *THY* 7.89–92; *TFYK* 35.27a–31a.
65 See the edict in *TTCLC* 66.368–69.
66 *CTW* 137.6a.
67 *THY* 7.93–94; *TFYK* 35.31b–33b.
68 On the T'ang conquest of the Hsüeh-yen-t'o, see *CHC* 3:230–31.
69 *TCTC* 198.6248; *THY* 7.94–95; *TFYK* 35.33b–34b; *TTCLC* 66.369.
70 *TCTC* 199.6249; *CHC* 3:234.
71 *WLTK* 50.27b–28a.
72 See *CHC* 3:251–55.
73 *TCTC* 201.6332.
74 See R. W. L. Guisso, *Wu Tse-t'ien and the Politics of Legitimation in T'ang China*
    (Bellingham, Wash., 1978), p. 115.
75 *TCTC* 201.6340; *THY* 7.96.
76 Cf. Guisso, *Wu Tse-t'ien*, pp. 28–29.
77 *THY* 7.96; *TFYK* 36.1b–2a.
78 *CTS* 23.884–85; Cf. the translation of Chavannes, *Le T'ai chan*, p. 181.
79 *CTS* 23.885; Chavannes, *Le T'ai chan*, p. 181.
80 See table 3 in Ishibashi, *Tendan*, pp. 91–92; Wang, "Chien tu chien shu k'ao,"
    2350–52.
81 See the memorial of Hsü Ching-tsung, *CTW* 151.25a–b.
82 *CTS* 23.885; Chavannes, *Le T'ai chan*, pp. 181–83. For a discussion of the

ways in which the jade and gold *kuei* and stone coffers were sealed, see Wang, "Chien tu chien shu k'ao," 2347–52.

83 *CTS* 23.886; Chavannes, *Le T'ai chan*, pp. 283–84; *THY* 7.97.

84 See Ishibashi, *Tendan*, table 3, p. 92.

85 *THY* 7.96; *TCTC* 201.6344, 6345; *TFYK* 36.2a.

86 See *TFYK* 37.2b–3b; Ishibashi, *Tendan* p. 94.

87 *CTS* 23.886; Chavannes, *Le T'ai chan*, pp. 185–87; *TFYK* 36.3b–4a; *TCTC* 201.6344–45.

88 *CTS* 23.888; Chavannes, *Le T'ai chan*, pp. 192–93; *HTS* 14.351; *TCTC* 201.6346.

89 *TFYK* 36.4a–b.

90 *CTS* 23.888; Chavannes, *Le T'ai chan*, pp. 192–93; *TFYK* 36.4b; *TCTC* 201.6346.

91 *TFYK* 36.4b, 51.18b.

92 *CTS* 23.888; Chavannes, *Le T'ai chan*, pp. 193–94; *HTS* 14.351; *TFYK* 36.4b–5a.

93 T'ai-tsung had also raised the possibility of performing the Feng and Shan at Sung-shan; see *WCKCL* 4.19b.

94 *TCTC* 202.6379; *TFYK* 33.6b; *THY* 7.101.

95 *TCTC* 201.6391, 6393; *THY* 7.101; *TFYK* 36.5a.

96 *CTS* 23.889; Chavannes, *Le T'ai chan*, p. 194; *THY* 7.102. For a case of opposition to Kao-tsung's plans, see *TCTC* 203.6410.

97 *CTS* 23.889–91; Chavannes, *Le T'ai chan*, pp. 194–99; *THY* 7.102–03.

98 *CTS* 23.890–91; Chavannes, *Le T'ai chan*, pp. 199–200; *TFYK* 36.5a–b; *THY* 7.104.

99 *THY* 7.104; *TFYK* 36.6a–b.

100 *CTS* 37.1376; *HTS* 35.919; *ChTS* 878.9941.

101 See Leach, *Culture and Communication*, pp. 77–79.

102 Mircea Eliade, *Images and Symbols*, pp. 42–51; idem, *Rites and Symbols of Initiation: The Mysteries of Birth and Rebirth*, trans. Willard R. Trask (1958; New York, 1965), p. 78.

103 See Hocart, *Kingship*, pp. 189–91.

104 *CTS* 23.882; *CTW* 147.16b.

105 On this theme, see Kaltenmark, "Religion and Politics," 38.

106 See *THY*. 7.104–23 for documents relating to the Feng and Shan of Empress Wu and Hsüan-tsung; also *CHC* 3:387–88.

107 Tsuda, "Kandai seiji shisō," 17:91.

108 See Watson, *Records*, 2:58–59; Kaltenmark, "Religion and Politics," 37–38.

109 Kurihara, *Shin-Kanshi*, pp. 39–42. Takeuchi sees this as a more general trend in Han rites, beginning around the time of the Former Han ruler Wen-ti; "Shiba Sen no Hōzenron," 97.

110 See *HHS* "Monograph on Ceremonial," p. 3169; Bielenstein, *Restoration of the Han Dynasty*, 4:175; Michael Loewe, *Chinese Ideas of Life and Death: Faith, Myth and Reason in the Han Period (202 BC–AD 220)* (London, 1982), p. 140.

111 *HHS* 1B.8a, commentator's note; "Monograph on Ceremonial," p. 3165; Bielenstein, *Restoration of the Han Dynasty*, 4:174.

112 On the theme of the more open character of the T'ang Feng and Shan, see Kaneko, "Kōtei saishi," 194; Ishibashi, *Tendan*, p. 94.

113 *CTS* 23.888.

114 *THY* 7.104.

115 *CTS* 23.898.

116 *CTS* 23.898–99; Chavannes, *Le T'ai chan*, pp. 224–25. On Hsüan-tsung's Feng and Shan, see also *THY* ch. 8; *TFYK* 35.7a–26b. For a study of the jade tablets Hsüan-tsung used in his Shan sacrifice, which were excavated in 1933, see Teng Shu-p'ing, "Two Sets of Jade Tablets in the National Palace Museum Collection," *National Palace Museum Bulletin*, 11:6 (Jan.–Feb. 1977), 1–17.

CHAPTER 10

1 E. R. Hughes, *Two Chinese Poets: Vignettes of Han Life and Thought* (Princeton, 1960), p. 57.

2 Arthur Waley, *The Poetry and Career of Li Po 710–762 A.D.* (London, 1950), p. 1.

3 The term Ming-t'ang is here to be understood as referring only to the building of this name and not necessarily to two structures often associated with it, the *pi-yung* and *ling-t'ai*.

4 See Fujikawa, *Kandai ni okeru reigaku no kenkyū*, p. 238.

5 See, for example, Henri Maspero, "Le Ming-t'ang et la crise religieuse Chinoise avant les Han," *Mélanges Chinois et Bouddhiques* 9 (1951):46–47; Bilsky, *State Religion*, 2:421n5. Cf. William Edward Soothill, *The Hall of Light: A Study of Early Chinese Kingship* (London, 1951), who sees the Ming-t'ang functioning at its height during the Chou dynasty.

6 Mikami Jun, "Meidō to iegata haniwa (II)," *Tōhō shūkyō* 28 (Nov. 1966):41; another, somewhat more inclusive list of functions, is offered by Wang Meng-ou, "Ku ming-t'ang t'u k'ao," *K'ung Meng hsüeh-pao* 11 (1966):222. Maspero, "Le Ming-t'ang," 2; Soothill, *Hall of Light*, p. 132; and Marcel Granet, *La pensée Chinoise* (1934; reprint ed. Paris, 1975), pp. 178, 318, contain lists of functions pertaining not only to the Ming-t'ang but also to the *ling-t'ai* and *pi-yung*.

7 Legge, *Li Chi*, 1:251–52, 256, 268–69, 271, slightly emended.

8 Maspero, "Le Ming-t'ang," 2; Granet, *La pensée Chinoise*, p. 178.

9 From the *Ming-t'ang wei* chapter of the *Book of Rites*; Legge, *Li Chi*, 2:31; see also 1:28.

10 Soothill, *Hall of Light*, p. 8.

11 James T. C. Liu, "The Sung Emperors and the *Ming-t'ang* or Hall of Enlightenment," in *Études Song: in memoriam Étienne Balazs*, ed. Françoise Aubin (Paris, 1973), p. 46n2.

12 Loewe, *Crisis and Conflict*, index, p. 329.

13 Hughes, *Two Chinese Poets*, p. 51n3. See also the use of this name by Bielenstein, *Restoration of the Han Dynasty*, 4:180–82.

14 Hamada Kaidō, "Meidō seido shikō," *Shinagaku* 9:3 (reprint ed. 1938–39):451, 452.

15 Mikami Jun, "Meidō no kigen to sono hatten ni tsuite no ichi kōsatsu (I)," *Tetsugaku* (Hiroshima tetsugakkai) 20 (Oct. 1968):19.

16 Mikami, "Meidō no kigen (I)," 17.

17 Mori Mikisaburō, "Getsurei to meidō," *Shinagaku* 8:2 (reprint ed. 1936):207; Wang, "Ku ming-t'ang t'u k'ao," 229.

18 Quoted in Maspero, "Le Ming-t'ang," 30–31.

19 *HS* 12.357; see also *TCTC* 36.1146.

20 On the significance of the various numbers associated with the Ming-t'ang, see Granet, *La pensée Chinoise*, chap. 3; on the numbers five and nine, see Soothill, *Hall of Light*, pp. 32, 36; on the number nine, see Schafer, *Pacing the Void*, pp. 75, 77; on the number seventy-two, see Kushitani, "Hōzen," 59, and Maspero, "Le Ming-t'ang," 9.

21 See, for example, the discussions of the Sui officials Yü-wen K'ai, *SS* 68.1592, and Niu Hung, *SS* 49.1302–03.

22 Hamada, "Meidō seido shikō," 453–54.

23 Hsü, "Liao-chi," 1–5; Ling, "Feng-shan yü Liang-ho-liu yü ti k'un-lun wen-hua," 25.

24 See Kwang-chih Chang, *Shang Civilization* (New Haven, 1980), pp. 133–34.

25 On Ming-t'ang structure, see Granet, *La pensée Chinoise*, pp. 178–81; Soothill, *Hall of Light*, chap. 10; and all of the articles by Mikami Jun cited here. After carefully reviewing the architectural dimensions of the Ming-t'ang furnished by the most important old Chinese sources, Maspero concludes that none of the authors could have had any firsthand knowledge of the buildings they described; "Le Ming-t'ang," 54. Cf. the view of Wang Shih-jen, "Han Ch'ang-an-ch'eng nan-chiao li-chih chien-chu (Ta-shih-men ts'un i-chih) yüan-chuang ti t'ui-ts'e," *K'ao-ku* 1963, no. 9:503.

26 See Mikami, "Meidō no kōzō ni tsuite no ichi kōsatsu," *Tetsugaku* (Hiroshima tetsugakkai) 13 (Nov. 1961):34–36; Maspero, "Le Ming-t'ang," 58; Wang Kuo-wei, "Ming-t'ang miao ch'in t'ung-k'ao," 1, ch. 3.

27 See, for example, Mikami Jun, "Meido to iegata haniwa (I)," *Tōhō shūkyō* 27 (Sept. 1966):48.

28 Legge, *Mencius*, pp. 161, 161n5.

29 See Watson, *Records*, 2:59.

30 See *Ta-Tai Li-chi* (*SPTK* ed.), 8.11a.

31 Mikami, "Meidō no kigen (I)," 11; Tetsui Yoshinori, "Konron densetsu ni tsuite no ichi shiron," *Tōhō shūkyō* 45 (1975):44. Functionally, it has been observed that this Ming-t'ang appears to resemble the T'ai-shan Ming-t'ang; Mikami, "Meidō to iegata haniwa (II)," 36, citing the view of a Ch'ing commentator.

32 Fujikawa, *Kandai ni okeru reigaku no kenkyū*, pp. 238–70; Mikami, "Meidō to iegata haniwa (II)," 42. Soothill, in the longest Western-language treatment of the subject, virtually ignores the contrasts between the T'ai-shan and suburban Ming-t'ang.

33 See chap. 9, n. 27.

34 Mori, "Getsurei to meidō," 233–24; Hattori, "Santō to shinsen shisō," 76–77; Mikami, "Meidō to iegata haniwa (II)," 40; idem, "Meidō no kigen to sono hatten ni tsuite no ichi kōsatsu (II)," *Tetsugaku* (Hiroshima tetsugakkai) 24 (Oct. 1972):46–47.

35 See Hattori, "Santō to shinsen shisō," 76–86.

36 Watson, *Records*, 2:64; Maspero, "Le Ming-t'ang," 5; Mikami, "Meidō to iegata haniwa (II)," 37.

37 Su Hsüeh-lin, "K'un-lun i-tz'u ho-shih shih chien Chung-kuo chi-tai," *Ta-lu tsa-chih* 9 (1954):336.

38 See Mitarai Masaru, "Konron densetsu no kigen," in *Shigaku kenkyū kinen ronsō* (Tokyo, 1950), pp. 191–210; Ling, "Chung-kuo ti feng-shan," 25; Sofukawa Hiroshi, "Konronsan to shōsento," *Tōhō gakuhō* 51 (Mar. 1979):85.

39 Eliade, *Myth of the Eternal Return*, pp. 12–18; idem, *Rites and Symbols of Initiation*, chap. 1; Mitarai, "Konron densetsu no kigen," p. 205.

40 Tetsui, "Konron densetsu ni tsuite," 33–44.

41 Eliade, *Myth of the Eternal Return*, pp. 86–90.

42 Van Gennep, *Rites of Passage*, p. 18.

43 Van Gennep, *Rites of Passage*, p. 20.

44 Van Gennep, *Rites of Passage*, pp. 192, 194.

45 See Turner, *The Ritual Process: Structure and Anti-Structure* (Chicago, 1969), pp. 94–96; idem, *Dramas, Fields, and Metaphors*, pp. 52–53.

46 Turner, *Dramas, Fields, and Metaphors*, pp. 245, 252, 258.

47 Eliade, *Rites and Symbols of Initiation*, xiii–xiv.

48 Eliade, *Mephistopheles and the Androgyne*, p. 21.

49 Tu Wei-ming, "The 'Thought of Huang-Lao': A Reflection on the Lao Tzu and Huang Ti Texts in the Silk Manuscripts of Ma-Wang-Tui," *Journal of Asian Studies* 39:1 (Nov. 1979):105.

50 Wang Meng-ou, "Ku ming-t'ang t'u k'ao," 222.

51 Mikami, "Mediō to iegata haniwa (II)," 41.

52 For example, in nine of the fifteen occasions Liang Wu-ti (rg. 502–55) is recorded as performing the suburban sacrifices, he also carried out ceremonies at the Ming-t'ang; Mikami, "Mediō to iegata haniwa (II)," 45.

53 SS 6.121; Kaneko, "Kōshi sōbyō no seido," 1526.

54 SS 6.121–22; *TCTC* 178.5540.

55 SS 49.1300–03. The memorial is mistakenly dated 583.

56 SS 68.1593.

57 *TCTC* 178.5540; SS 6.122. The biography of Niu Hung, SS 49.1305, however, attributes the failure to construct a Ming-t'ang to drought.

58 SS 68.1593; *CTS* 22.849.

59 *CTS* 22.849.

60 See *CTS* 22.849–53; *HTS* 13.337–38.

61 For his memorial, see *CTW* 141.1a–2b; *TFYK* 585.1a–3a.

62 *CTW* 147.20a–22b; *CTS* 22.851–52.

63 *CTW* 147.15a–b; *CTS* 22.852–53.

64 *CTS* 22.853.

65   *CTS* 22.853–55; *TFYK* 585.14a–16a.
66   See chap. 5, pp. 111, 115; and Kramers, *K'ung Tzu Chia Yü*, pp. 141–44.
67   Fujikawa, *Kandai ni okeru reigaku no kenkyū*, p. 255; *TCTC* 79.2495–96, note.
68   *HS* 74.3139, biography of Wei Hsiang; *CWTTT* 1:651.529.
69   *CTS* 21.821; *TT* 44.252b.
70   *CTS* 21.821; *TCTC* 199.6275.
71   *Hsiao-ching* (*SPTK* ed.), 9a.
72   See Legge, *Li Chi*, 2:202.
73   *CTS* 21.821; *TT* 44.252c–53a. *THY* 9A.145 incorrectly dates the memorial
     651.
74   See pp. 111, 115.
75   *CTS* 21.823; *TCTC* 200.6304; *TT* 43.247a–b; *THY* 9A.145–46.
76   *CTS* 21.826–27; *HTS* 13.335.
77   See also p. 48.
78   *HTS* 13.338, 37.9625; *TTCLC* 99.498.
79   *TCTC* 204.6447.
80   See Guisso, *Wu Tse-t'ien*, pp. 35, 46.
81   *CTS* 22.862–76.
82   *CTS* 22.862; Schafer, *Pacing the Void*, p. 18.
83   *CTS* 22.864; C. P. Fitzgerald, *The Empress Wu* (1956; reprint ed. London,
     1968), p. 132.
84   Liu Tzu-chien, "Feng-shan wen-hua yü Sung-tai ming-t'ang chi-t'ien,"
     Chung-yang yen-chiu-yüan min-tsu-hsüeh yen-chiu-so chi-k'an 18 (Sept. 1964):
     45–49 (English summary, pp. 50–51); Liu, "The Sung Emperors and the
     Ming-t'ang," 52–53.

CHAPTER 11

1   Joseph Needham, *Science and Civilisation*, vol. 3, *Mathematics and the Sciences
    of the Heavens and the Earth* (1959), p. 189; idem, "Time and Knowledge in
    China and the West," in *The Voices of Time*, ed. J. T. Fraser (New York,
    1966), p. 100.
2   Wolfram Eberhard, "The Political Function of Astronomy and Astronomers
    in Han China," in *Chinese Thought and Institutions*, ed. John K. Fairbank
    (Chicago, 1957), pp. 62–64; Paul Wheatley, *The Pivot of the Four Quarters:
    A Preliminary Enquiry into the Origins and Character of the Ancient Chinese City*
    (Chicago, 1971), pp. 385–86.
3   Needham, *Science and Civilisation*, 3:189; Frederick W. Mote, *Intellectual
    Foundations of China* (New York, 1971), p. 32.
4   Legge, *Shoo King*, pp. 18–22. On this passage, see Soothill, *Hall of Light*,
    pp. 120–23; Needham, *Science and Civilisation*, 3:186–88.
5   *HS* 30.1767.
6   Nathan Sivin, *Cosmos and Computation in Early Chinese Mathematical Astron-
    omy* (Leiden, 1969), p. 7. See also Needham, "Time and Knowledge,"
    p. 123.
7   Kiyosi Yabuuti, "Chinese Astronomy: Development and Limiting Factors."

in *Chinese Science: Explorations of an Ancient Tradition*, ed. Shigeru Nakayama and Nathan Sivin (Cambridge, Mass., 1973), p. 94.

8   Ho Peng-yoke, *The Astronomical Chapters of the Chin Shu*, p. 34; Yabuuti, "Chinese Astronomy," p. 95.

9   Sivin, *Cosmos and Computation*, pp. 52–53.

10 Needham, "Time and Knowledge," pp. 100–01.

11 See Sivin, "Chinese Conceptions of Time," *The Earlham Review* 1(1966): 86–89.

12 Sivin, *Cosmos and Computation*, pp. 64–69.

13 Wolfram Eberhard (with Rolf Mueller), "Contributions to the Astronomy of the Han Period III: Astronomy of the Later Han Period," in *Sternkunde und Weltbild im Alten China* (n.p., 1970), p. 182.

14 Based on the calculation of Sivin, *Cosmos and Computation*, pp. 10, 11n.

15 *HS* 21A.974–76; Sivin, *Cosmos and Computation*, pp. 16–17, 18; cf. Edmund Burke Ord, "State Sacrifices in the Former Han Dynasty According to the Official Histories" (Ph.D. dissertation, University of California, Berkeley, 1967), pp. 117, 282.

16 *HS* 21A.975.

17 *HS* 6.199, 25B.1245; *HFHD* 2:98; Sivin, *Cosmos and Computation*, p. 10; Bodde, *Festivals in Han China*, pp. 27–28.

18 See Bilsky, *State Religion*, 2:296–97. Bilsky notes that the changes that were made in the calendar, dynastic color, and related correspondences were not actually made final until the summer of 104 B.C.; 2:327–28.

19 Eberhard, "Contributions III," p. 188; idem, "Political Function of Astronomy," p. 66.

20 Yabuuti, "Chinese Astronomy," p. 96.

21 Eberhard, "Contributions III," p. 184. For a discussion of the Triple Concordance system, see also Sivin, *Cosmos and Computation*, pp. 11–19. The calendar served as the basis of the "Monograph on the Calendar" of the *History of the Former Han Dynasty*; Yabuuti, "Chinese Astronomy," p. 95.

22 See Sivin, *Cosmos and Computation*, pp. 19ff.; Yabuuti, "Chinese Astronomy," p. 92; Eberhard, "Contributions III," pp. 190–220.

23 Eberhard, "Contributions III," p. 190.

24 Needham, *Science and Civilisation*, 3:200–06; Yabuuti, "Chinese Astronomy," pp. 99–100; Wolfram Eberhard and Rolf Müller, "Contributions to the Astronomy of the San-kuo Period," in *Sternkunde und Weltbild im Alten China*, pp. 229–44.

25 *CTS* 32.1151–52.

26 *SS* 17.416.

27 *SS* 17.420–28; Yabuuchi Kiyoshi, *Zui-Tō rekihōshi no kenkyū* (Tokyo, 1944), pp. 8–11.

28 *SS* 18.459, 461–501; *CTS* 32.1152; Yabuuchi, *Zui-Tō rekihōshi*, pp. 14–17.

29 *SS* 17.428–35, 18.459–61; Yabuuchi, *Zui-Tō reikihōshi*, pp. 13, 17.

30 The calendars following the Ta-yen calendar of Hsüan-tsung's K'ai-yüan reign seem all to have been based on it, and were not independently conceived; Yabuuchi Kiyoshi, *Chūgoku no temmon rekihō* (Tokyo, 1969), p. 94.

31 Yabuuchi, *Zui-Tō rekihōshi*, p. 22; idem, *Temmon rekihō*, p. 94.

32 *CTS* 1.8, 79.2710–11; Yabuuchi, *Temmon rekihō*, p. 96.

33 Hiraoka Takeo, ed., *Tōdai no koyomi*, T'ang Civilization Reference Series no. 1 (Tokyo, 1954), pp. 6–7.

34 *CTS* 79.2710–11; *HTS* 25.534; *THY* 42.749–50; *CTW* 133.16b–17a.

35 Yabuuchi, *Zui-Tō rekihōshi*, pp. 25–26; idem, *Temmon rekihō*, p. 96.

36 *HTS* 25.534; *THY* 42.750.

37 For Fu's defense, see *CTW* 133.17b–19a.

38 For Wang's criticism of Fu's calendar, see *CTS* 79.2711–12.

39 *CTS* 79.2714; *HTS* 25.536; Yabuuchi, *Zui-Tō rekihōshi*, pp. 26–27; idem, *Temmon rekihō*, p. 96.

40 *HTS* 25.536; Yabuuchi, *Zui-Tō rekihōshi*, pp. 27–28; idem, *Temmon rekihō*, pp. 96–97.

41 Hiraoka, *Tōdai no koyomi*, p. 8.

42 Hiraoka, *Tōdai no koyomi*, p. 6; Yabuuchi, *Temmon rekihō*, p. 99n69.

43 Yabuuchi, *Zui-Tō rekihōshi*, p. 28; idem, *Temmon rekihō*, p. 97.

44 *HTS* 25.536.

45 *HTS* 26.559; *THY* 42.751. According to these same sources, at the time the Lin-te Calendar was promulgated, another calendar by the Grand Astrologer Ch'ü T'an-lo, called the *Ching-wei li*, was also published, and was used in conjunction with the Lin-te. But we know almost nothing about this second calendar.

46 On the role of *chia-tzu* years in inaugurating T'ang calendars, as well as their predecessors, see Yabuuchi, *Zui-Tō rekihōshi*, p. 59. Lin-te was the first *chia-tzu* year of the T'ang.

47 See n. 15 of this chapter.

48 *TTCLC* 82.475. The date given here for the edict, the ninth month of 665, is in error. See also *THY* 42.750–51.

49 Biographies: *CTS* 79.2717–19; *HTS* 204.5798. Li was assisted in his work by an Indian astronomer; Needham, *Science and Civilisation*, 3:202.

50 *CTS* 79.2718; *HTS* 204.5798; Yabuuchi, *Zui-Tō rekihōshi*, pp. 28–29; Needham, *Science and Civilisation*, 3:197; Schafer, *Pacing the Void*, p. 14.

51 Yabuuchi, *Zui-Tō rekihōshi*, p. 29; idem, *Temmon rekihō*, pp. 97–98.

52 See Sivin, *Cosmos and Computation*, pp. 14, 20.

53 Yabuuchi, *Zui-Tō rekihōshi*, p. 30; idem, *Temmon rekihō*, pp. 97–98. The common denominator was changed from time to time, depending on the age.

54 Yabuuchi, *Zui-Tō rekihōshi*, pp. 31, 32n5.

55 *PHT* 7.5b; Som, *Po Hu T'ung*, 2:548.

56 *CTS* 33.1216–17; *TCTC* 204.6462; *CHC* 3:304.

57 *PHT* 7.6b; Som, *Po Hu T'ung*, 2:550.

58 Eliade, *Myth of the Eternal Return*, p. 54.

CHAPTER 12

1 Turner, *Dramas, Fields, and Metaphors*, pp. 184–85.

2 The altars of state, *she* and *chi*, can be viewed as also functioning in this capacity, but they had decreased in ritual importance by T'ang times.

3   See Fukunaga, "Kōten jōtei."
4   See Arthur F. Wright, "The Formation of Sui Ideology, 581–604," in *Chinese Thought and Institutions*, ed. John K. Fairbank (Chicago, 1957), pp. 97–99.
5   *TCTC* 193.6073; *THY* 73.1312.
6   Lo Hsiang-lin, "T'ang-tai T'ien k'o-han chih-tu k'ao," in his *T'ang-tai wen-hua shih* (Taipei, 1963), pp. 54–87.
7   *CTS* 5.99; *TCTC* 202.6372.
8   For a discussion of the theory that the term *t'ien* may have similarly been used during the Spring and Autumn period to set apart the Chou kings (as *t'ien-wang*) from the self-proclaimed kings (*wang*) of the feudal states, see Taniga-wa Michio, "Goko jūrokkoku oyobi Hokushū no shokunshu ni okeru Tennō no shōgō ni tsuite," *Nagoya Daigaku bungakubu kenkyū ronshū*, 41 (*Shigaku* 14) (Mar. 1966), 96–97. Tanigawa traces the use of *t'ien-wang* during the regimes of the disunion period.
9   On the expansion of T'ang territory during Kao-tsung's reign, see *CHC* 3:279–86.
10 Jürgen Habermas, *Legitimation Crisis*, trans. Thomas McCarthy (Boston, 1975), p. 71. See also Thomas A. McCarthy, *The Critical Theory of Jürgen Habermas* (Cambridge, Mass., 1978), pp. 369–70.

Selected Bibliography

ABBREVIATED TITLES

CCC. Ta-T'ang ch'uang-yeh ch'i-chü-chu 大唐創業起居注. 3 *chüan*. Compiled by Wen Ta-ya 溫大雅. Prior to 627. *Ts'ung-shu chi-ch'eng* ed. Shanghai, 1936.

CHC. Cambridge History of China. 14 volumes projected. Vol. 3. *Sui and T'ang China, 589–906 Part I.* Edited by Denis Twitchett. Cambridge, 1979.

ChTS. Ch'üan T'ang-shih 全唐詩. 900 *chüan*. Compiled by Ts'ao Yin 曹寅 et al. 1707. Taipei, 1971.

CKCY. Chen-kuan cheng-yao 貞觀政要. 10 *chüan*. Compiled by Wu Ching 吳兢. 705–720. *Jōgan seiyō teihon* 貞觀政要定本 ed. Compiled by Harada Taneshige 原田種成. Tokyo, 1962.

CS. Chou-shu 周書. 50 *chüan*. Compiled by Ling-hu Te-fen 令狐德芬. Taipei, 1972.

CSTP. Chin-shih ts'ui-pien 金石萃編. 160 *chüan*. Compiled by Wang Ch'ang 王昶. 1805. Taipei, 1964.

CTS. Chiu T'ang-shu 舊唐書. 200 *chüan*. Compiled by Liu Hsü 劉昫. 940–45. Taipei, 1976.

CTW. Ch'üan T'ang-wen 全唐文. 1,000 *chüan*. Compiled by Tung Kao 董誥 et al. 1814. Taipei, 1965.

CWTTT. Chung-wen ta-tz'u tien 中文大辭典. 10 vols. Edited by Chang Ch'i-yün 張其昀. Taipei, 1973.

DJ. Daikanwa jiten 大漢和辭典. Compiled by Morohashi Tetsuji 諸橋轍次. 13 vols. Tokyo, 1955–60.

HFHD. History of the Former Han Dynasty. 3 vols. Translated by Homer H. Dubs. Baltimore, 1938, 1944, 1955.

HHS. Hou Han-shu 後漢書. 100 *chüan*. Compiled by Fan Yeh 范曄 (398–445). Taipei, 1972.

HS. Han-shu 漢書. 100 *chüan*. Compiled by Pan Ku 班固 (32–92). Taipei, 1972.

HTS. Hsin T'ang-shu 新唐書. 225 *chüan*. Compiled by Ou-yang Hsiu 歐陽修. 1043–60. Taipei, 1976.

HWTS. Hsin Wu-tai shih 新五代史. 74 *chüan*. Compiled by Ou-yang Hsiu 歐陽修. 1044–60. Peking, 1974.

HYSC. Hun-yüan sheng-chi 混元聖紀. 9 *chüan*. Compiled by Hsieh Shou-hao 謝守灝. 1191. *Tao-tsang* 道藏 fascicles 551–53. Reprint ed. Taipei, 1963.

KHMC. Kuang-hung ming-chi 廣弘明集. 30 *chüan*. Compiled by Tao-hsüan 道宣 (596–667). *SPTK* ed.

KYL. Ta-T'ang K'ai-yüan li 大唐開元禮. 150 *chüan*. Compiled by Chang Yüen 長說 and Hsiao Sung 蕭嵩. 732. Photolithographic copy of ed. of Hung Ju-k'uei 洪汝奎. 1886. Koten kenkyūkai 汲典研究會. Tokyo, 1972.

LC. Li-chi 禮記. 20 *chüan*. *SPTK* ed.

LS. Liang-shu 梁書. 56 chüan. Compiled by Yao Ssu-lien 姚思廉. 622–29. Peking, 1973.

LTCTC. Li-tai ch'ung-tao chi 歷代崇道集. 1 *chüan*. Compiled by Tu Kuang-t'ing 杜光庭 (850–933). *Tao-tsang* 道藏 fascicles 590–606. Reprint ed. Taipei, 1963.

NCS. Nan-Ch'i shu 南齊書. 59 *chüan*. Compiled by Hsiao Tzu-hsien 蕭子顯 (489–537). Taipei, 1972.

PCS. Pei-Ch'i shu 北齊書. 50 *chüan*. Compiled by Li Pai-yao 李百藥. 627–36. Taipei, 1974.

PHT. Po Hu T'ung 白虎通. 10 *chüan*. Compiled by Pan Ku 班固 (32–92). *SPTK* ed.

PS. Pei-shih 北史. 100 *chüan*. Compiled by Li Yen-shou 李延壽. Ca. 630–50. Peking, 1974.

SC. Shih-chi 史記. 130 *chüan*. Compiled by Ssu-ma Ch'ien 司馬遷. 58–76. Taipei, 1972.

SKC. San-kuo chih 三國志. 65 *chüan*. Compiled by Ch'en Shou 陳壽. 285–97. Taipei, 1973.

SKCSTMTY. Ssu-k'u ch'üan-shu tsung-mu t'i-yao 四庫全書總目提要. 40 *chüan*. Compiled by Yung Jung 永瑢 et al. Taipei, 1971.

SPTK. Ssu-pu ts'ung-k'an 四部叢刊. Shanghai, 1929.

SS. Sui-shu 隋書. 85 *chüan*. Compiled by Wei Cheng 魏徵 et al. 629–36. Taipei, 1976.

T. Taishō shinshū Daizōkyō 大正新修大藏經. Edited by Takakusu Junjirō 高楠順次郎. 1924–32. Reprint ed. Tokyo, 1960.

TCTC. Tzu-chih t'ung-chien 資治通鑑. 294 *chüan*. Compiled by Ssu-ma Kuang 司馬光. 1084. Taipei, 1962.

TFYK. Ts'e-fu yüan-kuei 冊府元龜. 1,000 *chüan*. Compiled by Wang Ch'in-jo 王欽若 et al. 1005–13. Reproduction of 1642 ed. Taipei, 1967.

THY. T'ang hui-yao 唐會要. 100 *chüan*. Compiled by Wang P'u 王溥. 961. Taipei, 1963.

TPYL. T'ai-p'ing yü-lan 太平御覽. 1,000 *chüan*. Compiled by by Li Fang 李昉 et al. After 983. 1935. Reprint ed. Taipei, 1968.

TT. T'ung-tien 通典. 200 *chüan*. Compiled by Tu Yu 杜佑 (735–812). Taipei, 1966.

TTCLC. T'ang ta chao-ling chi 唐大詔令集. 130 *chüan*. Compiled by Sung Min-ch'iu 宋敏求 (1019–79). Taipei, 1972.

TTLT. Ta-t'ang liu-tien 大唐六典. 30 *chüan*. Compiled eighth century A.D. Punctuated and annotated by Hiroike Senkurō 廣池千九郎 and Uchida Tomoo 內田智雄. Tokyo, 1973.

WCKCL. Wei Cheng-kung chien-lu chiao-chu 魏鄭公諫錄校注. 5 *chüan*. Compiled by Wang Fang-ch'ing 王方慶. Prior to 702. Annotated by Wang Hsien-kung 王先恭. Changsha, 1883.

WCTCS. Hsin-shih piao-tien Wen-chung-tzu Chung-shuo 新式標點 文中子中說. 10 *chüan*. Compiled by Wang T'ung 王通. Ca. 617. Shanghai, 1936.

WHTK. Wen-hsien t'ung-k'ao 文獻通考. 348 *chüan*. Compiled by Ma Tuan-lin 馬端臨. Taipei, 1964.

WLTK. Wu-li t'ung-k'ao 五禮通考. 262 *chüan*. Compiled by Ch'in Hui-t'ien 秦蕙田. 1753.

WS. Wei-shu 魏書. 114 *chüan*. Compiled by Wei Shou 魏收. 551–54. Peking, 1974.

TRADITIONAL CHINESE SOURCES

Chao I 趙翼. *Nien-erh-shih cha-chi* 廿二史箚記. 36 *chüan*. 1795. 2 vols. Taipei, 1965.

———. "Yang Huan ch'uan-kuo-hsi k'ao chih wu" 楊桓傳國璽考之誤. *Kai-yü ts'ung-k'ao* 陔餘叢考 ed. 43 *chüan*. Preface 1790. Shanghai, n.d.

Chin O 金鶚, comp. *Ch'iu-ku lu li shuo* 求古錄禮說. 15 *chüan*. In *Huang-Ch'ing ching-chieh hsü-pien* 皇清經解續編. 1,398 *chüan*. 1888.

Chin-shu 晉書. 130 *chüan*. Compiled by Fang Hsüan-ling 房玄齡. 644. Peking, 1974.

Chou-i 周易. 10 *chüan*. SPTK ed.

Chou-li 周禮. 12 *chüan*. SPTK ed.

Ch'üan Te-yü 權德興. "Hsien I erh-tsu ch'ien-miao tsou-i" 獻懿二祖

遷廟奏議. In *Ch'üan Tsai-chih wen-chi* 權載之文集. 50 *chüan*. *SPTK* ed.

Fan Tsu-yü 范祖禹. *T'ang-chien* 唐鑑. 24 *chüan*. 1086. Shanghai, 1980.

Hsiao-ching 孝經. 1 *chüan*. *SPTK* ed.

Hsü Sung 徐松. *T'ang liang-ching ch'eng-fang k'ao* 唐兩京城坊考. 5 *chüan*. *Chōan to Rakuyō (Shiryō)* 長安と洛陽(資料). T'ang Civilization Reference Series no. 6. Tokyo, 1956.

Kuan-tzu 管子. 24 *chüan*. Compiled by Kuan Chung 管仲. *SPTK* ed.

K'ung-tzu chia-yü 孔子家語. 10 *chüan*. *SPTK* ed.

Kung-yang chuan 公羊傳. 12 *chüan*. *SPTK* ed.

Lin T'ung 林侗. *T'ang Chao-ling shih-chi k'ao-lüeh* 唐昭陵石蹟考略. 5 *chüan*. 1697. *Ts'ung-shu chi-ch'eng* 叢書集成 ed. Shanghai, 1960.

Po Chü-i 白居易. *Po-shih ch'ang-ch'ing chi* 白氏長慶集. *SPTK* ed.

Shen Ch'in-han 沈欽韓. Han-shu shu-cheng 漢書疏證. Che-chiang kuan-chü k'an-pen. 1900.

Sung-shu 宋書. 100 *chüan*. Compiled by Shen Yüeh 沈約. 492–93. Peking, 1974.

Ta-Tai Li-chi 大戴禮記. 13 *chüan*. Compiled by Tai Te 戴德. *SPTK* ed.

T'ang-shih chi-shih 唐詩紀事. 81 *chüan*. Compiled by Chi Yu-kung 計有功. *SPTK* ed.

Tao-hsüan 道宣. *Hsü Kao-seng chuan* 續高僧傳. 30 *chüan*. Ca. 645. *T* vol. 50.

Wang Ting-pao 王定保. *T'ang chih yen* 唐摭言. 15 *chüan*. Ca. 955. Taipei, 1962.

MODERN CHINESE, JAPANESE, AND WESTERN SOURCES

Adachi Kiroku 足立喜六. *Chōan shiseki no kenkyū* 長安史蹟の研究. Tokyo, 1933.

Allan, Sarah. *The Heir and the Sage: Dynastic Legends in Early China*. San Francisco, 1981.

Arnold, Thurman W. *The Symbols of Government*. New York, 1962.

Balazs, Étienne. *Le traité économique du "Souei-chou."* Leiden, 1953.

Barth, Frederik. *Ritual and Knowledge among the Baktaman of New Guinea*. New Haven, 1975.

Beattie, John. "Ritual and Social Change." *Man* 1 (1966):60–74.

Benn, Charles D. "Taoism as Ideology in the Reign of Emperor Hsüan-tsung." Ph.D. dissertation, University of Michigan, 1977.

Berger, Peter. *The Sacred Canopy: Elements of a Sociological Theory of Religion*. Garden City, N.Y., 1967.

Bielenstein, Hans. *The Restoration of the Han Dynasty. Vol. 4, The Government. Bulletin of the Museum of Far Eastern Antiquities* 51 (1979):3–300.

Bilsky, Lester James. *The State Religion of Ancient China*. 2 vols. Taipei, 1975.

Bingham, Woodbridge. "The Rise of Li in a Ballad Prophecy." *Journal of the American Oriental Society* 61 (1941):272–80.

Biot, E. *Le Tcheou-Li ou Rites des Tcheou*. 2 vols. Paris, 1851.

Bloch, Maurice. *Political Language and Oratory in Traditional Society*. New York, 1975.

———. "Symbols, Song, Dance and Features of Articulation: Is Religion an Extreme Form of Traditional Authority?" *Archives Européennes de Sociologie* 15 (1974):55–81.

Bodde, Derk. "Authority and Law in Ancient China." *Journal of the American Oriental Society* Supplement 17 (1954):46–55.

———. *Festivals in Classical China: New Year and Other Annual Observances during the Han Dynasty 206 B.C.–A.D. 220*. Princeton, 1975.

Bokenkamp, Stephen. "Taoist Millenarianism and the Founding of the T'ang." An unpublished paper presented at the Conference on the Nature of State and Society in Medieval China, Stanford, California, 16–18 August 1980.

Burling, Robbins. *The Passage of Power: Studies in Political Succession*. New York, 1974.

Cammann, Schuyler. "Types of Symbols in Chinese Art." In *Studies in Chinese Thought*, ed. Arthur F. Wright, pp. 195–231. Chicago, 1953.

Chang Ch'ün 章羣. *T'ang-shih* 唐史. 2 vols. Taipei, 1958, 1965.

———. "Wang T'ung chih ssu-hsiang chi ch'i ying-hsiang" 王通之思想及其影響. *Chung-hua wen-hua fu-hsing yüeh-k'an* 中華文化復興月刊 10:2 (1977):80–84.

Chang Tsun-liu 張遵騮. "Sui-T'ang Wu-tai fo-chiao ta-shih nien-piao" 隋唐五代佛教大事年表. In Fan Wen-lan 范文瀾, *T'ang-tai fo-chiao* 唐代佛教, pp. 91–310. Peking, 1979.

Chao-ling wen-wu kuan-li-so 昭陵文物管理所. "Chao-ling p'ei-tsang mu tiao-ch'a chi" 昭陵陪葬墓調查記. *Wen-wu* 文物 1977, no. 10:33–40.

Chao Ling-yang 趙令揚. *Kuan-yü li-tai cheng-t'ung wen-t'i chih cheng-lun* 關於歷代正統問題之爭論. Hong Kong, 1976.

Chavannes, Édouard. *Le T'ai chan: Essai de monographie d'un culte Chinois*. 1910. Reprint. Taipei, 1970.

Ch'en Yin-k'o 陳寅恪. *Sui-T'ang chih-tu yüan-yüan lüeh-lun kao* 隋唐制度淵源略論稿. 1944. Reprint. Shanghai, 1946.

Chien Po-hsien 簡博賢. "K'ung Ying-ta Ch'un-ch'iu Tso-chuan cheng-i p'ing-i" 孔穎達春秋左傳正義平議. *K'ung Meng hsüeh-pao* 孔孟學報 20 (Sept. 1970):53–69.

———. "K'ung Ying-ta Shang-shu cheng-i pu-cheng" 孔穎達尚書正義補正. *K'ung Meng hsüeh-pao* 孔孟學報 19 (1960):155–74.

Ch'ien Mu 錢穆. "Lüeh-lun Wei-Chin Nan-Pei-ch'ao hsüeh-shu wen-hua yü tang-shih men-ti chih kuan-hsi" 略論魏晉南北朝學術文化與當時門第之關係. *Hsin-ya hsüeh-pao* 新亞學報 5:2 (1963):23–77.

Cohen, Abner. "Political Symbolism." *Annual Review of Anthropology* 8 (1979):87–113.

————. *Two-Dimensional Man: An Essay on the Anthropology of Power and Symbolism in Complex Society.* Berkeley and Los Angeles, 1976.

de Bary, William Theodore, et al. *Sources of Chinese Tradition.* New York, 1960.

des Rotours, Robert. *Traité des fonctionnaires et traité de l'armée.* 2 vols. Leiden, 1947.

Douglas, Mary. *Natural Symbols: Explorations in Cosmology.* New York, 1970.

Dull, Jack L. "A Historical Introduction to the Apocryphal (ch'an-wei) Texts of the Han Dynasty." Ph.D. dissertation, University of Washington, 1966.

————. "Kao-tsu's Founding and Wang Mang's Failure: Studies in Han Time Legitimation." An unpublished paper presented to the Conference on the Legitimation of Chinese Regimes. Asilomar, Monterey, California, 15–24 June 1975.

Easton, David. *A Systems Analysis of Political Life.* Revised and expanded edition. Chicago, 1965.

Eberhard, Wolfram. "The Political Function of Astronomy and Astronomers in Han China." In *Chinese Thought and Institutions*, ed. John K. Fairbank, pp. 33–70. Chicago, 1957.

Eberhard, Wolfram (with Rolf Mueller). "Contributions to the Astronomy of the Han Period III: Astronomy of the Later Han Period." In *Sternkunde und Weltbild im Alten China*, pp. 181–228. N.p., 1970.

Eberhard, Wolfram, and Rolf Müller. "Contributions to the Astronomy of the San-kuo Period." In *Sternkunde und Weltbild im Alten China*, pp. 229–44. N.p., 1970.

Edelman, Murray. *The Symbolic Uses of Politics.* Urbana, Ill., 1964.

Eliade, Mircea. *Images and Symbols: Studies in Religious Symbolism.* Trans. Philip Mairet. New York, 1961.

————. *Mephistopheles and the Androgyne: Studies in Religious Myth and Symbol.* Trans. J. M. Cohen. New York, 1965.

————. *The Myth of the Eternal Return or, Cosmos and History.* Trans. Willard R. Trask. Princeton, 1974.

————. *Rites and Symbols of Initiation: The Mysteries of Birth and Rebirth.* Trans. Willard R. Trask. 1958. New York, 1965.

Ellwood, Robert S. *The Feast of Kingship: Accession Ceremonies in Ancient Japan.* Tokyo, 1973.

Etzioni, Amitai. *A Comparative Analysis of Complex Organizations: On Power, Involvement and Their Correlates*. Rev. ed. New York, 1975.

Fehl, Noah Edward. *Li: Rites and Propriety in Literature and Life: A Perspective for a Cultural History of Ancient China*. Hong Kong, 1971.

Feuchtwang, Stephan D. R. "Investigating Religion." In *Marxist Analyses and Social Anthropology*, ed. Maurice Bloch, pp. 61–82. London, 1975.

Firth, Raymond. *Elements of Social Organization*. Boston, 1963.

———. *Symbols: Public and Private*. Ithaca, N.Y., 1973.

Fitzgerald, C. P. *The Empress Wu*. 1956. Reprint ed. London, 1968.

Forke, Alfred, trans. *Lun-Heng*. 2d ed. 2 vols. New York, 1962.

Fortes, Meyer. "Ritual and Office in Tribal Society." In *Essays on the Ritual of Social Relations*, ed. Max Gluckman, pp. 53–88. Manchester, England, 1962.

Fujikawa Masakazu 藤川正數. *Kandai ni okeru reigaku no kenkyū* 漢代における礼学の研究. Tokyo, 1968.

Fukunaga Mitsushi 福永光司. "Hōzensetsu no keisei (I)" 封禪説の形成. *Tōhō shūkyō* 東方宗教 6 (Nov. 1954):28–57.

———. "Hōzensetsu no keisei (II)." *Tōhō shūkyō* 7 (Feb. 1955):45–63.

———. "Kōten jōtei to Tennō daitei to Genshi tenson—Jukyō no saikōshin to Dōkyō no saikōshin" 昊天上帝と天皇大帝と元始天尊—儒教の最高神と道教の最高神. *Chūtetsu bungakkai hō* 中哲文学会報 2 (June 1976):1–34.

Fung Yu-lan. *A History of Chinese Philosophy*. 2 vols. Princeton, 1952.

Geertz, Clifford. *The Interpretation of Cultures: Selected Essays by Clifford Geertz*. New York, 1973.

———. *Negara: The Theatre State in Nineteenth-Century Bali*. Princeton, 1980.

Gluckman, Max. *Order and Rebellion in Tribal Africa*. New York, 1963.

———. "Les Rites de Passage." In *Essays on the Ritual of Social Relations*, ed. Max Gluckman, pp. 1–52. Manchester, England, 1962.

Goldhamer, H., and Edward Shils. "Types of Power and Status." *American Journal of Sociology* 45 (1939):171–82.

Goody, Jack. "Religion and Ritual: The Definitional Problem." *British Journal of Sociology* 12 (1961):142–64.

Goody, Jack, ed. *Succession to High Office*. Cambridge, 1966.

Grainger, Roger. *The Language of the Rite*. London, 1974.

Granet, Marcel. *Danses et légendes de la Chine ancienne*. 1926. Reprint ed. 2 vols. Paris, 1959.

———. *La pensée Chinoise*. 1934. Reprint ed. 1975.

Guisso, R. W. L. *Wu Tse-t'ien and the Politics of Legitimation in T'ang China*. Bellingham, Wash., 1978.

Habermas, Jürgen. *Legitimation Crisis.* Trans. Thomas McCarthy. Boston, 1975.

Hamada Kaidō 濱田恢道. "Meidō seido shikō" 明堂制度私考. *Shinagaku* 支那学 9 (1938–39; reprint ed.):447–76.

Hattori Katsuhiko 服部克彦. "Kodai Chūgoku ni okeru Santō to shinsen shisō" 古代中国における山東と神仙思想. *Ryūkoku Daigaku ronshū* 龍谷大学論集 392 (1970):74–94.

Hiraoka Takeo 平岡武夫, ed. *Chōan to Rakuyō (Chizu)* 長安と洛陽 (地図). T'ang Civilization Reference Series no. 7. Tokyo, 1956.

――――, *Chōan to Rakuyō (Shiryō)* 長安と洛陽(資料). T'ang Civilization Reference Series no. 6. Tokyo, 1956.

――――, *Tōdai no koyomi* 唐代の暦. T'ang Civilization Reference Series no. 1. Tokyo, 1954.

Ho Peng-yoke. *The Astronomical Chapters of the Chin Shu. With Amendments, Full Translation and Annotations.* Paris, 1966.

Ho Ping-ti. *The Cradle of the East: An Inquiry into the Indigenous Origins of Techniques and Ideas of Neolithic and Early Historic China, 5000–1000 B.C.* Hong Kong, 1975.

Ho Tzu-ch'eng 賀梓城. "'Kuan-chung T'ang shin-pa ling' tiao-ch'a chi" "關中唐十八陵"調査記. *Wen-wu tzu-liao ts'ung-k'an* 文物資料叢刊 3 (May 1980):139–53.

Hocart, A. M. *Kings and Councillors.* 1936. Reprint ed. Chicago, 1970.

――――. *Kingship.* London, 1927.

Holtom, D. C. *The Japanese Enthronement Ceremonies with an Account of the Imperial Regalia.* 2d ed. Tokyo, 1972.

Hsiao Kung-chuan. *A History of Chinese Political Thought, vol. 1: From the Beginnings to the Sixth Century A.D.* Trans. F. W. Mote. Princeton, 1979.

Hsü Chin-hsiung 許進雄. "Liao-chi feng-shan yü ming-t'ang chien-chu" 燎祭封禪與明堂建築. *Chung-kuo wen-tzu* 中國文字 19 (Mar. 1966): 1–5.

Hughes, E. R. *Two Chinese Poets: Vignettes of Han Life and Thought.* Princeton, 1960.

Ichikawa Mototarō 市川本太郎. *Bunchūshi* 文中子. Tokyo, 1970.

――――. "Zui no daiju Bunchūshi no shisō" 隋の大儒文中子の思想. *Kokushikan Daigaku jimbun gakkai kiyō* 国士舘大学人文学会紀要 3 (Mar. 1971):199–237.

Iijima Taketsugu 飯島武次. "Tō Kōsō Kenryō 唐高宗乾陵. *Kodai bunka* 古代文化 31:4 (1979):69–71.

Ikeda Suetoshi 池田末利. "Byōsei kō—seigen byōsū no mondai" 廟制考—制限廟數の問題. *Nippon Chūgoku gakkaihō* 日本中國學會報 11 (Oct. 1959):13–26.

Ishibashi Ushio 石橋尹雄. *Tendan* 天壇. Tokyo, 1957.

Kaltenmark, Max. "Religion and Politics in the China of the Tsin and the Han." *Diogenes* 34 (1961):18–43.

Kamada Shigeo 鎌田重雄. *Shin-Kan seiji seido no kenkyū* 秦漢政治制度の研究. Tokyo, 1962.

Kanai Yukitada 金井之忠. "Bunchūshi Chūsetsu no seitōron ni tsuite" 文中子中説の正統論に就いて. *Bunka* 文化 3 (1936):971–78.

Kanaya Osamu 金谷治. "Shinsen no keisei" 神僊の形成. In *Chikuma Shobō Sekai no rekishi* 筑摩書房世界の歴史, 3:239–57. Tokyo, 1960.

Kaneko Shūichi 金子修一. "Chūgoku kodai ni okeru kōtei saishi no ichi kōsatsu" 中國古代における皇帝祭祀の一考察. *Shigaku zasshi* 史学雜誌 87 (1978):174–202.

———. "Gi-Shin yori Zui-Tō ni itaru kōshi sōbyō no seido ni tsuite" 魏晉より隋唐に至る郊祀宗廟の制度について. *Shigaku zasshi* 史学雜誌 88 (1979):1499–1534.

———. "Tōdai no daishi, chūshi, shōshi ni tsuite" 唐代の大祀、中祀、小祀について. *Kōchi Daigaku gakujutsu kenkyū hōkoku* 高知大学学術研究報告 25:2 (1976):13–19.

Kao Ming 高明. *Li-hsüeh hsin-t'an* 禮學新探. Hong Kong, 1963.

Keightley, David. "The Religious Commitment: Shang Theology and the Genesis of Chinese Political Culture." *History of Religions* 17 (1978):211–25.

Kimura Eiichi 木村英一. "Hōzen shisō no seiritsu" 封禪思想の成立. *Shinagaku* 支那学 11:2 (1942–43; reprint ed.):179–217.

Klapp, Orrin Edgar. *Ritual and Cult: A Sociological Interpretation*. Washington, D.C., 1956.

Kramers, R. P. "Conservatism and the Transmission of the Confucian Canon: A T'ang Scholar's Complaint." *Journal of Oriental Studies* (Hong Kong) 2 (1955):119–32.

Kramers, R.P., trans. *K'ung Tzu Chia Yü: The School Sayings of Confucius*. Leiden, 1950.

Ku Chieh-kang 顧頡剛. "Shan-jang chuan-shuo ch'i yü Mo-chia k'ao" 禪讓傳說起于墨家考. *Shih-hsüeh chi-k'an* 史學集刊 1 (1936):163–230.

Künstler, Mieczyslaw Jerzy. "Deux biographies de Tcheng Hiuan." *Rocznik Orientalistyczny* 26:1 (1962):23–64.

Kurihara Tomonobu 要原朋信. *Shin-Kanshi no kenkyū* 秦漢史の研究. Tokyo, 1970.

Kushitani Michiko 串谷美智子. "Hōzen ni mirareru futatsu no seikaku—shūkyōsei to seijisei" 封禪にみられる二つの性格—宗教性と政治性. *Shisō* 史窓 14 (Mar. 1959):59–68.

Langer, Susanne Katherina. *Philosophy in a New Key; A Study in the Symbolism of Reason, Rite, and Art*. New York, 1962.

Lasswell, Harold D., and Abraham Kaplan. *Power and Society: A Framework for Political Inquiry*. New Haven, 1950.

Leach, Edmund. *Culture and Communication: The Logic by Which Symbols Are Connected*. Cambridge, 1976.

————. *Political Systems of Highland Burma*. 1954. Boston, 1965.

————. "Ritual." In the *International Encyclopedia of the Social Sciences*, ed. David L. Sills. 18 vols. 13:520–26. New York, 1968.

Leban, Carl. "Managing Heaven's Mandate: Coded Communications in the Accession of Ts'ao P'ei, A.D. 220." In *Ancient China: Studies in Early Civilization*, ed. David T. Roy and Tsuen-hsuin Tsien, pp. 315–41. Hong Kong, 1978.

Legge, James, trans. *The Chinese Classics*. 2d ed., rev. 5 vols. Hong Kong, 1961. Vol. 1, *Confucian Analects, The Great Learning, The Doctrine of the Mean*; vol. 2., *The Works of Mencius*; vol. 3, *The Shoo King*; vol. 4., *The She King*; vol. 5, *The Ch'un Ts'ew with the Tso Chuen*.

————. *I Ching: Book of Changes*. 1899. Reprint ed. Secaucus, N.J., 1964.

————. *Li Chi, Book of Rites*. 2 vols. New Hyde Park, N.Y., 1967.

Li Shu-t'ung 李樹桐. *T'ang-shih hsin-lun* 唐史新論. Taipei, 1972.

————. *T'ang-shih k'ao-pien* 唐史考辨. Taipei, 1965.

Ling Shun-sheng 凌純聲. "Chung-kuo ti feng-shan yü Liang-ho-liu yü ti k'un-lun wen-hua" 中國的封禪與兩河流域的昆侖文化. *Chung-yang yen-chiu-yüan min-tsu-hsüeh yen-chiu-so chi-k'an* 中央研究院民族學研究所集刊 19 (Mar. 1965):1–38.

————. "Pei-p'ing ti feng-shan wen-hua" 北平的封禪文化. *Chung-yang yen-chiu-yüan min-tsu-hsüeh yen-chiu-so chi-k'an* 中央研究院民族學研究所集刊 16 (Sept. 1963):1–82.

Liu, James T. C. "The Sung Emperors and the *Ming-t'ang* or Hall of Enlightenment." In *Études Song: in memoriam Étienne Balazs*, ed. Françoise Aubin, pp. 45–58. Paris, 1973.

Liu Tzu-chien [James T. C. Liu] 劉子健. "Feng-shan wen-hua yü Sung-tai ming-t'ang chi-t'ien" 封禪文化與宋代明堂祭天. *Chung-yang yen-chiu-yüan min-tsu-hsüeh yen-chiu-so chi-k'an* 中央研究院民族學研究所集刊 18 (Sept. 1964):45–49.

Lo Hsiang-lin 羅香林. *T'ang-tai wen-hua shih* 唐代文化史. Taipei, 1963.

Loewe, Michael. *Crisis and Conflict in Han China*. London, 1974.

————. "The Orders of Aristocratic Rank of Han China." *T'oung Pao* 48:1–3 (1960):97–174.

————. *Chinese Ideas of Life and Death: Faith, Myth and Reason in the Han Period (202 BC–AD 220)*. London, 1982.

McCarthy, Thomas A. *The Critical Theory of Jürgen Habermas*. Cambridge, Mass., 1978.

McKnight, Brian E. *The Quality of Mercy: Amnesties and Traditional Chinese Justice*. Honolulu, 1981.

————. "Patterns of Law and Patterns of Thought: Notes on the Specifications (*shih*) of Sung China." *Journal of the American Oriental Society* 102:2 (April–June 1982):323–31.

Maspero, Henri. "Le Ming-t'ang et la crise religieuse Chinoise avant les Han." *Mélanges Chinois et Bouddhiques* 9 (1951):1–71.

Mikami Jun 三上順. "Meidō no kigen to sono hatten ni tsuite no ichi kōsatsu (I)" 明堂の起源とその発展に就いての一考察. *Tetsugaku* (Hiroshima tetsugakkaî) 哲学 20 (Oct. 1968):11–23.

————. "Meidō no kigen to sono hatten ni tsuite no ichi kōsatsu (II)." *Tetsugaku* 24 (Oct. 1972):47–57.

————. "Meidō no kōzō ni tsuite no ichi kōsatsu" 明堂の構造に就いての一考察. *Tetsugaku* 哲学 13 (Oct. 1961):25–39.

————. "Meidō to iegata haniwa (I)" 明堂と家形埴輪. *Tōhō shūkyō* 東方宗教 27 (Sept. 1966): 35–48.

————. "Meidō to iegata haniwa (II)." *Tōhō shūkyō* 28 (Nov. 1966): 35–49.

————. "Shin, byō, meidō no kibo ni tsuite no ichi kōsatsu" 寝廟明堂の規模に就いての一考察. *Hijiyama Joshi Tanki Daigaku kiyō* 比治山女子短期大学紀要 6 (1972):11–24.

Mitarai Masaru 御手洗勝. "Konron densetsu no kigen" 崑崙傳説の起源. In *Shigaku kenkyū kinen ronsō* 史学研究紀念論叢, pp. 191–210. Tokyo, 1950.

Mitsunaga Shunsuke 光永俊介. "Kan Rikuchō bosei ni okeru ryōbo no shūhen" 漢六朝墓制における陵墓の周邊. *Tōhō kodai kenkyū* 東方古代研究 9 (Nov. 1959):32–40.

Miyakawa Hisayuki 宮川尚志. *Rikuchōshi kenkyū (seiji shakai hen)* 六朝史研究（政治社会篇）. Tokyo, 1956.

————, *Rikuchōshi kenkyū (shūkyō hen)* 六朝史研究（宗教篇）. Tokyo, 1964.

Moore, Sally F., and Barbara G. Myerhoff, eds. *Secular Ritual*. Amsterdam, 1977.

Mori Mikisaburō 森三樹三郎. "Getsurei to meidō" 月令と明堂. *Shinagaku* 支那学 8:2 (1936; reprint ed.):201–24.

Moroto Tatsuo 諸戸立雄. "Tō Taisō no Bukkyō shinkō ni tsuite" 唐太宗の仏教信仰について. *Akidai shigaku* 秋大史学 27 (1980):1–17.

Nagendra, S. P. *The Concept of Ritual in Modern Sociological Theory*. New Delhi, 1971.

Needham, Joseph. *Science and Civilisation in China*. 7 vols. projected. Cambridge, 1954–. Vol. 2, *History of Scientific Thought* (1956); vol. 3, *Mathematics and the Sciences of Heaven and Earth* (1959).

———. "Time and Knowledge in China and the West." In *The Voices of Time*, ed. J. T. Fraser, pp. 92–135. New York, 1966.

Niida Noboru 仁井田陞. *Tōryō shūi* 唐令拾遺. 1933. Reprint ed. Tokyo, 1964.

Nishida Tai'ichirō 西田太郎. "Kōsai no taishō to sono jiki to ni tsuite" 郊祭の對象とその時期とに就いて. *Shinagaku* 支那学 8 (1935; reprint ed):47–65.

Nishijima Sadao 西嶋定生. *Chūgoku kodai teikoku no keisei to kōzō* 中國古代帝國の形成と構造. *Tokyo, 1962*.

———. "Kandai ni okeru sokui girei—toku ni teii keishō no ba'ai ni tsuite" 漢代における即位儀礼—とくに帝位継承のばあいについて In *Enoki Hakase kanreki kinen Tōyōshi ronsō* 榎博士還暦記念東洋史論叢, *pp.* 403–22. Tokyo, 1975.

———. "Kōtei shihai no seiritsu" 皇帝支配の成立. In *Iwanami Kōza Sekai rekishi* 岩波講座世界歴史 vol. 4 (Kodai 古代), pp. 217–56. Tokyo, 1970.

Nunome Chōfū 布目潮渢. "Zui-Tō jidai no ketsusō to teiryō—Rakuyō kara Seian e—' 隋唐時代の穴倉と帝陵—洛陽から西安へ. *Tōyō gakujutsu kenkyū* 東洋学術研究 18 (Jan. 1979):21–46.

Ogata Isamu 尾形勇. "Chūgoku kodai ni okeru teii no keishō—sono seitōka no katei to ronri" 中国古代における帝位の継承—その正当化の過程と論理. *Shigaku zasshi* 史学雑誌 85 (1976):308–22.

———. *Chūgoku kodai no 'ie' to kokka—kōtei shihaika no chitsujo kōzō*— 中国古代の「家」と国家—皇帝支配下の秩序構造—. *Tokyo*, 1979.

———. "Kandai ni okeru 'Shin bō' keishiki—kodai teikoku no kunshin kankei ni tsuite" 漢代における「臣某」形式—古代帝国の君臣関係について. *Shigaku zasshi* 史学雑誌 76 (1967):1159–1203.

———. "Kōtei no jishō keishiki to sokui girei" 皇帝の自称形式と即位儀礼. *Yamanashi Daigaku Kyōikugakubu kenkyū hōkoku* 山梨大学教育学部研究報告 28 (Dec. 1977):100–08.

Ord, Edmund B. H. "State Sacrifices in the Former Han Dynasty According to the Official Histories." Ph.D. dissertation, University of California, Berkeley, 1967.

Ozaki Yasushi 尾崎康. "Gu Seinan no Tei-ō ryaku ni tsuite" 虞世南の帝王略について. *Shidō Bunko ronshū* 斯道文庫論集 5 (July 1967): 185–224.

Paludan, Ann. *The Imperial Ming Tombs*. New Haven, 1981.

P'an Chung-kuei 潘重規. "Wu-ching cheng-i t'an-yüan" 五經正義探源. *Hua-kang hsüeh-pao* 華岡學報 1 (June 1965):13–22.

Parsons, Talcott. "On the Concept of Power." *Proceedings of the American Philosophical Society* 107 (1963):232–62.

P'i Hsi-jui 皮錫瑞. *Ching-hsüeh li-shih* 經學歷史. 1924. Reprint ed. Hong Kong, 1961.

Rickett, W. Allyn. *Kuan-tzu: A Repository of Early Chinese Thought*. Hong Kong, 1965.

Sapir, Edward. "Symbolism." In *Encyclopedia of the Social Sciences*, ed. Edwin R. A. Seligman. 15 vols. 14:492–95. New York, 1930.

Schafer, Edward H. "The Auspices of T'ang." *Journal of the American Oriental Society* 83 (1963):197–225.

———. "Chinese Reign Names—Words or Nonsense Syllables?" *Wennti* (Yale University) 3 (July 1952):33–40.

———. *Mao Shan in T'ang Times*. Society for the Study of Chinese Religions Monograph no. 1. 1980.

———. "The Origin of an Era." *Journal of the American Oriental Society* 85 (1965):543–50.

———. *Pacing the Void: T'ang Approaches to the Stars*. Berkeley and Los Angeles, 1977.

Seidel, Anna. "Dynastic Treasures and Taoist *lu* Registers." An unpublished paper presented at the Conference on Legitimation of Chinese Regimes, Asilomar, Monterey, California, 15–24 June 1975.

———. "The Image of the Perfect Ruler in Early Taoist Messianism: Lao-tzu and Li Hung." *History of Religions* 9 (1969–70):216–47.

Shan-hsi sheng wen-wu kuan-li wei-yüan hui 陝西省文物管理委員會. "Shan-hsi Hsing-p'ing hsien Mao-ling k'an-ch'a" 陝西興平縣茂陵勘查. *K'ao-ku* 考古 1964, no. 2:86–89.

———. "T'ang Ch'ien-ling k'an-ch'a chi" 唐乾陵勘查記 *Wen-wu* 文物 1960, no. 4:53–60.

Shih Chang-ju 石璋如. "Han-T'ang ti kuo-tu ling-mu yü chiang-yü" 漢唐的國都陵墓與疆域. *Ta-lu tsa-chih* 大陸雜誌 6 (April 1953): 243–50.

Shryock, John K. *The Origin and Development of the State Cult of Confucius: An Introductory Study*. 1933. Reprint ed. New York, 1966.

Sivin, Nathan. *Cosmos and Computation in Early Chinese Mathematical Astronomy*. Leiden, 1969. (Reprinted from *T'oung Pao* 55 [1969]: 1–73).

———. "Chinese Conceptions of Time." *The Earlham Review* 1 (1966):82–92.

Sofukawa Hiroshi 曾布川寬. "Konronsan to shōsento" 昆崙山と昇仙圖. *Tōhō gakuhō* 東方學報 51 (Mar. 1979):83–185.

Soothill, William Edward. *The Hall of Light: A Study of Early Chinese Kingship*. London, 1951.

Som, Tjan Tjoe. *Po Hu T'ung*. 2 vols. Leiden, 1949.

Sternberger, Dolf. "Legitimacy." In the *International Encyclopedia of the Social Sciences*, ed. David L. Sills, 9:244–48. New York, 1968.

Strickmann, Michel. "The Mao Shan Revelations; Taoism and the Aristocracy." *T'oung Pao* 63 (1977):1–64.

Su Hsüeh-lin 蘇雪林. "K'un-lun i-tz'u ho-shih shih chien Chung-kuo chi-tai" 崑崙一詞何時始見中國記載. *Ta-lu tsa-chih* 大陸雜誌 9 (Dec. 1954):333–36.

Su Ying-hui 蘇瑩輝. "Wu-ching cheng-i ti-i-tz'u p'an-hsing yü Chen-kuan nien-chung shuo" 五經正義第一次頒行於貞觀年中說. *Kuo-li Chung-yang t'u-shu-kuan kuan-k'an* 國立中央圖書館館刊 (n.s.) 2 (Oct. 1968):29–33.

―――. "Ts'ung Tun-huang-pen hsien-ming-yeh lun Wu-ching cheng-i chih k'an-ting" 從敦煌本銜名頁論五經正義之刊定. *K'ung Meng hsüeh-pao* 孔孟學報 16 (Sept. 1968):181–93.

Swartz, Marc J., Victor W. Turner, and Arthur Tuden, eds. *Political Anthropology*. Chicago, 1966.

Takeuchi Hiroyuki 竹内弘行. "Shiba Sen no Hōzenron—Shiki Hōzensho no rekishi kijutsu o megutte" 司馬遷の封禪論―史記封禪書の歷史記述をめぐって. *Tetsugaku nempō* 哲学年報 (Kyoto Daigaku) 34 (1975): 91–111.

T'ang Yung-t'ung (Walter Liebenthal, trans.). "Wang Pi's New Interpretation of the *I-ching* and *Lun-yü*." *Harvard Journal of Asiatic Studies* 10 (1947): 124–61.

Tanigawa Michio 谷川道雄. "Goko jūrokkoku oyobi Hokushū no sho-kunshu ni okeru Tennō no shōgō ni tsuite" 五胡十六国および北周の諸君主における天王の称号について. *Nagoya Daigaku bunga-kubu kenkyū ronshū* 名古屋大学文学部研究論集 41 (Shigaku 史学 14) (Mar. 1966):91–103.

T'ao Hsi-sheng 陶希聖. "K'ung-tzu miao-t'ing chung Han-ju chi Sung-ju ti wei-tz'u (I)" 孔子廟庭中漢儒及宋儒的位次. *Shih-huo yüeh-k'an* 食貨月刊 (n.s.) 2 (April 1972):9–29.

―――. "K'ung-tzu miao-t'ing chung Han-ju chi Sung-ju ti wei-tz'u (II)." *Shih-huo yüeh-k'an* (n.s.) 2 (May 1972):81–97.

Teng Shu-p'ing, "Two Sets of Jade Tablets in the National Palace Museum Collection" *National Palace Museum Bulletin*, 11:6 (Jan.–Feb. 1977), 1–17.

Tetsui Yoshinori 鉄井慶紀. "Konron densetsu ni tsuite no ichi shiron" 崑崙伝説についての一試論. *Tōhō shūkyō* 東方宗教 45 (1975):33–47.

Ts'en Chung-mien 岑仲勉. *Sui-T'ang shih* 隋唐史. Peking, 1957.

Tsuda Sōkichi 津田左右吉. "Kandai seiji shisō no ichimen" 漢代政治思想の一面. In *Tsuda Sōkichi zenshū* 津田左右吉全集. 28 vols. 17:1–108. Tokyo, 1963–66.

Tsuruma Kazuyuki 鶴間和幸. "Kanritsu ni okeru funkyū kitei ni tsuite" 漢律における墳丘規定について. *Tōyō bunka* 東洋文化 60 (Feb. 1980): 1–21.

Tu Erh-wei 杜而未. *Chung-kuo ku-tai tsung-chiao hsi-t'ung* 中國古代宗教系統. Taipei, 1960.

————. *K'un-lun wen-hua yu pu-ssu kuan-nien* 崑崙文化與不死觀念. Taipei, 1962.

Tu Pao-jen 杜葆仁. "Hsi-Han chu-ling wei-chih k'ao" 西漢諸陵位置考. *K'ao-ku yü wen-wu* 考古與文物 1980, no. 1:29–33.

Tu Wei-ming. "The 'Thought of Huang-Lao': A Reflection on the Lao Tzu and Huang Ti Texts in the Silk Manuscripts of Ma-Wang-Tui." *Journal of Asian Studies* 39 (1979):95–110.

Tung Tso-pin. "The Chinese and the World's Ancient Calendars." In *A Symposium on the World Calendar*, ed. The Chinese Association for the United Nations, pp. 3–23. Taipei, 1951.

Turner, Terrence. "Transformation, Hierarchy and Transcendence: A Reformulation of van Gennep's Model of the Structure of Rites de Passage." In *Secular Ritual*, ed. Sally F. Moore and Barbara G. Myerhoff, pp. 53–70. Amsterdam, 1977.

Turner, Victor W. *Dramas, Fields, and Metaphors: Symbolic Action in Human Society*. Ithaca, N.Y., 1974.

————. *The Forest of Symbols: Aspects of Ndembu Ritual*. Ithaca, N.Y., 1967.

————. *The Ritual Process: Structure and Anti-Structure*. Chicago, 1969.

————. *Schism and Continuity in an African Society: A Study of Ndembu Village Life*. Manchester, 1957.

————. "Symbolic Studies." *Annual Review of Anthropology* 4 (1975): 145–61.

————. "Variations on a Theme of Liminality." In *Secular Ritual*, ed. Sally F. Moore and Barbara G. Myerhoff, pp. 36–52. Amsterdam, 1977.

Turner, Victor W., and Edith Turner. *Image and Pilgrimage in Christian Culture: Anthropological Perspectives*. New York, 1978.

Twitchett, Denis C. "The Sui (589–618) and T'ang (618–907) Dynasties: An Introduction." In *Essays on T'ang Society*, ed. John Curtis Perry and Bardwell L. Smith. Leiden, 1976.

Uchino Tairei 内野台嶺. "Tenshi shichibyōsetsu ni tsuite" 天子七廟説に就て. *Daitō bunka* 大東文化 17 (1937):23–43.

Utsugi Akira 宇都木章. "Raiki no kōrei ni tsuite no okusetsu" 禮記の郊礼についての憶説. In *Wada Hakase koki kinen Tōyōshi ronsō* 和田博士古稀記念東洋史論叢, pp. 175–85. Tokyo, 1961.

Van Gennep, Arnold. *The Rites of Passage*. Trans. Monika. b. Vizedom and Gabrielle L. Caffee. Reprint ed. Chicago, 1960.

Waley, Arthur, trans. *The Analects of Confucius*. London, 1938.

Wallacker, Benjamin. "Han Confucianism and Confucius in Han." In *Ancient China: Studies in Early Civilization*, ed. David T. Roy and Tsuen-hsuin Tsien, pp. 215–28. Hong Kong, 1978.

Walzer, Michael. "On the Role of Symbolism in Political Thought." *Political Science Quarterly* 82 (June 1967):191–205.

Wang Chih-hsin 王治心. *Chung-kuo tsung-chiao ssu-hsiang shih ta-kang* 中國宗教思想史大綱. 1931. Reprint ed. Taipei, 1965.

Wang Kuo-wei 王國維. "Chien tu chien shu k'ao" 簡牘檢署考. *Wang Kuan-t'ang hsien-sheng ch'üan-chi* 王觀堂先生全集.ed., 6:2349–52.

———. "Ming-t'ang miao ch'in t'ung-k'ao" 明堂廟寢通考. In *Kuan-t'ang chi-lin* 觀堂集林. 4 vols. 1:123–45. Peking, 1959.

Wang Meng-ou 王夢鷗. "Ku Ming-t'ang t'u k'ao" 古明堂圖考. *K'ung Meng hsüeh-pao* 孔孟學報 11(1966):221–29.

Wang Shih-jen 王世仁. "Han Ch'ang-an-ch'eng nan-chiao li-chih chien-chu (Ta-shih-men ts'un i-chih) yüan-chuang ti t'ui-ts'e" 漢長安城南郊禮制建築(大士門村遺址)原狀的推測. *K'ao-ku* 考古 1963, no. 9: 501–15.

Wang Shou-nan 王壽南. *Chung-kuo li-tai ch'uang-yeh ti-wang* 中國歷代創業帝王. N.p., 1964.

Watson, Burton. *Early Chinese Literature*. New York, 1962.

———. Ssu-ma Ch'ien: Grand Historian of China. New York, 1958.

Watson, Burton, trans. *Hsün Tzu: Basic Writings*. New York, 1963.

———. *Records of the Grand Historian of China, Translated from the Shih-chi of Ssu-ma Ch'ien*. 2 vols. New York, 1961.

Weber, Max. *The Theory of Social and Economic Organization*. Trans. A. M. Henderson and Talcott Parsons. 1947. New York, 1964.

Wechsler, Howard J. "The Confucian Impact on Early T'ang Decision-making." *T'oung Pao* 66 (1980):1–40.

———. "The Confucian Teacher Wang T'ung (584?–617): One Thousand Years of Controversy." *T'oung Pao* 63 (1977):225–72.

———. "Factionalism in Early T'ang Government." In *Perspectives on the T'ang*, ed. Arthur F. Wright and Denis Twitchett, pp. 87–120. New Haven, 1973.

———. *Mirror to the Son of Heaven: Wei Cheng at the Court of T'ang T'ai-tsung*. New Haven, 1974.

Wheatley, Paul. *The Pivot of the Four Quarters: A Preliminary Enquiry into the Origins and Character of the Ancient Chinese City*. Chicago, 1971.

Wheelwright, Philip. *The Burning Fountain: A Study of the Language of Symbolism*. Bloomington, Ind., 1968.

Wright, Arthur. F. "The Formation of Sui Ideology, 581–604." In *Chinese Thought and Institutions*," ed. John K. Fairbank, pp. 71–104. Chicago, 1957.

————. "Some Preliminary Reflections on Legitimation in Chinese History." Unpublished paper offered at the Conference on Legitimation of Chinese Regimes. Asilomar, Monterey, California, 15–24 June 1975.

————. *The Sui Dynasty: Unification of China,* A.D. 581–617. New York, 1978.

————. "T'ai-tsung and Buddhism." In *Perspectives on the T'ang,* ed. Arthur F. Wright and Denis Twitchett, pp. 239–63. New Haven, 1973.

Wright, Arthur F., and Edward Fagan. "Era Names and Zeitgeist." *Études Asiatiques* 5 (1951):113–21.

Yabuuti Kiyosi [Yabuuchi Kiyoshi]. "Chinese Astronomy: Development and Limiting Factors." In *Chinese Science: Explorations of an Ancient Tradition,* ed. Shigeru Nakayama and Nathan Sivin, pp. 91–103. Cambridge, Mass., 1973.

Yabuuchi Kiyoshi 薮内清. *Chūgoku no temmon rekihō* 中國の天文曆法. Tokyo, 1969.

————. *Zui-Tō rekihōshi no kenkyū* 隋唐曆法史の研究. Tokyo, 1944.

Yamazaki Hiroshi 山崎宏. *Zui-Tō Bukkyōshi no kenkyū* 隋唐仏教史の研究. Tokyo, 1967.

————. "Zuidai no gakkai no kenkyū" 隋代の学界の研究. *Risshō Daigaku Bungakubu ronsō* 立正大学文学部論叢. 37 (Mar. 1970):29–78.

Yang, C. K. *Religion in Chinese Society.* Berkeley and Los Angeles, 1970.

————. "The Functional Relationship between Confucian Thought and Chinese Religion." In *Chinese Thought and Institutions,* ed. John K. Fairbank, pp. 269–90. Chicago, 1957.

Yang K'uan 楊寬. *Chūgoku kōteiryō no kigen to hensen* 中国皇帝陵の起源と変遷. Trans. Nishijima Sadao 西嶋定生, Ogawa Isamu 尾形勇, and Ōta Yūko 太田有子. Tokyo, 1981.

Yen Keng-wang 嚴耕望. *T'ang p'u-shang ch'eng-lang piao* 唐僕尚丞郎表. 4 vols. Taipei, 1956.

Yoshikawa Sadao 吉川忠夫. "Bunchūshi kō" 文中子考. *Shirin* 史林 53 (Mar. 1970):225–58.

Yoshinami Takashi 好並隆司. "Kandai kōtei shihai chitsujo no keisei—teiryō e no shisen to gōzoku—" 漢代皇帝支配秩序の形成—帝陵への徙遷と豪族. *Tōyōshi kenkyū* 東洋史研究 35 (1976):211–42.

Yün Shih 尤時. "Chao-ling" 昭陵. *Wen-wu* 文物 1977, no. 10:60–62.

Glossary-Index